C000279921

WHAT HAPPENED TO THE BATTLESHIP

WHAT HAPPENED TO THE BATTLESHIP
1945 to the Present

CHRIS BAKER

NAVAL INSTITUTE PRESS
ANNAPOLIS, MARYLAND

Frontispiece: USS *Iowa* firing a 16in and 5in gun broadside
at Vieques Island, Puerto Rico, 1 July 1984. *(NHHC)*

Copyright © Chris Baker 2022
First published in Great Britain in 2022 by
Seaforth Publishing,
A division of Pen & Sword Books Ltd,
47 Church Street,
Barnsley S70 2AS

www.seaforthpublishing.com

Published and distributed in the United States of America and Canada by the
Naval Institute Press,
291 Wood Road, Annapolis,
Maryland 21402-5034

www.nip.org

Library of Congress Control Number: 2022933854

ISBN 978-1-68247-876-9

This edition authorized for sale only in the United States of America,
its territories and possessions, and Canada

Designed and typeset by Ian Hughes, Mousemat Design Ltd

Printed and bound in Great Britain

Contents

Preface

Tʜɪs ʙᴏᴏᴋ ʜᴀᴅ its origins around 1978. I had a long fascination with things naval, and with battleships in particular. As I read more widely it seemed to me that the books of that day took an oversimplistic approach to the inevitability of the end of the age of the battleship. In particular, I considered that the evidence of the Second World War pointed to a complex operational picture. Competing and fast-developing technologies in the surface, air and underwater domains struggled for supremacy. The diverse theatres across which the war was fought required different approaches and different types of forces to win each campaign. The battleship, operating alongside the aircraft carrier, was still very much part of this picture in 1945, and further technological developments after the war could also play to its inherent strengths. So, there was an argument to retain the battleship, or its modern guided missile-armed 'heavy ship' equivalent.

An early manuscript mainly researched and written in 1978–79 argued just this, but then the demands of a career in the Ministry of Defence and family life led to the work being suspended for nearly forty years. Little did I perceive at that starting point that many in the United States Navy and Marine Corps shared my perspective. The revival of the last surviving battleships was about to take place under the Presidency of Ronald Reagan. I followed the debate around those projects via the media, where it received quite a bit of coverage. The Soviet Union shared the vision of heavy surface warships as well, with their *Kirov* class of new guided missile 'battlecruisers'. The final chapters of the Cold War generated a substantial naval arms race.

Recently I decided to return to the subject. Although much more had been written about battleships in the intervening forty years, and much of it outstanding, there was still a tendency to focus on the early years of the twentieth century, and to treat the battleship story after 1945 as a mere footnote. This book is, I believe, the first to focus just on those later years, although it is necessary to reach back into the last years of the Second World War, and sometimes a little further, to provide context for what transpired after 1945. While much of the story does inevitably chart retrenchment, reductions and scrapping, I hope to show that these were more reluctant, intermittent, and longer drawn out than is generally reflected in published work.

This later battleship story is also a story of the struggle to find affordable security in post-war Europe and the wider world; of new rivalries and balances of naval power in the Cold War; of the role battleships played in early Western Union and NATO deterrence; and of their continued use in combat from 1945 to 1991.

So this book is not focussed on evidence to support an argument that battleships still had a role on the world stage, because that came to pass. Instead it aims to be a straightforward narrative of what happened to battleships between 1945 and the present day, together with some observations and analysis of the reasons why. In its later years the story is more focussed towards the United States as the possessors of the last battleships, but hopefully it also does justice to other nations up to the 1970s. The battleship story continues in the present, because although the last quartet of United States battleships did finally go into retirement in 2009, they and four of their predecessors still survive as museum ships, with their own continuing challenges against the ravages of time and tide. So the final chapter of the battleship story will continue to be written.

I am conscious that this narrative is a bit of a mixed bag, with access to original sources for much of the United Kingdom story, but relying much more on published sources for the other nations as Covid has disrupted potential research expeditions. I have also used information from the internet, which may not all be as thoroughly sourced or reliable but there is a wealth of detail and anecdote on the web and it is worth collecting into one place, and, with due warning, presented for what it is. Authoritative published sources quite often disagree about details and precise dates. Usually this is of little significance. Where it is more substantial, or primary evidence seems to contradict, I have done my best to present both interpretations as well as my view.

The narrative covers a span of seventy-five years, a dozen countries, and material ranging from global security and strategy, through national politics, budgeting, planning and programming, to the organisation of fleets and missions and the minutiae of daily life aboard ships. I have opted for a broadly chronological approach, but I have grouped material by theme and country as well to maintain some narrative coherence. Hopefully the result is informative to the specialist audience, but also entertaining and accessible to a general reader.

Thanks are due to Jon Day, Timothy Baker, Claire Baker and Edward Dismorr for reading early drafts and making helpful suggestions; to Timothy Baker for drawing the maps and Sue Rhodes for helping with the photographs. The staff at the National Archives at Kew, the British Library and the Hampshire County Archive have been most helpful with assistance to access their records. I am indebted to Ian Buxton at the Newcastle University Marine Technology Special Collection for access to his records and permission to use photographs. I have found the on-line collection of the United States Naval History and Heritage Command a valuable source of illustrations. Photographs referenced NHHC are used courtesy of Naval History and Heritage Command, and those referenced NARA courtesy of the US National Archives. I am grateful to Professor Tim Wilks for permission to quote from his father's Royal Air Force Logbook. And finally, my gratitude to Julian Mannering at Seaforth Publishing for his assistance and encouragement to get this project over the line.

Introduction

MUCH HAS BEEN written about battleships. Technical studies abound, as do histories of their operations in the twentieth century. They are the most argued over type of warship. Debate still rages about their strategic impact, design, utility, expense, vulnerability and effectiveness. Historians and naval analysts have tended to draw the curtain in September 1945 when Japan surrendered. Some adopt an even earlier cut-off.[1] To summarise their argument, the events of the Second World War were held to have shown that the battleship had become an expensive and vulnerable anachronism, a naval irrelevance in an era now dominated by the submarine, air power, and the aircraft carrier. Battleships only survived as long as they did, it was asserted, because decision-making admirals were hidebound conservatives, fixated by their formative experiences as young officers in the battleships and the old ways of naval warfare. They, along with their political masters who made the investment decisions, also remained blinded by the great power status and prestige that battleships attracted, in defiance of operational, technical and scientific progress. This, I suggest, is a view strongly coloured by hindsight.

Instead, the evidence shows that towards the end of the Second World War and immediately afterwards into the beginnings of the Cold War all the major naval powers saw things as much less clear cut, and their policies and investments reflected a continuing requirement for battleships as well as aircraft carriers. Many battleships remained active for a number of years, or were reactivated from reserve. A few still under construction in 1945 were completed as late as 1950. Others, half built, were retained for years on their slipways against the contingency of their eventually being required to come into service. One major power, the Soviet Union, began brand new, secretive and very ambitious battleship programmes after 1945. There was still a very pronounced and explicit worry about the battleship or 'heavy ship' balance of power through the 1940s, and what plans the rapidly developing Soviet Navy might have well into the 1950s.

Battleships that remained in service were put to all manner of work – as fleet flagships, command ships, troop transports, training ships, Royal Yachts, Presidential yachts, hearses, experimental vessels, target ships, prison ships, supply vessels for smaller ships, offensive gunfire support platforms, integral components of national, multilateral, Western Union and NATO task forces. Over this period battleships also met with a variety of fates, from the prosaic to the spectacular. Plans for the conversion and use of battleships as guided missile platforms in a post-war, nuclear-armed world continued to be made. Battleships saw action in the 1940s, '50s and '60s, and, after a hibernation in the 1970s, once again in the 1980s and '90s. It was 1992 before the United States Navy finally decommissioned the last of the four *Iowa*-class ships; and not until 2009 that the US Congress finally acknowledged that there would be no future requirement to reactivate them for gunfire support roles, and they were finally struck from the United States Naval Register.

Even after that, a contemporary echo of the enduring role and utility of the battleship is still being played out in the planning of the modern great power fleets. Despite cost pressures, numbers of naval platforms are everywhere being sacrificed for capability, and just as for the battleship planning of the 1920s and '30s, capability still generally means size. The size of post-war surface warships, and indeed submarines, has grown to exceed that of preceding classes and now matches the size of the Second World War cruiser. In some cases the new ships have become almost as large as their early battleship predecessors, confirming predictions from as early as 1945 that future heavy ships with long range anti-ship or land attack rocket weapons would remain part of the world's fleets. The hankering for a modern larger gun than that mounted by destroyers and frigates has been and remains a leitmotif of US Navy planning over the thirty years since their battleships finally went into reserve. The emerging People's Liberation Army Navy of China also now reflects this trend for ship displacement growth.

Instead of finishing the history of the battleship in 1945, I will start there at the point when the Japanese instrument of surrender was signed aboard a battleship, USS *Missouri*, in Tokyo Bay on 2 September, bringing the Second World War to its close. A brief revisionist analysis of the later stages of the war and the role that battleships played, or could have played, also helps set the scene for what followed.

New Mexico with Mount Fuji, late August 1945. *(NHHC)*

Indiana and Massachusetts, plus cruisers, photographed from *South Dakota*, the bombardment of Kamashi, Japan, 14 July 1945. *(NARA)*

CHAPTER ONE

2 September 1945

O<small>N THE DAY</small> of the Japanese surrender, ninety-five dreadnought battleships could still have been viewed around the world by an enthusiast. Eleven of them (eight American, two British and one Japanese) were in or around Tokyo Bay for the surrender itself. More than half of all the 175 dreadnoughts[2] ever built still existed in 1945, as did a handful of earlier ironclad battleships, and battleships converted to aircraft carriers before the war, some of which had also played a part in the hostilities. Some of these ships were damaged or wrecked, but many others had been pivotal to the conduct of the war, and in the thick of it until the very last days of hostilities.

The war in Europe had finished on 8 May 1945. Battleship-related naval activity in that theatre of war had been low since the sinking of the German *Tirpitz* by the RAF in Tromsø Fjord, north Norway, at the end of November 1944. However, that event in itself was the culmination of an extraordinary and sustained effort that the Allies had made to eliminate *Tirpitz*, *Scharnhorst* and the rest of the German surface navy heavy ships based in northern Norway over the preceding three years, in order to protect the Atlantic sea lanes and supply convoys to Russia. It showed what a profound strategic impact even one modern battleship could still have very late in the war. The lessons of the sinking of the *Scharnhorst* by the British battleship *Duke of York* at the Battle of the North Cape on 26 December 1943 – a purely surface action in near darkness and poor weather where aircraft played no part at all – resonated at the British Admiralty long afterwards into peacetime.

The campaign in the Mediterranean from 1940 to 1943 had been as much about the battleship balance of power as about air power. It was no coincidence that the United Kingdom's heaviest setbacks in the Mediterranean were in early 1942 when battleship losses there and in the Far East, combined with the threat of German heavy ships in the North Atlantic, meant she had no available battleships in the Mediterranean to counter the threat of the Italian battlefleet to her Malta convoys. Italy's major opportunities were squandered because it was desperately short of fuel to put its own battleships to sea; and because of excessive caution when Italian admirals had the chance to use them to strike decisive blows – a caution engendered in part by the moral superiority that the British battleships had established in surface actions during 1940–41. Nor was it a coincidence that the culminating moment of the war against Italy was the escape and flight of the Italian fleet – led by its battleships – from its own ports, under heavy German attack, to surrender to the Allies under the guns of the fortress of Malta in September 1943.

Three remaining German heavy ships outlasted *Tirpitz*: the battlecruiser *Gneisenau*, sister of *Scharnhorst*, and the pocket battleships *Lützow* and *Admiral Scheer*, sisters of *Graf Spee*. *Lützow*, plus the pre-dreadnought battleship *Schlesien*, remained in action in the Baltic Sea against the Soviet Red Army advance until very close to the end of hostilities, when all were finally scuttled or sunk at their moorings in the final weeks of the European war. In the Pacific, however, naval and amphibious operations continued against Japan at a pace, range and scale that planners had never imagined before 1941. The final actions of the war in the Far East, from the invasion of the Philippines in October 1944; the push against Japanese conquests in South East Asia; the battles for the two strategic outlying islands of Iwo Jima and Okinawa; and finally operations against Japan itself in the summer of 1945, all involved Allied fast striking forces arranged into task forces of aircraft carriers and battleships escorted by cruisers and destroyers. There was also extensive use of older, slower battleships providing gunfire support to successive amphibious landings, or for shore bombardment against strategic targets. Battleships of the US Navy, Royal Navy and French Navy were involved in these campaigns.

For their part the Japanese, increasingly bereft of effective air striking power as the war progressed, especially after the Battle of the Philippine Sea in June 1944, had used their battleships, all nine of them, in an extraordinary (and typically over-complex) operation to forestall the US invasion of the Philippines in October 1944. Despite the massive air superiority and overall material preponderance of the US Navy, the Japanese very nearly succeeded. They sacrificed two weaker fleets to do so. Their largely empty carriers acted as a decoy fleet to the north and drew away the bulk of the US Navy's air strike effort. Admiral William Halsey, in command of the US Navy 3rd Fleet, also planned to use his fast battleships finally to destroy them, and deployed these in a full-speed chase ahead of his carrier groups to do so. To the south a Japanese force with the two older battleships *Yamashiro* and *Fuso* tried to penetrate the Surigao Strait to reach the landing beaches, but were sunk by a larger force of old US battleships blocking their path.

The Americans had employed aircraft to attack the third, and most powerful, Japanese force the previous day as it approached from the west, and had sunk, after prodigious effort, the super-battleship *Musashi*. But the other four battleships plus heavy cruisers were undamaged and, after retreating briefly, reversed course in the night to achieve surprise and get in among the lighter US forces covering the landings at Leyte Gulf, and virtually to the beachhead itself. Many argue that the Japanese commander, Admiral Kurita, could and should have used his four surviving battleships and their numerous escorts to destroy the covering force of small escort carriers and the invasion fleet. They have wondered why he failed to press home the advantage on 25 October 1944 at Leyte Gulf, and what the impact on the final shape of the war might have been had he done so. Kurita's force would certainly have been destroyed once Admiral Halsey refocussed on that threat, but very severe disruption could have been inflicted on the invasion – it might even have been initially repulsed – and much amphibious capability that was later reused in the subsequent operations would have been destroyed.

As it was, Kurita lost his nerve and extracted all four battleships without serious damage the way they had come. There was to be no similar opportunity for Japan in the remaining ten months of the war. There is also a case for the Imperial Japanese Navy to answer as to whether it made effective use of its battleship advantage, gained by sinking all the US battleships at Pearl Harbor, during the campaigns of 1942. At the pivotal Battle of Midway in June 1942 the many Japanese battleships present were held back way behind their carrier force and played no effective role. Had they been thrown forward to threaten both Midway Island itself, and the US carriers, it is hard to see how the Americans could have made their decisive attacks against the Japanese carriers. And in the Solomon Islands campaign, although the Japanese did use their battleships, it was done piecemeal, allowing the US to pick them off.

Although the Imperial Japanese Navy was essentially a broken force after the Philippines campaign, it still had six battleships, and the launching of the enormous *Yamato*, the largest battleship ever built, against the Okinawa invasion fleet in April 1945 required an unprecedented aerial assault by more than 400 US planes to sink her. The remaining Japanese battleships were thereafter hamstrung by the absence of air cover and even more by critical shortages of fuel, but remained elusive targets. The last four ships (*Kongo* had been sunk by a submarine in November 1944) were only finally immobilised in their bases by overwhelming air attacks in the last few days of the war.

Most of those fighting and planning were expecting these 1945 operations against Japan to be the precursor to another lengthy and massive amphibious assault on the Japanese home islands, code-named Operation Downfall. Planning for this envisaged the deployment of twenty-four battleships in further operations along the same lines as those undertaken over the previous two years across the Pacific. Planning assumptions envisaged the war lasting until at least mid-1946, possibly into 1947. Instead, on 6 August 1945 Hiroshima was destroyed by the first dropping of the atomic bomb. Nagasaki followed three days later.

Above: *Haruna* at Kure, under attack by United States Navy 3rd Fleet aircraft, 28 July 1945. *(NARA)*

The Japanese leadership, faced with the reality of obliteration by this new, overwhelming weapon, elected to end the war. A ceasefire came into effect on 15 August, bringing the Second World War to an end.

The formal instrument of unconditional surrender was signed on 2 September 1945, not on the capacious deck of an aircraft carrier (they were mainly still at sea maintaining an insurance against renegade Japanese attacks), but with pomp and heavy symbolism, and under the gaze of 225 reporters and seventy-five photographers, as well as fifty-seven US admirals and generals and nineteen from the other Allied nations, on the deck of US Admiral Halsey's 3rd Fleet flagship, the battleship *Missouri*.

The spot chosen was on the starboard side of 01 deck in the imposing shadow of her 16in artillery and armoured conning tower. The UK's representative, Commander-in-Chief of the British Pacific Fleet, Admiral Sir Bruce Fraser, travelled across Tokyo Bay to the ceremony from his own flagship, the battleship *Duke of York*. He took with him a large mahogany table to be used for the surrender ceremony. At the last minute it transpired that, although grand, this table was not large enough for the signatories and surrender documents, and the Captain of *Missouri* had to scavenge a larger standard-issue folding table from the crew mess deck and render it presentable for the historic moment by rapidly covering it with a coffee-stained tablecloth from the officers' mess.[3]

The ceremony itself was brief. The Japanese delegation arrived at 0856 and 'at 0902 … the ceremony commenced and the instrument of surrender was presented to all parties'. It was over by 0925, whereupon the various dignitaries all left *Missouri*.[4] Battleships, then, were centre stage at the end of hostilities, as they had been throughout the previous six years. A review of the locations and status of the ninety-five battleships on 2 September 1945 shows how extensive their presence still was. It also throws up a number of little-known historical curiosities. The list that follows is intended to be comprehensive. It includes all ships built after 1905 (the year of the laying down of HMS *Dreadnought*) which were

Below: *King George V* anchored at Sagami Wan, Tokyo, 29 August 1945. Six other battleships are among the vessels just visible in the background – two *Idaho* class, *Missouri, South Dakota, Iowa* and *Duke of York*. (NARA)

The Surrender on *Missouri* – General of the Army Douglas MacArthur and Fleet Admiral Chester W Nimitz, with Admiral William F Halsey behind, approaching the assembled Allied representatives for the Japanese surrender aboard *Missouri*, 2 September 1945. *(NHHC)*

originally designed as battleships, and which mounted an all big-gun armament of 11in guns or greater. It excludes a handful of battleships converted into aircraft carriers in the 1920s after new battleships were forbidden by the Washington Naval Treaty (the US *Saratoga*, UK *Furious* and French *Bearn)*. It includes ships sunk, beached or scuttled, but which were still physically visible in August and September 1945. Visible, it should be emphasised, is not the same as viable. In some cases these were out and out wrecks, in some cases capable of refloating and repairing, as had happened to battleships frequently during the war. The list also includes battleships still under construction on 2 September 1945. I have excluded pre-dreadnoughts – battleships dating from before 1905 with mixed-calibre armaments – a few of which still existed; and also excluded the three Swedish Coastal Defence ships of the *Sverige* class, which although armed with 11in guns and heavily armoured, lacked seagoing battleship characteristics. (For the record the last of these survived until 1957.)

The battleships are listed by country, then by date of construction.[5]

United States of America (thirty-two ships)

Utah. Dating from 1909, she was demilitarised after the Washington Naval Treaty of 1922, and employed as a target ship thereafter. In 1945 she was partially capsized and wrecked at Pearl Harbor, Hawaii. Salvage attempts after the Japanese sank her on 7 December 1941 were abandoned in 1944. She remains there to this day, a national memorial.

Wyoming. Laid down in 1910, she was also demilitarised after the London Naval Treaty in 1930. She served through the Second World War as an anti-aircraft gunnery training ship in Chesapeake Bay on the US east coast. On 13 July 1945 she joined Composite Task Force 69, a unit established to conduct trials into methods of combating Japanese Kamikaze suicide attacks, which were taking a heavy toll on US warships.

Wyoming configured as a gunnery training ship, late 1945. *(NARA)*

This Task Force became the Operational Development Force US Fleet on 31 August 1945, a role that continued in the immediate post-war period at Casco Bay, Maine, testing new fire control systems.

Arkansas. Originally *Wyoming*'s sister ship, she remained fully operational as a battleship during the Second World War, based in the Atlantic, Mediterranean and Pacific. She was at Okinawa on 2 September preparing for further operations against mainland Japan.

New York. She had been laid down in 1911. Having fired 5,200 rounds of 14in main battery ammunition at Iwo Jima and Okinawa earlier in 1945, her guns were worn out, and required relining in preparation for the Japan invasion. She was undergoing this refit at Pearl Harbor, Hawaii, when the surrender came.

Texas. New York's sister, she was also at Okinawa on 2 September preparing for further operations against Japan.

Nevada. Dating from 1912, she was sunk at Pearl Harbor in December 1941, but salvaged, modernised and restored to operation by November 1942. She was in Buckner Bay, Okinawa, on 2 September 1945, and she departed for San Pedro, California, on 23 September 1945.

Oklahoma. Nevada's sister, she had capsized after the Japanese air attack at Pearl Harbor on 7 December 1941. She had been salvaged, righted and pumped out by 1943. The damage from seven torpedo hits was so severe that restoration to active service was finally ruled out in August 1944, but only because it would have taken longer than the projected duration of the war to mid-1946. She was patched up with temporary wooden bulkheads and concrete patches, and anchored at a remote corner of Pearl Harbor, where she lay in September 1945.

Oklahoma being righted at Pearl Harbor, 8 March 1943. *(NHHC)*

Pennsylvania torpedoed at Buckner Bay, Okinawa, with decks almost awash, 12 August 1945. *(NHHC)*

Pennsylvania. She was laid down in 1913, and was another Pearl Harbor survivor brought back into full service. On 12 August 1945 she was torpedoed at Buckner Bay, Okinawa, by a lone Japanese aircraft, the last major success of Japanese arms in the war. Damage aft was extensive, and 2 September found her under tow by two tugs on her way to the US base in Guam, where she arrived on 6 September for emergency repairs in a floating dock.

Arizona. Sister ship of *Pennsylvania*, she had been blown up and sunk at her moorings by a magazine explosion in Pearl Harbor during the Japanese attack on 7 December 1941. She was beyond salvage, and had been partially dismantled by 1945. The hull below the weather deck remains substantially intact, awash at the site where it sank, and now straddled by the National Memorial erected in the 1960s.

New Mexico. Dating from 1915, she had started the war in the Atlantic, but then served extensively in the Pacific. She was hit by

USS *Arizona* memorial, Pearl Harbor. *(NHHC)*

kamikazes on 6 January 1945 while shelling Japanese defences in the Philippines.[6] *New Mexico* had recovered from this and further Kamikaze damage sustained in May at Okinawa, and joined the Japan occupation force, entering Tokyo Bay on 28 August. While there, she was the subject of an iconic and much-reproduced photograph against the background of Mount Fuji, symbolising victory in the Pacific.

Mississippi, New Mexico's sister ship, was also part of the Japan occupation force, entering Tokyo Bay on 27 August.

Idaho. She was the third ship of this class, and she too was part of the occupation force, entering Tokyo Bay on 27 August.

Tennessee. She had been laid down in 1917 and was also repaired and modernised after extensive damage at Pearl Harbor. She had taken part in the later battles of the war and was at Buckner Bay, Okinawa, when the surrender took place.

California. She was *Tennessee*'s sister, and also a veteran of Pearl Harbor and of the later Pacific campaigns. She was covering the activities of an Allied minesweeper squadron in the China Sea on 2 September. In late September she landed US occupation forces in Honshu, Japan.

Colorado. She was laid down in 1919, and had fought across the Pacific. She had covered the airborne landings at Atsugi Airbase near

Tokyo on 27 August, and then was part of the Japan occupation force, in Tokyo Bay until 20 September.

Maryland. She was sister to *Colorado*, and, following extensive service to the end of the Okinawa campaign, she had returned to the USA for modernisation and overhaul, in anticipation of further employment in the Japanese invasion force. She was completing her work-up training off the US west coast on 2 September 1945.

West Virginia. The final ship of the *Colorado* class, she had undergone the most prolonged reconstruction of all the Pearl Harbor battleships before rejoining the fleet in September 1944, just in time to engage the Japanese battleships at the Battle of Surigao Strait (see above). On 2 September 1945 she was part of the surrender Task Force in Tokyo Bay.

North Carolina. The first of America's modern battleships dating from 1937, she was patrolling the Japanese coast on the day of surrender, arriving at Tokyo Bay on 5 September.

Washington. Sister of *North Carolina*, she was undergoing a refit at Puget Sound Navy Yard, Bremerton, Washington, between the end of June and mid-September.

South Dakota. Laid down in 1939, she had carried out the final shore bombardment of the war on 15 August, the very day of the Japanese surrender, and had arrived in Tokyo Bay as part of the occupation force on 29 August.

Indiana. *South Dakota*'s sister ship, she was patrolling the Japanese coast on the day of the surrender, and arrived in Tokyo Bay on 5 September.

Massachusetts. The third ship of this class, she had carried out her last bombardment of the Kamashai iron and steel works in Japan on 9 August. Uniquely among the twelve US Navy modern battleships, she was not required for the final act of the drama and had begun her journey back to the USA on 1 September.

Alabama. The final ship of the *South Dakota* class, she was also patrolling the Japanese coast on 2 September, and arrived in Tokyo Bay on 5 September.

Iowa. She had been laid down in 1940 and joined the war in August 1943. She had reached Yokosuka on 27 August 1945 to oversee the seizure and neutralisation of the naval arsenal, including that of the still partially operational Japanese battleship *Nagato*. She moved into Tokyo Bay on 29 August for the surrender.

New Jersey. *Iowa*'s sister ship had been overhauled at Pearl Harbor after her participation in the Okinawa campaign, and was returning to the theatre of operations when the surrender came. She had reached Buckner Bay, Okinawa, by 1 September. Later she proceeded slowly to

Japan, arriving in Tokyo Bay on 17 September. Although she missed the surrender, once there she served as flagship for the US occupation force until relieved by *Iowa* on 28 January 1946.

Missouri. The third *Iowa*-class ship, she had arrived in Tokyo Bay on 29 August 1945 and was prepared as the site for the formal signature of Japan's instrument of surrender on 2 September (see above). General Douglas MacArthur, Supreme Allied Commander in the Pacific, signed on behalf of the United States of America.

Wisconsin. The fourth *Iowa*, she was patrolling Japanese coastal waters on 2 September, and arrived in Tokyo Bay to join the occupation force on 5 September.

Kentucky. The fifth *Iowa*-class ship was still under construction at Norfolk Navy Yard, Portsmouth, Virginia, on 2 September. Building had begun in March 1942, but there was a prolonged hiatus from June 1942 to June 1944 as priority was given to amphibious shipping. She was some 70 per cent complete at the date of Japan's surrender.

Illinois. The sixth ship of the *Iowa* class was also under construction at the Philadelphia Naval Shipyard, Pennsylvania. She had been begun in December 1942, but construction proceeded slowly due to higher priorities. She was only some 22 per cent complete, and the contract was formally cancelled on 11 September 1945.

Alaska. The first of America's 12in-gunned large cruisers, a pet project of President Franklin D Roosevelt, she was laid down in 1941. She joined the war late in 1944 and in September 1945 she was part of the US North China Force, tasked to occupy Japanese-held territory in Korea and China. She sailed from Okinawa and reached Inchon, Korea, on 8 September. She moved on to Tsingtao in northern China by 27 September to support the 6th US Marine Division, who went ashore there.

Guam was *Alaska*'s sister. She had played a minor role in the 1945 campaigns. On 2 September she had been appointed flagship of the North China Force, and also reached Inchon, Korea, on 8 September, where she provided support for the occupation forces until 11 November 1945.

Hawaii. The third *Alaska*-class battlecruiser was under construction at the New York Shipbuilding Company, Camden, New Jersey. Construction was well advanced, and she was nearly ready for launching in September 1945. Construction continued and she was launched in November 1945.

United Kingdom (eighteen ships)

Centurion. This survivor of the Grand Fleet, laid down in 1911, had been demilitarised as a result of the Washington Naval Treaty of 1922. When *Nelson* replaced her in the fleet, she had been converted into a radio-controlled target ship in 1926–27, with all her guns removed. She served through the Second World War, including camouflaged as a dummy *King George V*-class modern battleship in the Eastern Fleet and Mediterranean. In this capacity she had even been used in mid-1942 as an escort to Convoy MW11 during Operation Vigorous, an unsuccessful attempt to resupply Malta. The aim was to persuade the Axis that the convoy had a battleship covering force when in reality there was none. Her final duty was as an anti-aircraft platform and block ship, deliberately scuttled on 7 June 1944 as a breakwater for the Mulberry harbour at Arromanches, in Normandy. She was badly damaged by the great storm of 19–22 June, breaking in two at the bows, but remained a functioning part of the outer breakwater. There she remained through 1945. She was eventually broken up for scrap where she lay, but detailed information on the how and when is difficult to find.

Iron Duke. Admiral Jellicoe's flagship at the battle of Jutland was laid down in 1912. She had survived the cull of the Royal Navy's older battleships following the London Naval Treaty of 1930 by virtue of partial demilitarisation. She still retained some of her 13.5in gun main armament, and had been converted into a training ship. She was bombed and damaged at Scapa Flow by the Luftwaffe early in the Second World War, but was beached and continued in active use as a harbour depot ship at the Flotta fleet base in Orkney. She remained at Scapa Flow until refloated for scrapping on 19 April 1946.

Queen Elizabeth. The UK's first 15in gun super-dreadnought had been laid down in 1912. She was active in the Allied campaign against Japan in the Indian Ocean until early 1945, when she was replaced by

Centurion sunk as Mulberry Harbour breakwater at Arromanches, Normandy, June 1944. *(NARA)*

Nelson. She had returned to the United Kingdom to become part of the Home Fleet, then an accommodation ship at Rosyth, Scotland. She had been placed in reserve there in August 1945.

Warspite. Sister ship of *Queen Elizabeth*, she had fought across the globe and finished her active service bombarding Walcheren in the Netherlands in September 1944. She was pretty much worn out. Severe damage had been inflicted to her on 16 September 1943 off the Salerno beachhead in Italy, when she became one of the earliest victims of a guided weapon, the German Fritz-X 1400 glider bomb. She had never been fully repaired. In September 1945 she was in reserve at Portsmouth, anchored to the reserve fleet buoy at Spithead.[7]

Valiant. Another of the *Queen Elizabeth* class, she was undergoing a long refit and repair at Devonport dockyard that had started in February 1945. This followed serious damage sustained at Trincomalee, Ceylon, on 8 August 1944 when the floating dock lifting her had collapsed under her.

Malaya. The final surviving *Queen Elizabeth*-class ship was also in reserve at Portsmouth, after her final active service bombarding the Normandy beachheads in June 1944. Since 15 May 1945 she had been serving as an accommodation ship for the Royal Navy Torpedo School and known as *Vernon* II.[8]

Revenge. She was laid down in 1913. Since May 1944 she had been in reserve, serving first at Gare Loch, Scotland, alongside her sister *Resolution* as part of the Royal Navy's *Imperieuse* stokers training establishment. The two ships were moved to Devonport to continue in this role from 11 December 1944.

Royal Sovereign. She was sister ship of *Revenge*. Following the defeat of Italy in September 1943 and the surrender of her fleet, Stalin had been pressing his allies for allocation of a modern surrendered Italian battleship as the USSR's share of the spoils of war. The UK felt strongly that it needed to retain control of the Italian fleet. Instead of a new Italian ship, Prime Minister Winston Churchill had agreed to give the USSR an obsolete British battleship. Since August 1944 *Royal Sovereign* had been loaned to the Soviet Navy, and was serving under the name *Archangelsk* with the Northern Fleet in the Kola inlet.

Ramillies. Another of the *Revenge* class, she was also in reserve since 31 August 1945 as a harbour training ship and accommodation ship at Portsmouth, where she was known as *Vernon* III. John Egerton Broome, famous as commander of the Escort Group in the doomed PQ17 Russian convoy of June 1942, was her captain from 1945 to 1946.

Resolution. The final surviving *Revenge*-class ship, her main armament had been removed in June 1944 to be used as spares for ships that wore out their own guns during the Normandy landing bombardments. Since December 1944 she had been in reserve, serving at Devonport as part of *Imperieuse* alongside *Revenge*.

Renown. Following the loss of her sister *Repulse* in 1941 she was now one of a kind, a 15in-gunned battlecruiser. Although laid down in 1915, she was much modernised before the Second World War. On 2 September 1945 she was at Plymouth in reserve in a training role. On 2 August 1945 she had hosted King George VI and President Harry S Truman for lunch as the latter returned to the USA from the Potsdam conference. Although old and lightly armoured, she was a fast and largely modernised ship, and was due to have started a refit to put her back into the war against Japan, but with the sudden end of that war the refit was cancelled in September.

Nelson. She was laid down in 1922. She was serving with Vice-Admiral Sir Arthur Power's East Indies Fleet in the Indian Ocean, leading the maritime operations that were steadily eroding Japan's hold on South East Asia. She had been at Trincomalee, Ceylon, when the Japanese ceasefire came into effect on 15 August. She then sailed to Penang, Malaysia, to lead the local surrender of Japanese forces there on 26 August, and agree terms for the British return to Singapore. She was at Penang on 2 September.

Rodney. *Nelson*'s sister ship had finished the war in Europe at Scapa Flow, serving as flagship of Admiral Sir Henry Moore, Commander-in-Chief Home Fleet. This duty finished on 22 May 1945, and she spent May to November 1945 in Rosyth.

King George V. Britain's first modern[9] battleship, laid down in 1937, had been in action with the British Pacific Fleet throughout 1945. On 29 July she undertook her final bombardment of industrial complexes on the Japanese mainland, the last occasion when any British battleship fired her main armament in anger. She was one of the eleven battleships in Tokyo Bay for the Japanese surrender on 2 September.

Duke of York. She was the sister of *King George V* and also laid down in 1937. As noted above, she was flagship of the Commander-in-Chief of the British Pacific Fleet, Admiral Sir Bruce Fraser, recently arrived from Australia, and she too was in Tokyo Bay for the surrender.

Anson. The fourth of the class (*Prince of Wales* having been sunk in 1941) was laid down in 1938. She had been *King George V*'s partner in the British Pacific Fleet until relieved by *Duke of York*. Following the ceasefire she had sailed from Australia via the Philippines, then joined the British Task Force that liberated Hong Kong from Japanese occupation, arriving there on 29 August 1945, and moving into Hong Kong harbour on 30 August, Liberation Day.

Howe. The last of the *King George V* class was laid down in 1938. Following a prolonged deployment in the British Pacific Fleet, she was being refitted in Durban, South Africa, at the date of the surrender ceremony, emerging from the dockyard on 10 September.

Vanguard. The last British battleship was in the final stages of construction at John Brown's shipyard, Clydebank. She had been begun as early as October 1941 when manpower and the slipway previously dedicated to construct *Duke of York* became available. She was originally expected to complete quickly because her 15in guns and turrets already existed in storage, but she had been progressively delayed because priority was given to construct aircraft carriers and destroyers. She was launched by Princess Elizabeth in December 1944, but in mid-1945 some 1,500 of John Brown's 4,000 workforce were still actively employed on her completion.[10]

France (twelve ships)

Condorcet. Her semi-dreadnought design was obsolete even before she was laid down in 1907. She had been disarmed and converted into a training ship as early as 1925, based in Toulon. She remained there through the war, initially under Vichy control until the German takeover in November 1942. She was scuttled by the Germans in July 1944 before the Allies overran the port. There she remained in September 1945.

Courbet. She was laid down in 1910. She had escaped from the German advance on Cherbourg in June 1940 to be impounded by the British at Devonport. After France had surrendered she was transferred to the Free French Navy. After later use at Loch Striven in the Clyde as a target ship for heavy bomb experiments, she was selected as a breakwater for the Gooseberry Harbour Number 5 off Sword Beach, Hermanville in Normandy. (Gooseberries were the code name for open beaches sheltered by sunken block ships, as opposed to Mulberries, which had port

Condorcet after being scuttled at Toulon. *(Alamy)*

facilities.) She was beached and scuttled there on 9 June 1944. She remained there through 1945, a few miles up the coast from *Centurion*, before being gradually salvaged for scrap after the war.

Océan. Sister of *Courbet*, she had been disarmed and became a harbour training ship in 1936, based in Toulon. There the Germans captured her along with *Condorcet* in November 1942. She was used by them for explosives experiments until sunk by Allied bombing in July 1944. She was later raised for scrapping, which began in December 1945.

Paris. Another sister of *Courbet*, she escaped from Brest in June 1940 and was also seized by the British in July. She was used at Plymouth as a depot ship and later as a barracks ship for the Polish Navy. Both she and *Courbet* had come to the attention of Mr A H Read, Chairman of the British Iron and Steel Corporation (Salvage) Ltd in the UK Ministry of Supply, who asked the Admiralty in November 1942 and again in July 1943 whether the two French ships could be made available as scrap to meet the pressing UK demand for metals. However, she survived in Free

Paris at Plymouth 1941. *(NHHC)*

French hands until the end of the European war. On 21 August 1945 she was transferred back to Brest naval arsenal.

Bretagne. Laid down in 1912, she blew up, capsized and sank in the harbour at Mers-el-Kébir, Algeria, on 3 July 1940 after being hit by 15in shells from HMS *Hood* during the controversial British attack designed to prevent units of the French fleet that would not submit to British control from potentially falling into German hands after the French surrender. She was still there, largely unsalvaged, in 1945.

Provence. *Bretagne*'s sister also dated from 1912. She had been more lightly damaged by the British gunfire at Mers-el-Kébir and returned to Toulon in November 1940 to become flagship of the Vichy navy's training division, moored alongside *Condorcet*, and scuttled by Vichy when the Germans seized the port on 27 November 1942. She was raised by Italian salvagers in July 1943, then sunk again by the Germans as a block ship in Toulon harbour in July 1944. She remained there in September 1945.

Lorraine. The third ship of this class, she had sailed to Alexandria, Egypt, in June 1940 and submitted to British control, thus avoiding the fate of the other French Mediterranean Fleet battleships. She had an active war in the Free French Navy, conducting her final shore bombardment against pockets of German resistance in the Gironde as late as 20 April 1945, just two weeks before the German capitulation. She was transferred to Toulon later in 1945.

Dunkerque. France's first modern battleship, dating from 1932, was badly damaged by the British operation at Mers-el-Kébir, and did not reach Toulon for full repairs until February 1942. She was still under repair there in the Vauban dry dock when partially demolished to frustrate the German takeover on 27 November that year. She was then bombed by the Allies, and further demolished by the Axis, with Italian salvage teams removing some scrap including the 13in gun barrels. The hulk was towed out of the dry dock by the Germans in 1944, and moored in Toulon roadstead.

Strasbourg. Dunkerque's sister ship had also been scuttled in Toulon by the Vichy Government on 27 November 1942, despite the unsuccessful intervention of a German Panzer on the dockside. She was raised by the Italians on 17 July 1943 and they began scrapping her. She was sunk in

Lorraine in a French port, 1945. (Alamy)

shallow water off Cap Saint Mandrier in the Bay of Lazaret after eight hits by Allied bombing on 18 August 1944. A pre-invasion plan to have her reconditioned in a US dockyard was cancelled due to the extent of the bomb damage discovered when the Allies retook Toulon in July 1944. After liberation *Strasbourg* was raised there in October 1944 (Garzke & Dulin say 1946), but was found to be uneconomic to repair as a battleship. She was in Toulon in September 1945.

Richelieu. She was laid down in 1935, but was barely complete when she escaped the German advance at Brest on 18 June 1940. She started the war under Vichy control at Dakar, Senegal, but went over to the Free French in November 1942. Eventually, after being refitted in the USA, she became part of the Allied East Indies Fleet and saw action alongside *Queen Elizabeth* against Japanese bases in South East Asia. She was returning to the front after a refit in Durban in August 1945. She had reached Trincomalee by 1 August. She left on 5 September to take part in Operation Tiderace, the surrender of Japanese forces in South East Asia.

Jean Bart. Sister of *Richelieu*, her escape from St Nazaire in June 1940 was even more hair-raising than *Richelieu's* because she was only partially completed. She had spent the war first as a Vichy ship at Casablanca, where she resisted the Allied invasion in November 1942,

Strasbourg damaged at Toulon, 1944. (Alamy)

exchanging fire with *Massachusetts*. After her capture and transfer to the Free French in November 1942, she was used as an accommodation ship while awaiting a viable plan for her restoration in the USA to serve as a Free French ship. Her only four 15in guns (out of a designed eight) had been removed to refit *Richelieu* in the USA. In August 1945 she had finally sailed from Casablanca to Cherbourg to use the only viable graving dock in France, which she entered on 12 November 1945 for underwater inspection while the French Government decided her future.

Clemenceau. The third ship of the *Richelieu* class, construction had started in the Salou graving dock of the Arsenal de Brest in January 1939. She was only about 10 per cent complete when captured by the Germans in June 1940. Although they grandiosely designated her 'Battleship R',[11] no work was ever done beyond towing her out of the dock to moorings at Landévennec. The hulk was sunk there by a US air raid on 27 August 1944. It was broken up for scrap after VE day, although it failed to find a buyer at first asking in 1948. As it was being towed to Poullic-al-Lor to clear the dockyard in September 1948 it broke in two and sank. The remains were only finally sold for scrap in August 1951.[12]

USSR (nine ships)

Oktyabrskaya Revolutsiya. She was the ex-Tsarist *Gangut*, Russia's first dreadnought launched in 1911. She spent the Second World War at Leningrad, and supported the Soviet advances in the Baltic during 1944. She was in service in the Baltic in September 1945.

Sevastopol. Second of the *Gangut* class, she was part of the Black Sea Fleet during the war and was in the port of Sevastopol, Crimea, from November 1944, having led the Black Sea Fleet back there during the Soviet advances.

Petropavlovsk. The third ship of this class, she was sunk at her moorings in Kronstadt harbour, Leningrad, by the Luftwaffe on 23 September 1941, and, partially raised, remained there throughout the war as a stationary battery, contributing to the defence of Leningrad.

Frunze. The Ex-Tsarist *Poltava*, she had been a hulk since a crippling fire in 1919. Various projects to repair her came to nothing and she was finally deactivated in 1939. Scrapping had begun in 1940, but she was still afloat when Germany invaded. She was run aground at Kronstadt naval base and used as a depot ship for small craft during the war. She was refloated in May 1944 and towed to Leningrad, where she remained in September 1945.

Sovietsky Soyuz. The first of Stalin's modern super-battleships, she was laid down in 1938 and under construction at Ordzhinikidze (Baltic) Yard, Leningrad, at the outbreak of the war in 1941. Construction was suspended on 10 July 1941, when she was some 20 per cent complete.

Sevastopol under way, Black Sea c. 1943. *(NHHC)*

Sovietskaya Ukraina. Sister of *Soyuz*, she was under construction at Nikolayev in the Black Sea and 18 per cent complete when war broke out and construction was suspended. The hull was captured by Germany in August 1941. Partially dismantled by them, she was then sabotaged in March 1944 as the Germans retreated, and was still a wreck on the building slipway in September 1945.

Sovietskaya Rossiya. The fourth ship of the class, she had only just been begun, and was maybe 1–2 per cent complete at Molotovsk, near Arkhangelsk, when construction was suspended in July 1941. Her sister *Sovietskaya Byelorossiya* had been broken up at the same facility in 1940 due to faults discovered in her construction.

Kronstadt. The first Soviet fast battlecruiser was under construction at the Marti shipyard, Leningrad, and possibly 5 per cent complete by June 1944.

Sevastopol(2): Sister ship of *Kronstadt*, she was in the early stages of construction at Nikolayev in 1945.

Italy (seven ships)

Conte di Cavour. She had been laid down in 1910 but, like all the older Italian ships, extensively modernised in the 1930s. She had been sunk by Swordfish aircraft from HMS *Illustrious* in November 1940 in the famous torpedo bomber attack on Taranto harbour. After salvage she had been moved to Trieste in the northern Adriatic in 1942. There she remained, initially under repair, then after the Italian surrender in September 1943, as a hulk under German control. She was sunk a second time by Allied air raids on 23 February 1945. She was raised a second time at the end of 1945, and scrapped in 1946.

Giulio Cesare. Sister of *Cavour*, she had evaded German air attacks to reach Malta when Italy surrendered on 8 September 1943. Following Italy's formal joining of the Allied side as a co-belligerent against Germany on 17 June 1944, she returned to the Italian base at Taranto, where she remained until December 1948.

Sovietsky Soyuz under construction at the Baltic Shipyard Ordzhonikdze, Leningrad, 28 March 1942. *(NHHC)*

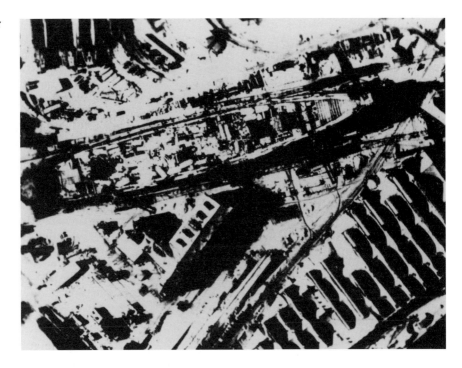

Caio Duilio. Dating from 1912, she too escaped to Malta and internment. Like *Cesare*, this was followed by a return to Taranto. She also spent time in 1945 in Sicily, at Syracuse and Augusta.

Andrea Doria. She was the sister ship of *Duilio* and followed a similar path. She was in Syracuse, Sicily, in September 1945, after surrendering at Malta in 1943, and a brief spell at Taranto following her return to Italian colours in June 1944.

Vittorio Veneto. The first modern Italian battleship, laid down in 1935, had survived the German guided weapon attacks that sank her sister ship *Roma*, and damaged her other sister *Italia*, to surrender at Malta on 9 September 1943. Because she was modern, capable and considered by

Andrea Doria. (Alamy)

Impero under guard of German soldiers at Trieste after September 1943 following the Italian surrender. *(NHHC)*

the British more susceptible to a counter-coup among fascist sympathisers in the crew, she was quickly moved on to Alexandria, Egypt, arriving on 14 September, and then on 17 October to Lake Amaro, the Great Bitter Lake in the Suez Canal. Plans to use her in the Allied war effort came to nothing, because the Royal Navy could not man her without putting other valuable ships into reserve and because of doubts about her condition and the dockyard effort required to rectify her. She remained interned in the Great Bitter Lake beyond September 1945.

Italia (Ex-*Littorio*). Her fate and movements were the same as her sister *Vittorio Veneto*, save that she picked up quite severe damage from a near miss by FX-1400 glider bomb on 9 September 1943. She too was in the Great Bitter Lake in September 1945.

Impero. She was the fourth ship of the *Vittorio Veneto* class, launched in 1939. Construction slowed during the war, and she was at Trieste by January 1942, around 70 per cent complete. She was never finished, instead being taken over by Germany in September 1943, used by the Germans as a target ship, then sunk in shallow water by Allied air raids on 20 February 1945.

Germany (six ships)

Derfflinger. Maybe the most remarkable of all the surviving battleships. Scourge of the British battlecruisers at Jutland in 1916, she had been scuttled along with the rest of the interned High Seas Fleet at Scapa Flow on 21 June 1919. She was the last of the ships to be salvaged by compressed air, coming back to the surface upside down as late as August 1939. In the normal course of events she would have been towed, upside down, following the rest of her fellow High Seas Fleet dreadnoughts to be scrapped by Metal Industries at Rosyth. But time ran out when the Second World War began days after her raising. For the duration of the war Rosyth was needed for other ship repair activity. So *Derfflinger* spent the entire war upside down, kept afloat by compressed air, anchored next to Rysa Little Island in Scapa Flow. A number of schemes were considered to scrap her in locations other than Rosyth, but all fell foul of technical difficulties because she was capsized, or the stringency of wartime resources. In Scapa Flow she remained in September 1945.

Lützow in the Kaiserfahrt Canal, with bomb craters, 1945.

Admiral Scheer capsized in dock at Kiel, 1945.

 Lützow. Dating from 1929, the pocket battleship had been sunk by RAF heavy bombers using 12,000lb Tallboy bombs in the Kaiserfahrt canal near Swinemünde (now Stettin) in the Baltic in March 1945.[13] However, she was on an even keel in shallow water and remained in action as a stationary gun battery, engaging advancing Soviet forces until her ammunition ran out on 4 May. Demolition charges were ineffective,

Gneisenau frozen in at Gdynia, probably winter 1945–46.

so she fell largely intact into the hands of the Red Army after the area was overrun.

Admiral Scheer. *Lützow*'s sister was sunk by RAF bombers in a mass air raid while being refitted at Deutsche Werke dockyard, Kiel, on 9 April 1945. Unlike *Lützow*, she had capsized.

Admiral Graf Spee. The final pocket battleship, she was famously scuttled off Montevideo, Uruguay, by her own crew on 18 December 1939 after the Battle of the River Plate, rather than re-emerge to engage the gathering Royal Navy forces. She had been salvaged only slowly from 1942 onwards, partially as a result of British attempts to glean intelligence about her equipment, but remained largely intact in 1945 and was visible offshore for many years after the war.[14]

Gneisenau. Laid down in 1935, she had been heavily damaged by air attack on 26–27 February 1942, at Deutsche Werke dockyard in Kiel. The battlecruiser was never fully repaired. She fell victim to Hitler's fury against the German surface navy after its failure to sink a lightly defended convoy to Russia in December 1942. She was due to undergo conversion at Gotenhafen to carry 15in guns instead of 11in, but instead she was

Settsu sunk off Kure, 9 October 1945. *(NARA)*

partially disarmed and eventually sunk by the Germans as a block ship at Gotenhafen (now Gdynia, Poland) on 23 (some sources say 27) March 1945, where she was captured by the Red Army in April.

Tirpitz. Sister of the *Bismarck*, she was completed in 1941. She had been capsized and sunk by RAF Lancaster bombers using the Tallboy in November 1944 in Alta Fjord, near Tromsø, Norway, but her keel and bilges were still above water in September 1945.

Japan (five ships)

Settsu. Japan's first dreadnought was launched in 1911. She had been disarmed in the 1920s under the terms of the Washington Treaty, but continued in service as a radio-controlled target ship. She was sunk in shallow waters by US aircraft at Kure naval base on the Inland Sea on 24 July 1945.

Haruna. The only survivor of a class of four fast battleships, she was launched in 1914. She was also sunk at her moorings in Kure naval base, Japan, by US Task Force 38 planes on 28 July 1945.

Ise. Launched in 1916, she had been converted to become a hybrid battleship/aircraft carrier in 1943 by removing the two aft turrets and superimposing a short flight deck. As the war reached its conclusion she was progressively damaged in air attacks and eventually sunk in shallow water near Kure on 28 July 1945.

Haruna sunk near Kure, 8 October 1945. *(NARA)*

Ise sunk off Kure, 8 October 1945. *(NARA)*

Hyuga. Ise's sister, and also converted in 1943, she too was run aground and sank after the air attack on 28 July 1945.

Nagato. Completed in 1920, she had been with Kurita at Leyte Gulf, but had been reduced to service as a coastal defence ship at Yokosuka naval arsenal in February 1945. She survived numerous US air attacks and was still afloat and partially operational at the point of the Japanese surrender. After the ceasefire she was secured by US sailors from *Iowa* on 30 August.

Brazil (two ships)

Minas Gerais. Only the third dreadnought battleship ever laid down, she was built by Armstrong and Whitworth at Elswick on the Tyne and laid down in early 1907, less than six months after the completion of *Dreadnought* herself. She had been refitted in the early 1940s but was still unfit for more than coast defence duties when Brazil entered the war on the Allied side in August 1942. She was anchored as a floating battery at Salvador for the duration of the war.

Sao Paulo. Delivered to Brazil by Vickers in July 1910, her condition was poor by the 1930s, and she was used as a coast defence ship. When

Hyuga sunk off Kure, 9 October 1945. *(NARA)*

Nagato at Yokosuka, 9 September 1945. *(NARA)*

Brazil declared war on Germany in August 1942, she was sent to Recife in this role, but saw no action and returned to Rio de Janeiro in 1945.

Argentina (two ships)

Rivadavia. Argentina's response to the perceived threat posed by the Brazilian battleships was built by Fore River Shipbuilding in the USA from 1910. She spent the war in Argentine coastal waters, preserving neutrality,

and made her last major cruise to the Caribbean between 29 October and 22 December 1945.

Moreno. Rivadavia's sister also spent the war in Argentine waters.

Chile (one ship)

Almirante Latorre. She was finally delivered to Chile in February 1921 after being requisitioned by the British Admiralty in 1914 and serving through the First World War in the Grand Fleet as HMS *Canada.* She was one of five dreadnoughts still operational in South American waters in 1945. She conducted neutrality patrols along the Chilean littoral during the Second World War and was still seagoing in September 1945.

Turkey (one ship)

Yavuz. The ex-German battlecruiser *Goeben*, whose sensational escape from the British Mediterranean Fleet to the Dardanelles in August 1914 had helped to trigger Turkey's entry into the First World War, continued to serve throughout Turkey's neutrality in the Second. She mainly divided her time between Istanbul and Izmir.

Summarising this list, of ninety-five dreadnoughts on 2 September 1945, twenty-nine were sunk, wrecked or damaged, awaiting their fate; seven were in service but in reserve or auxiliary roles and ten were still under construction or incomplete. That left forty-nine battleships still active, serving with nine navies. Twenty-six of the active ships belonged to the United States Navy, reflecting her precipitate rise to become the predominant political and military force in global affairs. Of these, twenty-four were in the Pacific theatre of war on 2 September 1945. The presence of ten Allied battleships in Tokyo Bay that day was designed as a crushing psychological blow to manifest US and UK military power towards any lingering embers of Japanese militarism that might have smouldered in the ruins of their empire.

CHAPTER TWO

Still Work to do

Admiral Sir Bruce Fraser, Commander-in-Chief of the British Pacific Fleet and later First Sea Lord, left, with Admiral Chester Nimitz, Commander-in-Chief US Pacific Fleet, aboard *Duke of York*, August 1945. *(Alamy)*

JAPAN WAS DEFEATED, but there was still a great deal for the Allies to do in the Pacific to unwind the chaos of four years of war. They needed to achieve three immediate objectives. One was to liberate the Japanese-occupied territories and establish secure administrations to allow a transition to peace. A second was to release, care for and repatriate prisoners of war and civilian internees. The third was to extend the occupation and administration of Japan itself. On 11 August 1945 Commander-in-Chief Pacific, General MacArthur, accepted Sir Bruce Fraser's offer of *King George V* plus the carrier *Indefatigable*, two cruisers and ten destroyers for the Japanese occupation force. Fraser's despatch to the Admiralty dated 6 December 1945 makes clear how complex were the arrangements for extracting prisoners of war from China, Hong Kong, Japan, Formosa and Hainan and arranging their repatriation.

Aircraft carriers were converted to be used as transports along with specialised ships.[1] His follow-up despatch dated 10 June 1946 estimated that in total 50,000 PoWs, internees and Dominion soldiers due for demobilisation were moved to their homes by the British Pacific Fleet in those nine months. The despatch also details the arrangements for selecting Kure as the port of entry for the British Commonwealth Occupation Force in Japan. Tasks of the naval party there included the cataloguing and destruction of enemy naval equipment, presumably including the sunken Japanese battleships in the vicinity of that port.

All these tasks had to be done against the underlying imperative of a further, and contrasting, objective, which was to move from a massive mobilised war footing ready for the assumed invasion of Japan to a peacetime military establishment and a peacetime defence budget in order to re-establish a peacetime economy as rapidly as possible. As part of that it was essential to get as many hostilities-only service personnel home as quickly as continuing tasks and available transport resources allowed. An immediate scaling down of the effort in the Pacific and Indian Oceans was an inevitable corollary, and most of the battleships that had been in action in August 1945 soon found themselves on the way home.

The US designated the return of troops to the Continental USA as Operation Magic Carpet. The War Shipping Administration used in all 370 warships and hundreds of merchant ships to repatriate an astonishing 8 million American military personnel from Europe, Asia and the Pacific to the continental USA as rapidly as possible. The battleships, particularly older ones, were used extensively for this task through to the end of 1945, because their size and scale of accommodation made it possible to transport hundreds if not thousands of troops at a time. Once home, the battleships' own early deactivation also directly released thousands more naval personnel to civilian life. The job began virtually immediately after the Japanese surrender. Vice Admiral Forrest Sherman led Task Force 11 from Tokyo Bay on 6 September with the battleships *New Mexico*, *Idaho*, *Mississippi* and *North Carolina* plus two aircraft carriers. Thousands of US Tenth Army personnel were picked up at Okinawa on the way back to the USA. The force proceeded via a brief stop at Pearl Harbor to discharge those heading for the west coast, before reaching the Panama Canal on 11 October. *Idaho* reached Norfolk, Virginia, as early as 16 October, where 229 of her crew were discharged for demobilisation.[2] *Missouri*, after her moment in the historic spotlight at Tokyo, also left on 6 September at 0502 with around 200 passengers aboard. She picked up 500 SeaBee construction workers from Okinawa for her return journey, along with forty sick cases for transfer to US hospitals.[3] Not only the SeaBees but 900 of her own crew of 2,700 were discharged for demobilisation immediately upon her arrival in the USA, also at Norfolk, on 18 October.[4]

A Magic Carpet ship – *Colorado* arrives at San Francisco, 15 October 1945. *(NHHC)*

Six more battleships were used for this purpose in the Pacific, making between one and five Magic Carpet trips each, mainly between Pearl Harbor and California. There were twenty such missions altogether by battleships. *Colorado* carried 6,357 men home during November and December.

Maryland's five trips conveyed over 8,000 until she finally moored at San Pedro, California, on 17 December. In the Atlantic, *Washington* was specially modified between 2 and 15 November to fit extra bunks for the troops. She sailed for Southampton with a reduced crew of only 919, compared to over 2,000 in her wartime configuration. This created enough accommodation on board to lift 1,664 US personnel back to their homes and families at the end of November. Oddly, after the trouble taken to assign and modify her, that was the only Magic Carpet mission that *Washington* took part in. The ex-battlecruiser, now aircraft carrier *Saratoga* with her voluminous hangar was particularly well suited to this task. On her many trips across the Pacific, she carried the largest number of returnees of any individual ship – 29,204.

One battleship, although heavily damaged, also participated in the Pacific troop transport task. *Pennsylvania* had taken two weeks of salvage work at Okinawa to be ready for tow to Guam, which took nine days at a speed of just 5 or 6 knots. Both her starboard propeller shafts were broken. On 7 September she was in the floating dock ABFD 3 at Guam and unloading ammunition. Seaman R D Sitzman fell from the brow of the ship to the bottom of the floating dock, and the log records that he died of multiple injuries. It took until 2 October to make her ready for the next leg of the trip, carrying forty-nine passenger officers and 350 marines. Her journey onwards to the west coast was fraught. She left on 4 October steaming at 13 knots on the two port shafts, and escorted by the cruiser *Atlanta* in case of trouble.

It came on 15 October, as she sustained further internal damage and flooding from the rotation of her number three propeller shaft, which had been distorted by the torpedo explosion. Divers had to be sent down to repair what the log describes as 'the patch'. Then on 17 October, which began at standard speed and 145 revolutions per minute, at 1054 she stopped all engines and hoisted the breakdown flag. It took over six hours for the divers to diagnose that the number three shaft was broken in the stern tube. Number three propeller and its shaft had to be cut away by divers before she could safely proceed, now on only one shaft out of four at a maximum of 9 knots. She finally made it to Puget Sound, Washington, USA, on 24 October at 1552. The passengers and hundreds of her own crew were discharged for demobilisation over the next few days, but she was still on duty on 27 October, fully dressed and hosting 11,700 visitors for Navy Day.[5]

The British battleships were not used in a comparable role, although there was some limited transportation of Dominion sailors back to Australia by *King George V*, *Duke of York* and *Anson*. The equivalent tasks for large-scale movement from the Indo-Pacific region to the UK (and for war brides to and from Australia) were undertaken by aircraft carriers including *Victorious*.

New Jersey and *Nagato* together at Tokyo Bay, 30 December 1945. (NARA)

But there was still much work for battleships in the East. Their value as command and control centres and flagships for taskforces was not extinguished by the end of hostilities. Their very large crews, typically around 2,000 all ranks, meant they could readily provide armed,

Guam at Jinsen (Inchon), Korea, 8 September 1945. *(NHHC)*

disciplined shore parties with a range of skills that assisted first in securing Japanese military assets, then in liberating and restoring to health the Allied prisoners of war and internees, and re-establishing key infrastructure. A battleship, first *New Jersey* from 17 September 1945 until 28 January 1946, then *Iowa* from January to March 1946, remained in Tokyo as flagship of the US Occupation Force in Japan. *Alaska* and *Guam* were the flagships and core of the US forces that ended the Japanese occupation in Korea, and assisted the Chinese Nationalist Government with the expulsion of Japanese forces from their northern provinces. *Alaska* was at Tsingtao in Northern China on 27 September, and remained in support of the US Marines there until 13 November. She returned to Inchon in Korea that day to pick up troops for a Magic Carpet run, and returned to Boston on 18 December, via San Francisco.

On 2 September 1945 there were five British battleships east of Suez. Their log books give a precise picture of the role they played in the transition to peacetime, and its occasional quirks and tragedies.

We have seen how *Nelson* and the French *Richelieu* participated in the takeover of Singapore and Malaya. *Nelson*'s log records long discussions with the Japanese envoys aboard the ship at Penang in northern Malaya every day from 28 August to 2 September 1945, the last session lasting until 2145 in the evening. These drawn-out negotiations were due to the inability of the local Japanese commanders to secure what they saw as the necessary authority from their chain of command based at Saigon to accede to the various British demands about security guarantees and de facto surrender. Details of the transfer of power back to Britain finally arranged, *Nelson* set off on 8 September to follow the spearhead of Operation Tiderace, the reoccupation of Singapore. Her transit of the Straits of Malacca was slow, with regular requirements to stream her paravanes to counter the known threat from mines. Unlike *Richelieu* a day later, she did not trigger one, although her paravane wires snapped on a couple of occasions requiring her to stop for repairs. She was also hampered by complete failure of the low-power electrical circuits early on 8 September, which deprived her of lights and the gyro compasses. She waited at the mouth of Singapore harbour for minesweepers to clear the channel, but was secure in harbour late on 9 September.

The formal surrender itself was signed by Lord Mountbatten, Allied Commander-in-Chief in South East Asia, aboard the cruiser *Sussex*. She had already been in Singapore for a week and had been the location of an earlier de facto surrender ceremony on 5 September.[6] *Nelson*'s log records an infantry landing craft coming alongside at 0710 on 12 September to convey the officers, landing party and Royal Marines band taking part in the official surrender ceremony. *Nelson* herself dressed ship with masthead ensigns and Union Flags to mark the surrender. It was 87°F at noon. Mountbatten came aboard himself the following day to address the ship's company, followed by ex-PoW officers for hospitality. *Nelson* stayed at Singapore until the end of the month, although to judge from the log her role in helping the colony get back on its feet seems to have been low key and consisted mainly in baking bread for despatch to the PoW camps and hospitals ashore. She left for Trincomalee on 30 September, passing *Richelieu* as she did so.

Nelson's journey home was uneventful. The advent of peace was manifested somewhat bizarrely, if traditionally, on 16 October when she stopped both engines to welcome King Neptune's Herald aboard. She crossed the equator at 0414 on 17 October, and at 0900 King Neptune himself, and his retinue, were welcomed aboard. She reached Kilindini, the harbour of Mombasa, East Africa, on 19 October, where she discharged eighteen officers and 234 ratings to *Howe* for further service in the Far East. On 22 October she resumed her voyage to the UK via Suez, where she would have passed the Italian battleships in the Great Bitter Lake, although her log, amidst all its myriad recordings of ships met, does not mention them – presumably because no courtesies were exchanged. *Nelson* moored at the South Railway Jetty, Portsmouth, at 1040 on 17 November 1945. The first job was to discharge five prisoners to the Royal Navy Barracks. Over the ensuing four days 723 ratings, nearly half the crew, left the ship, drafted to their home ports for discharge. Those that remained spent the next two weeks scraping the ship's bottom in D lock at Portsmouth. Christmas was celebrated at Portsmouth, but there was still work for *Nelson*, and on 29 December she sailed for Portland and the Home Fleet (see Chapter Six).[7]

Howe was the one battleship of the British Pacific Fleet not to get involved in the post-war activity. Her odyssey was indeed quite odd, almost as if the Admiralty did not know what to do with her. She lingered at Durban until 10 September, then went west to Cape Town for a visit between 14 and 20 September. Then she headed back east, and reached Kilindini, the main British base in East Africa, on 28 September. She had to wait there for three uneventful weeks until *Nelson* arrived. This triggered the first of a number of major churns for her crew, as 204 men left the ship to go home on *Nelson* but 243 joined her from the other battleship. On 27 October Stoker P Rooney fell off the dockside and was certified dead at 0100 the next morning. His funeral took place ashore that day. On 29 October the ship caught fire at the forward end of the pom-pom deck. It took fifteen minutes to extinguish.

Howe finally left Kilindini on 31 October after five weeks in East Africa, and called at the Seychelles on 6 November and then Addu Atoll in the Maldive Islands, which had been the secret 1942 Eastern Fleet emergency base, on 9 November. She reached Colombo in Ceylon on 12 November, where 102 men left the ship and fifty-four joined. On 15 November at Trincomalee on the opposite coast of Ceylon a further four left and fifty-two joined. She also welcomed aboard Lieutenant General Miles Dempsey, Commander of 14th Army, and other senior Army and RAF officers of his staff, bound for Singapore to command the newly re-established garrisons there. By 25 November *Howe* was in the Straits of Malacca. These were apparently no safer than three months before when *Nelson* and *Richelieu* had made the passage. Paravanes were put out and she went to damage control state 3. At 1031 on 26 November she opened fire on a mine in position 3 degrees 45 minutes N, 99 degrees 56 minutes E. Singapore was reached the following day. Fifteen men left the ship and fourteen joined. Mountbatten came aboard on 4 December to address the ship's company. But she did nothing more. If she had been intended for further service in the Pacific, that idea was scotched, and she set off westwards again on 7 December back to Colombo. There 273 souls left the ship and 255 joined, as well as Admiral Sir Arthur Power, stepping down as Commander-in-Chief East Indies. She made brief calls at Bombay and Aden (where eighteen men joined and four left her) before reaching the Suez Canal on 29 December. She left Port Said on New Year's Day. Sadly, Able Seaman R Wilkinson was not to see home. He died at 1415 on 1 January 1946 as a result of falling down a hatch in 'A' 14in barbette. He was buried at sea the next day. Avoiding the normal calls at Malta and Gibraltar, she sped home, reaching the South Railway Jetty at Portsmouth on 9 January 1946.[8]

King George V remained in Tokyo until late September 1945, before returning to Australia. She left behind 245 Royal Marines and sailors, who had been transferred to US landing ships as early as 20 August, to form part of the initial occupation force in Japan. As early as 7 September, at Tokyo, thirty-three of the crew also left the ship on draft for demobilisation. Her log records daily departures of US and UK ships, many carrying released PoWs away. Also each day Vice-Admiral Sir Bernard Rawlings, Second in Command of the British Pacific Fleet, would leave the ship for conferences with Admiral Fraser aboard *Duke of York*, and after his departure on 9 September for Hong Kong, for conferences with the US Admirals Halsey and Spruance, commanding the 3rd and 5th Fleets respectively. On 18 September the American admirals came aboard *King George V* for dinner and stayed overnight.

King George V left Tokyo Bay on 20 September, and reached Sydney, Australia, on 1 October. Rawlings hauled down his flag on 26 October, and the ship visited Melbourne from 27 October to 11 November. On the way back to Sydney she carried out what the ship's log calls 'MV' firings from the main armament (probably muzzle velocity) on 9 November. The number of rounds fired is not recorded.[9] At Sydney she underwent a short refit at the Cockatoo Island dockyard that lasted until 28 December. It was noted that her machinery was in good condition, with new boilers not expected to be required until 1954 (compared to the estimate of 1950 when she was first accepted into service).[10] On Monday, 7 January 1946 the ship's log recorded the embarkation of the Governor General of Australia for passage to Hobart, Tasmania:

King George V at Sydney, Australia, October 1945. *(Alamy)*

0625   Hands scrub decks.

0735   Hands employed cleaning and preparing ship for sea.

1000   Half mast colours for funeral of Signaller Wilkinson.

1100   Colours close up.

1315   Hands employed cleaning upper deck and slinging up wires.

1548   Their Royal Highnesses Prince William and Prince Richard and party come aboard.

1600   Their Royal Highnesses the Duke and Duchess of Gloucester come aboard for passage to Hobart.

1630   Slipped. Courses and speeds as required to leave Woolloomooloo Bay.

1705   Tugs cast off.

1725   Pilot disembarked.

1730   speed 13.5 knots, course 145 degrees (later 180 degrees).[11]

Hobart was reached on 9 January. Having dropped off the Governor General and hosted the usual round of parties for dignitaries as well as showing off the battleship to the public, she set sail for home. It was not a completely straightforward trip. On 17 January, 704 miles out of Hobart at 1005 both electric steering motors failed and the ship swung out of

control through nearly 180 degrees for twenty minutes while steam steering was connected. By 1030 she was back on course for Fremantle and at 1045 the log reported 'electric motors correct, changed back to ordinary steering'. Fremantle was visited, then Cape Town. On 13 February 1946, 1,260 miles north-west of Cape Town in the middle of the South Atlantic, a 14in sub-calibre firing took place between 0930 and 1008. Routine administration of the battleship was duly recorded every day. On 14 February Captain Schofield recorded a personal note in the log: 'I have this day admonished Temporary Lieutenant Theodore La Fontaine Fryett RNVR for having negligently performed the duty imposed upon him as a censor officer in that over a period of 6 months he failed to ensure that a large number of letters entrusted to him for censorship were despatched.' Via a final stop in Freetown, Sierra Leone, *King George V* finally tied up alongside the South Railway Jetty in Portsmouth Naval Base at 1205 on Saturday, 2 March 1946, back from the war at last. The next day 190 ratings left the ship, drafted straight to Chatham and Devonport for demobilisation.

Duke of York's movements as the flagship were dictated by the very broad responsibilities of Admiral Fraser. After the Japanese surrender, she left Tokyo on 9 September for Hong Kong (see below) and then went back to Japan on 21 September, and briefly relieved *King George V* at Tokyo before also travelling on to Sydney. Her logs for September and October 1945 are missing at the National Archive, but she left the Commander-in-Chief at Sydney sorting out the business of the British Pacific Fleet, and undertook a very leisurely trip to Tasmania between 3 and 21 November, which seemed to include very little official business, but did include a four-day ship's regatta at Norfolk Bay. This may have been evidence of Fraser's policy of keeping all his ships busy and on the move to forestall dissatisfaction among crews now increasingly pining for home.

Duke of York undertook a full-power speed trial on the return journey to Sydney. She re-embarked Admiral Fraser and made the return voyage to Hong Kong between 1 and 21 December via Fremantle and Singapore. It was punctuated by two tragedies. On 6 December at 1130: 'A/B G.D. Furness D/JX579806 died as a result of firing accident on No. 32 Oerlikon.' At 1655 the same day he was buried at sea 34 degrees 21 minutes South, 114 degrees 34 minutes East. Then, on passage from Singapore to Hong Kong, the first lieutenant, Lieutenant Commander May, was swept overboard and lost in the South China Sea at 0626 on 19 December. The log says it was a moderate NNE Force 3 wind, and after an hour's search at 0720 'Hope of recovering (which is then crossed through) Search for man overboard (Lt Cdr May RN) abandoned. Proceeded at 10 knots.' The ship's log only mentions May going overboard.[12]

Duke of York reached Hong Kong on 21 December 1945. On Christmas Eve she landed about 120 sailors and Royal Marines to relieve Kennedy Force, landed in August by *Anson*. On 16 January an initial detachment she had left behind in September came back aboard, but their replacements remained ashore providing support to the rapidly recovering colony until 8 March 1946. *Duke of York* then took Admiral Fraser to Amoy in China between 17 and 21 January. His despatches show how concerned Fraser was becoming about restoring full access by the Royal Navy to China after the war. This visit was part of his attempt to smooth matters. Chinese Nationalist Admiral Liu paid three separate visits to *Duke of York* on 18 January and Fraser went ashore to reciprocate. The rest of January and February were passed in harbour at Hong Kong with just two days at sea for exercises. The number of sick aboard the battleship rose steadily to thirty-nine on 8 March (*Duke of York* seems generally to have been a more sickly ship than the other battleships). It had been decided to base the British Pacific Fleet in Hong Kong at this point, so Admiral Fraser went ashore with his headquarters staff.

The battleship then spent two weeks in Japan, starting at Nagasaki on 15 March 1946, where the sole reason for the day trip was to allow a

Duke of York at Hong Kong viewed from Victoria Peak, probably in early 1946. (*Imperial War Museum*)

total of 576 sailors to be ferried ashore by Tank Landing Craft and 'landed for atom bomb tour'. She moved on to Kagoshima and then Kure on 19 March, and a further day excursion was mounted overland to Hiroshima. The final stop was Yokohama from 27 March to 2 April, whence she sailed again to Australia. Without the Commander-in-Chief aboard there were no senior visitors and a much lower level of drafting and personnel exchange than at earlier ports of call. So, it is hard to divine from her log the wider purpose of this visit to occupied Japan, unless, again, Admiral Fraser was just concerned to keep her busy. It is also likely, if not specifically mentioned, that the visit helped to support the establishment of the British Commonwealth Occupation Force at Kure from February 1946 onwards (see Chapter Five).

On the way to Australia one final time, *Duke of York* fired her 5.25in battery and undertook another full-power trial on the passage south. She was in the hands of the dockyard at Sydney between 15 April and 14 May 1946, when work was undertaken to improve the accessibility and drainage of the 14in mountings and to fit air conditioners.[13] A total of seventy personnel were drafted away from the ship. There was trouble of some sort on the night of 25–26 April as the log records Able Seamen Garside, Beveridge, Parritt and Vanhindle and Stokers Stewart, McCarl and Evans being placed under close arrest. She left Australia on 15 May 1946, the last departure of a British battleship from Australian waters, although the Americans were to be back some forty years later. *Duke of York* returned to Hong Kong for the final time on 29 May 1946. She picked up Admiral Fraser, now relieved as Commander-in-Chief in the Pacific. She also picked up sixty-four Royal Navy personnel and seventy-two from the Army for passage home, but drafted ninety-five off the ship as well for further duty in the Far East. *Duke of York* left Hong Kong on 7 June, initially for a very brief fuelling stop at Singapore, then via Colombo to Suez. The minutiae of naval discipline continued to be exercised. On Sunday, 23 June Captain Nicholl annotates the log in red ink: 'This day admonished Surgeon Commander M J Brosnan RN for improper behaviour in the wardroom at 2200 on 23 June.' There is no indication what the offender did. *Duke of York* took three days to transit the Suez Canal and exchanged a twenty-one-gun salute 'to the country of Egypt' on 30 June at Port Said. Then she went rapidly, via Malta and Gibraltar, to home.

Duke of York reached Plymouth on 11 July 1946 and secured to C Buoy. There were the usual immediate drafts, although on this occasion numbers are not given. Admiral Fraser disembarked the next day to continue his illustrious career: ennoblement, Commander-in-Chief at Portsmouth, and eventually to become the First Sea Lord. We shall meet him again in later chapters. He was closely followed at 1350 by the mysterious log entry '20 boxes left ship for Bank of England'. No further details are forthcoming – presumably it was gold bullion from Australia.

Anson's employment after hostilities was mainly in Hong Kong, although she and the aircraft carrier *Venerable* had initially been allocated to the relief of Singapore. The liberation of Hong Kong was entrusted to a task force led by Rear Admiral Cecil Harcourt, centred on *Anson*, *Venerable* and the carrier *Indomitable*. The task force sailed from Leyte in the Philippines on 26 August, and arrived off Hong Kong on 29 August 1945. Harcourt transferred his flag to the cruiser *Swiftsure* for the first entry into Victoria Harbour because the Australian minesweepers were still ensuring that the harbour was safe for the capital ships. They followed into the harbour the next day. *Anson* anchored at 1708 on 30 August and immediately despatched Royal Marine landing parties. The picket boat investigated a suspicious sampan at 2130. The next day she shifted berth to anchor off Kowloon.

There was initial disorder and some looting as Japanese authority collapsed. An urgent task was to establish security. About 1,000 men from the large ships of the fleet were landed and organised into two forces, Brown Force and Kennedy Force (named after their commanders), to patrol Hong Kong and Kowloon. They were soon reinforced by 3 Commando Brigade Royal Marines, which secured the New Territories. On 1 September *Anson* recorded: 'Lent the following officers for shore duty in Hong Kong for police and garrison duties. All remain on *Anson*'s books and will return when relieved by the Army. Cdr Kennedy in command, Lt Cdr Cameron, Lts Easton, Beattie, Coburn, Davies, Stuhe, Dowie, Dexter, Surgeon Lt Russell, Engineer Lt Bennett, Reverend G How, Sub Lts Hodges, Ffoulkes, Maj Baker-Creswell RM, Capt Miles RM, Lts Carruthers and Gathencole RM, Midshipmen Ballie-Hamilton, Burton, Jones, Mr Laiden, and Mr Adams, gunners. Also 200 ratings and 230 Royal Marine ranks, hereafter known as KENNEDY Force.' A further ninety-eight officers and men followed for Kennedy Force over the next week, making a total of over 550 from the battleship ashore.[14]

Meanwhile, normal shipboard duties carried on. Landing stores to sustain Kennedy Force was a major task. On 3 September at 1600 500 ex-Prisoners of War were entertained for tea and shown around the ship. The fluid situation in the Territory was exposed by the entry in the log on 7 September: '2330 Picket boat on anti-sabotage patrol intercepted 2 Japanese junks and captured 60 prisoners. Junks towed to Kowloon and turned over to MAK.' (probably Military Authorities Kowloon.) On 9 September at 1820 the log reports 'extinguished small fire in the blacksmith's shop. No damage.' *Anson* seemed prone to catching fire. There are half a dozen similar reports for the period 1945–46, many more than for her sisters.

A formal surrender by the Japanese did not take place until 16 September 1945 at Government House in the Central District. It was observed by Admiral Sir Bruce Fraser, who had arrived aboard *Duke of York* at 1500 on 14 September. *Anson* recorded: '1420 landed seaman guard (50 file) RM band and spectators. 1630 the Japanese surrendered Hong Kong unconditionally to Rear Admiral Harcourt representing Great Britain at ceremony in Government House. Fired a 21 gun salute in honour of the occasion. 2100 firework and searchlight display.'

Anson remained at anchor in Hong Kong harbour, with the exception of two brief trips to sea on 24–25 September and 1–4 October to ride out typhoon warnings. During the second trip she noted on 2 October: '1730 Junk breaking up, preparing to pick up crew. 1830 Chinese Mr and Mrs Kai and two paid hands on board. Was on passage to Hong Kong with a load of salt.' There was also a sojourn in Mirs Bay, west of the New Territories, between 27 October and 6 November. This was caused by an outbreak of disease in the ship. The log records her in quarantine from 25 October and the vaccination of the entire ship's company, but it does not say against what. There were then daily medical inspections until the all-clear. The passage back to harbour was used to exercise the main armament, with firing from A turret between 0941 and 0950 on 6 November.

Routine in harbour was occasionally disrupted. On 12 November at 1645: '1 cask of rum broken. 22 gallons of rum thrown overboard after breakage of cask.' On 16 November the Chief of the Imperial General Staff, Field Marshal Lord Brooke, visited the ship but only stayed twenty-five minutes. On 24 November Admiral Sir Andrew Chan Chak, Commander-in-Chief of the (Nationalist) Chinese Navy, came from Canton for a more leisurely visit. *Anson* then made a trip to Tokyo from 27 November to 12 December. Its only purpose seems to have been to pick up the Danish Consul to Tokyo, Mr Hansen and his wife, and the Swiss Legation party including nine women (Mrs Knoffle, it was noted, was eighty years old) and five children, all for passage to Hong Kong and thence onward to Europe. The log records their luggage as consisting of 140 large trunks, 105 suitcases and three pantechnicons each measuring 9 × 7 × 7 ft. There were also thirty crates, the property of Mr Assher, late British Consul General at Yokohama, and seventy Royal Navy personnel from the occupation force, also destined for Europe. There were gunnery drills on the return trip, with A2 14in gun being fired at 1440 on 10th December.

As noted above, *Duke of York* arrived to join *Anson* in Hong Kong on 21 December and Kennedy Force was relieved by the detachment from *Duke of York*. They came back aboard mainly over 22 and 23 December, with Kennedy himself rejoining with the final Royal Marine rearguard on Christmas Eve. After a quiet Christmas Day, on 26 December at 1534

Anson weighed anchor then sailed to Australia, via the Lombok Strait. Lombok was detected by radar at 0001 hours on New Year's Day 1946. She stopped over at Fremantle, where over 11,000 visitors were welcomed aboard, and she suffered her fourth minor fire in four months. Then it was on via Albany to Sydney. On the way she undertook a full-power trial in the Bass Strait on 16 January 1946. Her performance was poor. She generated 108,000 shp, and managed 214 shaft revolutions per minute, but a speed of only 25 knots, well below her design best. The captain was moved to write to Commander-in-Chief Pacific Fleet pointing out that the bottom of the ship was very dirty with extensive coralline growth, which he blamed on eighty-six days at anchor in Hong Kong. She was docked at the Captain Cook Dock, Sydney, between 26 February and 16 March 1946, where she was scraped and painted. The next full-power trial was south of Japan on 13 June 1946, when she was back to her best, developing 110,500 shp, 227 revolutions and 27.7 knots.

During her early days in Sydney at the end of January the wartime complement began to thin out. Eight officers and 280 ratings were drafted off the ship for passage to the UK. Before her docking, the next duty was a brief trip to Tasmania to pick up the Governor General, marooned there earlier by *King George V*. There was a gunfire demonstration for the Duke of Gloucester on 14 February during the passage back to Sydney. After emerging from the dock, she spent a week more in Sydney, suffering three more small fires, two on the same day. She went to sea on 28 March 1946 for a thorough shakedown cruise and exercises in Australian waters. This included firing practice for the main and secondary armament. On 2 April she fired five 14in rounds from each gun, a total of fifty shells. The rate of fire was leisurely in the extreme, Y turret taking five and a half hours to fire its twenty shells, A turret one hour eleven minutes for its twenty, and B turret fifty minutes for its ten. On 5 April there were simulated massed aerial attacks with thirty-two aircraft involved. *Anson*'s final trip to Sydney lasted from 6 to 10 April, on which day she left for Yokohama, and *Duke of York* arrived in Australia. The passage north was reminiscent of *Duke of York*'s in December, but with a happier outcome, because on 13 April in Force 6 winds, travelling at 14 knots, at '1033 ½ 2 men overboard starboard side. Stopped engines. Dropped starboard lifebuoy.1037 half astern both. 1107 ½ alongside men who were both saved and unhurt. 1108 proceeded, 14 knots.'

Anson arrived at Kure on 24 April for the last visit by a British battleship to Japan. She spent the next seven weeks shuttling between there, Yokohama and Kobe. A draft of 149 ratings left the ship at Yokohama, presumably for redistribution across the British Pacific Fleet still supporting the occupation forces. She left Japan on 12 June and was back in Hong Kong on 16 June. She finally sailed for the UK on 21 June, but she was still treated as a fully operational battleship, so 14in ammunition and cordite was transferred to her at sea that day south of Hong Kong from the Royal Fleet Auxiliary *Hickory Glen*. She called at Singapore and Colombo, where 189 more men left the ship, drafted to HMS *Gould*. Since May 1946 this had become the shore station hosting the British Pacific Fleet drafting pool of seamen, which had been moved from Sydney to avoid ships having to undertake the long dog-leg to Australia for drafts before service in the Northern Pacific. *Anson* reached Suez on 13 July, where she had to pump off oil in order to reduce the draft to 32ft 4in for the passage of the canal. She had to pause in the Great Bitter Lake, and the crew were allowed to go swimming off the ship. Again the officer of the watch did not remark on the presence of the Italian battleships, although at Port Said he did note that they passed the French *Bearn*, also on her way home from Vietnam (see below). This was the last time a British battleship transited the Suez Canal, and the last time one was seen in the East.

After the usual stops at Malta and Gibraltar, *Anson* arrived at Portsmouth, and was in C lock No. 3 basin at 1430 on 29 July 1946, the last of Britain's battleships to return from the war. The keenness of her crew to get back is possibly evidenced by the sick list, which had averaged fifteen to twenty every day of the voyage, but dropped to seven the day after she arrived and just three the day after that. On 30 July her captain proceeded on three weeks' leave. With *Anson* back on 29 July 1946, all Britain's battleships were in home waters for the first time since the eighteenth century.[15]

For France, post-war events took a rather different turn. In August the French Government decided to send an expeditionary corps to assist with the restoration of French colonial rule in Indochina. *Richelieu* and the ex-battleship, now aircraft transport, *Bearn* were envisaged as the core of its maritime component. Meantime, *Richelieu* became the last battleship casualty during the conflict, mined in the Straits of Malacca on 9 September as she made the passage south to Singapore from Penang. The mine exploded 17m to starboard of 15in turret number one. She stopped briefly, but was not seriously damaged – minor damage to the hull plating was sustained and 3,000 litres of wine were destroyed – and she limped into Singapore on 11 September, just in time for the formal surrender of Japanese General Itagaki on 12 September.[16]

The French commander, General Leclerc, having signed the Japanese surrender document in Tokyo on behalf of France, arrived in Saigon on 9 October. Meanwhile, Ho Chi Minh had declared Vietnam independent from France, on the very day that Japan surrendered. The situation on the ground in Vietnam at that point was a confused mixture of British security forces, deployed in the first instance during September because no French ground forces were available; released French Prisoners of War and internees; Vietnamese officials loyal to France waiting for their instructions; Japanese soldiers, who, authorised on behalf of the Allies, remained the de facto administrators and security presence for most of Vietnam; and Viet Minh forces seeking to take control of their country from all the above by revolutionary force.

France's naval squadron in the Far East, besides *Richelieu* and *Bearn*, also included two cruisers and two destroyers. *Richelieu* did not linger in Singapore, sailing back to Ceylon on the day of the formal surrender, 12 September, to pick up the 5th French Infantry Regiment for service in Vietnam. She arrived at Cap St Jacques at the mouth of the Mekong delta on 3 October 1945, where she anchored while the smaller ships in the squadron made their way upriver to Saigon with General Leclerc. *Richelieu* was then flagship, as well as command vessel for the 6th French Infantry Regiment in late 1945 and provided wider support, including medical, for French forces.

Leclerc soon wanted to extend French control northward from Saigon, and an operation was launched to secure the port and town of Nha Trang, some 200 miles up the coast. The Viet Minh had also begun to invest Nha Trang at the same time. *Richelieu* carried out a bombardment of Viet Minh positions on 19 October, firing 146 152mm shells and 800 100mm shells. The main armament was not used.[17] *Richelieu*'s marines were among the French troops who landed from the sea on 20 October 1945 to assist the remaining Japanese forces to control Nha Trang. The French–Japanese composite force soon found itself under pressure from the Viet Minh, who seized the railway junction. *Richelieu* and the other ships of the squadron came into action again on 22 October with a bombardment in support of the landing parties. This was instrumental in causing the Viet Minh forces to retreat. Nha Trang was secure. It was the last occasion that *Richelieu* fired her guns in anger.[18]

This was, of course, the beginning of the fruitless nine-year campaign France waged to secure control of Indochina, and of the thirty-year struggle for the future of Vietnam. The French Navy continued to play a major part in the war, in riverine warfare and also with gunfire support to her land forces from destroyers and cruisers. But *Richelieu*'s part in the Vietnam war (although not that of the battleship) was done. She departed the Indochina theatre on 29 December 1945 and arrived back in France at Toulon on 11 February 1946. Thence she progressed to Cherbourg for overhaul at the Homet drydock. *Bearn* stayed in Indochina for a few more months, and in December 1945 she transported twenty landing craft from Singapore to Vietnam, as well as contributing crews for them in that earliest phase of riverine warfare against the Viet Minh. *Bearn* returned to France during June and July 1946.[19]

CHAPTER THREE

Post-War Planning and the Battleship

EVEN AS THE Second World War drew to a close, the governments of the victorious powers were planning for their anticipated peacetime needs. The previous balance of naval power with its 5:5:3 ratios allocated by Treaty to the UK, USA and Japan had been heavily distorted by the outcome of the war. The USA and Britain now had an overwhelming predominance in materiel, technology and skills, but both needed urgently to cut their naval cloth according to peacetime need, and in the UK's case, progressive economic stringency. France was some way adrift of these two in terms of surviving naval critical mass, and even more heavily constrained in what she could achieve by industrial limitations, the requirement to rebuild a shattered nation after the war, and her increasingly debilitating colonial military commitments. Japan and Germany were smashed and would never be allowed to re-emerge as global naval powers. Italy, also defeated, had been reborn as a late co-belligerent against Germany, but would be subject to severe restrictions in the forthcoming peace process. The Soviet Union looked increasingly like the future political and military opponent of these Western powers, but in 1945 she was still a formal ally and nowhere near a comparable naval power. Her immediate interest was in consolidating her strategic position and wartime gains on the Continent of Europe, although Stalin also had strong aspirations for an ocean-going navy.

What role, then, for the battleship in this new world of the United Nations Organisation, guided rocket weapons and the atomic bomb? The war in the Pacific had seen the perfection of a template for naval warfare that had enjoyed unprecedented success in taking the fight from Hawaii, India and the Australian littoral, thousands of miles to Japan itself. The core of the fleets that did this was a fast striking force of aircraft carriers supported by battleships, roughly in a ratio of two to one. The carriers provided long-range striking power and air superiority to blunt the enemy air power. The battleships provided command and control, close-in anti-aircraft support, superiority in surface combat if the need arose, plus long-range shore bombardment. In tandem with this was an amphibious component based around new specialist shipping designed to deliver opposed landings across open beaches. This depended crucially on a bombardment component of older battleships and smaller warships, too slow to range with the carriers, but perfectly suited to reduce fixed shore defences, in the battleship's case no matter what their scale. Given the unbroken record of success for this force structure over three years of campaigning against the world's number three maritime power, little wonder then that in 1945 it was seen as a likely template for the future as well.

United States Planning

The United States Navy had begun planning for the post-war fleet in 1943.[1] They planned for an immediate post-war future from the perspective that the shape of the existing fleet was about right, but that its wartime size and disposition was unnecessary in peacetime, unaffordable and incompatible with readjusting the economy to a peacetime footing. That said, it took some time and a number of iterations before the hard reality of the post-war budget and manpower constraints was applied with full severity to the US Navy's own internal projections.

The initial work was done by a Special Planning Section under the Chief of Naval Operations, Admiral Ernest J King. It was headed by retired Rear Admiral H E Yarnell. Vice Chief of Naval Operations Admiral Frederick Horne supported retention of a large fleet with as many ships in commission as possible. Once he had Yarnell's plan, Horne took over responsibility for post-war planning. He forwarded 'Navy Basic Demobilisation Plan No. 1' to the Secretary for the Navy on 22 May 1944. Russia was designated a probable enemy because 'they would almost certainly build a fleet'. Demobilisation Plan 1 was rapidly superseded by Demobilisation Plan 2 on 9 June 1944, which slightly scaled down projected US Navy effort on the not unreasonable premise that the USA's allies would defend Europe and the Eastern Atlantic. These proposals called for a peacetime navy of 550,000 personnel and an annual budget of $3 billion. In view of the later figures that emerged, this amount was probably a significant underestimate of the resources a fleet of the projected size would need.

After only rudimentary staffing this plan was circulated as Navy Basic Post-War Plan No. 1 in April 1945. It assumed a fleet with three categories of ships: an active fleet manned at around 70 per cent of wartime complement; a reserve fleet for training manned at 20–30 per cent; and an inactive fleet reserve with ships out of commission and only caretaker crews. For capital ships the number envisaged was eight active battleships. Although not explicit in the Plan, bearing in mind the US Navy's propensity to deal with force structures by treating each class of ships as a single homogenous entity, this would include logically the five *Iowa*s, assuming the completion of the well-advanced *Kentucky*, and the three *Alaska* battlecruisers, assuming the completion of the well-advanced

Hawaii. There would be ten active fleet carriers. Six battleships (logically the modern *South Dakota*s and *Washington*s) and five fleet carriers would be in the training fleet; and seven and twenty-two respectively in the inactive fleet. These carrier numbers do not include the much smaller escort carriers, almost all of which were projected to be inactive.

There was some debate within the US Navy about the ratios between battleships and carriers. A more radical air component in the naval staff wanted to see more, potentially many more, carriers in commission, but there was a strong element of operational experience from the returning Pacific veterans that favoured a balanced force, very much a scaled-down version of the Second World War structure, retaining relatively more cruisers and battleships. If anything, Navy Basic Post-War Plan No. 1 was more battleship-heavy than the existing 3rd and 5th Fleet orders of battle. Had it been delivered, the US Navy would have had in commission altogether fourteen battleships and fifteen fleet carriers. However, James Forrestal, Secretary for the Navy, appeared to favour the air camp. His Fiscal Year 1945 Annual Report stated that 'Air Power has the main emphasis in the post-war Navy ... the carrier is the spearhead of the modern fleet just as the battleship was 25 years ago.'

The staffed and consolidated Navy Post-War Plan 1A thus differed in emphasis from Plan 1. Projected active battleships were cut to four

James Forrestal, Secretary for the Navy in 1945 (seen centre, as Secretary for Defense in December 1947, with Chief of Naval Operations Admiral Chester Nimitz, John L Sullivan, Secretary for the Navy (left) and James Kenney, Under Secretary for the Navy (right) and Mrs Nimitz. *(NHHC)*

Honourable Carl
Vinson, Chairman
House Naval
Affairs Committee
1931–47, then
Chair of the
House Armed
Services
Committee.
c. 1960. (NHHC)

(logically the completed *Iowas*), and carriers were increased to thirteen, although numbers in the proposed training fleet were unaltered at six and five respectively, so a total of ten modern battleships would have remained in commission, and eleven would be in the reserve, including, by inference, *Kentucky* and the three *Alaskas*. Eighteen fleet carriers would have remained in commission under this blueprint.

Meanwhile, the United States Congress became involved in the process via a House Concurrent Resolution (Number 80) sponsored by Chair of the House of Representatives Naval Affairs Committee Carl Vinson. Vinson was a strong advocate of a strong navy. He introduced the Resolution in hearings of the House Committee on Naval Affairs on 18 August 1945, just three days after Japan had surrendered. Testimony was given by Secretary Forrestal, Admiral Ernest J King, Chief of Naval Operations, Rear Admiral E W Borrough, Assistant Chief of Naval Operations for Logistic Plans and other officers.

Concurrent Resolution 80 asserted the responsibility of Congress to specify the size and shape of the post-war navy:

> Whereas it will not be necessary to retain for the Navy all of the ships, vessels or craft now built, building or authorized, and
>
> Whereas it is necessary for the Congress to determine the size of the immediate post-war Navy, giving due consideration to the security of the United States and its Territories and insular possessions, the protection of our commerce, and the necessity for co-operating with other world powers in the maintenance of peace ...
>
> Resolved by the House of Representatives (The Senate concurring), That it is the sense of the Congress that the Navy of the United States should consist of ships of the following type and numbers:
>
> Three large aircraft carriers ... twenty four aircraft carriers ... ten light aircraft carriers ... seventy nine escort aircraft carriers ... eighteen battleships, three large cruisers [the designation given here to the *Alaskas*], thirty one heavy cruisers, forty eight light cruisers, three hundred and sixty seven destroyers, two hundred and ninety six destroyer escorts and two hundred submarines.

This total force structure clearly matched what the US Navy wanted to such a degree that some prior staffing and collusion must have taken place. Forrestal's testimony supported it completely, and asserted the continuing need for a strong navy in the face of atomic bombs and rocket-guided weapons. 'If we were to give away our fleet today and rely wholly on the atomic bomb, we would lose control of the sea.'

With an eye to demobilisation, affordability and the economy, Forrestal's testimony proposed that only 30 per cent or approximately 300 of the ships enumerated in Concurrent Resolution 80 should constitute an active fleet in full commission, with approximately 100 in a 'ready reserve' manned with nucleus crews of about one third of full complement and engaged in training midshipmen and naval reservists. The remaining 60 per cent, about 700 major combatant ships, would be 'wholly out of commission, tied up, and with only caretaker crews aboard'. Dealing with the major units only, Forrestal proposed an active fleet of eight battleships, ten aircraft carriers and ten escort carriers. The ready reserve would be six battleships, five aircraft carriers and eleven escort carriers. This left seven old battleships, twenty-two carriers and fifty-eight escort carriers in the laid-up reserve.

Excluding the Marine Corps, Forrestal estimated that this fleet could be manned with between 500,000 and 600,000 personnel, of whom not more than 40,000 would constitute the caretaker crews for the laid-up reserve. More detailed testimony later by the Naval Staffs refined this caretaker figure downwards to about 27,000. Forrestal further estimated, with considerable caveats, that when compared with 1945 expenditure of $26 billion, the approximate cost of the Concurrent Resolution 80 fleet, manned as proposed, would be between $2.8 billion and $4 billion.

The House Committee then had a wide-ranging discussion around the proposals. Despite the assurances of the officials that this fleet was likely to be larger than any combination of any powers that could be ranged against it, there were still Congressional concerns that it was not big enough, that it should be treated as a floor rather than a ceiling for numbers, and that it proposed insufficient active ships to maintain strong active fleets in both the Atlantic and Pacific. The Congressional record includes some comparisons between the proposed US Navy and the British Empire, France and the Soviet Union. The balance of power in battleships was assessed to be eighteen to twenty in favour of Britain alone (excluding the *Alaskas* from the figures), and eighteen to thirty once France and Russia were in the balance. Quite where the Congressional staffers conjured the four imaginary British battleships from is not clear, unless they were assuming completion of four new *Lions* (see below) and retention of every old battleship. They were equally creative in the case of aircraft carriers, crediting Britain with thirty-seven (plus forty-two escort carriers). The real figure assuming the most generous conceivable combination of old ships retained and all ships laid down or programmed to be completed was about thirty-two. But the exaggerations, and the implicit assumption that the UK might be ranged against the US in future, were clearly designed to support a hawkish case for the largest possible US peacetime navy.

More detailed testimony confirmed that the proposed carrier task force would be based around two or three carriers and three battleships, based on Pacific War experience. There was a detailed discussion of battleship numbers and dispositions[2] including a debate, echoed in later testimony, as to why the 22 per cent complete *Illinois* had been cancelled and whether she could be reinstated and completed. It was further confirmed that with twenty-one battleships retained in the post-war fleet, six old battleships, all over thirty years of age, would be disposed of, possibly in experiments with the atomic bomb: *Arkansas, New York, Texas, Nevada, Pennsylvania and Mississippi* were among 222 obsolete vessels destined for scrapping under the plans. (So too was *Oklahoma*, although not included in these figures.)

But with no immediate naval threat, even with Vinson urging them on, the US Navy was up against irresistible wider political demands to cut spending and manpower. A little later, in November 1945, Congress also mandated a US Navy demobilisation plan requiring precipitate reductions from more than 3,380,000 men on active service in September 1945. Some 327,000 had to be out of uniform by Christmas, and 1,500,000 more by 1 April 1946. The peacetime active duty level was set at only 490,000 enlisted men, and was to be achieved by January 1947, requiring over 1 million more to leave in the latter part of 1946.[3] This was a very tall order in its own right, let alone set against the ambition of Post-War Plan 1A. In fact the US Navy's own initial demobilisation schedule testified to the House Naval Affairs Committee in October was even more precipitate. It would seem that the planners were having difficulty with the maths of running a peacetime fleet of the size proposed with the manpower they themselves requested.

The Concurrent Resolution and the hearings reflected that America had created in only four years the largest, most modern and most capable navy ever seen. It would have been feckless to waste entirely that asset, particularly its materiel, given recognised uncertainties in the post-war world order. But it also reflected the impossibility of manning more than a fraction of that fleet, and the need to train in peacetime against a potential future mobilisation requirement. Congress's solution, matching the Navy's own, was admirable in its simplicity. On the basis that the peacetime navy must be no more than around 500,000 men for reasons of fiscal stringency; and to achieve very rapid mass demobilisation; and to rebalance the economy by restocking the civilian workforce, in outline their plan would have kept about 30 per cent of the September 1945 fleet in active service including training, put 50 per cent into a care and maintenance inactive fleet, and disposed outright of about 20 per cent, representing the most obsolete pre-war ships. There was very little attempt to discriminate between ship types or capabilities in this early planning. Cuts were almost exclusively decided on the basis of ship age. This is why, thanks to the legacy of the pre-war naval treaties and the battleship building 'holidays', more old battleships were due for scrapping than carriers.

To summarise the plan arising from Concurrent Resolution 80, the 1,310 major combatants of the US Navy (battleships, carriers, cruisers, destroyers, escorts and submarines) were allocated into 317 active ships, 763 in the inactive fleet, and 230 being scrapped as obsolete. It was an almost complete endorsement of the US Navy's own Post-War Plan 1A. Of the twenty-seven battleships, the eight most modern and capable, the *Iowa*s and *Alaska*s, would remain fully crewed and operational. Six modern battleships would be in the training fleet. Seven pre-war types of late First World War vintage would go into reserve for use as amphibious bombardment ships. The oldest and least capable six and the hulk *Oklahoma*, as well as the trials ship *Wyoming*, would be scrapped. Of the aircraft carriers, twenty-four (including escort carriers) would be active and ninety-two placed in reserve. Only three were rated obsolete for scrapping. *Mississippi* was initially destined for scrapping but in the event was retained to replace *Wyoming*.

So the Congressional and Navy intent expressed through the period from mid-1944 to the end of 1945 did not differ greatly, although Congress and Forrestal adopted a more balanced ratio between active battleships and carriers than the US Navy was inclined to favour – fourteen battleships to twenty-four carriers for Congress, versus ten to eighteen for Post-War Plan 1A. The geopolitical rationale for retaining such a preponderant fleet, and its active component in particular, was rudimentary. Although protecting and promoting US interests were specified in the Western Hemisphere, Western Atlantic and the entire Pacific including the occupation of Japan, the tabulated comparisons of US Naval strength with that of other maritime nations were naive in the extreme. The mood of the hearings tended to regard the appropriate basis for planning as precautionary and isolationist. At best, to be a little more charitable, they made the assumption that the US would have to provide all the forces for dealing on behalf of the international community with any rowdiness or future threat.

But despite the strong consensus about need, the funding of the plans had yet to be addressed in any meaningful way. Secretary Forrestal's estimates given in his testimony in August 1945 proved way wide of the mark when in 1946 the Navy actually requested $6.235 billon to deliver Plan 1A, but the Bureau of the Budget offered only $3.96 billion, later raised under protest to $4.22 billion. Most of the shortfall was covered by cuts to ship construction and public works. By November 1946 the US Navy had terminated 63,338 wartime prime contracts worth over $16 billion. But it was impossible to protect the projected fleet entirely from the fiscal pressure, so the overall number of combatant ships retained had to be reduced from 1,079 to 965, including the cutting of four carrier air groups and fourteen large surface combatants from the active fleet, in order to balance the books. This became Basic Post-War Plan No. 2 in late 1946. The total of active battleships in this plan was now four, with thirteen fleet carriers. The aspiration to add *Kentucky* to the fleet seems to have been put on ice at this point. Just two battleships were envisaged in the revised training fleet together with three carriers, for a commissioned total of six battleships and sixteen carriers. Thirteen battleships were now destined for the inactive fleet along with twenty-one carriers. Total battleships planned for retention were therefore nineteen, of which now only five were of pre-war construction. The other eight inactive ships would be *Kentucky*, two *South Dakotas*, two *Washingtons*, and three *Alaskas*. The two older battleships newly made surplus by this cut were *Idaho* and *New Mexico*, and both were sold and scrapped in 1947.

Despite its economies, Post War-Plan No. 2 also very rapidly proved beyond the ability of the US Navy to sustain, when set against the money actually voted by Congress and the manning constraints. By June 1948 they were one fleet carrier, three escort carriers, two battleships and thirty-one escorts below the 965-ship target. Instead of the 550,000 naval personnel envisaged in initial planning, by June 1949 the total had sunk to 410,000, and a year later just prior to the Korean War to 381,000. The proposed Fiscal Year 1950 budget was expected to cut active carrier strength from eleven to eight, had the Korean War not intervened. The distinction between an active operational and a training fleet never became a reality as far as battleship participation was concerned, and the number of battleships active had dwindled very rapidly to just four by mid-1946, plus *Wyoming/Mississippi* in use or planned for use as trials ships. The four *Iowas* spent a considerable amount of their time in commission during the late 1940s, but largely undertaking the roles originally envisaged for other battleships of the training fleet. All the remaining fifteen (now including *Kentucky* and *Hawaii*) were already being reduced to inactive status and had become completely deactivated by the end of 1947.

Even then the US Navy was not able to keep the four *Iowas* in commission as envisaged by Plan 2. The number active dwindled to three in late 1947, two in June 1948, and just one, *Missouri*, in September 1948. Even she would have been mothballed as well, were it not for President Truman personally vetoing the recommendations of the Secretary for the Navy, and Secretary for Defence Louis Johnson, that this should happen.

The US Navy had a long history of 'mothballing' (which originally is literally what was done to preserve the fabric of internal compartments in the early ironclads) stretching back to the Civil War and the 1860s. A large programme to retain First World War destroyers after 1918 had eventually allowed the lend-lease programme to provide fifty to the UK in 1940, and many more of these ships also came back into US Navy service after they entered the Second World War. There were no mothballed battleships before the Second World War because of the requirement to scrap or repurpose them under the Washington and London Naval treaties, and the requirement to use demilitarised ships such as *Utah* and *Wyoming* for training.

Early preservation techniques and practices were haphazard. Learning lessons from the difficulties of reactivating their destroyers in the 1940s, the US Navy approached the preservation of the post-war inactive fleet with some care. A 'Readiness and Care of Inactive Ships' team had been in existence since 1944, trialling techniques on three old hulks. The key steps were getting the ship to a predesignated permanent berth; grouping them at these berths by type and class to increase maintenance efficiencies; and, crucially, using their existing operational crews to repair

Mothballs: Cruisers *Huntington* and *Dayton* with *South Dakota* (right) showing the distinctive igloos. Philadelphia Navy Yard, August 1961. *(NHHC)*

damage and defects before they were demobilised, and removing all stores, fuel and perishable material with less than a three-year life. Corrosion was then tackled with extra paint along the foam line and electric cathodic protection via currents passed through the water to slow down the rusting process underwater. Pooling of rainwater on exposed flat surfaces was eliminated, and three types of rust-proofing protection applied, designed to be optimised for external surfaces, machinery and parts such as valves in contact with water. Then plastic covering or structures (the distinctive aluminium igloos that can be seen on photographs of all major ships in the preservation programme) were placed over guns, radars and apertures. Finally, the interior of the ships, once sealed, was dried out and permanent dehumidification initiated to maintain the sealed ship as dry as possible.

The pace of demobilisation and post-war manpower shortages eventually meant that the application of these principles was less thorough on some ships than others, but battleships generally got the attention they needed. It was the thoroughness of this process that accounted for the long periods, typically up to a year for a battleship, which elapsed between the ships arriving at their permanent bases, going out of full commission and finally being decommissioned into their respective reserve fleets. Later on, manpower shortages meant corners had also to be cut in terms of the frequency and thoroughness of the periodic inspection regimes designed to keep the inactive ships ready. Nevertheless, taken in the round and set against other countries' efforts, this was an extraordinarily successful programme. At a cost of only $100 million, a total of 2,269 Second World War combatants and auxiliaries were preserved, including, eventually, all nineteen surviving battleships. Ongoing costs were minimal, especially once the original plan to retain skeleton crews for the larger ships, and divisional teams for groups of smaller ships, was abandoned due to post-war manpower pressure. Reactivation of these ships, for the Korean War, Vietnam War and later proved relatively easy, cheap and quick. Indeed, it could be argued that the programme ultimately had perverse consequences because ships were so cheap to maintain in reasonable condition that the incentives to dispose of them evaporated. Hence five of the older US battleships originally scheduled for preservation in 1945–46 were still on the books in 1959, around forty years old, unused during the Korean War, and given the existence of twelve more modern, much more capable ships, retained well beyond any plausible geopolitical or military scenario for their use. Even more egregious examples of retention of other types of ship were perpetuated into the twenty-first century. The last Second World War ships and the associated Reserve Fleet shore facility were not scrapped until 2011.

The five older US battleships scheduled for retention in the inactive fleet were mothballed and retained as part of this effort. Sisters *Tennessee* and *California* remained inseparable throughout their post-war journey. Together they left Okinawa for Japan on 20 September 1945 and spent three weeks around Honshu and at Yokosuka, providing a presence ashore and covering the landing of the US Sixth Army occupation forces. They left on 15 October 1945, designated Task Force 50.5, escorted by six destroyers and the oiler *Chemung*, with *Tennessee* carrying around 300 passengers, mainly US Navy Reserve enlisted men from a dozen other ships. They sailed via celebratory calls at Singapore from 23 to 26 October, Colombo, Ceylon, from 30 October to 3 November, and South Africa, carrying some South Africans for demobilisation at Cape Town, where they stayed from 15 to 19 November. These stops involved liberty, shopping, the exchange of hospitality with British and Empire officials, as well as exhibition baseball matches, which proved very popular. Then the force crossed the Atlantic, sighting both St Helena and Bermuda, before arriving back in Philadelphia at 1250 on 7 December 1945. The scale of immediate demobilisation on these returning battleships is shown by the fact that on arrival 754 of *California*'s crew were released. However, 1,375 still remained aboard as the ship gradually mothballed. One hundred and twenty-two officers remained aboard *Tennessee* in November 1945, but this shrank to eighty by February and forty-one in May. *California* went

The Pacific Reserve Fleet, Bremerton, Washington, 25 October 1951. Mothballed ships include five battleships: *Indiana, Alabama, Colorado, Maryland* and *West Virginia*, plus four fleet carriers. Battleships are top and bottom centre, with a carrier and six cruisers moored between them. *(NARA)*

into the Atlantic Reserve Fleet on 7 August 1946, and on 1 October there was a brief 'inactivating ceremony', placing *Tennessee* in an inactive state, in commission, in reserve. By December 1946 only four officers were aboard, with *Tennessee* occupying the southern end of dry dock No. 5, and the ever-present *California* the northern end.[4] They were only formally decommissioned, together, on 14 February 1947 at the Philadelphia Navy Yard, the whole process having taken some fifteen months in all. Sister ships *Maryland*, *Colorado* and *West Virginia* went through the same process in the Pacific Reserve Fleet, decommissioning between January and April 1947, before laying up at Puget Sound Navy Yard, Bremerton, Washington.

The modern ships soon followed. *North Carolina* arrived back from the war at Boston, Massachusetts, on 17 October 1945. She was placed out of commission in the Atlantic Reserve Fleet at Bayonne, New Jersey, on 26 July 1947. Her sister, *Washington*, was also there in reserve from 27 June 1947. *South Dakota* arrived at San Francisco on 27 September 1945 as flagship of the 3rd Fleet with Admiral Halsey aboard. On

20 January 1946 she began an overhaul at Philadelphia and decommissioned there, being placed in the Atlantic Reserve Fleet on 31 January 1947, along with *Massachusetts*, which was decommissioned on 27 March that year. *Indiana* reached San Francisco on 29 September 1945, but was overhauled at Puget Sound, where she was deactivated and became part of the Pacific Reserve Fleet at the beginning of 1947, along with *Alabama*, which arrived at Bremerton on 27 February 1946 for her inactivation overhaul, and went into Pacific Reserve Fleet at Bremerton on 9 January 1947. *Alaska* returned from the Pacific via the Panama Canal on 13 December 1945 and reached Boston Navy Yard on 18 December. By 1 February 1946 she was at Bayonne, New Jersey, where she went in commission into reserve on 13 August. She finally went out of commission on 17 February 1947. *Guam* transited the Canal a couple of weeks earlier than her sister, reached Bayonne on 17 December 1945 and went into reserve there on 17 February 1947, as part of the Atlantic Reserve Fleet.

United Kingdom Planning

In the UK there was a parallel process of post-war naval planning. It was also marked by a level of ambition for post-war reach and activity that was, with quite rapid hindsight, exposed as completely unrealistic. A rapid series of retrenchments and reprioritisations was required. In the UK's case this was accentuated by the more extreme levels of indebtedness and weak public finances arising from the war effort.

Against that backdrop there was also a lively official debate about the role and viability of the battleship. This had strong echoes of the battleship versus bomber controversies of the 1920s and '30s. As early as 15 May 1944 a memorandum titled 'The Empire's Post-war Fleet' was prepared for the Admiralty Board. It stated: 'Battleships and aircraft carriers are complementary and the enthusiast for one arm or the other must not be allowed to upset the balance. This war has proved the necessity of battleships and no scientific developments are in sight which might render them obsolete.'[5] The chief protagonist of the air case was Prime Minister Churchill's highly influential but often controversial Scientific Adviser, Frederick Lindemann, Lord Cherwell. He served as Paymaster General in the Cabinet until July 1945, and again when Churchill returned to power in 1951.

Cherwell had argued at the end of 1944 that the battleship was finished. He circulated a paper for the War Cabinet[6] designed to influence the allocation of resources in the 1945 Naval Estimates, in which it was anticipated that the Admiralty would bid for funds for the construction of new battleships. Cherwell doubted that battleships could in future survive attack from the air. This was because:

Frederick Lindemann, Lord Cherwell, battleship sceptic, as Paymaster-General, October 1951. *(Alamy)*

Battleship displacement had traditionally been used for armour against surface attack. In a new world of air and underwater threats insufficient displacement would exist for reliable protection against all three;

Shaped charge warheads were many times as lethal as conventional explosive delivery means, and would invalidate current armour schemes;

Guided glider bombs (as used successfully by Germany from 1943) would finally make stand-off high level bombing of ships effective, and would be more effective still incorporating new radar and television guidance technology;

Anti-aircraft defence was always at a disadvantage compared to air-to-surface attack because of the complexity of hitting faster moving aircraft targets in three rather than two dimensions;

The economics of producing aircraft and battleships would always allow a ratio of around one hundred to one in favour of aircraft, meaning that scale of air attack would swamp ship-based or carrier-based fighter defences;

Why have a battleship if it has to have a carrier escort, when the carrier itself can perform the battleship's anti-surface function?

Cherwell concluded: 'The handicaps of the battleship are fundamental and inevitable. In the struggle for existence the tortoise has achieved but a relatively humble niche; it is only in fable that it carries off the prize.'

The paper did not find favour in the Admiralty. The First Sea Lord was Admiral of the Fleet Sir Andrew Cunningham. He had been successful in command of the Mediterranean Fleet when he had battleships, and very hard pressed during early 1942 when they were sunk or damaged and none was available.

Although he was not particularly militant on the point of promoting

Admiral of the Fleet Sir Andrew Cunningham, First Sea Lord, at the launch of *Vanguard* on 30 November 1944, with Princess Elizabeth, A V Alexander (left) and Vice-Admiral Sir Frederick Walker (right). *(Alamy)*

battleships, at one point describing the completion of *Vanguard* as a waste, nor is there much evidence that he promoted the air arm. Little wonder then that a strong pro-battleship lobby existed at the Admiralty under his regime.[7]

The Cherwell paper was argued exclusively from scientific principle and judgement, and lacked any leavening of real operational analysis from the war. The Admiralty argued back, reasonably on the basis of their evidence, that the experience of the war illustrated the ambiguity of the battleship versus aircraft and aircraft carrier question, and also the effectiveness of battleships in new anti-aircraft escort and shore bombardment roles. Cherwell also ignored the likelihood that the technological advances he outlined could be used to serve defence as well as attack. The Admiralty spent the first half of 1945 staffing a response to the Cherwell paper. The correspondence within the Naval Staff is quite prolonged, but it is noteworthy that every Admiralty Branch and officer involved promoted or accepted the fundamental argument that battleships were required, and were complementary to aircraft carriers in a balanced fleet. There were no dissenting naval voices in 1945, in contrast to the more polarised opinions evident in the parallel US Navy debate.

Prime Minister Winston Churchill with First Lord of the Admiralty, and later Minister for Defence, A V Alexander. *(Alamy)*

The battleship case was also supported at the political level. Much of the delay in producing a response to Cherwell arose because the responsible Cabinet Minister, First Lord of the Admiralty Labour Party Politician A V Alexander, felt that the draft first submitted to him on 14 March 1945 was not as strong as it could be. He thought that Cherwell's case could be further weakened by being set against the historical background. Alexander's own redraft on 29 March was ten pages long. Cunningham felt it lacked punch and politely insisted on the original: 'The Naval Staff have devoted considerable time to the preparation of this reply, and their draft was most carefully scrutinised by the naval members of the Board.' Cunningham won his point. The main themes of the emerging response to Cherwell were:

> We depend on shipping which must be defended against air, surface and submarine attack. Long-range air attack can be defeated by carrier-based aircraft supplemented by ship-borne anti-aircraft artillery, for which the battleship is the most effective platform, especially in rough weather;
>
> The carrier itself must be defended against surface attack by the heaviest enemy unit, i.e. battleships. Carrier and battleship are therefore complementary to each other in forming the battlegroup, as used in the Pacific;
>
> When flying is possible the carrier can do the battleship's job; but often flying is not possible, at night or in poor weather, especially in the North Atlantic, which remained crucial for UK sea communications. In these conditions 'the battleship retains its former mastery'.
>
> The battleship will change – it will become the 'heavy support ship' for the carrier group. It will still carry the main anti-aircraft defence of the fleet, but in due course its offensive power might become a proven long range rocket weapon of equal power to 16in artillery. This could allow future battleships to be smaller, faster and more agile.

The Admiralty Plans Division was articulating this radical evolution of the battleship type as early as 6 February 1945:

> The very term 'battleship' is becoming obsolescent ... The battleship is virtually the heavy support ship ... The scientific advances of the next few years may improve the operational capability of the aircraft carrier in bad weather and may also make it possible to construct a heavy support ship whose offensive and defensive power are superior to the projected battleship of today, but whose displacement is

considerably less ... We have not yet reached the stage where we can give up the 16in gun but it is possible we shall be able to do so in some years' time in favour of a rocket weapon with a hitting power at least as great and with greatly improved accuracy. In the Admiralty view the change in battleship design will occur gradually in the next five to fifteen years.

In the meantime, the Admiralty envisaged a need to plan for a battle group-based mixed fleet, with conventional big-gun battleships alongside carriers. The papers supporting the arguments included these assessments:

> In spite of many forecasts during the last 20 years very similar to the paper under discussion [i.e. the Cherwell paper], the lessons of this war have shown that the battleship has been essential. Without them we could not have guaranteed our imports or supplied Malta and Russia ... During non-flying periods the battleship remains the deciding factor in any encounter between surface forces ... we cannot leave ourselves without battleships until the evidence that they have outgrown their usefulness is much more convincing than it is now ... The Admiralty agree that there will be a great change in the design of the battleship of the future. They emphasise, however, that the battleship in some form is certain to remain, in conjunction with the aircraft carrier, one of the principal elements on which sea power ultimately depends. As an insurance therefore, and in view of the time taken to build a capital ship, the Admiralty consider it essential to lay down the *Lion* and *Temeraire* [the next proposed battleships] as soon as possible.

The First Lord of the Admiralty eventually responded to the Cherwell paper in a further War Cabinet Memorandum dated 2 July 1945,[8] the immediate objective being to flesh out the case for the two new battleships included in the New Construction Programme, which he had also just put before the War Cabinet. The final version of the arguments reflected closely what had gone before. Although Brendan Bracken submitted the memorandum, having become the interim First Lord following Alexander's resignation when Labour leader Clement Attlee refused to continue the coalition Government in May 1945, it is evident that Alexander, as First Lord, was equally persuaded of the case.[9] In fact he had finally agreed the draft paper by the First Sea Lord responding to Cherwell on 24 April 1945, but indicated he would hold his formal response back until the New Construction Programme for 1945 went before Cabinet.

The final articulation of the Admiralty view to the War Cabinet was:

The Admiralty fully agree that the design of all warships must be continually examined in order that they may keep pace with contemporary weapon developments. We make no exception for battleship design. In fact it is all the more necessary that the design of a warship at once so vital to the security and so costly to the purse of the nation should be kept constantly under review in the light of developments in both naval and air warfare ...

Our object is to seek out and destroy the enemy forces which would otherwise be capable of severing the sea communications on which the life of the Empire depends. This being so ... in order to achieve this object balanced forces must be available, capable of overwhelming any enemy concentration, whatever type of ship that concentration may contain. It is therefore necessary in the Admiralty view for our fleet to contain battleships in order to ensure the destruction of enemy heavy ships ...

The reason for the inclusion of the battleship in a balanced force is that being capable of carrying heavy guns and a large quantity of ammunition for them she can strike the heaviest blows and keep on striking those blows under any conditions of geographical position, weather or light. This potentially is a more important factor than the power to survive blows ...

Moreover, the battleship being equipped with a powerful A.A. [anti-aircraft] armament can contribute more than any other type of ship to the A.A. gun defence of herself and the ships with which she is in company.

Modern war experience has shown that the battleship is just as much required to give the aircraft carrier heavy cover as the aircraft carrier may be required to give fighter protection to the heavy ship. In short the two types are complementary ...

The battleship, in fact, provides a sure means of destroying the enemy heavy ship: bombers can be countered by fighters, but there is no counter to the heavy ship, adequately protected by fighters, except from suitable surface forces. Thus so long as any potential enemy possesses heavy ships, the battleship will remain an essential part of our fleet ...

The war experience of the *Scharnhorst* action (on which particular emphasis was laid because of its clear-cut lesson that the heavier broadside had won the day in very poor conditions where aircraft could play no part); the Battle of Cape Matapan, where a superior force of British battleships had destroyed an Italian fleet at night; the *Bismarck* action; and Leyte Gulf were all adduced as evidence for the battleship's continuing relevance. But the Navy was alive to the wind of change too:

It is likely that the 'battleship' of the future will bear little resemblance to the battleship as we know it. For example, if the rocket weapon replaces the gun it may be possible to build a smaller ship which will still fulfil the essential requirement of the 'battleship' – i.e. the ability under all conditions to seek out and destroy the most powerful ships of the enemy …

But we cannot afford in the interval of waiting for such developments, to fail to provide the best which can at present be devised for this purpose …

Rather disappointingly after its visionary flourish, the paper ended, in deference to Alexander's earlier views, with a backward-looking reference to what it saw as the continuing and undiminished relevance of the final conclusion of the 1936 report of the Inskip Committee, set up to investigate the vulnerability of the capital ship to air attack: 'The advocates of the extreme air view would wish this country to build no capital ships (other powers still continuing to build them). If their theories turn out well founded we have wasted money, if ill founded, we would, in putting them to the test, have lost the Empire.'

While this debate played out in the context of the 1945 New Construction Programme, across the Admiralty wider work continued on the future size and shape of the post-war fleet. An Admiralty paper dated 6 March 1945,[10] and staffed at the same time as the Cherwell response, set out the wider context for the role of the battleship in planning the post-war fleet. The Admiralty was very much aware that there would be a need to justify the size, shape, role and cost of the fleet in peacetime. A baseline peacetime manning assumption of 220,000 was made: modest by comparison with the 650,000 then in naval uniform, but, as the Naval Personnel Branches pointed out, ambitious when measured against 1939 pre-mobilisation active duty manpower of just 133,000. The political assumptions were both unimaginative and conservative. The basis of imperial defence, it was assumed, would be control of sea communications that the fleet was required to exercise, worldwide. This implied a need for a large number of cruisers in active commission to be spread globally on foreign stations. Although Germany and Japan would initially be completely disarmed, future resurgence and aggression could not be ruled out. War with the USA was 'unthinkable' and in most conditions she would be an ally. But trust could not be placed in a future World Security Organisation, and a paramount need would be to keep Britain strong and self-reliant for security through the status of her armed forces. There was no specific mention of the Soviet Union (then, of course, still a formal ally).

It was held that the post-war fleet should consist of 'battleships, carriers, cruisers and destroyers, supported by a fleet train [stores ships and tankers] and supplemented by an adequate force of shore based aircraft'. It was held that a battleship 'could not operate within range of carrier based or shore based aircraft without the protection and striking power afforded by naval aircraft. To avoid undesirable limitation in the freedom of movement of the battlefleet, the aircraft must accompany the force in carriers.' The war 'had proved the necessity of battleships, and no scientific development is in sight which might render them obsolete'. As to its function, 'Besides providing anti-aircraft support to all classes of ship, the battleship is the most powerful unit for destroying the enemy surface forces once they are brought to gun action. A heavier broadside than the enemy is still a very telling weapon in a naval action.' The carrier was allocated the role of 'long range weapon of offence', as well as air defence. The battleships and carriers could only be few in number because of their expense, and would need cruisers and destroyers in larger numbers to protect them. The battle group, called a 'composite squadron', could be formed of two battleships, four aircraft carriers, six cruisers, and eighteen destroyers plus a fleet train of supply vessels. It could operate if required in two divisions of a battleship plus two carriers each, the minimum for operational efficiency.

Uncertainty about a post-war world made planning the size of the active versus the reserve component of a fleet difficult. The paper therefore opted for a minimum active strength judged necessary for the defence of the empire and its communications, plus a reserve of ships to bring forward in time of tension or general war. The overall numbers envisaged were twelve battleships (of which six would be active in peacetime, and six in reserve); twenty-four carriers (twelve active and twelve in reserve); and fifty cruisers (of which only seventeen in reserve, the larger active proportion reflecting the peacetime focus on global presence and trade protection). Smaller ships included 126 fleet destroyers (63 in reserve) and 190 escorts (154 in reserve). The peacetime manning requirement was estimated at 170,000 from the UK, with the Dominions making up the balance to 220,000 in total.

A third draft of this paper on 27 April 1945, which was discussed by the Sea Lords on 4 May, set out the proposed worldwide distribution of these forces in peacetime. There would be three main fleets, the Home Fleet with three battleships and four carriers in commission, the Mediterranean fleet with two of each, and an Australian and East Indies Station fleet with one battleship and two carriers. There would additionally be a carrier in each of the West Indies, South Atlantic, Indian Ocean and China/Pacific stations, making the total six battleships and twelve carriers in commission.

By 13 August 1945 this work had evolved into a paper submitted to the First Sea Lord by the Deputy Chief of the Naval Staff.[11] In the covering note he said: 'Although the development of the Atom Bomb (dropped just one week before) may radically alter the conception of war, the full implications of this new discovery may not be known for some time. Its impact on naval operations cannot at present be gauged.' The paper slightly evolved the political assumptions in the earlier drafts. It now assumed that Germany and Japan would be completely disarmed, and that the UN Organisation would ensure that they remained so. But 'there will still exist in Europe and Asia potential disturbers of the peace. Such nations possess navies and shipbuilding resources … which could threaten the safety of our sea communications.' The USSR was clearly meant here, although, as we shall see, the Admiralty also had an eye to the continued possession of battleships by Italy and France as well.

The paper went on to identify Home Waters and the North Atlantic as crucial. The required navy there should include 'heavy forces sufficient to destroy a similar enemy force … The heavy forces will be built around a core of battleships and carriers and will contain cruisers and destroyers.' In the Pacific and Indian oceans the emphasis was more on the carrier, but battleships might also be required. The total wartime requirement was seen as eight battleships plus two in reserve, eight fleet carriers plus two in reserve, twenty light fleet carriers plus three in reserve, and thirty-five cruisers. Some 112 destroyers, 220 escorts and eighty-five submarines would complete the wartime fleet. Because battleships and carriers took several years to build, the war reserve in those categories should be maintained in peacetime, giving a total requirement for ten battleships, ten fleet carriers and twenty-three light fleet carriers. In peacetime, however, the focus would be on training, and the number of active ships in commission was projected as just four battleships, four fleet carriers, ten light fleet carriers, thirty-two cruisers (almost all of these being in commission to reflect the focus on worldwide trade protection), sixty-four destroyers, fifty-six escorts and forty-five submarines. A total of 170,000 men were needed to man this force, plus 30,000 from the Dominions, for a slightly reduced peacetime navy manning requirement of 200,000.

The Admiralty Plans Division issued the final version of this paper as C P D 0140/45 on 12 September 1945 as guidance for post-war planning. The only change was a drop in the number of fleet carriers from ten to nine. It noted that: 'In peace there will be a reserve fleet of the order of [six battleships] … The majority of these ships already form part of the fleet, the remainder are well advanced in their construction.' So, to achieve the ten ships required altogether, this implied retaining the five modern ships that would soon be available (four *King George V* class and *Vanguard*), and in addition the older *Nelson*, *Rodney*, *Queen Elizabeth*, *Valiant* and *Renown*, but with no direct reference made to the need to lay down new battleships to replace them in due course.

Looking at the 1945 analyses of needs and solutions with long hindsight, it reflects pretty faithfully the way the maritime war was actually being fought in its final months, and the near-contemporary perceptions of the lessons of the conflict. It also closely parallels the US thinking, although I have found no evidence that the two navies formally shared their plans at this early stage. There is a clear shift in emphasis between battleship and carrier when compared to pre-war assumptions. In 1939 the ratio of carriers to battleships was 1:2. Henceforth it was envisaged early in 1945 as 2:1, and eventually as thinking developed, around 3:1. It was, scaled up to meet Atlantic and Mediterranean needs, the fleet with which the Royal Navy was fighting the Pacific War.

The weaknesses in the analysis of the strategic context as it soon emerged are maybe forgivable in 1945. The absence of a plausible immediate and existential naval threat to UK interests that might justify a larger fleet than that of 1939 was offset by genuine uncertainty about how the new world order would evolve, and a determination to be well prepared for all future eventualities, in contrast to the scramble to rearm in the late 1930s. The underplaying of the degree of co-operation between allies, which was explicit in the war just finishing and implicit in the new United Nations Organisation, reflected bitter experience of the failure of the League of Nations before the war. It was also arguably an echo of the pre-war position where the UK was striving to be a global power and at least a global military equal of the United States, and the UK knew that the interests and values of the two powers did not always precisely coincide (for example on colonial policy). There was at that point no inkling in the planning of the more explicit co-operation and collective security approach eventually to be delivered by the Western Union and NATO. The failure to anticipate the rapid end of empire with its fundamental impact on the required fleet, and the change in focus away from remote overseas stations reflected a more general stasis of thinking about Britain's role in the world.

The inability, just a few weeks after it was dropped, to address the impact of the atomic bomb and the nuclear age is also understandable. Also very soon to become painfully evident is that, just as in the United States, there was no effort to consider properly the resource implications of what was proposed. The scale of effort envisaged in these 1945 plans was completely unsustainable in the face of the UK's post-war demobilisation and its economic realities.

The beginnings of detailed post-war battleship planning in the UK, matching real ships to paper requirements, can be seen from as early as July 1944.[12] The Director of Naval Plans advised the Ordnance Department that after the Pacific War the Royal Navy envisaged keeping the twelve most capable battleships. Although not specified, this must have included the badly shattered *Warspite* and the slow *Ramillies*, unless Naval Plans were counting on incorporation of the Italian battleships *Vittorio Veneto* and *Italia* into the Royal Navy (see below). It excluded *Royal Sovereign*, whose fate with the USSR would have been uncertain at that point. This meant that only *Revenge*, *Resolution* and *Malaya* of the existing ships were expected to be scrapped, together with their guns because there was a sufficiency of 15in artillery to support the remaining ships. The twelve ships it was planned to retain match the initial strategic assumptions for a post-war fleet from early 1945.

But by February 1945 the Director of Gunnery and Anti-Aircraft Warfare was assuming only four 15in battleships would need supporting logistically, and in April 1946 the Director of Naval Ordnance was confirming that spare 15in equipment would only be needed for the new *Vanguard*, plus *Queen Elizabeth*, *Valiant* and *Renown*. He confirmed that *Warspite* would be broken up, although her gunnery equipment was required for spares. The other ships for which no future ordnance requirement was now envisaged were *Ramillies*, and, by implication, *Royal Sovereign* once she was back in British hands. This left a planned battlefleet of ten existing ships (the four 15in ships noted above, four *King George V* class, *Nelson* and *Rodney*), which matched the slightly modified assumptions about future fleet requirements of August and September 1945. The post-war picture was clarified in October 1945 in a paper for the Defence Committee of the Cabinet. This specified that the maximum number of ships to be scrapped or otherwise disposed of if not required by the Admiralty for non-operational purposes included five battleships: the three 'Rs', *Malaya* and *Warspite*. This proposal was approved by the Cabinet on 29 October.[13]

However, there was no getting away from the fact that half of this proposed battlefleet was old, indeed very old. Against this backdrop of strategic thinking, and the perceived ongoing requirement for ten battleships, what then of the plans for new British battleships? *Lion* and *Temeraire* were the next projected generation of British battleships. They had already been approved as part of the 1938 New Construction Programme as scaled up versions of *King George V* (40,000 tons, nine 16in guns). They were to be part of a class of four ships. Building both had begun in 1939, but they were cancelled in September that year and dismantled in 1940 because shipbuilding effort was needed for other ships that would take less time to get into action during the then-envisaged (and badly under-estimated) duration of the war. Various redesigns based on war experience were then undertaken, with the requirements for speed and more sophisticated protection gradually making them much larger ships. There was a dilemma because by 1945 the full staff requirement for a new battleship, based on experience from the war, implied a ship of around 59,000 tons, 950ft long, costing £13,250,000, and for which there were virtually no available docking facilities.

A 'Battleship Committee' was therefore set up by the Admiralty under Rear Admiral R M Servaes to look at the issue from a semi-independent perspective. This was less a committee proper than a focussed staff effort to boil this one issue down to its essentials. Servaes had previously been an Assistant Chief of the Naval Staff, and was given a captain deputy and a secretary, with a room next to the Admiralty Boardroom. He worked at speed over a three-week period in April 1945 consulting widely in a series of bilateral meetings with the Naval Staff departments.[14]

Servaes's final report was delivered to the First Sea Lord on 1 May 1945 towards the end of the Cherwell paper staffing.[15] It is interesting not only for its technical analysis but for its strategic appreciation, where the threat from the emerging world power of the Soviet Union was first clearly articulated. Servaes, no doubt reflecting the parallel staff work noted above, was of the view that the battleship was the basis of the strength of the fleet. The battleship was the most powerful unit for destroying the enemy surface forces once they were brought to action. A heavier broadside than the enemy was still a very telling weapon in a naval action. Countries likely to maintain battleships after the war were assessed as the USA, Russia and France. War with the USA could be ruled out, but the size and capability of her fleet might cause others to build new ships in competition. It was too early to say what France would do, although the constraints of her need for post-war reconstruction, and possible priority for army and air force requirements were (rightly as it turned out) seen as substantial constraints on the theoretical battleship and aircraft carrier programmes she might sustain.

So far as Russia was concerned, the report (for which the analysis came from the Director of Naval Intelligence-DNI) was (for intelligence) quite categoric. Stalin's pre-war battleship programme was noted. DNI felt Russia could build two if not three battleships simultaneously. Pre-war technical deficiencies could be overcome by using captured German machine tools and engineers, plus the captured Skoda works in Czechoslovakia for armour plate. The Soviet avidity for technical details of UK ships, and the degree to which they could exploit their knowledge of the (admittedly old) *Royal Sovereign* was noted, with disapproval. 'The desire of the USSR to possess a large modern battlefleet has recently been reiterated in the Soviet press, and there can be no doubt that the USSR will proceed to fulfil this aim after the war with all the energy of which she is capable ... The USSR will proceed unwaveringly to carry out the intention to build capital ships.'

Servaes concluded that to keep a future battleship within sensible bounds of cost and to give it more docking options, dimensions of roughly 850ft length × 115ft beam × 34ft draught, giving about 44,000 tons to play with, were preferable to the full staff requirement at 59,000 tons. More of these smaller ships could be afforded, which would also avoid putting too many eggs in too few baskets. The requirement for 16in guns and protection for the magazines against the equivalent weapon, and protection of decks against 2,000lb bombs, was accepted as necessary. So was an anti-aircraft battery on the scale of *Vanguard*'s, able to deal with six simultaneous targets; plus the need for a top speed of 29 knots to operate with the carrier task force. It would therefore be necessary to make compromises to stay within the assumed available displacement. These would be achieved mainly by accepting less protection over the machinery spaces than over the magazines: 11½in thickness of side armour and 4in of deck armour, much less than *Vanguard*'s 14in and 6in respectively, and only sufficient to defeat dive bombing below about 5,000ft. It was also accepted that the ship could carry only six 16in guns, all mounted forward in imitation of the most modern French designs. Servaes signed off by saying: 'We believe a ship embodying the above characteristics provides a fair balance between mobility, firepower and protection.' Servaes's report was noted by the First Sea Lord, but there does not seem to be any evidence for subsequent detailed ship design based around it.

At around the same time, the draft First Lord memorandum on 1945 New Construction was shown to Prime Minister Churchill, requesting a private discussion before it went to Cabinet. Churchill in turn sent a personal memorandum to the Chancellor of the Exchequer. He said: 'I think it would be well to spend the £250,000 put down for the *Lion* and *Temeraire* in the year 1945. But the whole question of battleship building will eventually have to come up for consideration after the war in the light of the increased power of air.'[16]

Lion and *Temeraire* were duly included in the Navy's submission for the 1945 shipbuilding estimates, submitted to the War Cabinet by interim First Lord of the Admiralty Brendan Bracken on 29 June 1945.[17] Costing an estimated £13,250,000 each, they absorbed nearly three-quarters of the overall new programme of just £37 million, as the remainder consisted only of a few minor vessels and auxiliaries. Expenditure on their construction would have peaked at £4.5 million in each of 1948 and 1949. Overall the two ships absorbed around 20 per cent of the total planned construction budget from 1946 to 1951, including all the previously approved construction programmes (which included a number of fleet carriers). The paper sought just 'preliminary work on *Lion* and *Temeraire*'. It explained that 'only our newest battleships are being sent to the Pacific and in view of the possibility of casualties among them, and the age of the rest of our battle fleet, I consider that we can delay no longer steps to maintain our effective strength in Capital Units. I therefore feel justified in asking for Cabinet approval to place orders as necessary to enable *Lion* and *Temeraire* to be laid down as early as possible. I hope this will be in 1946, but in any case I regard it as important that their completion should not be delayed beyond the end of 1952. I propose that *Conqueror* and *Thunderer* (the third and fourth ships of the class) remain deferred for the time being.'

There does not seem to have been a formal Cabinet discussion of this proposal. Events overtook it. First, it proved one of the very last gasps

Clement Attlee,
Prime Minister,
July 1945–
October 1951.
(Alamy)

of the Churchill Government, as Parliament had already been dissolved on 15 June and the 1945 General Election took place on 5 July and returned the Labour Government. Second, just a few weeks later the war against Japan came to its unexpectedly swift conclusion without any battleship casualties having been sustained.

Alexander, reappointed as First Lord of the Admiralty in the new Government by Prime Minister Clement Attlee, submitted a further 1945 New Construction (Revised) Programme to Cabinet on 22 November 1945. With the war over, and the need for economy pervading Labour discussions on defence, within the Admiralty the decision to suspend/cancel *Lion and Temeraire* had been endorsed initially at a meeting chaired by Cunningham on 15 October 1945, and then by the Admiralty Board with Alexander again in the chair on 7 November.[18] Alexander explained to his Cabinet colleagues that the last Government had proposed a new construction programme based on the need for the Navy to build up for the Far Eastern War. With the end of the war the basis of the new construction programme for 1945 had changed and priority in the shipyards now had to go to merchant ship construction as part of post-war reconstruction. New naval construction would be adjusted so as to proceed immediately only with a very few vessels needed to replace deficiencies of outstanding importance, and to proceed slowly with or to defer construction of vessels that, although needed for the post-war Navy, could be ordered later and used as a cushion to absorb the shock of any fluctuations in the merchant ship market. A further advantage of delaying the substantive programme was that this would enable advantage to be taken of research into the lessons of the war. The revised programme included only one submarine, two escorts and two survey ships, plus auxiliaries, and its total cost was only £3 million, compared to the £37 million envisaged in June. There was just the bald statement: 'The preliminary work on *Lion* and *Temeraire* has ceased.'[19]

There were no naval new construction estimates submitted in 1946. At a Sea Lords meeting on 5 March 1946 Cunningham was recorded as saying 'he was uncertain whether we should embark on replacement of battleships yet, although we might eventually have to evolve some new type of ship to take their place'. The meeting concluded: 'The question of replacement of capital ships must be suspended until the situation is clearer.'[20] This was reflected in the First Lord's Statement on Defence Estimates for 1946, where he said (speaking of the four *Lion* class): 'It is not intended to proceed with any of these four ships. Future decisions upon capital ships will, of course, depend on many factors and I am not in a position to make any statement at present.' The 1947 programme was, like that of 1945, very constrained by resources, and was not considered in the Admiralty as remotely representative of the needs of a post-war fleet.[21] The 1947 Statement contained no mention of the battleships, or the suspension of preliminary work on them in 1945. The main clue to their ultimate demise is in a Plans Department note dated 12 September 1946.[22] On battleships it said:

> CAPITAL SHIPS (Proposed post war strength = 10)
> By 1956 the state of the existing battleship force will be five effective ships 10 – 16 years old, two over 29 years and three some 40 years old.
>
> It is therefore apparent that in 10 years' time our first line strength will consist of but five ships with five more semi-effective ships suitable only for bombardment or convoy protection.
>
> PROPOSALS
> The construction of further Capital Ships should be suspended for the time being. If it is found that some type of Capital Ship is required and a modern design in the light of research and development can be agreed, it will be possible from the point of view of building capacity to commence a programme of new construction any time after 1949.

The document did not receive Admiralty Board approval, but there is no evidence of dissent from this position in its Naval Staff circulation. The future heavy ship with an assumed guided weapon armament was still alive, but the Royal Navy would not commence work on another conventional big gun battleship. The Plans Department proposals did include plans to lay down eight aircraft carriers and seven cruisers between 1949 and 1954, showing how long-term priorities were beginning to change. Economic conditions and manpower realities would, almost immediately, make even those plans unrealistic and undeliverable. D K Brown and George Moore say that *Lion* and *Temeraire* died at this point but development of the 16in Mark IV gun intended for the ships continued as a low priority until 1948.[23] Of five Mark II and Mark III 16in gun barrels actually built, one was relined after the war and used up to November 1947 to fire forty-seven rounds of a new longer shell using flashless powder, with satisfactory results, but no further trials were conducted. Approval to stop the development of the 16in gun, mounting and ammunition was asked for in September 1948, but Admiralty worries about the wider policy implications of losing the industrial capability to design and manufacture such weapons led to a prolonged staffing. The First Sea Lord was only invited to give his approval on 20 July 1949 once the Controller of the Navy was satisfied that no future battleships mounting such weapons were likely.[24]

Notwithstanding the pause on *Lion* and *Temeraire*, the centrality of the battleship to Royal Navy thinking continues to show through in papers from 1946 and later. The Director of Plans was minuting Vice Chief of the Naval Staff on 23 January 1946 that it was hoped to have one battleship in the Mediterranean by March 1947, and ultimately two, plus two in the Home Fleet, although manning constraints would force two of these ships to be held in reserve for the present. And on 27 May 1946 Deputy Chief of Naval Staff was suggesting that the tactical organisation of the fleet (for war-fighting) should be based on Heavy and Light squadrons, the former to have at least one battleship, two carriers, three cruisers and thirty escorts.

This was reflected in Cabinet Defence Committee discussions. On 15 February 1946 the Committee agreed to reduce naval manning to 144,000 for 1946–47, which would mean withdrawing both the battleships then in the Pacific by the middle of the year. By the end of the year it was planned to have three battleships in the Home Fleet, two with reduced complements, and six in reserve, alongside four carriers, all at reduced complement, and nine in reserve.[25] By the end of 1946 a paper for the Cabinet Defence Committee was setting out a requirement for four training battleships and one for 'police forces' plus one in reserve as there would be insufficient warning time of a major conflict to build new. It said:

> It will be noted that the requirement for battleships has been placed at six. This is a lower figure than in any previous assessment. This reduction is however considered acceptable for the time being in view of:
>
> The increased power of naval aviation in maritime warfare and the possession of fleet carriers which will join with the battleships to form the combined striking power of the battlefleet.
>
> The present non-existence of a potential enemy battleship force of anything approaching equal strength.[26]

However, the paper noted that the UK possessed additional older battleships and stated that: 'If war should come within the next ten years these old ships might prove of great value for escorting important convoys, shore bombardment and other duties ... Furthermore they may prove very useful for experiment and development in the mounting of rocket weapons and in the evolution of the future form of the capital ship. It would therefore be folly to dispose of them prematurely and it is considered that all should be retained in reserve.'

In January 1948, despite intervening economic shocks and manning challenges, the Director of the Tactical Staff Division prepared a paper for the Vice Chief of Naval Staff on the role of the battleship saying: 'It is necessary for our fleet to contain battleships in order to ensure the destruction of enemy heavy vessels.' It goes on to reiterate much of the exact language from the 1945 papers, and includes a twenty-page historical survey of the positive contribution of battleships in the war, drawing on senior German Prisoner of War evidence as well as the earlier Admiralty assessments.[27]

Development of battleship main armament ammunition also continued during the late 1940s. In April 1946 the Ships Target Trials Committee made the testing of a new 14in shell designed to attack the upper works of capital ships a top priority for experiments in September 1946 using the cruiser *Caledon*. Although that trial did not happen, there were fifteen separate investigations of attacking ship armour with improved designs of heavy shells between 1945 and 1948 under the auspices of the Ordnance Board. The Board expressed their concern about the loss of industrial expertise in this field when it was suggested in September 1948 that this work stopped, in parallel with the proposal to stop 16in gun development. Despite misgivings, agreement was reached to stop the development work and manage with existing stocks of 14in and 15in shells to support the UK's five remaining battleships. The stocks were massive. On 29 October 1948 the UK held 16,340 15in shells, exceeding *Vanguard*'s and the two 15in gun monitors *Roberts* and *Abercrombie*'s requirements over three-fold; and 18,640 14in, against an expected requirement of 13,000 representing three years' war expenditure for the *King George V*s.[28]

French Planning

In France the pressure on the post-1945 defence budget was at least as great as Britain's, and there was much more national reconstruction to do. More than 400,000 buildings had been completely destroyed and 1,400,000 damaged by the conflict. There was also the growing drain of the colonial campaign in Indochina, and this on top of a large budget deficit run up by the Vichy regime before 1944. There were manning difficulties to sustain a post-war navy. These also affected the rebuilding of capacity in the dockyards and ship construction, and the Navy dockyard infrastructure was severely damaged during the war. But on the positive side, the Free French Navy had been making a worthwhile contribution with the Allies to the war since 1943, and some important naval assets and infrastructure were still in existence after its conclusion. In 1945 the French Navy was operating 365,000 tons of shipping, much of it on loan via Lend-Lease. The total had dropped to 226,000 tons by November 1947.

In *Richelieu* and *Jean Bart* France potentially had two of the largest, fastest and most modern battleships in the world. France had seen the lessons of the war, and knew she needed aircraft carriers too. *Bearn* was too old and slow to operate in the front line, and France only had one other escort carrier, *Dixmude*, on lend-lease. A study into the reconstruction of the French Navy, specifically the naval air arm, in May 1945, projected that the battle group/task force ought to consist of a balanced mixture of aircraft carriers and battleships, supported by escorts. Each task force ought ideally to contain one battleship, two carriers, four cruisers and twelve destroyers. This reflected the structure of contemporary US and UK task forces in the Pacific and Indian Oceans.[29] The French Navy hoped to have a minimum of four such groups based in the Atlantic, Mediterranean, Indian Ocean and Pacific. A study to plan the size of the Navy dated 1 January 1946 therefore set out the grandiose ambition for a fleet with a total tonnage of 750,000, including eight fleet carriers, four battleships, four escort carriers and one training carrier.[30]

The history of post-war naval planning in France followed a very similar trajectory to that in the USA and the UK. The initial level of ambition reflected a desire to bestride the world stage on a scale much larger than had ever been achieved in the 1930s. This was rapidly scaled back to reflect an assumed level of affordability, which itself was rapidly and repeatedly revised downwards through the 1940s as the real impact of successive economic crises and the overriding priority of civil reconstruction bit hard. So the January 1946 plan was soon amended to propose just two battle groups, plus a convoy escort force and coastal defence forces. Each battle group would have one heavy (27,000-ton) and one light (16,000-ton) carrier accompanied by *Richelieu* and *Jean Bart*. The latter was to be completed and the four carriers built from scratch. Three other carriers, *Dixmude*, *Commandante Teste* (converted from a seaplane carrier) and one leased from the UK would be the heart of the convoy escort force. This required a naval shipbuilding programme of 265,000 tons of combat ships, spread out over eleven years. The total cost would be 98 billion francs at 1946 prices, of which the aircraft carriers would absorb 24 billion and *Jean Bart* around 2 billion.

The French Navy reworked these plans over the next few years, but the broad parameters remained the same. The '1950 Plan' covering the decade 1950–60, which was evolved from 1947 to 1949, envisaged maintaining just 300,000 tons of combat shipping, of which the two battleships absorbed 70,000 tons, and three heavy and two light aircraft carriers 100,000 tons.[31] The implication was that besides continuing to complete *Jean Bart* and operate both her and *Richelieu*, France still needed to acquire four aircraft carriers (having secured *Colossus*, renamed *Arromanches*, from the UK on loan in 1946). It proved an unrealistic programme set against the wider national challenge. Financial crises and resourcing difficulties led to the cancellation of France's home-built aircraft carrier project, PA-28 (*Clemenceau*), in 1949. France's eventual accession to NATO that year opened up the avenue of further assistance from the United States, and the acquisition of two light fleet carriers 'off the shelf' in 1950 and 1952, which became *La Fayette* and *Bois Belleau*. The indigenous carrier project was deferred until the late 1950s and eventually bore fruit as *Foch* and *Clemenceau* in the 1960s. Through it all, however, a trickle of resource was maintained to refurbish *Richelieu* and push *Jean Bart* towards completion.

CHAPTER FOUR

Bikini Atoll

L OOMING OVER POST-WAR planning of many sorts, but especially military planning, was the existence of the atomic bomb. It was a high priority to build on the first analysis of its effects undertaken at Hiroshima and Nagasaki. The US Navy (and US Army Air Force) wanted to undertake an early trial of the effects of atomic weapons on ships. This possibility was already in the mind of James Forrestal, Secretary of the Navy, when testifying to Congress on 18 August 1945. Lewis Strauss, later Chairman of the Atomic Energy Commission, but then on the personal staff of the Secretary for the Navy, claimed the credit for suggesting the tests to Forrestal[1] by sending him a memorandum a couple of days earlier, saying 'if such a test is not made there will be loose talk to the effect that the fleet is obsolete in the face of this new weapon, and this will militate against appropriations to preserve a post-war navy of the size now planned'.

Senator Brien McMahon made a public proposal for tests on 25 August, and wanted to use captured Japanese ships as the targets. The US Navy Chiefs of the Bureau of Ships and Bureau of Ordnance wrote a joint letter to the Chief of Naval Operations on 1 October 1945: 'The appearance of the A bomb has made it imperative that a programme of full scale tests be undertaken to determine the effects of this bomb, both underwater and above the water against ships of various types.'[2] CNO approved the tests on 16 October 1945, and went public with the intent in outline on 27 October. This was a purely United States programme, although observers from the fourteen member states of the United Nations Organisation Atomic Energy Commission, even the USSR, were allowed to witness the tests, as were members of Congress and 124 representatives of the press.

By dint of its earlier links to the Manhattan Project constructing the bombs and its broader wartime special relationship with the US military, the United Kingdom managed to get a more privileged special observer status, and information about the plans. Indeed, the Admiralty made suggestions to the Americans about the proposed target array, which they considered too concentrated to allow survival of the instrumentation intended to record the effects of the explosions. The terms of reference for the UK observer team of ten, led by Captain S W Roskill RN, included to assess 'the technical and scientific results obtained from the 1946 atom bomb tests, with particular reference to the relationship between the distance of each ship from the zero point of the burst and the damage caused to each unit ... further, to make recommendations about the design of warships and defence equipment of the future in order to reduce the effects of damage by atomic bomb attack ... finally to review in general terms the technical and tactical implications of the introduction of the atom bomb on naval warfare.'[3] In the immediate aftermath of the Hiroshima and Nagasaki bombs the Admiralty was tending towards pessimism about ship survivability. The Director of Plans guessed that underwater atomic explosions might be lethal to ships at 3 miles distance. The new vulnerability of ships to aircraft attack suggested that fleets should operate dispersed, and consist of many low-value units to make them unattractive targets for the A-Bomb.[4]

The potential for the test and the interpretation of its results to become an inter-service dispute and even an existential question for the United States Navy was recognised early on, and planning proceeded jointly between Navy and Army from a very early stage, under the auspices of the Joint Chiefs of Staff. There was also a Presidential Education Commission of four Congressmen and five scientists to assess the results free from service bias, as well as a US Joint Chiefs of Staff Education Board. President Truman endorsed the plans for the tests on 10 January 1946, and the following day the Joint Chiefs appointed Vice Admiral William H P Blandy to lead the exercise.

The US went public with the plans for the tests on 24 January 1946, when Admiral Blandy gave detailed testimony to Congress. The *Washington Post* that day carried a banner headline 'Famed dreadnought to be atomised' over a picture of *New York*. 'Four Battleships head array set for Navy/Army Test' the paper continued.

The tests were designated Operation Crossroads. The logistics were massive, and in their scope and detail unprecedented because of the requirement to capture scientific data. Some 42,000 personnel were involved in supporting the tests, organised under a US Navy–US Army group called Joint Task Force 1 under the command of Admiral Blandy. The support fleet had 123 vessels and 156 planes. The US Navy also assembled ninety-five assorted target vessels (the British report says eighty-two vessels) to evaluate the impact of atomic blast on a wide range of different types of ships. The events were recorded by four television transmitters, 750 cameras, 5,000 pressure gauges and 25,000 radiation recorders. A total of 204 goats, 200 pigs and 5,000 rats, mice and guinea pigs were transported across the Pacific to assess the impact of radiation on living creatures.[5] The chosen site was Bikini Atoll at the northern end of the Marshall Islands chain in Micronesia – sparsely populated, remote, but within B-29 bomber range of US bases and large enough to anchor the Joint Task Force, support the troops on land and set out the array of target ships inside a sheltered coral atoll.

Vice Admiral William H P Blandy USN, Commander of Joint Task Force 1 for the Bikini atom bomb tests in 1946. *(NHHC)*

The US decided to expend its oldest battleships on these tests, as they were anyway due for scrapping under the various post-war plans. Veterans and legislators from New York, including Governor Thomas E Dewey, and from Pennsylvania, petitioned for their States' namesake battleships to be preserved as shrines and museum ships, but Joint Task Force 1 replied: 'It is regretted that such ships as the USS *New York* cannot be spared.'[6] So during spring 1946 *Arkansas*, *New York*, *Nevada* and *Pennsylvania* made their way back across the recently fought-over Pacific, to be prepared for testing.

Nevada at Pearl Harbor en route to Bikini, 9 May 1946. *(NARA)*

Saratoga was also there, one of only two carriers in the tests, alongside four cruisers and sixteen destroyers. The ships were left in battle-worthy condition, all guns and sensors still aboard, machinery working, and loaded with varying amounts of ammunition and fuel (33 per cent in *Nevada*, 50 per cent in *Arkansas* and *Pennsylvania*) to simulate operational conditions. Demands that they all carry full loads of fuel and ammunition were rejected because of fears that ships might sink and deprive the scientists of the detailed ship-by-ship data on the force and effects of the explosions, which were a key deliverable for the tests. *Saratoga* had armed aircraft ranged on deck. *Pennsylvania* was not fully battle worthy, as she had never been fully repaired after the torpedo hit in August 1945. The ships were also used as platforms on whose exposed decks were placed a wide variety of Army stores and equipment, so that its survivability close to nuclear explosions could also be assessed.

The deck log for *Pennsylvania* for 1946 gives a detailed insight into the preparations. She was de-ammunitioned and dry-docked at Bremerton in January. On 9 March she started re-ammunitioning with seventy-three 14in shells and 600 powder charges, plus 4,400 5in shells and charges. On 13 March two army tanks were loaded aboard, and two more followed on 19 March. On 20 March D B Alfred of Movietone News reported aboard for passage to Pearl Harbor. By 31 March she was under way for San Pedro, California, still only able to steam on port engines at 12 knots. Her thirty-one officers (contrast with her wartime complement of well in excess of one hundred) included a watch-keeper, Lieutenant (Junior Grade) J Edward Snyder Jnr, who was to go on to command *New Jersey* during her 1960s recommissioning. *Pennsylvania* left San Pedro on 28 April for Pearl Harbor, where she refuelled, took on a little more ammunition and spent five more days in dry dock. Captain Bushell called on Admiral Blandy on 15 May, and Blandy and his staff came aboard for an inspection the following day, when the log records *New York* getting under way for Bikini. *Pennsylvania* followed on 20 May, making her way across the Pacific increasingly slowly, managing only 8 knots by the time she arrived on 31 May.[7]

Nagato flying the US flag at Yokosuka, 12 October 1945, flanked by US Navy maintenance auxiliaries. *(NARA)*

The ex-Imperial Japanese Navy battleship *Nagato* was also selected as a target ship for the tests. She was the largest (38,000 tons), most modern and most heavily armoured of the heavy ship targets, if not the most seaworthy after her rough handling at the hands of the US 3rd Fleet in July 1945.

In mid-March 1946 she departed from Yokosuka to the United States base at Eniwetok in the Marshall Islands. A total of 180 American

sailors supplemented the Japanese crew. The voyage was fraught. Her condition was poor and she could only use two out of four propeller shafts, travelling at 10 knots. She leaked badly as wartime damage had not been fully repaired, and broke down completely on 28 March after trying to take in tow the cruiser *Sakawa*, Japan's other Bikini target ship, which had also broken down previously. *Nagato* was listing a substantial 7 degrees to port when rescued by US tugs two days later. Eniwetok was finally reached on 4 April at a speed of only 1 knot. There, *Nagato* was patched up and managed an improvement to 13 knots on the final leg of the trip to Bikini Atoll.

Once at the atoll, preparations intensified. After various inspections, *Pennsylvania* left her anchorage at Berth 225 on 5 June and carried out mooring tests outside the atoll, moored to a deadman on Oruk island in tandem with three other ships including the cruiser *Salt Lake City*. This was in accordance with a plan issued by Rear Admiral Fahrion, Commander JTF 1.2, which may have been a rehearsal for target array mooring for a possible deep-water bomb test. However, after dark on 8 June the wind rose and shifted to the south-east, and the mooring arrangements were abandoned as the other ships were in danger of grounding on the reef. The next morning *Pennsylvania* was back inside the atoll at Berth 225.

Pennsylvania at Bikini atoll, 15 June 1946. *(NARA)*

A fortnight of visits, inspections, loading of photographic and radiation monitoring equipment, and practising of evacuation and reboarding protocols followed. On 20 June the phased evacuation of the ship began in preparation for the 'Queen Day' dummy run by the B-29 bomber. The day 22 June saw the final pre-test inspections and commencement of closure of the ship. At 0850 Major Calhoon of the Biological Test Materiel Section came aboard to deliver four rats. Queen Day was postponed from 23 to 24 June due to bad weather, when the 'last minute group' of just sixteen personnel left the ship at 0336. The practice bombing runs were at 0815, and the dummy bomb was dropped at 0914. Later that day the 'last minute group' and boarding teams A and B reboarded, and restored power, one boiler and general services, completing the practice sequence. On 28 June *Pennsylvania* received twelve goats and nine pigs 'for medical research purposes'. On 29 and 30 June the close-down and evacuation procedures were repeated, while numerous visitors were still coming aboard including Congressman Michael J Bradley of Pennsylvania for a brief topside inspection. Around midnight various shipboard equipments intended to be left running during the test failed and the last-minute party spent three hours trying without success to restore them. Then at 0335 it was time to disembark, leaving the ship to her fate.[8]

Nevada prepared as the Bikini target ship – unnaturally bright due to her orange colour scheme. *(NARA)*

The battleships were all anchored very close to the target ground zero, the point on the sea surface above which the bomb was supposed to explode. *Nevada* was picked as the aiming point itself for the first test, which was to be a bomb dropped from a plane. The battleship was, bizarrely, painted a bright orange from end to end to assist the aim of the B-29 Superfortress bomber.

The bombs used at Bikini were Fat Man-type plutonium implosion devices, of comparable design and yield to the one used on Nagasaki. They were the equivalent of about 23,000 tons of TNT. The first test was designated 'Able', and, after considerable debate about the experimental value of an explosion high up that would spread moderate damage more widely, versus a low-level one that was expected to inflict heavier damage over a smaller area, it was planned as the latter – an air burst at an altitude of 500ft.

There was a competition to select the very best B-29 crew in the USAAF; a successful and accurate 'Queen Day' rehearsal a few days before on 24 June; good conditions on the day itself; a number of practice runs over the lagoon on the day itself; and a bright orange target 600ft long. Despite all this, come the real thing on 1 July 1946, the bomber missed

The Bomb – Test Able on 1 July 1946. *(NARA)*

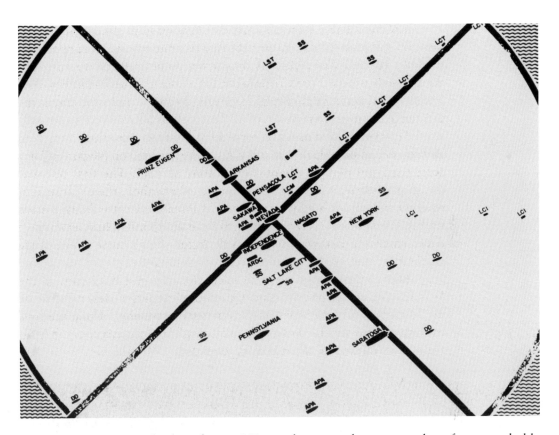

The target array enlarged from the original to show the positions of the battleships. (NARA)

Nevada by about 650 yards, enough to save her from probable annihilation. The error also placed *New York* and *Pennsylvania* significantly further away from the blast than had been planned. There was heated debate about the inaccuracy of the drop, with the Army blaming the ballistics of the bomb and the Manhattan Project bomb designers blaming poor meteorological data. Shurcliff says, illogically, that a dozen different explanations were all examined and ruled out due to incontrovertible evidence. Maybe the simple one was the best – that as the whole experience of the war at sea had repeatedly shown, high-level ballistic bombing of ships still could not be done with anything approaching pinpoint precision. In the event this miss meant that *Arkansas* was also 650 yards away from the explosion, *Nagato* 850 yards, *New York* and *Pennsylvania* 1,500 yards and *Saratoga* 2,500 yards.[9]

Five smaller ships near ground zero were vaporised or capsized by the explosion. But despite their proximity, all the battleships and *Saratoga* stood up to a nuclear bomb remarkably well. Even on *Nevada* there was only superficial, albeit widespread damage. Photos in the Admiralty report show wrecked seaplanes on her quarterdeck, and damage to the funnel, spotting top, radars, aerials and gunnery directors, the lightest anti-aircraft fittings plus other flimsy exposed structures. But the hull of the ship, armoured areas and most superstructure remained largely intact, and there were no sympathetic detonations of fuel or ammunition. *Arkansas* was similarly affected. The photo of *Nagato* shows her severely scorched on the port side exposed to the blast, but with little structural damage. The British report concluded: 'Beyond one mile from the explosion there was practically no damage, and crippling damage was confined to within half a mile.'[10] It found that gun and torpedo armaments were little damaged, and there was no evidence of blast entering the turrets, where exposed cordite charges were unaffected. There were minor fires aboard some of the ships, but only due to ammunition, stores and other flammable equipment having been deliberately left exposed on the decks. The British team assessed that the blast damage to the lighter funnels and ventilation ducts, spreading into the boiler rooms on the ships closest to the blast, would have resulted in a temporary complete loss of steam and hence propulsion to those ships.

Having noted the advanced age and poor seaworthiness of some of the battleship targets, the British observers concluded that a modern battleship could survive an air bust explosion of this magnitude at as little as 250 yards distance, albeit heavily damaged.

There was also little lasting contamination of the hulls from this first explosion as most fallout was sucked into the stratosphere in the mushroom cloud. Had there been a modicum of warning in a real attack, allowing crews to take shelter, previously undamaged vessels might have been able to continue to steam and fight even after close exposure to an atomic attack, albeit with damaged sensors and some casualties. A more serious problem for ships very near the explosion would have been the effect on the crew of the immediate intense fireball and the gamma and neutron radiation burst associated with proximity to the nuclear fireball. Various animals were tethered on the ships to assess these effects, and it was found that exposed animals were dead within two days, while even those in some of the armoured positions, but above the upper deck, died from radiation exposure a few days later. To stand a reasonable chance of survival from this radiation burst the crew would have had to shelter deep within the ships. In the run-up to the tests the Bulletin of Atomic Scientists had opined that: 'a large ship about a mile away from the explosion, would escape sinking, but the crew would be killed by the deadly burst of radiations from the bomb, and only a ghost ship would remain, floating unattended in the vast waters of the ocean'.[11] The British observers were more optimistic. Their casualty estimates arising from radiation exposure were 100 per cent of exposed personnel up to 1,000 yards, 65 per cent at 1,500 yards and 10 per cent at 2,000 yards. In between decks the corresponding estimates were 20 per cent at 500 yards, 10 per cent at 1,000 and 5 per cent at 1,500, with no radiation casualties among those

Test Baker on 26 July 1946, half a second after explosion. Left to right are *Pennsylvania*, *New York*, *Saratoga*, *Salt Lake City*, *Arkansas*, *Independence*, *Nagato* and *Nevada*. (NHHC)

stationed behind armour even at the closest distance. Effects would vary locally depending on the direction of the explosion and the precise amount of ship structure between personnel and the radiation source.

For that first test 'Able' on 1 July 1946, *Nagato* was only 850 yards from the explosion. Nevertheless, she survived with only light damage. A boarding party assessed the damage, ran her machinery for thirty-six hours without any difficulties and prepared her for the next test. The same was done for the other ships. *Pennsylvania* was reboarded according to the previously exercised plan, despite the need to extinguish a small fire during the afternoon. The radiological monitors gave the initial all-clear at 1905 to reboard the following day, and A and B teams were aboard at 1155 on 2 July. By 1455 the entire ship was declared radiologically clear. While numerous instrument inspectors came aboard, the crew relit number three boiler and had restored all services to normal operation by 2305. The test animals were removed on 3 July and further testing of equipment including main engines was completed, all satisfactorily. On 9 July the Royal Navy inspection team, led by Roskill, came aboard for over an hour. Other visitors included Congressman Albert J Engel of Michigan.[12]

The ability to reboard and operate the ships was relatively encouraging for those who wished to argue the continued relevance of navies in the atomic age. Given a little warning for crews to take shelter, it seemed as if larger and heavily armoured ships with some dispersal in a task force type of formation could survive atomic attack even at very close quarters and remain reasonably operational. The second test, called 'Baker', was to prove a very different matter.

This was an underwater explosion 90ft below the surface of the lagoon set off from a tethered barge on 25 July, and designed to simulate nuclear attack on a harbour. Its characteristics differed greatly from Able. The area affected by the blast was less overall but its impact on ship structures and operation was more severe. There was a huge column of water thrown up – initially estimated to be at least 10 million tons, but possibly only 2 million – which partly vaporised and then saturated almost all the target ships as it descended.

Two seconds after the explosion. *(NHHC)*

Six seconds after blast showing the *Arkansas*'s 'slot' to the right of the water column. (NHHC)

Arkansas was only 250 yards from the second bomb and she suffered what must be the most spectacular demise of all the battleships. First she was badly crushed from end to end by the underwater shock wave, then almost immediately lifted by this water column, then dumped directly onto the floor of the atoll 180ft below. She can be seen, momentarily, in what looks like a vertical position, on the right-hand side of the water column in the film taken of the explosion from the shore of Bikini Atoll, before the expanding water column completely engulfs her. Some observers thought she was so lifted, but the British observers took a different view, that the photographic evidence showed the gap in the water column where *Arkansas* had been, and there was no evidence that she was lifted.

It hardly seems to matter. Rather quaintly, the bureaucracy of the US Navy only then kicked into action. Four days after her destruction she was formally decommissioned, and nineteen days after that she was formally stricken from the Navy list. The British observers noted: 'It is reasonable to suppose that nothing could have saved her, the whole of her structure would have been holed and shaken by the pressure wave and the extremely high velocity particles which bombarded her. She may have broken up and the descending water may have hastened her end. It is also conceivable that she may have fallen into the large cavity which must have been left by the water which was thrown up and that she was swamped by the rush of water which would have rapidly flowed into this cavity. No doubt all of these features contributed to her early demise.' In fact, *Arkansas* did not break up. The wreck is indeed crushed all along its length, and capsized, but substantially intact today and along with the rest of Bikini a UNESCO world heritage site and scuba diving destination.[13]

The 'water hammer' effect was similar to that seen from the underwater detonation of mines and near-miss heavy bombs near the hulls of ships during the war, but on a much larger scale. Some underwater damage was inflicted on the other battleships that were further away (*Nagato* 800 yards, *New York* 1,000, *Nevada* 1,100, *Pennsylvania* 1,200), but generally it did not appear serious. There was also a significant tsunami effect, with a wave 100ft high near the centre of the blast, which was particularly devastating for *Saratoga* at only 400 yards from ground zero. She lost her superstructure and all aircraft and fittings on deck.

New York returns to Pearl Harbor from Kwajalein, 14 March 1947. *(NARA)*

Underwater damage resulted in progressive flooding and her capsize and sinking a few hours later. *New York* was left substantially intact, and was eventually towed back to Pearl Harbor for evaluation of the damage.

Pennsylvania also survived well, although it was noted on 27 July that she was slightly down by the stern and had a small oil leak. Although the Director of Ship Materiel cleared her for initial reboarding on 27 July, this was rescinded, and further decontamination efforts using foam sprayed from salvage tugs continued. She was finally reboarded only on 8 August, when work focussed on pumping out the flooded stern compartments. Following the decision to abandon decontamination efforts on 10 August, she was towed to Kwajalein Atoll some 200 miles away between 21 and 24 August, where she was again inspected and closed up with canvas coverings across all openings. She was formally decommissioned on 29 August 1946.[14] There she remained for eighteen months undergoing radiological and structural assessment. She was deliberately scuttled there on 10 February 1948.

Nagato was only 800 yards from the underwater burst. She survived the 'water hammer' effect and the tsunami with little apparent damage and a 2 degree list after the test. However, it was not possible to reboard her and assess what had happened in detail because of the radioactivity from the water column. Some underwater damage had obviously been sustained because the list increased very gradually over the following five days, possibly as a result of reopening of her wartime damage or of taking on quantities of sea water that had been pumped over her during the attempted decontamination. *Nagato* eventually capsized and sank, unseen, during the night of 29–30 July 1946. *Nevada*, the original Test Able target ship, survived the two tests, and was also eventually returned to Pearl Harbor via Kwajalein.

The British observers concluded that in terms of structural damage, all ships would be sunk within 500 yards of such an underwater explosion, and all within 800 yards disabled, but there would be no significant structural damage beyond 1,200 yards. Instead, it was the unexpected characteristics of the water column from the second test, and its irradiation of the entire exposed surfaces of the ships it engulfed, which ultimately did the most telling damage. Despite large scale, if primitive, attempts to clean and wash down the targets to decontaminate them, all the ships immersed by the column remained dangerously irradiated by the fission products of the explosion. A further major problem was the microscopic dispersal of the 10 kilograms or so of plutonium that did not experience fission in the explosion of the bomb. This was very difficult to detect using the technology of the time, but if it remained coating the exposed surfaces of the ships then eventually it would be ingested or inhaled by crews and manifest its acute toxic properties. The British observers noted: 'There is little hope for any men exposed to radioactive spray from the explosion.' They would receive a fatal dose within one day of exposure to weather decks and superstructure. The water column, called by the British 'the cloud', contaminated an area about 4,000 to 5,000 yards in diameter.

The decontamination efforts were persisted with for two weeks, against the protests of some of the radiological advisers, until it was decided on 10 August that the health risks of working aboard or close to the target ships were too great for the sailors thus exposed and with only very rudimentary radiation protection. *Pennsylvania*'s log records on 11 August: 'In accordance with CTG1.2 despatch of 102258Z all decontamination work was halted.' The previous three days had been spent pumping out flooded compartments, including those damaged by the torpedo at Okinawa, although the radiological survey showed a tolerance permitted on the weather deck of only forty-five minutes to two hours. The boarding parties also successfully relit boiler No. 2 and steamed for ninety minutes. After the decision to abandon decontamination it was still necessary to put boarding parties aboard from 16 to 21 August to continue pumping, undertake the final Director of Ships Materiel inspections and prepare the ship for towing, but no one was living aboard, as the parties returned to the accommodation ship USS *Niagara* after duties.[15] It was therefore impossible to repeat the original plan, as carried out after Able, to put proper crews back aboard the ships to evaluate damage more fully, operate their machinery, and prepare for a third planned test explosion in deep water. That test, 'Charlie', which was in any case scheduled to take place rather later due to the unsolved challenge of anchoring and monitoring the bomb, and bringing the bomb and the target array together in deep open water, was therefore cancelled.

The UK had hoped to increase its stake in the trials by offering surplus ships of its own for the third test, assuming that it would have been in early 1947,[16] but these aspirations were extinguished by the Presidential decision to postpone it indefinitely, announced on 9 September 1946. It was speculated by the British that this was due on the one hand to a belief from General Leslie Groves, Head of the Manhattan Project, that the test was superfluous and extravagant given the extrapolations that could be made from 'Baker' (a view that the UK underwater damage experts strongly rejected), and also that the sheer scale of Joint Task Force 1 made it impossible to sustain the Bikini effort into 1947 given the cutbacks in the US Navy vote and the need for more rapid demobilisation. A deep ocean test was eventually reinstated in 1955 (Test 'Wigwam'), but with a much larger weapon and using only simulated submarines as target vessels. The British observers at Bikini instead extrapolated their own estimates for the impact of 'Charlie' from what they had observed of 'Baker'. They expected a more powerful underwater pressure pulse to sink or disable ships at about three times the range of Baker, so 1,500 to 2,500 yards, but the contaminating water column would be smaller. But both they and the Admiralty were very disappointed that 'Charlie' did not take place to enable the validation of what were perforce very speculative conclusions.

Overall the results of the Bikini tests were fairly intuitive. The largest and most heavily protected ships – the battleships – survived the best. Their degree of physical resilience to 20 kiloton explosions between 600 and 1,600 yards distant was probably greater than expected. Aircraft carriers and their exposed aircraft were more vulnerable – the light fleet carrier *Independence* was extensively wrecked by the first explosion. Task forces could probably survive attack by a single airburst bomb, but were likely to be severely degraded by wide area damage of their upper works, notably their radars, range finders and communications, and within a few days also by some acute radiation casualties. An underwater burst proved ultimately more effective at this sort of kilotonnage because of the irradiating impact of the vaporised water column denying safe access to the contaminated ships, rather than the direct physical damage it inflicted. *Pennsylvania*, *New York* and *Nevada* could never be safely and economically decontaminated for conventional scrapping.

The British observation team plotted the scientific results of the two tests against their assessments of the impact on the ships had they been in action, and then against a series of likely tactical dispositions. For the airburst test 'Able' they estimated *Nevada* and *Arkansas* disabled, mainly due to widespread loss of their sensors; *Nagato* damaged with heavy casualties; and the other heavy ships undamaged. For the underwater test 'Baker' they observed *Arkansas* and *Saratoga* actually sunk; estimated *Nagato* disabled; *New York* and *Nevada* damaged with heavy casualties; and *Pennsylvania* undamaged but with heavy casualties. Atomic attacks on large ships concentrated in harbour (Portsmouth is the example used in the report) or lighter shipping relatively closely concentrated during amphibious assaults would prove the most damaging scenarios. Attacks on convoys or on fleets at sea would be much less effective given the typical dispersal distances in use during the Second World War. Using the template of the cruising formation of the British Pacific Fleet in 1945, they estimated that one airburst could not expect seriously to affect more than one ship in a twenty-one ship squadron. One underwater burst could sink at most one capital ship if accurately delivered, and potentially leave two more contaminated by the water column, but those other ships could be expected to be able to manoeuvre once the bomb had exploded and be able to avoid the radioactive spray. Dispersal, the observers concluded, was the best defence, and the submarine was likely to be the most survivable platform.

The longer-term significance of the Bikini tests as a determinant of the future of naval warfare and detailed fleet characteristics is debatable. The yields of weapons increased dramatically from the mid-1950s with the arrival of the Hydrogen bomb, first tested in 1952. This meant the weapons became strategic rather than tactical. However, given that the USA settled on mass production of an 18 kiloton Mark 4 nuclear bomb after further tests in 1948, smaller than the yields at Bikini, the conclusions of the Bikini observers about tactics and survivability in a tactical nuclear war remained operationally valid for at least the next decade or so. And, despite the increased explosive power delivered by the atomic bomb, at the yields of the 1940s and early 1950s it was still just a large bomb rather than a complete game changer. There would still be a need for considerable aiming precision to sink capital ship targets with ballistic bombs, which could not always be expected in attacks on moving and defended high-value targets in the open sea, and given the considerable height from which these bombs would need to be dropped to allow the bombers to get clear of the effects. There was also the question of air defence against the bomber, which for some years before bombs could be manufactured smaller would have to be a large land-based plane, hence easier to defend against than naval aircraft, and the fact that the overall inventory of bombs remained very small over this period, so target selection would be a difficult judgement.

These assumptions were reflected in later UK planning, for example in Exercise Trident, a table-top seminar held at the Royal Naval College, Greenwich, in April 1949. It suggested that the Russian A-bomb threat in its chosen 'Exercise year' of 1957 would come from Bikini-style weapons and that the most likely attack would be a high-level air burst designed to affect mass areas, or a low airburst designed to incapacitate capital ships. In either case the weapon would have to be carried by a large and vulnerable bomber and dropped from high level, which would make it not very accurate. The conclusion of Trident was that use of these weapons was not very economical against ship targets at sea.[17] The simulated atom-bombing of the Fleet by the RAF in exercises between 1948 and 1953 also tends to confirm that the precision needed to sink or disable capital ships with such weapons was still hard to achieve.

A lasting lesson, reflected in Cold War ship design henceforth, was the need to provide protection against radiation. An over-pressure nuclear citadel to ensure the interior of ships remained uncontaminated, and a built-in wash down system, tested in the UK on the trials cruiser *Cumberland*, became fundamental characteristics of future surface warship designs. Less evident, but as important, were the modifications to ships' funnel designs to make them resistant to wide-area blasts, and avoid the loss of steam that the Bikini observers noted as a likely effect of the airburst weapon on *Nevada*.

CHAPTER FIVE

Thinning the Ranks

WHILE MANY BATTLESHIPS remained active in various roles (see Chapter Six), the period between late 1945 and the outbreak of the Korean War in June 1950 did see the ninety-five battleships of September 1945 dwindle steadily in number. As the post-war recovery gathered pace there was a large and pressing requirement for recycled iron and steel to use for reconstruction projects, and this played its part in sending battleships to the breakers although each one, weighing in at around 25,000 tons of scrap, only amounted to 0.25 per cent of the UK's 11.5 million tons requirement for metals in 1948.[1] The pace of battleship decommissioning and scrapping, and indeed that for all classes of warships, picked up.

Underpinning this thinning of the battleship ranks were three factors. First, a number of the ships were to useful intents and purposes wrecks and write-offs. Their restoration to service, while in some cases technically feasible, was neither militarily justified, nor economic. Second, the political reality of the new world order dictated that the erstwhile Axis naval powers, Germany and Japan, would not be allowed to retain or restore their battleships. Italy too would face explicit battleship constraints in her Peace Treaty. And third, because of the prolonged battleship building holiday after the Washington Treaty of 1922, and nearly two decades where investment went into modernising old ships instead of replacing them, many of the ships still serving in 1945 were old, obsolescent, and worn out from war service.

Japan
All the Japanese ships except *Nagato* were progressively broken up in 1946–47 after a directive from Supreme Command of the Allied Powers dated 19 February 1946. *Settsu*, sunk at Kure where she had been built, was raised in June 1946, and scrapped there at Harima shipyard by August 1947. *Haruna* was also raised in 1946 and broken up through to 1948. *Ise* was scrapped where she sank at Kure without being raised between 9 October 1946 and 4 July 1947. *Hyuga* was raised on 2 July 1946 and broken up in dry dock by Harima Zosen Yard at Kure by 4 July 1947.[2] The British Commonwealth Occupation Force based at Kure from February 1946 had lead responsibility for demilitarising Japan. This included destruction of the infrastructure that had supported the battleships. The task included the disposal of hundreds of guns, including the 16in and 18in spare barrels for the *Nagato* and *Yamato* classes, and thousands of heavy shells.[3]

Tirpitz at Alta Fiord, Tromsø, 1954. *(Alamy)*

Germany

The German ships lasted a little longer. The Russians laid claim to *Lützow*, and raised her in 1947. Some sources say she was scrapped from 1948 onwards[4] but it seems more likely, according to Soviet archives, that she was expended as a target and sunk as a result of Soviet weapons trials in the Baltic on 22 July 1947.[5] *Tirpitz* was scrapped where she lay in Alta Fjord, close to the island of Hakoy. Work lasted from 1948 to 1957, by which point some 80 per cent of the structure had been removed. The large working platform used to demolish her can still be seen there at low water.

Graf Spee was never comprehensively salvaged, and her remains were visible for many years after the war. The wreck is in very shallow water just off Montevideo's main shipping channel and is still easily accessible. Since February 2004 Uruguayan salvage teams have recovered a 5.9in secondary armament gun, the main rangefinder and other memorabilia. In 2007 it was reported that the whole wreck was to be raised as it represented a hazard to shipping, and that film director James Cameron, of *Titanic* fame, was filming this operation. However, nothing seems to have come of this and in May 2016 the Uruguayan Navy confirmed that the wreck was 90–95 per cent buried into the mud.[6]

Admiral Scheer was capsized at the Deutsche Werke dockyard in Kiel. She too was partially broken up in situ through the 1940s, until the remains were abandoned and covered over with rubble as part of a plan to expand the dockyard facility. *Gneisenau* lingered in Gdynia. Although it ordered the removal of the ship in 1947, it took the Polish Government until 12 September 1951 to seal and refloat her. Scrapping proceeded thereafter. Her aft (Caesar) turret had been removed in 1943 following Hitler's tantrum about the uselessness of the German surface navy, and remounted as a coastal defence battery at Austratt Fort, Trondheim, Norway, where it remains today, accessible as part of a museum. It remained an operational fort under Norwegian control until 1968 and the turret made its final 11in firing in 1953. [7]

Italy
Of the two Italian wrecks at Trieste in the Adriatic, which had become the new front line in Cold War tensions between Italy, the Western Powers and Yugoslavia's Tito, the hulks of *Conte di Cavour* and *Impero* were also gradually salvaged. Brescia says *Cavour* was capsized, and scrapped from 1946,[8] although M J Whitley says she was not refloated until 1951–52 and finally scrapped from 1952 to 1953. *Impero* had remained upright when sunk and was raised in late 1947. Whitley says she was scrapped at Venice from 1948 to 1950.[9]

United Kingdom
In the United Kingdom the first ships to go after the war were *Derfflinger* and *Iron Duke*. They had spent the whole conflict a few miles apart in Scapa Flow, the one anchored near Rysa Little island, afloat but upside down after her salvage; the other upright but beached at Flotta. The Royal Navy continued to require the dry docks at Rosyth after the war for repair of other ships, so *Derfflinger* was unable to follow her High Seas Fleet predecessors to be broken up there. In July 1946 Metal Industries instead acquired a new lease of the ex-Admiralty wartime logistic facility at Faslane, in Gare Loch on the Clyde, as their main shipbreaking site to replace Rosyth. *Iron Duke* had been purchased by Metal Industries in February 1946 for only £8,000, refloated at Scapa Flow in April and towed to Faslane, arriving on 19 August after four days at sea, delayed by high winds and seas.

However, unlike Rosyth, there was no dry dock at Faslane to accommodate *Derfflinger*. The standard method of scrapping an upright ship was by progressively removing top weight so that the ship floated higher and higher, drawing less and less water, allowing lower levels to be accessed and scrapped in turn while the ship still floated. Eventually so little would remain as to allow the final remains of the hulk to be beached

at high tide and completely dismantled at low tide. The upside-down *Derfflinger*, however, presented a very significant technical challenge. Because of the protrusions of her superstructure below the hull, she was drawing far too much water to get alongside or to scrap on the beach. If her exposed hull was breached in the scrapping process the compressed air inside that allowed it to float would escape and she would sink again.

The solution was for Metal Industries to lease, in addition to Faslane, Admiralty Floating Dock No. 4, now also surplus to requirements and also moored on the Clyde. Its 32,000-ton lifting capacity was adequate to accommodate the weight of the battlecruiser, although her two deepest protruding turrets first had to be cut out from inside the ship by divers to reduce her draught. Even then the remaining draught, at 39ft, was so great that the dock had to be sunk 8ft below its normal submerged depth to ease her in. In September 1946, using six tugs, *Turmoil*, *Dextrous*, *Empire Jean*, *Empire Mascot*, *Metinda II* and *Metinda III*, *Derfflinger* made the same upside-down tow from Scapa Flow as her High Sea Fleet predecessors, but this time westwards around Cape Wrath and to the mouth of the Clyde, arriving at Greenock on 12 September.

She was docked in AFD 4 on 12 October and gradually raised. The dock with her inside was then towed alongside at Faslane on 15 November. There *Derfflinger* was reunited with *Iron Duke*. As 1947 progressed (and the Clyde Fleet Review took place just around the

Derfflinger is eased into the floating dock No. 4 in Gare Loch, October 1946. *(MTSC)*

The dock has been pumped out and *Derfflinger* is moved towards Faslane, November 1946. *(MTSC)*

Rosneath peninsula, see Chapter Six), the two protagonists of Jutland lay in adjoining berths and were inexorably cut to bits. In September 1948 Metal Industries resold the remains of the *Iron Duke* hulk to Smith and Houston of Port Glasgow, where she arrived on 30 November 1948 for final demolition.[10]

A number of the UK battleships still in service in 1945 were by warship standards old or even obsolete. Twelve of Britain's Second World War battleships dated from the First World War, and by 1945 the nine survivors were at least twenty-eight years old. Furthermore, they had all

Iron Duke (left) and *Derfflinger* (right) alongside at Metal Industries Ltd, Faslane. *(MTSC)*

suffered hard usage in the conflict, and in some cases were well and truly worn out. The four *Revenge* class were very slow by modern standards, able to steam only 21 knots at best, versus the 27 or greater now needed for carrier task group operations. They plus four more ships (*Nelson, Rodney, Warspite and Malaya*) had undergone no significant modernisation to Second World War standards of protection or anti-aircraft armament. There was very unlikely to be a case to refurbish or maintain any of these ships in commission, or even in reserve in straitened times. This was especially so given that there were still eight other more recent or more extensively modernised and capable battleships available to the Royal Navy. Nonetheless, as we have seen, initially the Admiralty saw a need for more than eight battleships as part of the planned post-war fleet, and only slowly grasped the reality of budget, manpower and infrastructural constraints on retaining them.

A decision was therefore made in principle in October 1945 to scrap only the oldest, least capable ships – *Warspite, Malaya, Revenge, Resolution and Ramillies* – when their present duties as training and

accommodation ships were completed. In approving this at the War
Cabinet the Ministry of Supply noted the acute need for scrap metal.[11]
However, all the ships except *Warspite* remained in use for the immediate
future, and there was no immediate announcement of the decision. Lord
Hall, First Lord of the Admiralty, finally explained to the House of Lords
on 29 January 1947: 'Noble Lords will realise that a number of ships
which were used during the last war were very old ships ... I speak in
terms of very great pride of the work which was done by the battleships
of the *Malaya* and *Warspite* class, ships well over thirty years old. But
ships like human beings get older and past their serviceable age. That can
be said of quite a number of ships which the Admiralty and His Majesty's
Government felt it was no longer necessary to retain, and they had to be
scrapped. This was done with a very great pang of regret ...'[12] The
announcement itself was a peculiar fudge, in response to a Notice on the
Order paper by Lord Howe that related to the transfer of Royal Navy
vessels to other Powers. The references to *Malaya* and *Warspite* were
buried deep in his response and the other battleships were not mentioned

at all. Lord Hall clarified in a debate over a year later, on 8 March 1948, that only 'two of our older capital ships had already been placed on the scrapping list – Namely *Malaya* and *Warspite*. Others, *Ramillies, Resolution and Revenge,* had previously been declassified as fighting ships and have been in use for non-combatant purposes.'[13]

In practice only *Warspite*, which had been on the disposal list since 31 July 1946, was immediately available at the beginning of 1947. The other ships were still employed as training and accommodation ships. In March 1945 the Royal Navy's Engineer in Chief had explained that *Revenge* and *Resolution* would both be needed in this role at Devonport if conscription into the Navy continued. Eventually it was hoped to build a proper training establishment ashore, but due to other pressures that was considered unlikely to be achievable during the first ten years of peace (i.e. until about 1957). 'In the meantime *Revenge* and *Resolution* together form a suitable establishment and their retention is necessary.' In February 1945 the Director of Plans at the Admiralty noted that *Ramillies* was the *Vernon* accommodation and turret drill ship, and that the commitment was expected to last five years.[14]

So, of the battleships that had fought the Nazis, *Warspite* became the first to go, but not quietly. There were calls to preserve her as a museum ship, but they did not amount to much of a campaign. The question was raised in the Houses of Parliament by Commander Noble, MP, in a written question on 29 January 1947, the same day that Lord Hall announced *Warspite*'s scrapping. He asked whether 'consideration will be given to preserving at Portsmouth a battleship, veteran of both wars, in similar manner to HMS *Victory*; and what is the additional yearly cost if this ship was also used as an accommodation ship instead of one of those so used at present'. Mr Dugdale, the Parliamentary Secretary, replied for the Admiralty: 'It has been decided that the scheme is not feasible for many reasons. Such a ship would either occupy valuable berthing space alongside or would indefinitely occupy a capital ship dock which cannot be spared. To preserve a steel ship against deterioration and to keep her presentable would require constant work and expense and would make an unjustifiable demand on manpower. The possible solution of combining the duty of accommodation ship with those of a relic has also been considered. To be of any value as an accommodation ship, however, a battleship would require extensive alteration to provide classrooms, messing accommodation etc. Furthermore the public could not be given constant access to what would be in fact a Naval Establishment. In these circumstances I have not thought I would be justified in having the additional annual cost calculated.'[15]

With so many other well-known battleships still in existence and no immediate expectation of their complete disappearance, *Warspite*'s case was probably not so obvious as it became in hindsight. And, whatever her historic merits, she was in very poor shape, still heavily damaged from her 1943 bombing. She would have been very expensive to repair, let alone preserve, at a time of biting post-war austerity.

In the event no rescue plan could be delivered, and she was instead sold to Metal Industries in November 1946 for £101,000. They planned to scrap her at the Faslane facility. In August 1946 *Warspite* left her buoy at Spithead and went into Portsmouth dockyard for the last time to have various fittings removed. This included the whole main armament of eight 15in guns, which had been specifically requested by the Director of Naval Ordnance on 19 March 1946 as part of a plan to maintain a 15in gun operational and spares pool for the remaining battleships and the monitors *Roberts* and *Abercrombie*. The process took seven months. On 12 March 1947 she went back to Spithead to join *Malaya* and *Queen Elizabeth* – three sisters together at the reserve anchorage for the last time. She departed on 18 April bound for the Clyde, under tow by the tugs *Bustler* and *Metinda III* (the veteran of the *Derfflinger* tow). A towing crew of eight was aboard the battleship. She was not to get very far.

As a fighting ship *Warspite* had a reputation for being difficult to handle. She had performed an uncommanded full circle with a jammed rudder under the guns of the whole High Seas Fleet at a critical moment of the Battle of Jutland. Twenty-seven years later, while being towed to the safety of Malta after being bombed and immobilised off Italy, she had broken free and drifted sideways out of control through the Straits of Messina in September 1943. On 20 April 1947 she encountered a fierce

Three sisters at anchor: *Warspite*, *Queen Elizabeth* and *Malaya* at Spithead, April 1947. *Warspite's* 15in and 6in guns have been removed at Portsmouth Dockyard. *(Author's collection)*

westerly gale as she headed down the English Channel. As darkness fell and winds reached 70mph, one of the tow lines snapped off Land's End. *Metinda III* stayed attached to the battleship, but could not on her own control *Warspite* as she drifted back up the Channel, shipping large amounts of water as the seas broke over her forecastle and the 15in turrets worked loose. *Bustler* managed to reattach her tow line during the following afternoon, but the weather had not abated. All the struggling tugs could manage was to crab *Warspite* northwards into Mount's Bay in search of some shelter. She dropped anchor 3 miles offshore late in the evening of 21 April. Still the weather raged. In the Bristol Channel the same tempest drove the merchant ship *Samtampa* onto rocks at Porthcawl, and the whole crew of the Mumbles lifeboat died attempting the rescue. Altogether there were forty-seven fatalities in that tragedy. Back in Mount's Bay at 1630 on 23 April, despite being partially in the lee of the land, *Warspite* broke loose from her anchors and drifted out of control eastwards across the bay. She ran aground first of all on Mountamopus Ledge off Cudden Point. At high tide she drifted clear and was carried a further 500 yards to the east, where she grounded on the rocks at Prussia Cove. Her bows had been damaged and she flooded by the head, stuck fast and listing to port.

The Penlee lifeboat was launched at 1730 to lift off the eight men of the towing crew, who must have endured a traumatic and very uncomfortable four days. Their ordeal was not over because the lifeboat was faced with 30ft waves as it neared the stricken vessel. The coxswain was Edwin Madron. *Warspite* was too close to shore to risk a rescue on the sheltered starboard side. Instead, he took the lifeboat down a channel only 40 yards wide between the more exposed port side of the battleship, and rocks over which seas were breaking further offshore. It was too rough to fire a line across and keep it taut, so instead he had to manoeuvre the lifeboat, full ahead then full astern as each wave passed, for over half an hour, maintaining position while holding his vessel close enough to the battleship to allow the eight men to jump across the gap, but not so close as to be smashed on the anti-torpedo bulge that protruded from the ship's side at the waterline. One by one the towing crew jumped as the decks of the battleship and the lifeboat came level at the crest of each wave. Finally all were safely off, and the lifeboat returned to Newlyn to land them that evening. Edwin Madron was awarded the RNLI's Silver Medal for this outstanding feat of seamanship and endurance.[16]

When the weather calmed down the stranded battleship quickly became a tourist sensation. People had picnics on the cliffs and local fishermen ran boat trips to see the leviathan up close. Metal Industries, whose investment and focus was in the fixed plant at Faslane, decided to cut their losses and claimed £149,000 for her loss from their underwriters.

She was then sold on to Bennet and Brewis of Bristol on 28 August 1948 for £25,000.[17] To begin their salvage they opted to lighten her as she lay on the rocks. There was not much visible progress through 1947, 1948 and 1949, to judge by pictures taken in April that year.

Bennet and Brewis then sold the hulk to the Wolverhampton Metals Company Ltd of Wednesfield in early 1949, following an earlier contract of August 1947 to deliver to them the non-ferrous scrap, estimated at 1,250 to 1,500 tons. Most of the upper superstructure and some of the 15in gun turrets had gone by the time Pathé News filmed her from a boat around mid-1950. As little heavy salvage could be done in such an exposed position, the three years passed at Prussia Cove were also used to make her airtight for a refloating attempt by P Bauer (Salvage) Ltd of London. This involved using twenty-four compressor pumps to try to expel the water from her hull. A large crowd and the media gathered to watch on the cliff top. Again, a rising gale frustrated these efforts. There was

Warspite on the rocks at Prussia Cove, Cornwall, May 1947. *(Alamy)*

insufficient depth at high tide to float *Warspite* clear of the reef. One of the salvage boats, *Barnet*, was herself holed in the rising seas, and drifted ashore at Long Rock a few miles away.

A further attempt in August 1950 was blessed with better weather, and was partially successful. They got her off the Prussia Cove rocks, round Cudden Point and back into Mount's Bay proper, where she was beached off Marazion, just west of St Michael's Mount. Some further salvage was undertaken. Further sealing of the hull to improve buoyancy also took place, and on 11 November 1950 yet another attempt was made to refloat her. The contrariness of the battleship still persisted. The tug *Masterman* went aground on Hogus Rocks after failing to tow her. Her fellow tug *Tradesman* got the hawser wire wrapped around her propeller trying to pull *Masterman* off.

The records of the Wolverhampton Metals Company, owners of the wreck, show that they took over direct responsibility for the salvage from Bauer's on 25 January 1952, and that they had to start assembling new salvage equipment and a crew from scratch. This was the job of Mr Frank Wilson. It was he who employed the jet engine compressors, loaned by the Ministry of Supply, with advisers provided from Rolls-Royce. *Warspite* was successfully lifted by this method on 12 May 1952, and moved inshore by a quarter of a mile. She grounded across a deeper channel and broke her back as the tide fell. Pathé News put a camera team aboard to record the work of the salvage crew at this point. The ship was awash at high tides, making work very difficult even in the calmest weather. The film shows the compressor pumps coming aboard again for another refloating attempt. British Pathé's soundtrack opined that *Warspite* had beaten the scrap men twice and that she might do it again: 'Thirty Thousand tons of old fighting spirit, alone with her battle against time.' They were not far wrong.

This, it transpired, was her final resting place. There she remained for around four more years, gradually being broken up. She was still not going quietly. In 1952 the Dutch steamship *Albatross* was being used to transport some of the salvage from Penzance to Hull. On 23 December she also went aground on St Catherine's Point, Isle of Wight. The crew was rescued but the ship and her *Warspite* cargo were lost. In Mount's Bay, the *Warspite* hulk gradually diminished. In order to speed up work, Wolverhampton Metals decided to remove the 21-ton lower armour plates intact, so a 25-ton crane had to be purchased to lift those. Further attempts to refloat her were still being made, but she came apart at the fracture where her back had broken in May 1953, and this meant she could be pulled just a little further up the beach on 27 June 1953. By this stage Wolverhampton Metals had recovered about 5,000 tons of steel. *Warspite* finally disappeared from recognisable view in around 1956, although sources conflict on the dates. But the lowest parts of her hull, sunk in the sands, still defied the scrappers. If you go down to the tideline at very low water west of St Michael's Mount, as I have done, you will still find fragments of metal there, the last remnants of Britain's most famous battleship.[18]

Malaya had spent the immediate post-war period as an accommodation ship at Portsmouth for the *Vernon* Torpedo Training School. She had been approved for scrapping at the same time as *Warspite*, but lingered for the best part of a year in her auxiliary role. She was much more placid than her sister. Eventually sold to the British Iron and Steel Corporation (BISCO) and allocated for breaking up to Metal Industries on 20 February 1948, she arrived for scrapping at Faslane on 12 April without any untoward incidents, and was torched over the next year or so.

Revenge and *Resolution* continued in reserve service as accommodation and training ships at Devonport through 1946. Eventually the stokers training school of which they were a part also encompassed the battleships *Renown* and *Valiant*, the latter fresh out of her expensive refit, as well as the aircraft carrier *Unicorn*. These ships were all jointly commissioned as HMS *Imperieuse* on 21 June 1946. They were reduced to reserve again by October 1947. *Imperieuse* herself was paid off on 1 June 1948. This meant the end of the line for the old battleships. *Resolution* was placed on the disposal list in February 1948 and allocated

Revenge (left) with *Royal Sovereign* at Thomas W Ward's scrapping facility, Inverkeithing, 1950. *(MTSC)*

to Metal Industries for breaking up, arriving at Faslane on 13 May. *Revenge* was placed on the disposal list on 8 March 1948 and allocated to Thomas Ward & Co. in July. She arrived at their facility at Inverkeithing in the Firth of Forth on 5 September 1948.

The requirement for *Ramillies* to support HMS *Vernon* also finished much earlier than had been anticipated in 1945, and she too was placed on the disposal list in December 1947 and sold on 20 February 1948 to BISCO, who allocated her to Arnott & Young. She arrived at their yard in Cairnryan, Galloway, for breaking up on 23 April 1948. In common with all Arnott & Young's battleships, she was dismantled alongside a jetty first, before the remaining hulk was transferred to the facility at Troon, Ayrshire, where it could be dragged up the beach on each tide as it was progressively demolished. The remains of *Ramillies* reached Troon for final demolition on 22 October 1949. She was drawing only 7ft 10in forward and 10ft 5in aft, compared with 33ft when complete in her deep-load condition. Probably only 7,000 tons or thereabouts of her structure was left. Demolition was completed on 30 August 1950.[19] One of *Ramillies*'s 15in guns was eventually preserved and is the right-hand gun, looking from the front, placed outside the Imperial War Museum in Lambeth, London.[20]

France

Across the English Channel on the Normandy invasion beaches, *Courbet* gradually met her end. The wreck was sold in 1946. Photographs show her substantially intact then, with main armament still in place. The mayor of Hermanville had hopes to preserve her and the rest of the gooseberry breakwater ships as a tourist attraction, but this was impractical given their exposed position, and *Courbet* was gradually broken up in situ by a consortium of shipbreakers based in Ouistreham, and then by three

Courbet scuttled as a blockship off Hermanville, Normandy.

successor companies up until the beginning of the 1970s. The remains were still visible during a very low tide in March 1967, and a substantial wreck remains on the seabed, 1,300 metres off the beach, marked today by a yellow and black cardinal buoy bearing her name.[21] Meanwhile, at Toulon, *Océan* was raised and scrapped from September 1945. *Condorcet* was also raised in late 1945 and eventually sold for scrap, finally being broken up around 1949.[22]

United States of America

Oklahoma alongside Iowa at Pearl Harbor, 1944. Note the discrepancy in size between dreadnoughts of different generations. (NHHC)

Just three weeks after *Warspite* deposited herself on the Cornish rocks, on the other side of the world another battleship began, and also failed to complete, her final voyage to the breaker's yard. *Oklahoma*, still lying at Pearl Harbor with *Arizona* and *Utah*, had been auctioned for scrap with an estimated tonnage of 24,300 at the New York Naval Shipyard on 26 November 1946. She was sold to Moore Drydock Co. of Oakland, California, on 5 December 1946 for $46,126. Moore planned to scrap her in San Francisco. In view of the ship's symbolic significance as a Pearl Harbor casualty, a farewell ceremony was planned for her arrival in California, to feature Governor of Oklahoma Roy Turner and 500 other guests.

She set off from Pearl Harbor under tow of two tugs, *Hercules* and *Monarch*, from Puget Sound Tug and Barge Co. of Seattle, on 10 May 1947. In contrast to the usual UK practice, there was no towing crew aboard the battleship to keep an eye out for trouble. Captain George Anderson of *Monarch* later recalled that there was no reason to suspect trouble. For the first twenty-four hours everything seemed to be going well, then it was noticed that the *Oklahoma* was developing a list to port (the side damaged by the Japanese torpedoes). During the next four days the list increased steadily to about 30 degrees. The tugs radioed the Coast Guard at Hawaii for instructions and were told to return. Close to midnight on 16–17 May, 540 miles north-east of Hawaii and in 18,000ft of water, *Oklahoma* suddenly straightened up. The tug crews became aware that they were going astern and gaining speed. Behind them the lights of the *Oklahoma* disappeared. *Monarch* was probably saved by the prompt release of the towing brake on the cable, which completely unreeled, snapped off and disappeared into the Pacific still attached to the plunging battleship. *Hercules* had an even closer call as her stern had already gone underwater as the tug went backwards and the crew could not disconnect the winch. Just as it seemed she would be dragged under by *Oklahoma*'s 23,400 tons, the winch gave way and the tug was free. The sinking was recorded at 1.40 am on 17 May.[23]

The two tugs searched the area at daybreak, but *Oklahoma* was gone and there was no wreckage. An official enquiry found no absolute cause for the sinking, but it seems beyond argument that the ship flooded progressively, and quite quickly, through the holes from the original torpedo damage. *Oklahoma*, despite getting the necessary certificate to undertake the voyage, was probably significantly less seaworthy than *Warspite* because of the fearful damage from 7 December 1941. As there was no passage crew aboard there was no opportunity to monitor her seaworthiness during the three days of the tow as she took on water and developed a progressive list that eventually reached a dizzying 30 degrees. By the time the tugs radioed Pearl Harbor to ask for advice and were told to return, it was far too late.

Sister ships *New Mexico* and *Idaho* dating from 1917 were not required in the reserve fleet after the Publication of Post-War Plan No. 2. *Idaho* was towed from Norfolk, Virginia, to Hawkins Point, Baltimore, Maryland, on 24 June 1946, where she was moored alongside *Texas*, from whom she received power. The remaining crew transferred away or lived aboard *Texas*, and the final log entry on 3 July 1946 reads: 'In accordance with Commander Norfolk Group 16th Fleet despatch 261230 of June 1946, USS *Idaho* was this date placed out of commission in reserve in a caretaker status.'[24] *New Mexico* was decommissioned at Boston, Massachusetts, on 19 July 1946, and along with *Idaho* and *Wyoming* was sold to Lipsett Inc. on 13 October 1947 for scrapping. *New Mexico*'s final journey was also fraught, with echoes of *Warspite* and *Oklahoma*, but in the end it had a more conventional ending.

Lipsett wanted to scrap all three battleships at a facility it had initially leased at Newark, New Jersey, during the war to scrap the gigantic French liner *Normandie*, which had famously keeled over at her pier in New York harbour in 1943 after catching fire and having too much firefighting water pumped into her. But Newark City officials led by Mayor Vincent J Murphy wanted Lipsett and the Navy to give the lease up so that they could proceed with a $70 million redevelopment of the waterfront that had been agreed with the Port of New York Authority. It is evident from the contemporary reporting that Murphy was using the press to sensationalise his and the City's position. According to Associated Press on 11 November 1947, Murphy used a remembrance day parade to tell reporters of a decision to pit the city's 'navy' of two fireboats against the battleship, which was by then en route from Boston. 'The fireboats, the *William J Brennan* and the *Michael P Duffy* are 35 feet long and manned by a captain and crew of five. They carry a ton of foam powder and pumps as offensive weapons.' 'I have given orders to the Fire Department and the Police Department,' said Public Safety Director John B Keenan after a conference with Murphy, 'to employ whatever measures necessary including the hiring of a tugboat to block the channel completely. I am not going to stand by and watch the Port of Newark become a perennial graveyard for navy ships.'

The next day, 12 November, AP reported the story as 'Newark Navy Gets Respite: Battleship's Tug Disabled'. The towing tug *C Heywood Mesik* had cast off from *New Mexico* in rough seas about 35 miles off the Port of New York, fearing for her own safety. The other tug, *Dorothy Anne Mesik*, continued the tow that day on her own, but also had to cast off that evening as the seas got rougher still. *New Mexico*, with a passage crew of three, was left adrift overnight. On the morning of 13 November she had been lost to sight, drifting somewhere off the busy New York shipping lanes. Fortunately she remained buoyant, survived the rough seas, and she was found later in the day 58 miles off New York by a US Coastguard plane. The tugs linked up again and the tow continued.

As the fireboats maintained their vigil, the battleship approached. Lipsett prepared its own tugs to contest the passage with the City's fireboats. The Chamber of Commerce of Santa Fe, New Mexico, announced its decision to make a formal protest against the perceived slur by Newark to their state's namesake battleship. Under Secretary of the Navy James Kenney held a meeting in Washington to defuse the impending confrontation. The deal brokered by Kenney was that the three battleships would be scrapped at Newark, but they would be the last ships to go there.

New Mexico, Idaho and Wyoming being scrapped at Newark, New Jersey, early 1948.

Furthermore, they would all have to be demolished within nine months, or Lipsett would incur penalties of $1,000 per day. Then the facility would be turned over to Newark City for the redevelopment project. So, having waited for favourable tides, *New Mexico* arrived in Newark on 19 November 1947 and came alongside not to protests and obstructions, but to be greeted by a friendly salute from the fireboats, a warm welcome from mayor Murphy, and even the razzamatazz of marching bands and drum majorettes.[25]

Lipsett managed to keep its side of the bargain. *Idaho* and *Wyoming* followed to Newark within ten days.Photographs from December 1947 show all three together at the pier, with *New Mexico* already without turrets or superstructure. Another photo in January 1948 shows the scrappers progressing below her forecastle and *Idaho* also reduced to her main decks. *New Mexico* was gone by July 1948, and the nine-month deadline for demolishing all three was achieved.

It remained to dispose of the three surviving Bikini target battleships. In Chapter Four we saw that *Pennsylvania* had been scuttled by the

Nevada (right) and New York (left) at Pearl Harbor on 8 June 1948, before being expended in Pacific Fleet target practice. (NARA)

US Navy off Kwajalein on 10 February 1948. *Nevada* and *New York* were both recovered to Pearl Harbor in 1946/47, and also studied extensively in an effort to understand the persistence of radioactive contamination.

However, it proved impossible to decontaminate them sufficiently thoroughly to allow a commercial sale for scrap. Instead the Pacific Fleet decided to expend them for target practice. On 8 July 1948 *New York* was subjected to an eight-hour pounding by ships and aircraft carrying out full-scale battle manoeuvres south of Pearl Harbor, which finished her off. She eventually capsized, but remained afloat for some time upside down leaking oil into the sea. The Pacific Fleet steamed past her inverted hull.

Nevada suffered the same fate on 31 July, but this time with *Iowa* helping to administer the punishment to her fellow battleship. *Nevada* was subjected to aerial bombing and successively larger-calibre shelling by destroyers and cruisers, culminating with *Iowa*'s 16in main battery. Having survived Pearl Harbor and two atomic bombs, *Nevada* had proven credentials as a tough nut, and her designer's faith in the 'all or nothing' distribution of armour, of which she was the first global exponent in 1914, was again amply demonstrated. Even *Iowa*'s barrage could not sink her. An aerial torpedo finally finished her off and her radioactive hull sank in 15,000ft.

New York (bottom left) capsized after Pacific Fleet target practice July 1948. *(NARA)*

CHAPTER SIX

Peacetime in the Royal Navy

Nelson leading the Home Fleet from Portland, *Illustrated London News*, 23 April 1946. *(Mary Evans Library)*

As their older battleships met their various fates, the world's navies gradually settled into peacetime routine and a peacetime establishment. For Britain it was planned that both the Home Fleet and the Mediterranean Fleet would revolve around a carrier/battleship core when resources allowed, and that for battleships the stringencies of

budgets and manpower during a period of mass demobilisation would mean that only the five most modern battleships, four *King George Vs* and *Vanguard*, would be active. *Nelson*, although slow, was in pretty good condition and also stayed in commission through 1946 and into 1947 while *Vanguard* was completed, and while three modern ships were still in the Far East. *Queen Elizabeth* was also still active in the winter of 1945–46. Following docking at Rosyth in November 1945 she sailed south at 12 knots via Cape Wrath and arrived at Portland on 7 December, classified as a training ship with a complement of 414. She spent December and January at Portland with *Nelson*, then shifted to Portsmouth on 1 February 1946, having been reduced to Category A reserve. Captain Ellis relinquished command on 13 February and two days later she took up her reserve station at the Motherbank Buoy, Spithead, at fourteen days' notice for steam. Formal acceptance into Category B reserve, with a complement of just 140, eventually followed on 23 October 1946.[1]

Initially *Nelson* was flagship of the Home Fleet with Admiral Sir Neville Syfret embarked, and she deployed to Portland in that role on 29 December 1945. *Nelson* led the first post-war Home Fleet Spring Cruise to Gibraltar and Lisbon between 7 March and 5 April 1946.

The Home Fleet carried out extensive exercises on outward and return legs, as reported by British Pathé. Although no aircraft carrier was available, the 10th Cruiser Squadron, *Birmingham*, *Bellona* and *Dido* went on for a further three-week cruise in the West Indies. It was not all plain sailing. On the way to Lisbon both *Nelson*'s engines failed at 2003 on 21 March. She had to haul out of line to port and hoist 'Not under control' lights while the problem was sorted out. At Lisbon the President and the Prime Minister of Portugal both visited the ship. Admiral Syfret signalled the Admiralty after the visit, concerned at the contrast between the very enthusiastic reception by Portugal – the visit had monopolised the Portuguese press for a week – and what he perceived as the indifference of the UK media, with the impact this might have on Portuguese attitudes in future.[2] On the return trip there were anti-submarine exercises. *Nelson*, screened by her destroyers, was attacked by seven submarines. Because the UK's 'S'- and 'T'-class submarines could only manage 7 to 8 knots when submerged, in order to simulate an attack by the 15-knot submarines that had been built by Germany, and for which the technology was now in the hands of the Soviet Union, *Nelson* was only allowed to steam at 14 knots and the destroyers at 16 knots. Many of the RAF sorties to simulate air attack on the squadron failed to find the fleet at all, and there were no naval carrier aircraft available. *Nelson* returned to Spithead on 5 April, passing *Queen Elizabeth* and *Warspite* at anchor on her way into harbour.[3]

On 10 April 1946 the Home Fleet flagship became *King George V*, which moved out to Spithead on 6 May, and thence on a short visit to

Guernsey to mark the first anniversary of the Channel Islands' liberation from the Nazis. The focus of Home Fleet Activity, as before the war, was an annual summer cruise of some five to eight weeks' duration in home waters. British Pathé film clips celebrated these evolutions and show the fleet, including battleships, setting out for the cruises in 1946, 1947 and 1948. In 1946 *King George V* set off on 7 June and led the fleet to Torbay, Falmouth, Aberystwyth, Bangor, Oban and Fleetwood, returning to Portland on 9 August. While at Falmouth on 8 July, according to the ship's log a Russian commodore and thirty Russian students from '*Tepek*' visited the ship for an hour and a half. The Cold War had yet to freeze hard, but the visit was sufficiently unusual to be reported to the Admiralty in a little more detail. The Russian vessels, led by '*Tepek*', were ex-German war prizes on passage to the Black Sea. Although the senior officer was described as a Lt Commander Korsch, a second visit aboard *King George V* was made by two 'Commodores' (possibly commissars?) D V Yakolev and N Orzarawaki and forty Russian sailors. They were entertained and a tour of the battleship took place, although it was confined to the upper deck and mess decks. The visit was cordial and friendly, and conversation was 'entirely non-technical', although the political tensions between their nations were acknowledged and regretted by the naval men.[4]

King George V returns to Portsmouth from the Pacific, 2 March 1946. (Alamy)

King George V had a quiet autumn at Portsmouth and Portland, before going to Devonport on 20 November 1946. There de-ammunitioning began on 9 December at No. 1 Battleship Trot (mooring). It carried on until the end of January. The ship's log records a typical day at No. 1 Trot on 27 January 1947:

> Wind E, force 3, visibility c. 6 miles, 0400 temperature 30 degree air, 40 degrees sea. 5 men on the sick list.
>
> 0630   Hands called.
> 0750   Ammo lighter secured port side forward.
> 0805   Hands fall in and continue de-ammunitioning.
> 1000   One rating on draft to HMS Dolphin
> 1015   2 ratings left ship to draft to HMNB
> 1030   Water boat secured.
> 1120   Water boat cast off.
> 1200   Hands to dinner.
> 1220   Stores and NAAFI boats secured.
> 1225   NAAFI boat cast off.
> 1315   Hands fall in. Employed as a.m.
> 1320   10 midshipmen arrived on board for instruction.
> 1335   Stores lighter cast off.
> 1420   Naval Store boat alongside
> 1500   Naval Store Boat cast off.
> 1545   De-ammunitioning ship completed.
> 1600   Hands to tea.
> 1700   Emergency party mustered.
> 2045   Rounds correct.
> Starboard and 2nd Port watches granted leave 1600 – 0730.[5]

On 3 February the battleship moved using tugs from the trot to No. 10 Dock in Devonport. In her lightened state draught forward was only 28ft 1½in, aft 31ft 1¼in. By 1550 she was secure in the dock. She stayed there until 12 June, then to the east wall of the dockyard, which she did not leave while her refit proceeded for the whole of 1947. She remained in Devonport for a further five months in 1948, hosting visitors to Navy Days during early May, before she finally proceeded to sea for the first time in eighteen months on 25 May 1948 to run up and down the degaussing range.[6] The next day she completed a full-power trial in the English Channel to the Wolf Rock and back. She maintained over 220 revolutions for six hours, the maximum being 224.7, which drove her at 27.2 knots. She spent the remainder of 1948 and the early part of 1949 uneventfully in the Training Squadron, at Dartmouth, Portland, Torquay and Portsmouth.[7]

Meanwhile *Nelson*, relieved of flagship duties in April 1946, spent a couple of months at Portsmouth. On 28 April the log records Annabel Lee Christine Bailey being christened on board. This tradition, using the ship's bell, still continues in the Royal Navy, and would continue for a few more years on the other active battleships, but Annabel was the last child to be christened on *Nelson*. In the summer *Nelson* became part of a newly created Home Fleet Training Squadron together with *Howe* and *Anson*. The Naval Secretary wrote to the First Lord on 28 June 1946 saying that the Commander-in-Chief of the Home Fleet had requested the establishment of a 'Rear Admiral Training Battleships' to co-ordinate the work of these three ships: 'The CINC does not consider that the squadron can go to sea yet owing to manning difficulties, but in due course he foresees the ships being able to do short cruises in company with the fleet.' A V Alexander approved the creation of the post on 8 July, and Rear Admiral Harold Hickling was appointed to fill it.[8] He came aboard *Nelson* for the first time on 10 August at Portland, and thereafter used her as his flagship. Defying the predicted manning difficulties, she went to Torbay for a week at the end of August and again at the end of September, and exercised at sea off Weymouth between 1 and 11 November.[9]

The Training Squadron at Portland, 1946 – Nelson, Anson and Howe. (Mary Evans Library)

In the New Year of 1947 *Nelson* was at sea again on 21 January with *Anson* and *Howe*, the whole Training Squadron plus *Duke of York* as the new flagship of the Home Fleet, practising royal salutes and manoeuvring as a squadron. *Howe*'s log records that the ships did three

separate runs down the English Channel to perfect their station keeping and the timing of the firing of the Royal Salute and Cheering ship. All this practice was because on 31 January 1947 the Training Squadron and the Home Fleet headed into the English Channel to meet *Vanguard*, carrying His Majesty King George VI and the Royal Family, departing on the Royal tour to South Africa. *Howe*'s log again records that at 1545 on 31 January she took aboard BBC and press representatives for Operation DTM (presumably standing for 'Departure of Their Majesties'). On Saturday, 1 February at 0957 she dressed ship with masthead ensigns. At 1040 the saluting guns crews were closed up, and at 1045 the lower deck was cleared and hands massed on the starboard side of the fo'c'sle. A Royal Salute was fired by the entire Home Fleet, between 1058 and 1100, and the King ordered 'Splice the Mainbrace'. At 1103 *Vanguard* passed *Howe* and was cheered by the hands on the fo'c'sle. *Duke of York*'s log together with the Home Fleet orders issued for the day adds the detail that she led the starboard column including *Anson* and the Fleet Carrier *Implacable* plus cruisers and destroyers, with *Nelson* leading *Howe* in a Port column. The columns were three and a half cables (2,100 yards) apart, and *Vanguard* steamed between them on an opposite course. It was stirring stuff, but also, unsensed by participants at the time, the end of an era. It was to be the last occasion that five British battleships, or indeed five battleships of any nation, were ever at sea steaming in company together. Such a concentration of force had become very unusual in the Royal Navy since before 1939 given the dispersed nature of operations and battle groups in the Second World War. Sadly, although the press were given access and the weather was decent, no film or photographic record showing the five battleships in company seems to have survived.[10]

This was also the last time that *Nelson* went to sea with intent. She spent the remainder of 1947 in the Training Squadron but did not leave Portland when the rest of the squadron went on its cruises. On 22 September she began her journey out of the active fleet, first to Portsmouth to transfer personnel and equipment to the carrier *Victorious*, which was taking over her training role at Portland. The Admiralty had decided to put *Nelson* into reserve in the Firth of Forth, so on 16 October she headed down the English Channel, through the Irish Sea, around Cape Wrath and, at 1118 on 20 October, under the Forth Bridge. At 1203 engines stopped for the last time as she moored at the buoy off Rosyth Naval Base. On 21 October Captain Everitt left the ship. On 27 October at 0830 Ammunition Lighter 'Vic 99' came alongside, and at 0840 'A' ammunitioning party closed up and commenced de-ammunitioning 'A' 16in turret. The log records the detail of this process over the next six weeks, revealing the scale and complexity of having a battleship fully armed and equipped for war, as she still was over two years after returning from the Far East. A total of 1,072 16in shells were unloaded, well over 1,000 6in shells, all their cordite, eighty 4.7in practice rounds, 85 boxes of 3-pounder, and 12 of 6-pounder shells; 261 boxes of 20mm ammunition, 125 boxes of .303 and 11 of .455 rifle ammunition; 723 boxes of assorted primers, fuzes and detonators, and 500 cases of 2-pounder pom-pom ammunition. There was much more besides, except the less zealous of the watchkeepers did not bother to record the exact details every day. The last entry of *Nelson's* log on 31 December 1947 shows her slipping quietly into history:

0755	Hands employed cleaning ship and mess decks
1030	Water boat '*Zeal*' alongside
1155	Water boat '*Zeal*' slipped
1200	Hands to make and mend clothes
1548	Sunset
1605	1 PO Radar Mechanic on draft to RNB (P)
1700	Exercise Fire Parties
1900	Land cinema patrol
2355	Guard boat hailed.

However, this was not quite the last act for *Nelson* – see Chapter Eight below.

Howe also had a quiet time in the Training Squadron during 1946. She was de-ammunitioned at Portsmouth in the second half of January and was docked there during February. She sailed for Portland on 20 March. As in the Far East, her logs reveal the constant human churn involved in manning a battleship, but also the process of downscaling the crew to a peacetime training role, and to allow demobilisation. In January 1946 twenty-eight officers and men joined the ship, but 185 left. In February forty-three joined, and 279 left. And in March forty joined and 418 left. The net reduction in three months after arriving in the UK from the British Pacific Fleet was 771 personnel. Further trickle draftings eventually reduced her complement to the 626 authorised for this class of ship in the Training Squadron, although this figure excludes the instructors and trainees themselves.[11] Training Squadron duties began in earnest on 1 July 1946 with the first references to men under training going to instruction. This new raison d'être for the ship did not seem to impress the watchkeepers for the first couple of months. The 'MUT' references have been inserted in the log later on, squeezed between existing entries in a different handwriting. Maybe Admiral Hickling had inspected the log and asked what was going on? *Howe* did not get further than Torbay during the latter half of 1946, and after she arrived at Portland only went to sea all told for fifteen out of 286 days that year.[12]

Correspondence sheds light on the challenge of manpower shortages and the dilemma of running *Howe* with a much reduced crew as an active ship, at the same time as maintaining her for her war role. On 4 July 1948 her commanding officer, Commander F N Elliot, explained to Commander-in-Chief Plymouth his concern about the deterioration of the main 14in armament by that date. As a training ship, the armament had been placed in a state of preservation and all ammunition landed. Guns were plugged and working spaces brought up to a high state of preservation. Thirty-three able seamen were included in the complement to maintain the main armament. The baseline assumption was that the ship would be permanently at Portland and only raise steam for safety reasons, and no outside commitments would be accepted. But in summer 1946 it had been decided that the ship would go to sea, and that a standard of appearance equivalent to a ship in full commission would be needed. The consequence was that the armament seamen were appropriated for other duties, only ten now remained, and 'if the main armament of the ship is to remain available for service at a month's notice, very early steps must be taken ...'[13]

Anson had spent three months at Portsmouth after her arrival from the Far East. In contrast to *Nelson*, her future role in the Training Squadron was deemed not to require ammunition, so the armaments so recently topped up off Hong Kong were unloaded again at No. 6 buoy. She sailed to Portland on 19 October 1946 and saluted the Flag of Rear Admiral Training Battleships with a thirteen-gun salute. *Nelson* returned the salute with seven guns. *Anson* spent the next few months at Portland, going to sea on just three occasions to manoeuvre with her fellow battleships (see above). She took over briefly as Training Squadron flagship on 22 November 1946. After the Royal rendezvous with *Vanguard* there were a couple of short trips to Torbay and Falmouth in the first half of 1947, otherwise she was anchored at Portland. The day 29 April 1947 was a typical one in the Training Squadron:

0615   Starboard watch and men under training scrub decks.
0810   Starboard watch of the hands and M.U.T [Men Under Training] wash paintwork.
0830   M.U.T to divisions on the quarterdeck.
0900   M.U.T to instruction.
0900   20 ratings on draft to RMB Chatham, 6 ratings on draft to RNB Devonport, 9 ratings on draft to RNB Portsmouth.
0925   HMS *Aisne* [a Battle-class destroyer] leaves harbour.
1315   Hands continue washing paintwork.
1500   HMS *Aisne* enters harbour.
1950   One rating joined ship from RNB Chatham.
2100   Rounds correct.[14]

After her return from the Far East *Duke of York* continued at Plymouth for most of the rest of 1946. On 15 July the crew spent the day unloading 'Food for Britain', which she had carried all the way from Australia. The Lord Mayor of Plymouth and Lord Wakehurst, the Lord Lieutenant of Devon, came aboard at 1145 for a ceremony to accept the food. A substantial part of the crew was drafted away, 137 leaving on 27 July alone. De-ammunitioning took place at No. 1 Battleship Trot from 22 July until 20 August. She was then undergoing maintenance and docking until the beginning of December, when some minimal re-ammunitioning took place. On 7 December she went to Portland and the Commander-in-Chief Home Fleet, still Admiral Syfret, came aboard on 9 December as she took over from *King George V* in the flagship role.

While the Royal Navy was demobilising and settling into a peacetime routine, the Training Squadron was being developed, and the last ships were returning from the Far East, in early 1946 the Royal Navy's newest battleship was approaching completion in John Brown's shipyard at Clydebank. *Vanguard* turned out to be the last British battleship, and like *Hood*, which had left the same building yard twenty-six years before, she was a one-off, fast and aesthetically very pleasing, so she always enjoyed a glamour and special status with the Navy and the public. She was also by a substantial margin the largest warship ever built in the UK, eclipsing *Hood* by over 4,000 tons, creating a record that stood for seventy years until it in turn was eclipsed by the delivery of today's aircraft carriers *Queen Elizabeth* and *Prince of Wales*.

Vanguard existed because it was believed as early as 1939 that the retention in storage of spare 15in guns and turrets from earlier classes of battleship, which were normally the longest lead item if building such a ship from scratch, would allow her to be rushed to completion by 1942. This would help redress the challenge to British power posed by the projected completion dates of the latest German and Japanese battleships. But delays with the design meant that she could not be ordered before March 1941. Although she was eventually given A1 priority after the war with Japan started, and work on the cruiser *Bellerophon* was halted to transfer labour to her, wartime building priorities chopped and changed and shortage of skilled labour hit the schedule, so she was again delayed. This had the advantage that it allowed the design to evolve substantially. War experience saw the modification of watertight integrity and improvements to electrical generation and distribution systems and portable pumps, deficiencies in which had contributed to the loss of the modern *Prince of Wales* in 1941. Also learned from that sinking, the spacing between the inboard and outboard propellers was increased to reduce vulnerability to a single torpedo hit. *Vanguard* was also redesigned with a distinctive flared bow to improve sea-keeping, once it was discovered that the *King George V* class took excessive water over the bow in even moderate seas. Her anti-aircraft armament was ten of a new design of six-barrelled Bofors 40mm Mark Six anti-aircraft mountings, as well as a new Twin-Stabilised mounting on B turret. The total number of 40mm guns carried was eventually seventy-three, requiring her to carry over 90,000 rounds of ammunition.

This, together with other additions and improvements, meant that, in common with the *King George Vs*, her displacement grew significantly beyond what had been planned, from 49,200 tons in 1942 to 51,420 tons as completed. As early as 16 January 1947 the Admiralty was concerned about 'very high stresses' on the ship's hull, and instructions were issued that the mean draught of the ship was to be limited to 35ft by keeping the midships fuel oil tanks empty to avoid strain on her structure. This saved about 1,000 tons of potential weight, but by 1954 she had added a further 500 tons through various modifications and limitations had to be imposed on her ammunition stowage as well.[15]

Vanguard was launched by the eighteen-year-old Princess Elizabeth (her first ship launch of many) on 30 November 1944. Tragedy struck at John Brown's fitting out basin on 16 September 1945 as she approached completion when a build-up of methane gas was ignited by the fitting out activity. Two employees were killed by the blast and six others injured. *Vanguard* was commissioned on 25 April 1946 for contractor's trials under command of Captain W G Agnew CBE, CVO, DSO. The ship's log begins on that day and for the next few months reveals in great detail the process of putting a new ship through her paces to iron out equipment defects, work up an efficient crew able to deal with any manner of manoeuvre, emergency, or problem of warfare, and to work out what she was actually capable of in relation to the contractual specifications. The log also reveals the workings of the sinews that allowed the Royal Navy to operate in all weathers, worldwide:

0700   Hands preparing for arrival of drafts
0845   Arrived first draft seamen from RNB Portsmouth
0930   Arrived draft of boys [boy seamen]
1110   Arrived draft of stokers and Royal Marines
1305   Seamen and marines exercised in falling in by divisions, watches, special parties
1700   Divisions. Commissioning ceremony.[16]

During the next week she prepared intensively for sea. It was evident that Agnew and the Admiralty saw her first and foremost as a fighting battleship. While still alongside at John Brown, the log records three separate 15in gun crew drills, drills for the 5.25in secondary armament

Vanguard on trials, Clyde Estuary, 1946. *(NHHC)*

control parties and the engine room exercising the highest states of damage control. *Vanguard* moved for the first time down the Clyde on 2 May, with the order 'obey telegraphs' given at 1117 and the cables slipped at 1124. By 1135 she was proceeding down the river. Before she anchored at Tail of the Bank off Greenock that afternoon there were turning and anchor trials, and a number of runs across the degaussing range to establish and neutralise her magnetic signature (not at all a hypothetical exercise in early 1946 given the ongoing task of wartime mine clearance in European waters).

Vanguard was still building up her crew. Forty-seven more men joined her that first day at Greenock, and they continued to trickle in over subsequent weeks. On 3 May she was embarking Bofors anti-aircraft ammunition and the day after she began embarking 15in and 5.25in cordite and ammunition. Now she had some practice ammunition, all the guns crews were again exercised on 6 May. Her public debut was on 8 May when representatives of the BBC and the press came aboard. The week finished with manoeuvring and mooring trials and further runs across the degaussing range. Princess Elizabeth renewed her association

with the ship by coming aboard in the Clyde at 1030 on Sunday, 12 May to attend the blessing of the ship by the Chaplain of the Fleet. She then undertook a full tour of the ship with lunch before leaving at 1445 to a formal cheer from the new ship's company.[17]

The sea trials around the Clyde and in the Irish Sea were generally successful. They were certainly intense, often lasting through entire weekends, and involved using all of the ship's equipment in a variety of scenarios so that she could be formally accepted by the Royal Navy as fit for purpose. The week after the dedication ceremony saw the trials of the 40mm armament while travelling at up to 27 knots, to establish the impact of vibrations on its effectiveness; plus trials and the first test firings of the 15in and 5.25in guns. These do not seem to have been at targets and besides proving the workings of the turret machinery and their crews, they were intended mainly to calculate the impact of blast from the guns on the ship's superstructure. Firing, especially the main armament, at bearings too close to the axis of the ship resulted in damage to the ship and harm to exposed personnel. R A Burt[18] says that twenty-four full broadsides were fired from the 15in guns and twenty-three broadsides from the

5.25in. No details are recorded in the ship's log, but when the guns, which had been relined before fitting to *Vanguard*, were measured for barrel wear on 2 July 1946 they were recorded as having fired between twelve and twenty effective full charges.[19] This is consistent with Burt's figures because some of the firing would have been with reduced charges of cordite that generated only one quarter or one sixteenth of the wear of a full charge.

The radars were tested against aircraft targets and an accompanying destroyer. There were two full-power trials. During the second on Sunday, 19 May she gradually worked up to 250 revolutions per minute and a speed (not precisely recorded) in excess of 27 knots. The next morning she was conducting anti-submarine warfare evolutions with a total of five submarines and a destroyer escort, on her way to Liverpool. There, she was briefly docked in the Gladstone Graving dock (the only dock close to the trials area large enough to take her), where she was secured by 1515 on 20 May and de-ammunitioned.

The purpose of the docking was to clean the bottom, now eighteen months in the water, so she could undertake the formal speed, power and fuel-consumption trials that required as clean a ship as possible. It was also a chance to take on stores and for leave, as well as to top up the crew and begin that constant churn that was so much a part of the post-war Royal Navy. A few of the ship's company, after less than a month with the ship, began to be released for demobilisation. She also continued her public duties. The Mayor of Liverpool, the Commandant and officers of the Imperial Defence College and eleven Members of Parliament were among her visitors in Liverpool. The dock was flooded up on 15 June, and the next day the crucial inclining experiments were done by shifting weight across the upper deck to establish her stability and metacentric height.

She sailed from Liverpool on 17 June and carried out more anti-submarine warfare (ASW) exercises on the way back to Greenock. There followed four more weeks of intense trials, steaming, manoeuvring with all conceivable combinations of engines, boilers and screws, with and without rudder. Speed runs established her power curves across the measured mile off Arran. Between 1205 and 1315 on Friday, 28 June she made six runs over the measured mile at full power. Top speed recorded in the log was 31.5 knots, although the timekeepers formally adjusted this later to a mere 31.47 knots at 136,000 shp and 255 revolutions. The only significant issue revealed throughout the trials was some hull vibration at certain engine revolutions, which was blamed on interactions between the inner and outer propellers. This was eventually corrected by the replacement of three-bladed by five-bladed propellers in her 1949 refit.[20]

Then it was time to join the Navy. She went first to Devonport via further ASW exercises for another brief docking, then up the Channel for

Vanguard speed trials, 1946. *(NHHC)*

exercises featuring attacks by motor torpedo boats, before meeting the Home Fleet and saluting the Commander-in-Chief aboard *King George V* on 9 August. From the 12 August she was refitting at Portsmouth for two months and received what must be one of the most eclectic visiting parties to any ship – 250 tenants of Windsor Great Park on 10 October. The second half of October and much of November was spent ammunitioning the ship with all calibres. This finished on Saturday, 30 November, and she was ready for a shakedown cruise to Gibraltar between 4 and 20 December, involving a whole series of continuing trials and exercises. Although there was by now an ulterior motive for her reliability and efficiency, the evidence in her logs is clear that beneath the polished and painted skin this was a fully trained, armed and equipped fighting battleship.

One particular role that was envisaged for her in the post-war world was to undertake 'Special Duties' – code for acting as a Royal Yacht. So, after her formal acceptance by the Admiralty on 9 August, rather than immediately take her place in the fleet it was decided that *Vanguard* would undergo a short refit in order to modify her to carry the Royal Family to

Vanguard overhead shot, 1946. *(NHHC)*

South Africa in 1947. This Empire tour harked back to similar voyages, also undertaken by battleship, in the 1920s. It had originally been conceived early in 1946 and Sir Andrew Cunningham gave his blessing to *Vanguard*'s participation before he left the First Sea Lord billet in May that year. The cruise was designed to reinforce links between the UK and the Dominions following the shared sacrifices of the war, but it was also about getting the ailing King out of the UK winter to more pleasant climes. The actual Royal Yacht *Victoria and Albert* was over forty-five years old, had never been outside European waters, and at this time was not fit to go to sea, having spent the war as a depot ship in Portsmouth harbour. She needed new boilers, and in the event she was retired, eventually to be replaced in 1954 by the new *Britannia*. South Africa was chosen as the destination for the trip partly in order to bolster the position of loyalists in the Union, led by Prime Minister Jan Smuts, against the backdrop of rising support for the racist Afrikaans nationalism of Daniel Malan's National Party.

Refitting a brand new battleship to carry the Royal Family seems a luxury viewed from today's perspective. The need for modifications becomes more understandable when one looks at the nominal roll for the visit.[21] Not only had the ship to carry the King, Queen and two princesses in the style to which they were accustomed, but also thirty-eight in the Royal party – ladies in waiting, private secretaries, medical officers, equerries, police officers, dressers, maids, hairdressers, valets, footmen and a press contingent. In addition to them there were forty members of the ship's company described as the Royal Retinue – cooks, stewards and telephonists – as well as the full Royal Marine Band and Drums to provide ceremonial music, numbering fifty-six. The ship herself was fully crewed to ensure no mishaps during the voyage, and a total of 1,975 souls made the trip. According to the ship's cover, her normal war complement was 1,427, and the special complement approved for this Royal duty 1,663.[22] The Royal accommodation took up the entire aft shelter deck, an area of about 5,000 sq ft. As shown in the commemorative brochure published for the trip, there were separate dining, day and sleeping cabins for the monarch, day and sleeping cabins for the Queen, sleeping cabins for the princesses, bathrooms, cabins for the Private Secretary, valets and maids, and a large pantry. 'No effort has been spared to render it as suitable and comfortable as possible for the Royal party. It will be entirely self-contained and will have its own galley and its own telephone switchboard. Some of the furnishings will be specially made. Others will come from the Royal Yacht Victoria and Albert, and some from Naval Stores. The general colour scheme will be that chosen by Her Majesty the Queen, and it is hoped that the whole suite will provide a pleasing and comfortable temporary home for the Royal party.'

The brochure goes on to enumerate 'some interesting facts about HMS *Vanguard*'. Besides the ship's dimensions and armament, we also learn that she has 2,000 miles of electrical cable and 6,750 light bulbs run off 3,720kW of generating capacity. She could distil over 100,000 gallons of water per day, some of which would be used to dilute the 1,400 gallons of rum carried on the voyage. The conversion cost was £170,000, and its extravagance was questioned at the time by some Members of Parliament.

January 1947 was spent sprucing up the ship. The King's Equerry, Lieutenant Commander Peter Ashmore, came aboard for two days on 6 January to check that facilities and arrangements were satisfactory. The Royal party embarked at the South Railway Jetty Portsmouth at 1640 on 31 January 1947. The crew had begun the previous two days by shovelling snow off the decks, and it was only 25°F (-4°C) on 30 January. This was one of the harshest UK winters of modern times, but despite warnings about the inclemency of the conditions, the Royal Navy decided to start the trip aimed at improving the King's health by making him inspect not one, but two guards of honour, one from the naval base ashore, then one on the ship, before having to endure a ceremonial sunset ceremony on the quarterdeck. Most of the King's immediate family came to see him off: his mother, HM Queen Mary, brother HRH Henry, Duke of Gloucester, sister,

HRH Mary, the Princess Royal, and sister-in-law HRH Marina, the Duchess of Kent, left the ship after the ceremonies. Nine of the dockyard craftsmen who had worked on the creation of the royal apartments were presented to the Royal Family. Then Rear Admiral and royal cousin Viscount Dickie Mountbatten, soon to be appointed the last Viceroy of India, Lady Mountbatten, Mrs Agnew and Sir Geoffrey Layton (Commander-in-Chief Portsmouth) and Lady Layton came aboard for dinner with the King.

Vanguard was finally on her way at 0720 the next morning in poor visibility and more snow. Fortunately the weather improved after passing the Nab tower. An air escort of RAF Mosquitos and Sunderlands was able to fly past. A Home Fleet Escort of two cruisers and a destroyer accompanied her for the rendezvous with the Home Fleet flagship and Training Squadron battleships off Portland on 1 February. Just after the junction of the five battleships, a Royal Navy helicopter touched down briefly on the quarterdeck and then took off carrying mail and photographs. The remarkable day was even capped off by a sixth battleship, as Richelieu, flying the flag of Rear Admiral F P Jourdain, sortied with two destroyers from Cherbourg and closed to within one mile of Vanguard to render her a royal salute as well. As there is no mention of this rendezvous in the records of the otherwise meticulous planning undertaken for the voyage, maybe it was a spontaneous gesture by France.

The Royal Family endured a south-easterly gale off Ushant that evening, which blew all through the next day and strengthened to Force 9 on 3 February, when there were further royal salutes from the Portuguese warships Bartholome Diaz and Dao Inez. Implacable, which had joined the escort on 1 February, undertook flying training on 4 February. The Home Fleet escort stayed with Vanguard as far as the Canary Islands, with the fleet making a steady 17 knots. In his Report of Proceedings dated 11 May 1947, Captain Agnew recorded that on 6 February: 'I was put to bed with the top of my feet poisoned, probably caused by the dye from my socks being rubbed into the skin when dancing the previous night. Fortunately I was not completely hors de combat and was able to command the Squadron from my sea cabin and a chair on the Compass Platform.'[23] He was still incapacitated on 10 February and had more trouble with his feet later in the trip. By 7 February the weather was calm enough for the Royal Family to take the royal barge to tour all the ships of the escort. The next day at 7 degrees north of the equator, the Home Fleet turned for home, and the cruiser Nigeria, flagship of the South Atlantic Station, took over as escort for the rest of the voyage. Ships of the South African Navy eventually completed the escort when she arrived in Cape Town on 17 February 1947. On 9 February Vanguard refuelled at sea from the Royal Fleet Auxiliary tanker Brown Ranger.

Later the same day, whatever his earthly dominions, the King Emperor George VI had to make way for the emissaries of another realm. The log records that at 2100 the ship was hailed from ahead and ordered to stop. She stopped and was boarded by 'Dolphinius, clerk to the court of his most oceanic and turbulent majesty King Neptune', who read the traditional proclamation. The next day the log records the arrival of Neptune himself and the holding of the Crossing the Line ceremony, including at 0920 'presentation of gifts and orders by King Neptune to HM the King and HM the Queen', then at 0930 'HRH the Princess Elizabeth and HRH the Princess Margaret inducted by King Neptune in the mysteries of the seven seas ...' The weather worsened as the Cape of Good Hope approached, and on two successive days an attempt to lower pontoons to paint the ship's starboard side for the grand arrival had to be abandoned, so on 17 February at 0930 *Vanguard* moored at the new Duncan Dock in Cape Town, rust streaks and all.

Governor General Mr G B Van Zyl and Prime Minister Smuts greeted the Royal party as they stepped ashore, and things aboard *Vanguard* returned to nearer normal. Three days of cleaning the ship followed, then she was on parade again to salute the departure of the Royal train from the dockside as the King set off for the interior of the continent. Next day she was open to visitors on 22 and 23 February, with 16,800 being hosted, and over 2,000 having to be turned away. The day 28 February was a less successful one. It began at 0335 with the fire party summoned to a small blaze in No. 73 mess, extinguished by 0410. Later on there was a much more serious fire in the starboard computer room,

Vanguard arriving at Cape Town with the Royal Family, 17 February 1947. *(NHHC)*

nerve centre for the ship's anti-aircraft fire control. This burned for over two hours between 1434 and 1645. This was substantially the most serious of the very many fires reported in UK battleship logs between 1945 and 1954. Midway through the attempt to fight it the hands were piped to tea, but tea had to be served in the mess decks as the fire had caused a power failure in the cafeteria and smoke rendered the dining halls unusable. Although *Vanguard* carried on as a Royal Yacht, the damage from this fire effectively put half her anti-aircraft armament out of action, and was to require a prolonged overhaul on her return to the UK.

Vanguard spent a further week in Cape Town, then embarked the Governor General, thirty-five South African members of parliament and eighty-six Sea Cadets for passage round the Cape of Good Hope to Simon's Bay. Poor weather delayed the sailing for a day, but on 7 March the guests were witness to 5.25in and Bofors demonstration firings. On 10 March she moved 100 miles north of Cape Town to Saldanha Bay, conducting a full-power trial and making 28 knots on the way. Shipboard routine was normal, and exercises were conducted with the South African Navy, but it was an out of the way place with few leave opportunities and only 350 visitors came aboard while she was up there. Agnew's report of proceedings emphasised the Nationalist sympathies of the local farming community, although their friendliness and hospitality were also noted. Thirty-five men were on the sick list by the time Vice Admiral Clement Moody, Commander-in-Chief of the South Atlantic Station, came aboard on 22 March. There were further 5.25in gunnery demonstrations from P1 and P2 turrets on 21 and 24 March on the way back to Simon's Bay. *Vanguard* then worked her way up the east coast of South Africa with pauses at Mossel Bay, East London and Port Elizabeth, before finally getting alongside at Durban on 1 April, where 11,000 visited the ship. She left Durban on 8 April and was back in Cape Town on 11 April. The final fortnight there was spent sprucing up the ship, hosting a further 6,893 visitors, and a dance on the quarterdeck that lasted until two in the morning. Two days were spent embarking £15 million of gold bullion.

On 20 April the Royal Family's White Train arrived at the quayside, and on 21 April *Vanguard* fired a twenty-one-gun salute for the twenty-first birthday of Princess Elizabeth. Three days later the royal entourage embarked, and the ship sailed for home at 1605 on 24 April. The journey back took in a stop at Saint Helena on 29 April, where the Royal Family took the barge to go ashore for the afternoon, and Ascension Island on 1 May, where the ship made just a ten-minute stop offshore, as the log puts it 'to allow the inhabitants of Georgetown to greet their Majesties'. The next day the Home Fleet escort, now led by the carrier *Triumph*, arrived and *Nigeria* peeled off to visit Freetown, Sierra Leone. On 10 May Princess Elizabeth was allowed to drive the ship, on the throttle and at the wheel. The next evening *Vanguard* moored at the South Railway Jetty and the Duke of Gloucester arrived to greet his brother. After a last night aboard the King inspected his final guard of honour of the trip at ten o'clock, and the Royal Family disembarked, followed by the entourage and baggage, and on 14 and 15 May, by the bullion.[24]

Although the tour was on the surface a great success, and achieved its political objectives as a showcase for the links between UK and Dominions, as well as for the role of the Royal Family, and especially the young Princess Elizabeth, it was a troubled voyage. There is no hint of this in Agnew's Report of Proceedings, or the ship's log, but the correspondence in First Sea Lord's papers[25] leaves no room for doubt. The reasons for this were complex. The churn of personnel as the Royal Navy slimmed down after the war played its part in weakening bonds of command and experience among the officers and senior ranks. So too did the overcrowding in the ship. Unrest found expression through dissatisfaction with the new cafeteria-style dining arrangements. *Vanguard* was the first major ship to have communal dining halls instead of the traditional arrangements where messes collected their food from the central galley, but took it away to distribute and eat in their individual mess living areas. This novelty was positively emphasised in the ship's publicity brochures, but was not popular with conservative lower-deck opinion, and the facilities in *Vanguard* proved too small for the numbers embarked, causing queuing and the need for up to three sittings at mealtimes. The quality of the food itself was criticised in subsequent official reports.

The visit to Gibraltar in late 1946 had featured incidents ashore that were viewed as beyond the norm of sailor's high spirits, and in the view of Commander-in-Chief Portsmouth, Admiral Sir Geoffrey Layton, the drunkenness had not been suitably punished at the time. By contrast, Captain Agnew believed that the ship's company had behaved exceptionally well in the first thirteen days alongside at Cape Town, with only eighteen cases of drunkenness in that period. 'From what I hear ashore the ship's company are behaving very well indeed.' Furthermore, there seem to have been a few seamen aboard who were active agitators, and who were linked to and sympathetic towards newspaper stories written around that time by the left-wing journalist Hannen Swaffer in *The People*, *The Daily Herald* and *The Daily Mirror*, criticising conditions in the Navy, and in particular the contrast between living standards for officers and for enlisted men.

The initial visit to Cape Town was a success, although lavish hospitality extended to the crew by the inhabitants was also assessed to be a contributing factor as it made the return to seagoing duty more stark. With the Royal party disembarked and touring South Africa, the ship spent two weeks at Saldanha Bay exercising with units of the South

African Navy. Shore facilities were rudimentary, and there was anyway difficulty landing men because of unfavourable weather and heavy swells. Captain Agnew received an anonymous letter expressing dissent during this period and criticism became more widespread among the crew over the period 22 to 24 March. Agnew reported on 29 March that the crew were complaining about being treated like cattle; forty-six seamen-torpedomen had specifically complained about poor food; the lack of shore leave since Cape Town was grating; and there was 'much talk and grumbling on the lower deck'. *Vanguard* was next due to visit Port Elizabeth, but on 26 March Captain Agnew signalled Vice-Admiral Moody that he intended to curtail the visit to ten hours, elaborating the next day that 'the primary reason for shortening the visit was discontent among the ship's company'. Partly in response to remonstrations from the mayor and dignitaries of Port Elizabeth, the full visit was reinstated, although there were again problems getting men ashore due to the weather and swell at the exposed anchorage, and a local tug had to be used instead of the ship's boats.

Moody was so concerned that he directed an extraordinary signal to Agnew on 6 April while *Vanguard* was at Durban: 'Do you feel quite repetition quite confident that you will be able to adhere to your programme up to arrival at Portsmouth?' Agnew replied three hours later with a blunt 'Yes'. By this time thoroughly alarmed, Moody came aboard *Vanguard* again, and on 8 April reported to the Admiralty: 'I have been considerably worried about the morale of HMS *Vanguard* during her stay in South African waters.' Moody was directly critical of Agnew's handling of the dissent, by choosing to broadcast his messages to the crew by Tannoy instead of 'clearing lower deck' to speak to them face to face; by not keeping them busier during the period at Saldanha Bay; and by not making robust attempts to find the ringleaders. Moody thought that some petty officer seamen may also have been implicated in fomenting the trouble, as well as junior ranks. Matters did not end there. Although the papers do not reveal who made the decision (the implication of the file is that it was the First Sea Lord himself), by the time *Vanguard* was back at Cape Town between 11 and 24 April, she was also visited by an MI5 officer, Major H F Boddington, who had been sent out to South Africa to make a more thorough investigation.

His dense five-page report dated 2 May 1947 to the First Sea Lord, written on his return to the UK, pulled no punches. Boddington was of the view that some crew members had direct links to Hannen Swaffer, who had been using their information to stir discontent from as early as July 1946. When the ship reached South Africa, much of the less reputable local press was already focussed on corroborating the earlier Hannen Swaffer stories. Discipline ashore in Gibraltar in December 1946 'was disgraceful. It was also obvious that the discipline and morale of some of the ship's company of HMS *Vanguard* which was already known to be the ship selected for the Royal cruise was not all that one would expect from a ship's company selected for such an important mission.' Boddington criticised the new feeding arrangements, in part because they allowed the exposure of impressionable seamen to the views of a few agitators. The captain's Tannoy broadcasts about restriction of shore leave had been greeted with booing and uncomplimentary remarks. The ship was overcrowded, and the men cramped, and the contrast with the generous officers' accommodation was exploited by malcontents.

Boddington then touched on the ship's future programme. On reaching Portsmouth one watch was to get eleven days' leave, and the ship would then go to Devonport to be reconverted from her Royal configuration, where the other watch would get their eleven days leave, before *Vanguard* went to the Clyde to host the Royal Family again for the King's Review in July. Worried about crew morale, Agnew had signalled the Admiralty requesting this be changed, but had been told the planned programme would be adhered to. Boddington said: 'On receiving this information I felt that unless both watches were given leave in Portsmouth, the old hands, particularly those residing in the Portsmouth and London areas, might join hands with the few discontented seamen-torpedomen and the possibility of the ship not sailing to Devonport had to be seriously considered.' Boddington also felt that discontent might be stirred by the distribution of honours and awards in relation to the cruise and recommended that 'a much larger percentage of awards should be given to the lower deck than had already been recommended'.

Summing up, he reports that at Cape Town he told Moody, Agnew and Executive Officer Commander Lamb, 'that from the many sources with whom I had come in contact and from my own observations when in *Vanguard* I felt that the Divisional and junior officers of the wardroom had little contact with or knowledge of their men and that their welfare was not uppermost in their minds ... I came to the conclusion that there are a few petty officers and still more so leading hands who are nowhere near to standard ... I am of the opinion that the discontent and unrest has been brought about by a very, very small minority of young seamen ... who have been led astray by one or two trained "agitators" who in the past perhaps served in HM Ships where we have had incidents of a similar nature ... a very small number of Sea Cadets were given passage in the ship. Among them there was one, possibly two who although young in age were well educated and I think trained in propaganda ... I know that at least two when ashore spread themselves considerably in regard to conditions in the ship and more or less confirmed some of the statements made in the past by Hannen Swaffer ... From my own observations when in HMS *Vanguard*, particularly when being escorted by ship's officers to another part of the ship for interviews, the discipline and morale were not good. Examples have been given to the Second Sea Lord ...'

Boddington made a series of recommendations, the more immediate of which were carried out. The scale of rations for the crew was to be maintained at the higher overseas rate until within one day's steaming of Portsmouth. The captain was to conduct a close review of the new messing system and decide whether it could be operated in capital ships. On the return voyage the King was personally to announce an extra three days' leave for the crew under the Royal Prerogative, and that both watches would get their leave in Portsmouth. This he did on 11 May. *Vanguard*'s programme was to be altered to fit in the extra leave and to allow her reconversion at Devonport. She was not to be used by the King during the Clyde Review. She was to be paid off, i.e. the crew dispersed to other active ships, as soon as the programme allowed, and recommissioned with a new crew. The list of honours and awards for the trip was to be withheld until a full investigation had been undertaken. Boddington even suggested that: 'Their Lordships may consider reviewing the Training programme with a view to intensifying and extending if possible the training period, ashore and afloat. Junior Officers, Petty Officers and leading hands must be made to realise the need for discipline and accept responsibility.'

The First Sea Lord was moved to write to Sir Percy Sillitoe, Director General of the Security Services, to thank him for Boddington's efforts. He also telephoned Sir Geoffrey Layton, Commander-in-Chief at Portsmouth, asking him to get to the bottom of things. Layton reported on 14 May 1947 that he had interviewed Agnew immediately upon his arrival. 'I told him to get hold straight away of the Commander and respective divisional officers and tell them to find out who the delinquents were ... This he has now done but with completely negative results ... I am of the opinion that even a Board of Inquiry would now be abortive and even do more harm than good on account of its publicity. My own view, for what it may be worth is that during the long period alongside at Portsmouth [August to November 1946] with a full ship's company on board discipline became lax and the Captain and Executive Officers failed to appreciate this and unfortunately the result was that the standard of discipline amongst the executive branch was not up to what it should have been in any ship, more particularly one which was destined to carry out this highly important mission.'

Layton agreed with Moody's concern about Agnew's broadcast communications style. He recommended that the ship's commander should be replaced, and that at least two new senior executive officers with strong disciplinarian streaks plus two or three similar divisional officers should also join the executive branch of the ship. A new and very experienced master at arms was sent to the ship as well, arriving as early as 16 May.

Boddington's inquiries were also renewed aboard *Vanguard* in late May when the ship arrived back in Portsmouth. He narrowed down the trouble to seamen-torpedomen in Messes numbers 75, 76 and 77, with Messes 79 and 81 also possibly implicated. Two individuals, able seamen, were named (now redacted on the papers) and further investigations of their backgrounds undertaken. His initial views were that the trouble was not externally inspired.

The final chapter in this tale of woe was written by First Lord of the Admiralty, Lord Hall, in a note to the Prime Minister on 28 May. Hall had also interviewed Agnew and Layton. Although he began with a fairly balanced assessment that the trouble was not as serious as had been feared, nevertheless he agreed with the First Sea Lord that *Vanguard* should be paid off and a new crew provided for her. This would happen straight after they returned from leave and the ship would then proceed to Devonport for repairs to the High Angle control system, modifications to the canteens and removal of the Royal fittings, but in such a way that these could be reinstalled at much less expense. He had also spoken to the King and obtained his agreement that the ship would not be used by His Majesty during the Clyde Review.

So *Vanguard* retired under a bit of a cloud to Devonport. Ironically the severity of the damage from the computer room fire and the length of time expected to repair it meshed with the disciplinary requirements for the complete change in ship's programme and for what was essentially a clean sweep of the ship's crew. The log shows numerous officers in the executive and engineering branches being replaced in short order after arriving at Portsmouth. Around 150 of all ranks had already left the ship by the time Agnew handed over to Captain Parham on 29 May. The number on the sick list was twenty-one on Agnew's final day in command, zero on Parham's first. Routine continued, Nicholas Anthony Canning Higham was christened aboard on 31 May, and the ship de-ammunitioned between 2 and 16 June. On 20 June she reduced to a steaming party complement and 630 men left the ship that day to various destinations. She sailed to Plymouth on 26 June, via air defence and anti-submarine exercises at Portland. This included the bizarre evolution of no fewer than seven submarines surfacing in her immediate vicinity, no doubt each claiming to have sunk her. On 27 June she was at No. 6/7 Wharf in Devonport Dockyard, where the crew was further whittled down to care and maintenance complement. Agnew duly got his KCVO from the King, but his career did not prosper. After serving as Director of Personnel Services in the Admiralty he retired at his own request in 1949.

Meanwhile, the Navy reviewed the experiment of the much-vaunted central messing and dining hall system that had been blamed for much of the trouble. The First Sea Lord read the seven-page report on 1 July 1947. The dining halls in *Vanguard* were too small, there was too much queuing and the intimacy of the mess system had been lost. There was 'a sense of gloom, depression and silence during meals' as men could no longer sit with their messmates.[26] Nevertheless, central messing did continue to be introduced in the fleet – you can get a good idea of what the system looked like by touring HMS *Belfast* in the Pool of London.

None of *Vanguard*'s troubles entered the public domain, and the Royal Navy was soon back in its stride. The 1947 Home Fleet cruises were more ambitious than those of 1946. *Anson*, now as flagship of the Training Squadron, and *Howe* made a foray to Torquay and Mevagissey, Cornwall, from 19 to 27 February, before *Howe* went into dock at Portsmouth for a quick scraping during April. Her log records Force 6 to 8 winds between 20 and 23 April, the period when *Warspite* was going aground on the Cornish coast. (*Duke of York*, also at Portsmouth, records Force 9 on 23 April.) *Howe* returned to Portland on 9 May, then, with *Anson*, visited Torbay again at the end of May and in the first week of June. They returned to Portland, then set off again on 7 July, and travelled north via, variously, Falmouth, St Ives, Milford Haven, Fishguard (where, bizarrely, *Howe*'s log records her 'embarking potatoes' at half past nine in the evening on 9 July), Douglas, Isle of Man and Bangor, Northern Ireland.

Duke of York, as flagship of the Home Fleet, had meanwhile led a more varied and active existence. After parting company with *Vanguard* on 1 February, she had rendezvoused with the Home Fleet cruisers and destroyers and taken the Commander-in-Chief and the Home Fleet on exercises in the Atlantic, then on to Gibraltar and into the Mediterranean to Villefranche-sur-Mer for a week. Among the many civic duties, the log noted on 15 February that a party of fifty French girls arrived on board from the Société France-Angleterre. Back to Gibraltar, she then proceeded to Funchal, Madeira, where the military and civil Governors both came aboard. Lieutenant (Supply) R E Symons missed the last liberty boat and was admonished for being absent without leave between 0030 and 0330 on 7 March. Further exercises followed during the return voyage. During this period *Duke of York* undertook pom-pom and limited 5.25in firings, but although exercised in ranging and indication trials with the 4th Destroyer Flotilla, the main armament does not seem to have been fired.

On 31 May she set off once again accompanied by three cruisers and six destroyers, via a rendezvous with the Training Squadron at Torbay, westabout to Norway. A three-week cruise took in Stavanger, Molde, Andalsnes, Odda and Kristiansand. At Molde, 1,000 libertymen were allowed ashore and a beer bar and 8,000 bottles of beer were specially imported for them into this normally 'dry' town. *Duke of York* and the fleet were more in tune with local customs later on, providing a searchlight display and fireworks to the traditional 21 June celebrations in Kristiansand. She returned to the east coast of Scotland, calling at Rosyth on 28 June. There she passed an American squadron, including the battleships *New Jersey* and *Wisconsin*. 'The usual courtesies were exchanged,' reported the Commander-in-Chief laconically.[27] *Duke of York* then went north about Scotland again, via exercises at Scapa Flow and a visit to Portrush, Northern Ireland. By 18 July the three active British battleships were together again, and with the aircraft carriers *Illustrious*, *Venerable*, the Second Cruiser Squadron and other Home Fleet units, gathered at Tail of the Bank anchorage in the Clyde estuary off Greenock. A couple of days' rehearsal followed before, on 22 July, still fresh from their exposure to the fleet aboard *Vanguard*, the Royal Family again honoured the Royal Navy with a Clyde Fleet Review.[28]

This review had its origins with orders by the First Sea Lord in May 1946. There was little enthusiasm in the Admiralty. The Director of Plans said on 21 May: 'In view of the extreme paucity of available resources, it appears to D of P questionable whether the review would serve any useful purpose other than to stress that we had reached our nadir of naval impotence.' Planning nevertheless proceeded on the assumption that it was not a formal fleet review of the type last carried out for George VI's coronation in 1937, but a Home Fleet visit to the Clyde that would be attended by the King. It was difficult to square this lower-key approach with the gathering of such a large fleet, not seen since the war, and with the level of ambition with which the various civic authorities in Scotland soon embraced the prospect. The official papers reflect this dilemma as the plans took shape. The early assumptions about participating units showed all five available battleships taking part, along with four carriers, five cruisers and fifty-two destroyers. *Vanguard* was withdrawn on 21 May 1947, although the printed orders for the Clyde event by Commander-in-Chief Home Fleet dated 1 June still assumed she would be there. *Nelson* could not make it either, so in the event *Duke of York*, *Howe* and *Anson* plus two carriers anchored in line just off Princes Pier, Greenock, from 18 July. It was still an impressive collection of British naval power.[29]

For *Duke of York* the big day began with a fire in the main naval store discovered at 0355. It was extinguished by 0410. The Prime Minister Clement Attlee and Mrs Attlee were aboard by 0945, and the Royal Family at 1015. They left for *Anson* at 1120, but returned in the evening for dinner with the Commander-in-Chief. The evening finished with a Royal 'At Home' hosting 500 officers of the Home Fleet. *Anson*'s log for 22 July records that the Royal Guard and band paraded on the quarterdeck at 0930. The Prime Minister and Mrs Attlee came aboard at 1135, closely followed at 1145 by their Majesties the King and Queen, the Princess Elizabeth, the Princess Margaret and Lieutenant Philip Mountbatten. *Anson*'s and *Howe*'s ships' companies marched past the Royal Family, who then proceeded to watch cutter racing from the ship (*Anson* won) before the party departed at 1425. There was at least one further march past aboard one of the aircraft carriers (probably *Illustrious*), captured for posterity by Pathé News. The next afternoon, 23 July, the King came back aboard *Duke of York*, from where he watched an amphibious display. At 1420 he boarded Motor Torpedo Boat No. 2016 to tour the fleet. *Anson* and others cheered the Royal procession along the fleet. Shortly thereafter the Minister of Defence, A V Alexander, and the First Lord of the Admiralty, Viscount Hall, came aboard *Anson* and passed a couple of hours visiting the ship. They then went on to *Duke of York*. That evening it was the turn of *Illustrious* to host all the dignitaries. At 2250 the whole fleet fired a Royal Salute to bring the review to an end.

Although she had provided sailors for the march past, *Howe* had to be content with a back seat for this review. Her band played at Helensburgh on 19 July, but in fact they did not belong to the ship and were brought up specially for the review from the Royal Marine Depot at Chatham. *Howe* was also hosting Mr Norman Wilkinson, the eminent maritime painter and war artist, inventor of dazzle camouflage in the First World War and poster artist promoter of the London and North Eastern Railway. Presumably he was aboard to paint scenes of the review, but once embarked, the log makes no reference to his activities. Although Wilkinson had a prolific output in terms of oil paintings of fleet reviews, including the Coronation Reviews of 1911, 1937 and 1953, and a prolific output of paintings of the Clyde estuary, both maritime and railway related, I cannot find any references to or evidence of a finished work by him depicting this particular event.

Besides hosting the King and other dignitaries and providing bands and teams for sporting events against teams from the communities of the Clyde, the battleships also had organised visits from around 1,000 people a day, from groups as diverse as the Boy Scouts, Boys Brigade, Girl Guides, Sea Cadets, the Association of WRNS, the Clyde River Patrol Association, the Institute of Engineering Inspection, hundreds of children from Glasgow, Paisley and Gourock, and a group of 100 from Singer Sewing Machines in Clydebank. The Royal family departed the Clyde on the cruiser *Superb* on 24 July for a private visit to the Isle of Arran, and on 27 July the battleships, carriers, and the remainder of the 2nd Cruiser Squadron sailed from the Clyde. It must have been an impressive sight.

The return journey reinforced the Navy's links with other nations of the UK, taking in stops at Dundrum Bay, County Down, Holyhead, Aberystwyth, Swansea, Tenby, Newquay and Penzance, before Portland was regained on 6 August 1947. *Anson* then went into No. 10 Dock at Devonport on 10 September for her bottom to be scraped and painted before exercising briefly in Torbay on 20 October. Back in Portland on 27 October, she did not stir from C Buoy in the harbour until 5 May 1948, over six months of unvarying routine and harbour training. *Howe* took over as flagship of the Training Squadron, now commanded by Rear Admiral P Enwright, on 5 September. She too had a quiet winter, going to sea for just eleven days in the next eight months, including a week at Torquay in October and an anti-submarine warfare exercise in February 1948.

Duke of York was also very quiet following her return to Portland at the end of July 1947. The days 6 and 15 October were, however, noteworthy for undertaking some 14in main armament firings in the Portland training area; according to the ship's log all fired from B turret. There were also 5.25in firings on the 15 October. The battleship returned to Portsmouth on 23 October and remained there until 25 May 1948, the only events outside normal routine recorded in the log being the half-masting of her colours on 1 and 2 February to mark the assassination of Mahatma Gandhi.

This was the period over the winter of 1947–48 referred to in official papers as the immobilisation of the Home Fleet, when manning difficulties reached such proportions that only a handful of ships based in the UK were fully capable, although those on foreign stations were less affected. On 1 March 1948 a report on the state of the Home Fleet to the First Sea Lord referred to *Duke of York* as 'immobilised'. She needed to have her quadruple pom-pom and single Bofors anti-aircraft armament reinstalled. A and Y 14in turrets were reduced to one month's notice for maintenance, as was 50 per cent of the 5.25in and remaining close-range armament. Her radar equipment was in poor shape due to maintenance constraints.[30] But better times were round the corner. Her refit at Portsmouth between 13 April and 20 August saw six Bofors Mark VII mountings fitted, as well as refuelling-at-sea equipment.[31] She was briefly at sea in May, June and July 1948 for exercises including pom-pom firings. Replenishment-at-sea trials took place on 14 August and 12 September, which we can infer were preparation for her acting in this role for her smaller consorts during the forthcoming cruise. On 16 August she began a major ammunitioning at Portsmouth's South Railway Jetty that lasted until 25 August. The last entry which we have in her log is her sailing to St Ives, and conducting Bofors firings on the way.

Her logs for September 1948 onwards are not at the National Archive, so regrettably there is no day-by-day record available for the

Duke of York leaves Portland for the Home Fleet cruise to the West Indies, 23 September 1948. *(Alamy)*

period when she was flagship for the Home Fleet cruise to the West Indies and South Africa in autumn 1948. It seems that *Duke of York* joined up with the 3rd Aircraft Carrier Squadron in Home Waters in September 1948. There is excellent Pathé footage of their departure, including the other battleships then at Portland. According to the sparse record in the ship's book,[32] after departing Portland on 23 September the fleet split, with the aircraft carriers cruising to South Africa and the Commander-in-Chief, now Admiral Sir Rhoderick McGrigor, taking the battleship and the 2nd Cruiser Squadron to the West Indies. Barbados was reached on 9 October, Tobago on 18 October, Antigua on 1 November, Jamaica on 4 November, Norfolk, Virginia, on 16 November, and Bermuda on 25 November, before the fleet recombined in home waters around 3 December and returned to home ports on 14 December. It was the last such visit by a British battleship to the Western Atlantic.

Manning the active fleet remained a big challenge. There is correspondence in the First Sea Lord's papers from late October 1948, where the Commander-in-Chief, writing from Antigua, argues vehemently against a plan to keep the carrier *Implacable* running at the turn of the year by drafting 145 men from *Duke of York* straight to *Implacable* immediately on their return to UK, which would cause those men to have missed their Christmas leave.[33]

Despite the lack of a battleship log, we do have some insight into *Duke of York*'s activities in December 1948 from the Admiralty records of Exercise Sunrise. These manoeuvres simulated the passage of a convoy and naval escort (the Home Fleet) from the UK to northern waters, and it being attacked by 'Russian' forces (units based in the UK). *Duke of York* had recombined with the three aircraft carriers, with sixty-six aircraft embarked, three cruisers and eighteen destroyers. The 'Russian' forces were assumed to be a weak surface force, but strong in submarines (eighteen took part in the exercise) and in land-based aircraft (over one hundred from the RAF). These latter were allocated two 'Atom Bombs' to use against the Home Fleet.

The Home Fleet sailed from the Azores on 7 December and planned to strike the 'Russian' base at Plymouth with its carriers when about one hundred miles to the west. Poor weather meant only the thirteen Barracuda aircraft could fly on all the days of the exercise. The Vampires, Sea Furies and Fireflies could only fly on the afternoon of one day, and the report bemoans the poor performance of the light fleet carriers. 'These ships were performing a duty for which they would most probably be required in war. The fact that they were unable to operate their aircraft is regrettable.' The strike on Plymouth had to be cancelled. Meanwhile, the 'Russian' air forces failed in their initial simulated atom bomb attack, unable to find the Home Fleet, despite closing it to within 30 miles. A second attack was pressed home and Coastal Command dropped its 'Atom Bomb' at 0300 on 12 December. The appropriate disposition of the Home Fleet to meet atomic attack was given considerable thought, including in consultation with US Navy Admiral Radford, who was riding with *Duke of York*. In the event they adopted 'Disposition No. 22' with the high-value targets, the battleship and three carriers, in a box formation about 10 nautical miles square. This was held to ensure that no more than one ship could be lost or seriously damaged by a single bomb, but still provided a reasonable degree of anti-submarine protection. Retrospectively, the Commander-in-Chief suggested they could be much closer for anti-submarine effectiveness without increasing the atomic bomb risk. In this particular instance the bomb was dropped 4,500 yards from the cruiser *Dido* and 6,700 yards from the nearest high-value target,

Vengeance. Based on the analysis after the Bikini Tests, that particular attack would have been ineffective.[34]

Back in the Training Squadron, 5 May 1948 saw the beginning of an extended cruise where *Anson* and *Howe* travelled first to Scapa Flow and then Rosyth. *Howe* was loaned 101 ratings from other ships to bring her complement up to a level where she could operate as a fleet unit. The ships conducted air plotting exercises on their way up the Irish Sea, then on 12 and 13 May they took part in extensive exercises with the Home Fleet carrier *Implacable* and cruiser *Superb* plus escorts in the northern North Sea, code-named 'Dawn'. There were dummy torpedo attacks on the big ships, and then practising defence against high-level bombing attack. The next day it was anti-submarine warfare exercises with much zigzagging of the fleet in formation. However, through all this the big guns remained silent – indeed no ammunition for them was being carried. Despite the excitement, in *Howe* the log records that the Men Under Training went to their classes as usual. Reflecting the degree of austerity imposed on managing the Navy, her log also records the specific permission from the Admiralty to burn fuel at greater than economical speeds during the exercise (although she does not seem to have exceeded 18 knots). The return trip took in the refuelling at sea of the destroyers *Dunkirk*, *Agincourt* and *Corunna* by *Howe* on 15 May. This evolution was a very common practice in the British Pacific Fleet in 1944–45 and vital to keeping the Task Forces at sea for long periods as the destroyers lacked the fuel endurance to operate for long without topping up. *Anson* went to Portree in Skye, Bangor, Northern Ireland, and Falmouth before Portland was reached on 28 May. She went to sea again on 7 July and then spent a couple of weeks at Torbay in the first half of August. *Howe* ended the Exercise Dawn trip at Plymouth on 18 May, where she handed back the temporary additions to the crew and began a refit that was ongoing in No. 10 dock on 31 August 1948. According to the ship's book,

Anson with *Victorious* in the Bay of Biscay on 7 July 1949, taking part in Exercise Verity. The cruisers *Montcalm* and *Superb* are following. *(Alamy)*

this lasted until 28 June 1949.[35] *Anson*'s and *Howe*'s logs also seem to be lost for the period from September 1948 onwards. We know from the ship's book that *Anson* was docked in No. 10 Dock, Devonport, from 18 February to 24 March 1949.[36] Then she went to Portland, and was flying the Flag of Rear Admiral Anstice Commanding the Training Squadron by June 1949 when she took part in Exercise Verity, the first joint naval exercises undertaken by the new Western Union powers. The Western Union emerged from the Anglo–French Treaty of Dunkirk in 1947 that provided for mutual defence assistance in the event of an attack, and encompassed the three Benelux countries as well after the Treaty of Brussels in March 1948. Its Defence Organisation dated from 28 September 1948. 'Verity' is little known today, but was significant as the first multilateral defence exercise of the Cold War. Sixty vessels from four nations took part, with the Dutch providing a cruiser and France the carrier *Arromanches* and cruiser *Montcalm*. Commander-in-Chief Home Fleet, still Admiral McGrigor, commanded the exercise. The UK contingent, besides *Anson*, also included the carriers *Implacable*, *Victorious* and *Theseus*.

Fifty of the ships had assembled for the exercise in Mount's Bay, Cornwall, by 30 June. The Borough of Penzance printed a souvenir programme price 6d. It said: 'To the men of the British, French and Netherlands navies, the people of Penzance extend a most hearty welcome and express the hope that they will carry away with them very happy memories.' Events organised for the visit included tea dances at the Winter Gardens, open air dancing on the promenade and a dance at Newlyn fish market. The combined bands of *Anson* and *Theseus* played at Morrab Gardens.[37]

In contrast to the dancing, the exercise itself was kept simple to overcome the novelty of navies working together, and the language challenges. Serial Four was a bombardment exercise by the cruisers, but

Anson, still presumably without ammunition, did not take part. The exercise then simulated the defence of a convoy approaching the English Channel. *Anson* and *Victorious* took part in serial Five on 4 July, as part of the 'Blue Force' convoy, which was attacked by submarines of three nations. The French submarine *Mille* fired a torpedo at *Anson* from 2,500 yards off her starboard bow at 1350. However, she had previously been detected by the escorting destroyer *Solebay* at 1342. HMS *Trespasser* was more skilful, penetrated both escort screens and attacked *Anson* from only 450 yards after dark. A further round of submarine attacks took place on 5 July, with *Anson* in command of the convoy and *Arromanches* operating as an independent hunter-killer ASW group. The Home Fleet's Firefly, Sea Hornet, Firebrand and Sea Fury squadrons all took part, as did the RAF. The culmination of the exercises on 6–7 July saw further attacks by submarines, a high-speed attack by French motor torpedo boats and high-level formation bombing by radar from 16,000 to 18,000ft by Lancasters and Lincolns of No. 19 Group, RAF. Finally there were some minesweeping evolutions around the Isle of Wight. Afterwards McGrigor told the press: 'The object of these manoeuvres is to show that we are willing and able to work together in case of aggression. I can say straight away that it's been a very great success.'[38]

King George V had joined the Training Squadron as well after her 1947 refit. A week after 'Verity' she too showed her paces, doing a full-power trial in the English Channel on 12 July 1949, and achieving her designed horsepower of 110,000 and speed of 27 knots. But the decision to reduce her and her sisters to reserve had already been taken (see below).

Vanguard continued her post-South Africa refit for the first eight months of 1948. Prime Minister Attlee and First Lord Hall visited the ship on 1 May. The captain of HMS *Excellent*, the Royal Navy gunnery school, reported on the successful completion of the gunnery control trial for the refurbished starboard computer room on 24 May.[39] There were occasional basin trials of the machinery, and some re-ammunitioning. A petty officer was injured by a 15in shell during this activity on 11 May. From 14 to 17 May the ship was open to visitors during Plymouth Navy Days. Master John Derek Napper, son of Lt Napper, was christened aboard on 3 July. Reflecting the officer of the watch's sense of history passing, he recorded in the log *Renown*'s last passage from Devonport on 3 August, and *Valiant*'s on 11 August as HMS *Imperieuse* shut down and these famous ships made their final journeys north to the scrapyard. On 31 August 1948, after fourteen months and four days being repaired and refitted, *Vanguard* finally went to sea again, down the English Channel to Mevagissey. The next few days were spent in the Channel shaking down: 5.25in firing on 1 and 2 September, the degaussing range and machinery vibration trials. On 17 September the Parliamentary Secretary to the

Admiralty Mr Dugdale came aboard to spend a few days on the ship on passage to Gibraltar. She arrived on 21 September.

There followed an intense period of trials and gunnery practice in the Atlantic and Mediterranean designed to prove all elements of her armament and its repaired control systems. If the number of references in the ship's log is a guide then in terms of gunnery it was rather more intense than the initial shakedown trials of 1946. The implication is that in late 1948 the Admiralty still saw *Vanguard* as much more than a showboat – she was first and foremost an operational warship. However, the log also shows that she was hampered by crew shortages. She probably carried only sufficient gun crews for half the 15in and 5.25in guns. Almost all the specific references to firings in the ship's logs are to the forward 15in turrets, A and B, and the forward 5.2in turrets P1, P2, S1 and S2. On 30 September 1948, 200 army personnel from the Gibraltar garrison came aboard to witness 5.25in firings. The next day A and B 15in turrets were in action for fifty minutes carrying out sub-calibre shoots against the destroyer *Childers*, acting as the target. More 5.25in firings took place that afternoon. Both main and secondary armaments fired again on 2 October. *Vanguard* then went to Malta from 4 to 13 October, and while based there carried out 15in sub-calibre shoots on 13 October, full calibre on 15 October, A and B turrets firing at full charge against targets 19,000 and 16,000 yards distant on the 18 October, and again on 4 November (the only time on this cruise that X and Y turrets were manned) and 5 November, when she opened fire at a range of 22,850 yards – still well short of her theoretical maximum of over 29,000 yards. The Bofors 40mm guns were fired on four occasions over this period, and the 5.25in batteries were exercised on six occasions.

These exercises were marred by a fatal accident on 21 October. The log states '0955 Mne [Marine] Bray killed in P2 turret. Plymouth X5591, Marine Bray, Edward Thomas aged 19 years 6 months, nationality Irish, last place of abode Schoolhouse, Monkstown, County Dublin, was caught between fixed and moving structure of 5.25in gun turret and crushed was killed instantly. Accidental death from shock due to penetrating fracture of the ribs and haemorrhage into the thorax and abdomen.' He was buried ashore at Malta the following day.[40]

Vanguard was back in Gibraltar on 8 November, and returned to Devonport on 12 November, via more Bofors firings in the Atlantic. She was in time to fire a Royal salute on 15 November in honour of the Royal birth (Prince Charles), and hosted the First Lord of the Admiralty and the Lord Chancellor for a visit on 5 December. She had originally been selected for a second 'Special Duties' task to take the King to Australia and New Zealand in the winter of 1948–49, but he was too ill to make the voyage, so instead she returned to Gibraltar on 3 February 1949 and then entered the Mediterranean, with Commander-in-Chief Mediterranean assuming operational control over her on 6 February. She undertook a further round of gunnery exercises with all calibres. The 15in shoots were on 17, 22, 23 and 24 February. On the last of these all the 15in turrets were fired sequentially in short order between 1628 and 1647, indicating that the crew had been augmented since the 1948 exercises. The culmination of these efforts was on 1 March 1949, when at 1045 an 8-gun broadside was fired. As this was sufficiently noteworthy to be highlighted in the log, it was probably the only UK battleship full broadside fired after 1945 and the final time a broadside was fired by a British battleship. See Appendix One for further evidence concerning firings by British battleships.

Vanguard spent the early part of 1949 in the Mediterranean. She went to Gibraltar for combined Home and Mediterranean Fleet exercises in early March, then visited Algiers between 16 and 21 March. She went on to Toulon, then Naples on 28 March.[41] The log for April is missing, but by 1 May she was back in North Africa at Tripoli. On the way back to Malta she took part in further exercises, including on 2 May 15in and 5.25in bombardments of Filfla, a barren islet off the south of Malta. She was in Grand Harbour from 6 to 15 May, and open to visitors. These

Vanguard's firing practice off Malta, 16 May 1949. She is firing a four-turret 15in salvo. *(Imperial War Museum)*

Vanguard straddles the target, 16 May 1949. (Imperial War Museum)

included Chelsea Football Club, on a post-season tour to Malta and fresh from their 6-0 thrashing of United Services Malta, who were photographed on the quarterdeck under the 15in guns. On 16 May she was back at sea and firing all calibres of guns, with the 15in opening fire at 1532. This exercise was extensively photographed by the Royal Navy both from accompanying ships and aircraft, and there is evidence that all four turrets fired simultaneous salvos on this occasion (see IWM photos), although the ship's log lacks details.

There followed a whirlwind tour of the eastern Mediterranean, starting at Venice on 19 May. On Sunday, 22 May Princess Margaret, visiting the city as part of her tour of Italy, renewed her acquaintance with the ship, coming aboard between 1025 and 1450. She attended divine service and telephoned the King from the communications centre to wish her grandmother Queen Mary Happy Birthday. *Vanguard* returned to Malta via Palermo and the exchanging of gun salutes with the US carrier *Coral Sea*. While at Malta the Italian battleship *Duilio* paid a visit, and on 1 June passed *Vanguard* to port at 0850, saluting the Commander-in-Chief. The Italian Vice-Admiral E. Oliva came aboard at 0955. *Vanguard* fired a twenty-one gun salute and extended further hospitality the next day to mark the foundation of the Italian Republic. *Duilio* left Malta on 4 June, and *Vanguard* followed on 13 June for further fleet exercises including submarine and aircraft attacks on the formation, and at 1845, 15in and 5.25in firings on two destroyers.

She next went via Famagusta in Cyprus to Port Said on 17 June, where a twenty-one gun national salute to Egypt was fired, and many senior British officers from the Canal Zone came aboard. She was at Beirut in the Lebanon on 22 June, where a party was landed to travel to Damascus, eighty-six ratings were landed for a tea dance, and the cricket team was landed on 24 June (opponents and result not recorded). There was an alarm on the morning of 25 June, when a frogman was reported

Vanguard at anchor. *(NHHC)*

on the port side at 0340. At 0405 the ship assumed damage control state B, and for thirty minutes charges were dropped from the motor boat to deter whatever activity might have been going on. The log records that she left the port, as planned, at 0635 that morning. Next she visited Rhodes, Salonika and Athens, where on 30 June the Commander-in-Chief hosted dinner for the King and Queen of the Hellenes, at which Field Marshal Jan Smuts was also a guest. Despite a major military drawdown in 1947, the UK was still heavily committed in Greece to support the Government to face down the communist insurgency, so *Vanguard*'s presence at the point when the civil war was about to swing decisively against the communists was as significant as that of USS *Missouri* in 1946

at the point when its post-war phase was just beginning (see Chapter Seven). The King and his children toured the ship the next day, and the Commander-in-Chief called in his turn on the Greek Commanders-in-Chief and the Prime Minister.

The next stop for *Vanguard* on 6 July was Taranto, where Admiral Oliva came aboard again, then Navarin, Malta, to pick up personnel bound for the UK, and back to Tripoli to embark 'His Excellency the Emir Senussi of Cyrenaica and his retinue', for passage to Marseilles, dropping him on 14 July. The UK had supported the Senussi order in the declaration of an independent Cyrenaica on 1 March 1949, with the Emir as its leader. However, the UN overturned a UK–French–Italian plan to run Libya as three protectorates under their mandate and insisted on a united Libya. The Emir, as King Idris, returned to lead the country from 1951 until he was ousted by Colonel Gaddafi in 1969.

After this intensive criss-crossing of the Mediterranean in support of British diplomacy and security initiatives, *Vanguard* returned to the UK, reaching Devonport on 21 July. Patricia Jane Landerson and Jane Elizabeth Bambrook were christened aboard on 24 July, and fifty Belgian girls visited the ship the same day. She de-ammunitioned during August, for a brief docking in Devonport between 29 August and 20 September, during which the new five-bladed propellers were fitted to her inner shafts to try to cure the vibration problems. Following intensive trials with the new propellers over the measured mile off Arran between 25 September and 6 October, during which she was again based at Greenock, she returned south to Devonport. On 10 November 1949 she steamed to Portland and the next day took over from *Anson* as flagship of the Training Squadron when Rear Admiral Evans-Lombe and his staff came aboard.[42]

Vanguard's new life at Portland saw a range of new challenges. On 9 January 1950 her log records: 'I have this day had occasion to admonish Father Michael Barry, Roman Catholic Chaplain, Royal Navy, for having, on the 9th day of December 1949 obtained a bottle of whisky from the ward room wine steward, contrary to the King's Regulations and Admiralty Instructions Article 619 paragraph 3. {signed} W Gladstone, Capt.' On 28 January she sailed in company with the Home Fleet including the carrier *Implacable* and the 4th and 6th Destroyer Flotillas, and went down to Gibraltar again. Only Bofors firings took place on this trip and she was back in Portland on 15 February. In early March she went up the Channel as far as Dover, then to Portsmouth, and by mid-May, Plymouth, where she once again hosted Navy Days on 27 and 28 May. She visited Torquay between 9 and 13 June, and was back at Portland later that month when the Korean War started (although not an event considered worthy of recording in her log). We will pick up the story of her life in the 1950s later.

CHAPTER SEVEN

Peacetime for the United States and France

IN THE UNITED States the immediate post-war focus had involved mothballing rather than scrapping (see Chapter Three). We have seen how *Arkansas*, *Nevada*, *New York* and *Pennsylvania* fared at Bikini and afterwards. *Texas* from this elderly cohort, sister of *New York*, had managed to escape the beady eye of Admiral Blandy and JTF 1. Instead of Bikini, she made her way to San Jacinto, Texas, to become a State Memorial (see Chapter Fifteen). *Wyoming* continued to serve as a trials ship for anti-aircraft systems on the Atlantic seaboard based at Casco Bay, Maine. Ensign Jimmy Carter, later to become 39th President of the United States and play his own not inconsiderable part in the later stages of battleship history, joined her as a very junior officer in April 1946.

But by 1947 time was up for the old ship, and she was decommissioned on 1 August at Norfolk, Virginia. The crew, however, remained battleship sailors because most were transferred to operate *Mississippi*.

Mississippi had one of the most active post-war careers of any battleship. She had returned from the war to Norfolk, Virginia, on 27 November 1945. She was selected for conversion to a gunnery training and trials ship in place of *Wyoming*, and work started from 15 February 1946 and completed in April 1948. While in dock she was briefly flagship of the Operational Development Force and of Battleships-Cruisers Atlantic Fleet. She was recommissioned not as BB-41, but redesignated as AG-128. As part of the Operational Development Force she spent the next four years of her career based at Norfolk, investigating gunnery problems and testing new weapons. It was logical to select another old battleship to replace *Wyoming* in this role. She was big enough to mount a variety of different weapons, gunnery directors and radars simultaneously, and to accommodate additional personnel for training.

Midshipman Jimmy Carter, USN, who served aboard *Wyoming* in 1946. *(NARA)*

Mississippi
c. 1948 in her
gunnery training
configuration,
with one 14in
turret. *(NHHC)*

Initially she retained her aftermost 14in turret, as there was still a theoretical requirement to train crews for the two 14in ships, *California* and *Tennessee*, which were being retained in mothballs during this period. But the other three turrets were removed to create the space for the same mixture of 5in, 3in and 40mm types mounted by *Wyoming*, representing the main types of light gun mountings used by the post-war US Navy. A little later *Mississippi* also acquired on A barbette a 6in twin 47-calibre fully automatic turret of the sort mounted on the *Worcester*-class cruisers. She was also planned to have had the triple 8in 55-calibre automatic mounting fitted on the *Des Moines*-class heavy cruisers, but in the event this was never installed because the US Navy already had plans to develop both medium- and long-range guided weapons, and *Mississippi* was assigned to become the first ship to mount the system that eventually became Terrier, and carry out its first test firings at sea (see Chapter Twelve).[1]

Apart from the trials and training in *Mississippi*, and the rapid reduction of all other ships to inactivation, and then the reserve fleets, peacetime activity was soon confined to the four *Iowa*-class ships. *Iowa* herself arrived back in Seattle on 15 October 1945 with her Magic Carpet contingent, then conducted some training at Long Beach before returning to Japan on 27 January 1946 to relieve *New Jersey* as flagship of the 5th Fleet at Tokyo. This deployment took place despite her captain's view that so many of the regular crew had been demobilised as to make her condition hazardous.[2] She returned to the US again on 25 March 1946, exercising and training with the Pacific Fleet, often embarking reservists and midshipmen for training. This routine went on for two years, interrupted only by a brief excursion to Vancouver, British Columbia, and her overhaul in 1947. It climaxed in the Pacific Fleet live firing exercises of July 1948, where the target, 65 miles south-west of Oahu, was her fellow battleship (and Bikini survivor), *Nevada*. In September 1948 the US Navy began a further post-war reduction in manpower and active ships, as part of which *Iowa* began deactivation at San Francisco, and went into the Pacific Reserve Fleet at Bremerton, Washington, on 24 March 1949.

New Jersey, initially as flagship of the 5th Fleet under Admiral Raymond Spruance, stayed in Tokyo Bay commanding US naval forces in Japanese waters until relieved by *Iowa*. She took back over 1,000 US-bound troops when she departed on 28 January 1946, arriving at San Francisco on 10 February. She spent the rest of 1946 on the west coast and being overhauled at Puget Sound. Then in 1947 she returned to Bayonne, New Jersey, where she had a fourth birthday party on 23 May 1947, attended by dignitaries including New Jersey Governor Alfred E Driscoll and former Governor Walter E Edge. Between 7 June and 26 August she sailed for northern Europe as part of the first Training Squadron cruise to those waters since before the war. Over 2,000 Naval Academy and Navy Reserve Officers Training Cadre midshipmen got seagoing experience on this trip. It was commanded for part of the time by Admiral Richard L Connolly, Commander Naval Forces Eastern Atlantic and Mediterranean, who hoisted his flag in *New Jersey* at Rosyth on 23 June. By 2 July she was at Oslo in Norway, where King Haakon VII inspected the crew during the visit. She then came back via a visit to Portsmouth in mid-July, which included hosting Sir Bruce Fraser and despatching twenty cadets to Buckingham Palace for a reception hosted by King George VI. She sailed on 18 July for exercises in the Caribbean and Western Atlantic. She spent autumn in New York City as flagship of Battleship Division One. There in the naval shipyard she began deactivation on 18 October 1947, and was put out of commission in the Atlantic Reserve Fleet on 30 June 1948.

Wisconsin sailed from Okinawa on 23 September 1945 with another Magic Carpet contingent of GIs. She was at San Francisco by 14 October, and spent Christmas on the West Coast, before transiting the Panama Canal on 11 January, and reaching Hampton Roads, Virginia, on

18 January 1946. She spent a few months in overhaul at Norfolk, where her crew dwindled to around 600, not enough men even to get her under way.[3] But in the autumn, thanks to the drafting of an additional 1,600 crewmen in the space of two weeks, she made the first post-war cruise by the US Navy to the Pacific coast of South America, transporting President Truman's personal representative and Chief of Staff, Fleet Admiral William Leahy, to the inauguration of the new President of Chile, Gabriel González Videla. In a preview to later overseas visits by US Presidents with 'The Beast' armoured limousines, Leahy had his own transport, a black Packard, carried to South America on the battleship, lashed down next to No. 3 turret. *Wisconsin* reached Valparaiso, Chile, on 1 November 1946, visited Callao, Peru, from 9 to 13 November and La Guaira, Venezuela, from 22 to 26 November. The presidents of all three countries toured the ship. In 1947 she settled into the training ship routine, taking naval reservists on two-week cruises from Bayonne, New Jersey, to Guantanamo Bay in Cuba or to the Canal Zone. Typically the battleships carried a crew of 1,100 for such work, judged just enough for the safe operation of the ship, plus 900 midshipmen or reservists. The British battleships were able to function as seagoing training ships with complements of 620–720.

During June and July 1947, in company with *New Jersey*, *Wisconsin* also took midshipmen to northern European waters, the first post-war cruise in that sphere. The spontaneous outpourings of UK generosity and hospitality to the US Navy were much commented upon. The enlisted crew had to be pressed into service alongside the officers to accept all the offers of hospitality made by the host nation in Edinburgh and Portsmouth. The senior US officers were hosted to dinner aboard HMS *Victory*. After further work along the east coast of the USA, in January 1948 *Wisconsin* came back to Norfolk, Virginia, where she too began deactivation, before going into the Atlantic fleet reserve on 1 July.[4]

This left *Missouri* as the only active US battleship during late 1948 and into 1949, at a time when, albeit only for a few more months, the UK was (just about) managing to run four active battleships. *Missouri* had a slightly more varied post-war experience than her sisters. After the surrender in Tokyo Bay, she ceased to be 3rd Fleet flagship as early as 5 September, and left for home the following day, via Guam, picking up the usual demobilising passengers. She got to Pearl Harbor on 20 September, then pressed on direct to the Atlantic. She paused briefly at Norfolk, Virginia, to have the Japanese Surrender commemorative plaque mounted on her deck at the site where the document had been signed, before reaching New York, where she became flagship of the Atlantic Fleet under Admiral Jonas Ingram.

On 27 October, while she was lying at the Navy Yard berth in the Hudson River, a twenty-one-gun salute was fired for the Commander-in-

President Harry
Truman boarding
Missouri at the
New York Navy
Day celebrations,
27 October 1945.
(NARA)

Chief as President Truman came aboard at 1438 for Navy Day celebrations. He spent just over an hour aboard the ship.[5] The next day the famed Hollywood actors Katharine Hepburn and Fredric March broadcast a war bonds drive from the ship. When she was opened to the public there was a crazy rush for souvenirs. Anything not nailed down was at risk, including porthole scuttles. Visitors even scraped handfuls of souvenir grease out of the gun barrels. After three weeks in the public eye, on 14 November the battleship crossed the bay to Bayonne, where she was de-ammunitioned. She was then overhauled and dry-docked at New York Navy Yard, Brooklyn, where even more material from the battleship where the war had officially ended went missing into the hands of a notoriously sticky-fingered workforce.[6] *Missouri* survived it all and undertook a short shakedown cruise to Cuba in the New Year.

Back in New York, on 21 March 1946 she then undertook possibly the strangest mission of a post-war battleship, and received the remains of the late Turkish Ambassador to the United States, Munir Ertegun. Ertegun had a fascinating diplomatic career, serving under the Ottoman

Missouri (centre) with *Yavuz* (right, in dazzle camouflage) at Istanbul, 5–9 April 1946. *(NARA)*

Emperors until 1920, then transferring his allegiance to Ataturk during the Turkish War of Independence. He served the Turkish Republic at the League of Nations, and then as Ambassador in Switzerland, France, the UK and finally from 1934 the USA. He was famous for his love of jazz and the promotion of many contemporary musicians through appearances at his avant-garde diplomatic parties. His son, Ahmet, thus musically influenced, went on to found the famous Atlantic rock 'n' roll record label. Ertegun senior was Dean (the longest-serving ambassador) of the Washington diplomatic corps when he died in November 1944. His wish was to be buried with his ancestors in Istanbul, so *Missouri* eventually carried the body across the sea, via Gibraltar, and on 5 April arrived in the Bosphorus. She fired a nineteen-gun salute in honour of the late ambassador, and was herself saluted by the host dreadnought, *Yavuz*.

Of course, there was much more to the visit than simply acting as the most extravagant hearse in history. This was the first trip to the Mediterranean by a US battleship since the war and the first to Istanbul for twenty-four years. It was all about showing US support for Turkey at the beginning of the Cold War, and the usual niceties were observed, with

Another view of *Missouri* with *Yavuz. (NARA)*

US officers dining aboard *Yavuz*. The deployment also encompassed Greece, then just slipping into civil war between the communist-backed Second World War resistance movement, and the pro-Western restored government in exile. The USSR was pressing for concessions in the Dodecanese Islands (Greek, but occupied by Italy since the First World War) to be included in the Italian Peace Treaty, and also wanted access for her shipping through the Dardanelles Straits. The USA was already exercising a de facto doctrine of containment of the USSR's potential expansion, and *Missouri*'s trip was trumpeted in the media as a symbol of the US interest in maintaining both Greece's and Turkey's independence. So after leaving Istanbul on 9 April, she stopped over at Piraeus, Greece, on 10 April, staying for over two weeks. A subsequent stop in Naples performed the same function to help cement Italy to the West. It also gave the chance for the ship's Roman Catholic contingent to travel by special train to Rome for a blessing by Pope Pius XII. Although an obvious success, and the foundation for a permanent US naval presence in the Mediterranean, the next visit to those waters by a US battleship was not until 1955.

Missouri returns to Norfolk from the Rio Conference, with President Truman aboard, 19 September 1947. *(NARA)*

Missouri returned to the USA via further port calls at Algiers and Tangier. After only a three-day turnaround at Norfolk, she went to Puerto Rico to join Admiral Marc Mitscher's 8th Fleet exercises, the first full-scale Atlantic Fleet Training manoeuvres after the war. Later in the year, on 13 December during practice firings, *Missouri* herself inadvertently became the target when she was hit by a star shell intended to illuminate the real target. Fortunately no one was injured. During 1947 she conducted further training cruises. Then followed another piece of heavy symbolism in support of the US post-war order as she visited Rio de Janeiro on 30 August 1947 for the Inter American Conference for the Maintenance of Hemisphere Peace and Security. This saw the signing of the Rio Treaty, which extended a US security guarantee to all its signatories (originally virtually all the Latin American nations). The Brazilian authorities presaged their tactics for the hosting of the 2014 Football World Cup and 2016 Olympics by clearing the streets of undesirables. Over 1,000 suspected thieves and pickpockets were arrested in advance of the ship's arrival. President Truman once again came aboard to celebrate the signing on 2 September and hosted Brazilian President Eurico Dutra.

Truman was then joined by his family on 7 September and the ship took them, plus forty reporters, back to the USA, arriving on 19 September. The voyage was enlivened by traditional 'crossing the line' ceremonies, and by a 16in practice shoot. Truman had to keep in touch with Presidential business during the voyage, and a special personal Presidential State Department cipher was used, with the code known only to *Missouri*'s Captain Dennison and his communications officer. Halfway back to the USA a signal was received warning Truman that President Tito of Yugoslavia was threatening to invade the Italian territory of Trieste, still occupied by Allied forces since the end of the war. Dennison brought the telegram to Truman in his cabin, where he was playing poker with his staff. Truman read it without disclosing the contents and to the bemusement of those present said: 'Tell the Son of a Bitch he's going to have to shoot his way in.'[7]

Missouri spent the next six months being overhauled in New York, then the rest of 1948 undertaking midshipman and reservist training cruises to the Caribbean. During these duties she again made history by becoming the first battleship to operate a helicopter detachment of two Sikorsky HO3S-1s on her quarterdeck. In November 1948 she spent three weeks on a cold weather training cruise in the Davis Strait between Greenland and Baffin Island, during which icebergs were used for 16in target practice. The next year was spent on Atlantic Fleet command exercises and two midshipman summer training cruises.

A further overhaul at Norfolk followed between 23 September 1949

Missouri on a midshipman cruise and commemorating the fourth anniversary of the Japanese surrender aboard her, 2 September 1949. *(NARA)*

and mid-December. She got a new captain, William D Brown, towards the end of the overhaul. Brown had thirty years of US Navy experience, but was a wartime submariner and had never commanded a ship larger than a destroyer. He successfully took *Missouri* to sea on 23 December for a shakedown off Cape Hatteras and returned to Norfolk the following day. His next outing was rather briefer and more spectacular.

Missouri sailed for a Caribbean shakedown cruise at 0725 on 17 January 1950. The exit from Norfolk naval base to Chesapeake Bay is narrow and involves a starboard turn after passing Old Point Comfort, then a 13-mile transit down a narrow dredged deep water channel south of the Thimble Shoal. The water over Thimble Shoal is as little as 12ft deep, and the edge of the channel shelves up to it quite abruptly. *Missouri* was due to run along a new acoustic range set up by the US Navy along the northern side of the deep water channel. This was part of the very early testing of technologies that could identify the acoustic signatures of individual ships, and hence contribute to the creation of more sophisticated underwater warfare sensors and weapons. As the subsequent inquiry found, this trial was not properly briefed to all those navigating the ship that morning. There was also confusion about the marking of the range, which had five buoys shown on the charts, but retained only two of them by the time *Missouri* began her voyage.

She correctly identified the buoy marking the start of the acoustic range, which she should have passed to port, but Captain Brown then mistook two buoys further north intended to guide fishing vessels over the shoal as the next markers for the acoustic range, and headed directly for them, out of the dredged channel. After a debate about the proper speed at which to run along the range, he also ordered an increase in speed to 15 knots. This meant that *Missouri* was accelerating and steaming straight out of the channel and heading for the Thimble Shoal. The executive officer and helmsman both warned the captain with increasing urgency that he was standing into danger, but Brown ignored their advice and pressed on with his northerly course. The result was that *Missouri* ploughed at considerable speed through and onto the sand and mud, 1½ miles west of the Thimble Shoal light. Her momentum meant that she strayed over three ship lengths off the deep water channel. Despite last-second attempts to twist her and turn her back south, at 0817 she grounded hard, travelling at 12 knots. She was in a deep load condition displacing 57,666 tons, and grounded at the top of an unusually high tide. She was bodily lifted some 8ft above her usual waterline and was stuck fast with a ground loading estimated at 11,700 tons. Her draught forward was only 27ft 7in (versus what should have been 35ft 4in floating in that condition) and aft 31ft 3in versus 36ft 9in before grounding.

The good news was that the weather was calm and clear, and the shoal was soft, so underwater damage proved negligible, mainly inflicted by an old anchor embedded from a previous seabed wreck. Also, thanks to quick awareness by some of the battleship's engineer officers who were on deck and witnessed the grounding, they were able to shut down all the main engine sea water intakes for the condensers before they ingested too much sand, which, had it happened, would have meant major repairs. However, the extent of the grounding along the whole hull blocking these intakes meant that using her own main engines to free her would not be possible. Tugs made an attempt to tow her later that day but were not successful. A major salvage operation then got under way, led by Rear Admiral Homer N Wallin, Commandant of the Navy Yard at Norfolk. He had been instrumental in salvaging nineteen of the twenty-one ships sunk by the Japanese at Pearl Harbor, so was no stranger to big challenges.

The grounding was a very public event, only a mile off the Virginia shore. It was also only a mile from US Army Fort Monroe, and there was plenty of inter-service joshing while *Missouri* was so prominently stuck aground. Around 10,000 members of the public wrote to the Navy Department with suggestions about how to recover the ship. Her predicament was also exploited in the Soviet *Red Fleet* magazine, which opined that the incident showed the low level of American naval proficiency. Some of the revelations in the Board of Inquiry tended to support them, such as the fact that the seaman stationed at the navigation plot to act as the 'talker' to relay messages between the captain on 08 level deck and the navigator's plot on 04 level was virtually inarticulate under questioning. However, the ultimate laugh would be on the Soviets themselves, as *Missouri* was recovered rapidly enough to make decisive interventions against the communist forces in Korea only a few months later.

Despite the public's suggestions, Admiral Wallin was pretty clear about his plan. The only way to get her off the shoal was to lighten the ship dramatically, and for two intensive weeks, before the next high tides once again worked in favour of the salvage effort, an estimated 11,758 tons of ammunition, fuel, food, anchors and cables and other stores were offloaded by a string of auxiliary vessels and lighters. The final element of lightening the ship was the removal of most of the crew on 30 January – another 80 tons saved. This reduced the estimated ground loading to less than 1,000 tons. In the meantime salvage vessels and dredgers had been busy making a new deep channel 2,500ft long from her stern to simplify manoeuvring her back into the main shipping channel, as well as removing sand from around the ship and loosening the harder compacted areas with high-pressure air hoses to allow a twisting manoeuvre that it was hoped would free her. Pontoons were attached to her sides to help lift the ship a little further. Winches were attached to her deck with their cables run astern to kedge anchors embedded in the sand bank to provide extra power for the attempt. Three destroyers made high-speed runs up the shipping channel in the hope that their wakes would reduce the suction of the mud, but this tactic was abandoned when the resulting waves played havoc with the tugs stationed to try to pull her off.

Although 2 February was the day selected for the main effort with the most favourable tides, a refloating attempt by way of a dress rehearsal took place on 31 January. It failed because *Missouri* became impaled on a previously undetected wreck, and because the tugs at her bow applying the twisting torque were not properly deployed. The next day they tried again, and on 1 February 1950 in heavy fog sixteen tugs and two salvage vessels managed to get her off and backwards up the newly dug escape channel to deep water. Thence she was towed back to Norfolk, with battle

Opposite: *Missouri* aground on Thimble Shoal, with tugs in attendance, January 1950. *(NHHC)*

ensigns flying, as the ship's band played 'Missouri Waltz', 'Anchors Aweigh' and 'Nobody knows the Trouble I've Seen'. Fortunately, despite such a hard strike, the damage was very moderate, with some slight buckling to the bilge keels, and punctures from the undetected wreck holing three of her fuel tanks. It only took five days in dockyard hands for her to be fully repaired. To find the space to repair *Missouri* at short notice her incomplete sister *Kentucky* was floated out of her dry dock at Norfolk Navy Yard.

The unfinished *Kentucky* being moved from Norfolk, Virginia, to Newport News on 20 January 1950 to make room for *Missouri* in the dock at Norfolk. *(NARA)*

Missouri carried out a fully successful post-repair trial as early as 8 February. Although the battleship was quickly back in action, it was curtains for Captain Brown. He pleaded guilty at his court martia, was relieved of command and demoted 250 places in the captain's seniority list. He never commanded a ship at sea again, and reportedly attempted suicide. Captain Irving T. Duke eventually took over to sail her to Korea. The extent of *Missouri*'s damage has been the subject of much speculation since the incident, maybe reflecting its prominence in the public eye in 1950. There were later claims in the Proceedings of the US Naval Institute

of a cracked main armament barbette and a bent keelson, with a permanent speed limitation to 15 knots. These were recycled in later official publications such as the 1969 narrative of the *New Jersey's* tour in Vietnam, and even resurfaced as evidence for the opposition during the battleship recommissioning debates in Congress in the 1980s. It is mystifying (or maybe not in our present world of conspiracies and fake news) how such stories got any subsequent traction when set against the facts of successful repair, rapid deployment and then redeployment in a fully operational condition to Korea, and three years of further unrestricted operations with the active fleet in the 1950s.[8]

France

In France, the ambitious plans to build back after the war meant focussing effort on *Richelieu* and *Jean Bart*. According to one authority, in 1946 the Marine Nationale briefly looked to rehabilitate *Strasbourg* and convert her into a light carrier, but the plan was cancelled due to a lack of funds.[9] It seems unlikely that this was a serious option in view of her damage and the complexity of the project. Wisely, France opted for off the shelf carrier options, but not before seriously considering the conversion of *Jean Bart*.

Both *Richelieu*, and particularly *Jean Bart*, needed a lot of work in 1945 to bring them into full commission. *Richelieu* arrived in Toulon from the Far East on 11 February 1946. She made one brief Magic Carpet-type trip, taking 1,000 Senegalese soldiers back to Dakar on 19 February, then went to Cherbourg, arriving on 7 March to be overhauled in the Homet dry dock. In August 1946 she emerged, and her initial mission was to go to Portsmouth, carrying the first tranche of French sailors destined to become the crew of *Colossus/Arromanches*. From August to November she undertook an autumn cruise to the Mediterranean and North Africa, calling at Casablanca, Arzew, Mers-el-Kébir and Dakar once more, also taking in Portugal, and returning to Cherbourg on 12 December. We have already noted her emergence and salute to *Vanguard* and the Royal Family on 1 February 1947 in the English Channel – the last meeting between these two ships. (They would have been at Portsmouth together the previous August.) Between 15 and 20 April 1947 *Richelieu* took the President of the Republic, Vincent Auriol, on a visit to Dakar, Senegal, her third since the war. In 1947–48 she was the flagship of the 'Force d'Intervention', which was the closest France got to fulfilling the ambition for balanced task forces to support either UN or national operations. It consisted of 'Groupe Richelieu', a cruiser group and the carrier group centred on *Arromanches*. The force's commander, Vice Admiral Jaujard, found that the antiquated command spaces in *Richelieu* were not up to his requirements. A new transmission centre and Combat Information Centre were required and it was hoped to modernise them during a refit in Brest from June to August 1947, but funds for work on this scale were not available. The emergency budget of autumn 1947 had the objective of shoring up the franc and expenditure was severely constrained. As part of this belt tightening there was a moratorium on all new expenditures. This period also saw considerable crew churn and low morale as her complement was reduced due to manning difficulties from 1,375 to 1,100.[10]

Richelieu's 15in guns were also modified at this time to cure a long-identified problem where the blast from the firings of the quadruple turret interfered with the trajectory of the salvo. This resulted in excessive dispersal of the shells at the target, varying from 950 to 1,710 metres. A very slight delay was built into the firing of the outer guns, which resulted in dispersal reducing by two-thirds in gunnery trials carried out at Mers-el-Kébir in May 1948 during a second deployment of the Force d'Intervention. The ship fired sixty-eight rounds while moored to the jetty to improve the accuracy of the measurements. Dispersal was now a maximum of 580m with an average of 300, at a range of 25,000m.

Richelieu at Salin d'Hyeres, near Toulon, 1952. *(H Landais collection)*

The 100mm anti-aircraft battery was also by this stage very antiquated, its design dating from 1931. It had slow rates of fire and fire control algorithms that could not cope with modern, fast-moving aircraft.

Proposals for new German 10.5cm mountings, or an improved 1945 version of the French 100mm mounting as now intended for *Jean Bart*, were both considered in 1949. But these mountings each had twice the weight of those already aboard *Richelieu* (27 tons vs 13 tons). Fitting them would have required bulging the ship (adding blisters to the hull on either side, as was being done for her sister) to retain her stability and keep the armoured deck above the waterline. The financial climate of 1949 precluded such expensive modifications, so she kept her original armament.

Following her return to Brest on 29 May 1948 *Richelieu* then languished for a while. She was docked at Cherbourg in August and September 1948, with the crew reduced to 750. She went into reserve on 1 April 1949, with priority for scarce resources being given to the completion of *Jean Bart*. *Richelieu*'s delayed and cost-constrained major refit finally began at Brest on 1 January 1950, and lasted until 24 November 1951. She had been modernised rather haphazardly during the war and since, and the French Navy recognised that her sensors and anti-aircraft systems were no longer state of the art. But funds were not available for a rebuilding as radical as *Jean Bart*'s so she retained much of her wartime armament, was never bulged and did not get the new anti-aircraft directors as fitted to her sister. Instead the refit focussed on complete overhaul of the machinery and the main and secondary armaments. All eight 15in guns were relined or replaced by pre-war spares recovered from their wartime use in German shore batteries. The machinery overhaul at least was a great success: *Richelieu* sustained an average speed of 31.5 knots when she did her full-power trials on 15 February 1952.[11]

The decision to complete *Jean Bart* was made on 12 February 1945. But it was to be a long tortuous process, partly because of the work needed to rectify war damage; partly because of the weak state of French dockyards and industry generally; partly because although completing her was a firm priority, money and manpower shortages were major constraints; and partly because the ambition to fit her with the most modern all-French anti-aircraft battery led to long delays while the various equipment completed development and trials. *Jean Bart* had been rushed out of St Nazaire so quickly in 1940 to escape the approaching Panzers that much equipment was not installed. She only had two out of four propellers, and by 1945 no 15in guns as the four that were originally aboard had been purloined by *Richelieu* for her 1943 US refit. *Jean Bart* had also been extensively, if superficially, damaged during the Allied invasion of Morocco in November 1942 by aircraft and by shelling from *Massachusetts*. Options to take her to the USA in 1943 for a makeover alongside *Richelieu* were rejected by the Americans. A significant drawback was the lack of 15in guns to equip her. So she had to await the liberation of France before work started. Damage to the dockyards in France and shortage of funds meant that refurbishment was a slow process. So for example, while she arrived in Cherbourg on 29 August 1945, she had to lie alongside the Homet jetty for over two months awaiting the clearance of a basin so a detailed engineer's survey could be carried out. This took place between 11 November and 20 December. She moved to Brest on 11 February 1946, and from 11 March was in No. 8 basin for repairs to the hull and the fitting of new, more spacious superstructures.

During 1945–46 the French Navy debated whether there was any merit in completing *Jean Bart* as an aircraft carrier. Her intrinsic merits and capabilities were set out in a note by the Navy staff dated 20 June 1945.[12] She could do 32 knots, and hence keep up with and provide air cover to *Richelieu*. She would be very robust with her armoured citadel, and could carry three squadrons of aircraft. This transitional plan would give France a carrier able to operate with *Richelieu* by 1950. There was a meeting of the French Navy Board (the Conseil Superieur de la Marine) on 21 September 1945 at which Louis Kahn, chief of naval construction, presented the alternative options of completing her as a 40,000-ton aircraft carrier or as a battleship. Studies had been undertaken that showed she could be converted to carry up to fifty-four aircraft at a cost of about 5 billion Francs (approximately $100 million US or £25 million), with the work taking five years. The case to do so was advocated by Rear Admiral Pierre Barjot, the most outspoken cheer-leader for French naval aviation. Admiral Lemonnier, Chief of the Naval Staff, was less convinced. The conversion was judged uneconomic, as the air wing would be too small to be effective, and a new carrier with much larger aircraft capacity would cost no more than the conversion. Khan was in favour of completing her as a battleship because in his view conversion would require the removal of around 14,000 tons of structure and radical remodelling of the ship's interior, while her fine lines would always restrict the capacity of a hangar to around forty aircraft.[13] Completion of *Jean Bart* as a battleship would only cost 2 billion Francs, although it would take around three to four years to complete manufacture of the main armament and ammunition. Eight new 15in guns would need to be manufactured. The result would provide a command ship with excellent anti-aircraft capability and for use in a shore bombardment role. The choice was between having, by about 1950, either a poor-value carrier based on *Jean Bart*'s hull, or a modern battleship *and* a new-build carrier of around 15,700 tons with an aircraft capacity similar to the battleship conversion, for about the same price. They decided to complete *Jean Bart* as a battleship. The decision was bemoaned by the air power advocates among the French admirals. Barjot was outraged and expressed a belief that there was a critical mass of officers at the top of the Navy in favour of the battleship type and prejudiced against naval aviation. Lemonnier assured the minister that this was not so. The Navy perfectly understood the importance of naval aviation and wanted to secure an aircraft carrier as soon as possible. The unanimous opinion of all the more junior officers consulted was that the conversion of *Jean Bart* to a carrier should have been pursued if she had been less advanced in construction, but as things stood, it made more sense on technical and financial grounds to complete her as a battleship and look for other carrier options. Lemonnier himself favoured construction of an unarmoured carrier, which would be easier for France to build herself.[14]

Work on battleship *Jean Bart* therefore continued, albeit painfully slowly. On 26 November 1947 she emerged from the basin to lie alongside the still incomplete armament jetty at Brest, and her guns and equipment were gradually added. L'État Major Général de la Marine had resumed the manufacture of 15in guns for the ship in 1945, when two were completed at the ordnance factory at Ruelle in the Charente. Three more new guns followed in 1946 and four in 1947. Two stayed at Ruelle for proving, and the other seven were eventually mounted in *Jean Bart*. Her eighth and final gun was one originally mounted in *Richelieu* and removed during her US refit in 1943, and since then held by the US Ordnance depot at Dahlgren, Virginia. The decision to upgrade the anti-aircraft battery, to mount both the new French 1945 model 100mm enclosed mounting (twelve twin turrets), and the new twin 57mm mounting (fourteen twin turrets), plus their directors, radars and other modern equipment meant that the addition of top weight became a major concern. In addition the projected crew requirement had increased from 1,550 as originally designed to around 2,500. Calculations showed that on her projected new

Jean Bart, still incomplete, at Brest in 1949. *(Robert Dumas)*

displacement the armoured deck would be below the waterline, making her very vulnerable to flooding in a damaged state, even if the armour was unpenetrated. The solution was to fit an external bulge of 1.1m depth along the entire length of the armoured citadel. This work in No. 9 basin took from 20 March to 9 October 1948. The propeller shafts were also repaired at this point.

On 4 December 1948 she was finally ready for a short sea trial in the approaches to Brest. There is Pathé news film footage of this excursion, showing her being manoeuvred by tugs, then in the roadstead under her own steam, with the number two 15in turret trained to port. Although the 15in main and 6in (152mm) secondary battery is installed, there are still no main armament directors, no anti-aircraft armament and very few fittings of any kind on the superstructure. A more extensive trip of 1,000 miles to Belle Isle took place from 8 to 11 January 1949. This was followed by firings of the 15in guns on the Ile de Groix ranges, and full-power trials on 16 January. She now displaced 48,180 tons fully loaded, but still managed a top speed of 32.13 knots at 180,000 shp. This makes her the second-fastest battleship ever, only marginally bested by the exceptional *Iowa* class.

Trials and repairs followed over the next few months, but the ship was formally commissioned at the end of January 1949, the last new battleship in the world to be commissioned. Although this is commonly quoted as her completion date, she was still far from finished, and was not declared ready for front-line service until 1955, more than eighteen years after her keel had been laid. In 1949 she became part of a battleship squadron with *Richelieu*, under the flag of Rear Admiral Branellec. In practice this was a toothless force with *Richelieu* laid up in reserve and *Jean Bart* seemingly languishing with very little progress since the burst of activity at the turn of 1948–49. She did sea trials from 6 to 9 February 1949 following damage to No. 1 boiler room sustained during the January steaming. Firing trials continued at Groix on 1 June 1949, but there then seems to have been a period of nearly a year through until April 1950 at Brest with very little activity, and, to judge from contemporary photos, very little obvious progress towards completion. There was still no anti-aircraft battery (other than interim mountings of 40mm and 20mm guns). Production of the 100mm and 57mm guns was delayed because of credit difficulties.[15]

Meanwhile, on 15 April 1950 L'État Major Général de la Marine decided to create a new grouping of vessels in the Mediterranean, and *Jean Bart* was finally let off the leash, passing under command of Vice-Admiral Lambert in the Mediterranean fleet. She did some final trials around Brittany from 27 April until 17 May 1950, then left Brest on 20 May 1950, and joined up with the Mediterranean Squadron. She then made a series of calls and exercises along the Tunisian and Algerian coasts between 25 May and 13 June, before returning to her wartime haven of Casablanca on 15 June. Admiral Lambert finally hoisted his flag in her on 23 June at Casablanca, and she left on 26 June and returned to Brest on 30 June. She seems to have been at Brest for the next ten months before conducting further trials and training in May, June and July 1951. She was moored alongside the Quai d'Armement for the whole of 1952. It was only at this point that the new 100mm and 57mm guns with the associated fire control radars were finally available to be fitted, and the interim 40mm anti-aircraft armament was removed.[16]

It is convenient to note the passing of the older French battleships at this point. *Paris* continued as a depot ship for the flotillas of the 2nd Maritime Region at Brest for over a decade after her return from the UK, finally being sold for scrap on 21 December 1955, redesignated as Q64 and broken up at La Seyne, Toulon, from 1956. Salvage work on the wreck of *Bretagne* in Mers-el-Kébir was desultory for over a decade after her sinking. She was finally cut up in situ and scrapped from 1952 to 1954 to make way for expansion of the French military base. *Lorraine* remained based at Toulon and undertook a cruise to Calvi and Algiers in 1946. She was in active fleet service until February 1947, when she was immobilised due to personnel shortages. She was then used first as a stationary gunnery training ship until 1950, then as a barracks ship until decommissioned on 29 November 1952, stricken in 1953 and sold that December to be scrapped at Brégaillon, Toulon, from 1954. The hulk of *Dunkerque* remained neglected in Toulon Roadstead until sold for final demolition on 30 September 1958. As for *Strasbourg*, she was used as an experimental ship to test the impact of underwater explosions in the Bay of Giens near Toulon. She spent a decade in this role, before being sold on 27 May 1955 for 458 million francs ($1,208,000) for scrapping at Toulon. The very slow progress to scrap some of the older French ships seems peculiar given that Director of Naval Construction Louis Khan had identified shortages of steel as one of the major constraints in pressing ahead with construction of France's indigenous aircraft carrier in 1946.[17]

CHAPTER EIGHT

Cuts to the Royal Navy

EVEN AS THE crowds gathered on the cliff tops of Prussia Cove to wonder at *Warspite*'s predicament, a more far-reaching predicament faced Attlee's Labour Government concerning the collapsing UK economy. The affordability of defence as a whole, including the maintenance and manning of the Navy, came under intense scrutiny. In summer 1947 the UK was still working to the post-war fleet template set out in autumn 1945, which involved one battleship active in the Home Fleet, three in the Training Squadron, and six in reserve, for a total of ten battleships available in case of general war (*Vanguard*, four *King George Vs*, *Nelson*, *Rodney*, *Queen Elizabeth*, *Valiant* and *Renown*).

Discussions at the Admiralty Board on future defence policy and Navy peacetime requirements in July 1947 slightly modified this. A paper submitted to the Board on 26 July 1947 identified three tasks for the Navy in peace: forming a nucleus for expansion in wartime; training for war; and providing a police force to protect and further British interests, which also served as a source for any UN contribution. The total fleet requirement for this, including Dominion contributions, was eight battleships, ten fleet carriers, twenty-five light carriers and thirty-five cruisers. There would also be 135 destroyers and 332 escorts, with a front-line air strength of 1,000. Mobilisation would require 382,000 personnel, with peacetime strength to be 191,000. The overall cost of this fleet would be £236 million in 1948–49, rising to £465 million by 1954–55.

There would be two large tactical training forces, one in Home waters and one in the Mediterranean, each consisting of one battleship, three carriers, three cruisers and thirty destroyers; and a light tactical training force of two carriers, a cruiser and sixteen escorts. Two more battleships would be harbour training ships, and two carriers occupied with trials and training. One battleship, four carriers and fourteen cruisers would form the core of the police force. The wartime requirement was six battleships and thirty-one carriers. The paper noted: 'No allowance has been made for the replacement of existing battleships by more modern Capital Ships. Should R&D show this to be necessary and also indicate the lines on which it should be done, further heavy expenditure would be necessary.' The maintenance requirement for the projected fleet therefore assumed battleship numbers would be dwindling from ten in 1948 to nine in 1949, eight in 1951 and six by 1957 as the older ships reached the ends of their economic lives.

The 26 July paper recognised that this scale of effort was an ideal informed by strategic and intelligence assessments, but that it was unlikely to be achievable in the prevailing economic climate, nor could the necessary naval manpower be generated. It accepted that the introduction of the tactical training forces be abandoned for the time being and that only three or four battleships would be in commission in peacetime, two with reduced crews, and only eight carriers, with 185 front-line aircraft.

A second paper by the Secretary dated 28 July 1947 revised the proposed programme to meet an anticipated overall defence expenditure cap of £600 million, of which the Navy might receive £180 million. The main penalty was borne by new construction, which was all but eliminated for five years, and only four carriers would be modernised, condemning the rest to obsolescence because they could not operate new aircraft types. There would be a total of three battleships and nine carriers operating between 1948 and 1953, and 190 front-line aircraft. The reserve fleet would also take a big hit to save on manpower and maintenance, with many ships being put up for disposal.[1] At the Admiralty Board on 31 July it was gloomily accepted that the plans were incapable of delivery because of shortage of capacity in shipbuilding and dockyards, and that there was no hope of the Government authorising expenditure on the scale envisaged in the memorandum.[2]

A V Alexander, erstwhile First Lord of the Admiralty, but since 1946 the co-ordinating Minister of Defence, had recognised early in 1947 that the post-war plans for imperial defence were wildly unaffordable. There were also reinforcing arguments to rebalance the economy by further reducing the 1,070,000 regulars of all three services still in uniform, as well as reducing the UK's armed forces overseas footprint to lessen the UK balance of payments burden. There is an early hint of this retrenchment and its impact on the battleships on 7 January 1947, even before the *Warspite* announcement was made, when the Admiralty staff was minuting that: 'The First Lord [Hall] requires as soon as possible the savings in manpower and money which would arise if *Nelson*, *Rodney*, *Queen Elizabeth*, *Valiant* and *Renown* were scrapped,' and also the manpower required to hold them at Category A (immediate readiness) and B (extended) reserve.[3]

Alexander eventually set out his thinking for the Cabinet Defence Committee in a lengthy paper titled 'Defence Requirements', DO (47) 68 dated 15 September 1947. His initial guidance to the Chiefs of Staff at the beginning of 1947 had been that the nation could not afford a long-term defence budget greater than £600 million a year. The work over the summer by the service departments had produced bids that were likely to exceed £900 million annually. 'It followed that some drastic change of policy which hitherto the Chiefs of Staff have followed would be necessary.' Based on a £600 million ceiling, 'it must be accepted that the risk of a major war is ruled out during the next five years, and that this risk will increase only gradually in the following five years ... if attacked we must fight with what we have.'[4] This was a new and very explicit version of the controversial 'Ten Year Rule' from the inter-war years.

Within competing bids, priority needed to be given to forces giving a visible show of deterrent and deployable strength, and to long-term research and development investment. The Navy should be maintained at the minimum level needed to safeguard sea communications, undertake overseas commitments, and to provide a nucleus of strength from which to expand in a future emergency. 'This policy will require a scaling down of Naval Plans, more especially as regards large capital ships. It implies concentration on the naval air arm and retention of cruisers and below in adequate numbers.'

Looking specifically at the financial year 1948–49, Alexander realised that his £600 million target could not be reached so quickly, but he nonetheless proposed trimming a revised and reduced Chiefs of Staff bid for £825 million to just £711 million. This would be achieved by drastic manpower cuts from just over 1 million previously approved for March 1948 across the three armed services to 713,000 in March 1949. The Navy's share would be a reduction from 178,000 to 147,000, and a contraction in the budget from an estimate of £211 million to between £150 and £163 million.[5] The consequences for the Navy included a large scrapping programme for the ships currently held in reserve, to include five battleships, eleven cruisers and up to sixty destroyers and frigates. Active strength in the Home Fleet would come down to one battleship, one carrier, three cruisers and eight destroyers (plus the Training Squadron). All new construction would be suspended, except one aircraft carrier, and all modernisation of older aircraft carriers was to be deferred. The Navy was not the only service to suffer. For comparison, the Army was to reduce from 113 to seventy-two regular infantry battalions, of which only twenty-four would be fully operational.

This was a drastic programme. Its fiscal imperative was reinforced by the 1947 convertibility crisis. The terms of the US agreement to loan the UK $3.75 billion in July 1946 to pay for the UK's overseas security commitments included the requirement to make sterling convertible one year later. Within a month of the start of convertibility nations with sterling balances had exchanged them for dollars and drained almost $1 billion from the United Kingdom's reserves. This forced the Government to suspend convertibility and begin drastic cuts in domestic and overseas expenditure. The pound was inevitably devalued from $4.02 to $2.80 in 1949.

Against this background, and given the extent of continuing and intractable overseas garrison commitments, in the absence of a clear and present large-scale international crisis with a naval dimension, the Admiralty was unlikely to prevail in any rearguard action to retain a larger reserve navy, or the older battleships. But the reluctance to bite the bullet is evident in Lord Hall's memorandum of 5 December 1947, which, he said 'does not include the scrapping of the five battleships on which I am not prepared to take a decision without further consultation with my colleagues in the Defence Committee and without their being more fully apprised of the strategic, political, financial and manpower implications than was possible when DO(47)68 was under consideration.' A draft of the paper for the Defence Committee reinforced Hall's reluctance, arguing that: 'In these circumstances I conclude that a decision should now be taken on the scrapping of at any rate of *Nelson* and *Rodney* and that the scrapping of the other three capital ships named should also be considered.' The cost of keeping all of them in reserve was thought to be very small, just £25,000, and only 400 men at a further cost of £100,000 would be needed as ship keepers. Vice Chief of the Naval Staff, Vice Admiral Sir John Edelsten, responded on 6 December arguing against half measures: 'there can but be only one conclusion and that is to scrap the lot. This continued vacillation over these ships is intolerable and throwing out of gear the restoration of the fleet ... these ships are of little worth and we cannot afford to spend a penny on them. First Sea Lord Sir John Cunningham still sat on the fence, minuting on 8 December that 'the only ship which so far we can say might be of any value in a future war is the *Renown*'.[6]

The formal Admiralty response to Alexander's paper came on 15 December 1947, as DO(47)96 by the First Lord of the Admiralty, Lord Hall entitled 'Disposal of certain HM Ships'. It made minor suggestions to amend the scrapping schedule for cruisers and escorts, which were otherwise accepted in principle, but requested Cabinet Defence Committee endorsement for the scrapping proposals for the five battleships. The first argument was a table setting out the relative strengths of the UK and other navies in battleships, divided into effective modern units and others. The US was assessed to have fourteen of the former, six of the latter, the UK five of each, France two modern ships and one older one (*Lorraine*), Russia five older ones (including a distrustful double counting of *Royal Sovereign* and their yet to be delivered Italian war prize), and Italy two old ships. The Turkish and South American dreadnoughts were also tabulated for completeness.

The paper continued: 'It can be seen that in certain circumstances we might have to guard against a possible combination of two effective modern battleships, three effective but not modern and four very much less effective units, i.e. the total European battleship strength ... At present the Royal Navy has five effective modern ships and five others. Allied to the United States we should have nineteen effective modern battleships and eleven others. If our five less effective units were scrapped, we should be left in the Royal Navy alone with five effective modern ships, which by themselves are considered more than a match for the five best units which could in the worst possible case be operated against us … It is clear that from considerations of our own defence and the balance of sea power, even without aid from the United States, the retention of more than our five most modern battleships is hard to justify under the present circumstances of urgent need for economy in money and manpower, even when we consider the possibility of all the foreign Capital Ships in Europe coming to be at the disposal of an enemy. The capacity of any potential enemy to challenge control of our sea communications by embarking on a programme of new construction must of course be constantly watched and provided against.' It is striking that at the turn of 1947–48, in none of these papers is the potential for carriers and their aircraft to redress the balance of surface power argued or discussed.

DO(47)96 continues with a brief discussion of the advantage conferred at any hypothetical future disarmament conference by retaining the five older ships as bargaining counters. The paper then lists the considerable cost required to maintain the five ships in fighting trim, which would nonetheless still require acceptance of their fundamental limitations in terms of age and speed. *Nelson* would cost £2 million to refit. *Rodney* 'is in extremely poor condition and has of necessity been berthed in a graving dry dock as she would otherwise have sunk at her moorings through continual leaks'. She would take not less than £2 million and two years to rectify. *Renown* would take £1 million and eighteen months, *Valiant* an extravagant £750,000 despite her recent major refit at Devonport, and *Queen Elizabeth* £1 million and eighteen months in dock. This total of at least £7 million was the bare minimum required to put the ships into a state of preservation in reserve. A further £4 to 5 million would be needed to bring them into service at a later date. The necessary dockyard resource would be substantial, and could be provided only at the expense of reductions in the maintenance of the active fleet. The 400 personnel required to keep these ships in even the lowest category of reserve had already been predicated as savings as part of the wider challenge to man the Navy within the 147,000 long-term ceiling.

The paper also provides an interesting sidelight on the fate of *Lion* and *Temeraire*, and the future Heavy Ship: 'There is no intention at present of embarking on a programme of Capital Ship replacement and there cannot in my mind be any question of doing so at least until the results of research and development have progressed sufficiently to throw more light on the form and armament of the Capital Ship of the future.' So, at the end of 1947 the missile-armed heavy ship was still distantly anticipated, but the Royal Navy would have to manage with just five conventional battleships in the interim.

Lord Hall concluded: 'In the circumstances outlined the Naval Staff are satisfied that there will be no use in their present condition for the five battleships under consideration for the next ten years. Their value even if modernised as far as practicable at the considerable cost indicated, would be doubtful and we shall in any event require the money for the modernisation of our Aircraft Carriers which must be given first priority. I agree and conclude that a decision should now be taken on the scrapping of *Nelson*, *Rodney*, *Queen Elizabeth*, and *Valiant*, and that the scrapping of *Renown* should also be considered.'

Given the coinciding views of the Naval Staff, First Lord and Minister for Defence, and the economic backdrop, it is not surprising that no voice of protest was raised at the Cabinet Defence Committee discussion of this paper on 19 December 1947. The minutes state: 'There was general agreement that in the light of the considerations set out in DO(47)96 all five battleships should be scrapped and that provided the decision to scrap these ships was announced in suitable terms as part of a process of modernising the fleet, it would have no adverse effect either in the UK or abroad.'[7] The case to save *Renown* because of her higher speed was debated, but rejected. Prime Minister Attlee approved the terms of the Parliamentary announcement on 18 January and it was made by the Civil Lord, Mr Walter Edwards MP, in Parliament on 21 January 1948. In view of potential sensitivities about the perception that losing these ships might cause, the Prime Minister was advised by his office to consider attending the announcement in person.

Mr Edwards said: 'The battleship strength of the Royal Navy has been under review in the light of the age and material condition of the ships concerned and their possible value in a future emergency ... as a result of the review the Admiralty have come to the conclusion that of the capital ships remaining in the Royal Navy, *Queen Elizabeth*, *Valiant*, *Renown*, *Nelson* and *Rodney* are likely to be of the least value as fighting ships. The possibility of maintaining the battleships in reserve was taken into consideration but they would be costly to maintain in this state both in money and manpower. Moreover, if they were to be of any value in a future emergency they would need extensive refits and modernisation, which, in view of the heavy costs and labour involved, could not be justified during the next few years. Even if the work was done, the vessels would fall considerably short of the standard and capabilities of modern construction. In particular their speed could not be increased to such an extent as to render them capable of taking their place in a modern fleet. In view of the above considerations, instructions have been issued that these vessels should now be scrapped ... The Admiralty is satisfied that these reductions do not reduce the effective strength of the Navy below that required to meet any emergency which is likely to arise in the foreseeable future.'[8]

Parliamentary reaction on the day was muted. Only Sir R Ross argued for the retention of *Nelson* and *Rodney*. Many of the questions concerned the potential scrap benefit of the decision, which Mr Edwards, probably conservatively, estimated at 82,000 tons. There was a more robust objection by the House of Lords at a debate on 8 March 1948, again initiated by Lord Howe, with a number of contributors viewing the international signal such a decision would send as very regrettable, but Lord Hall naturally stuck to his guns.

It was, nevertheless, felt necessary to reassure the Dominion governments by telegram the same day as the Parliamentary announcement that the decision had been given very careful consideration, and that: 'Apart from the United States which has fourteen modern battleships, there are in existence in the world only two modern French battleships and some four or five ancient vessels which even together would not provide an effective combination against our strength of five modern vessels.' This footnote to the discussion reflects its whole tenor, that the decision to do without these five ships was justifiable purely on the basis that the battleship balance of world power was still the appropriate yardstick by which to make such judgements. Had the answer in this like-for-like comparison been less clear cut then no doubt more sophisticated arguments might have been made about the overall balance of naval strength, where the UK's relative preponderance in carriers and other surface ships would also have counted. But it is revealing that two and a half years after the war ended a Cabinet debate could still be couched in such traditional, one-dimensional terms, and also that the UK Government could be thinking in terms of a complete European collapse placing all French and Italian battleships intact in hostile hands.

Further evidence of continuing battleship-centred thinking in the UK Government during 1947 is also revealed by the discussions during that year about the final fate of the surrendered Italian battlefleet. We have seen how Sir Andrew Cunningham feared, and Churchill coveted, the two modern *Littorio*-class battleships *Vittorio Veneto* and *Italia*. Churchill had minuted in early October 1943, only three weeks after the Italian surrender: 'We cannot afford to allow units of the Italian Navy to remain idle whether at Alexandria or elsewhere. My present idea is to suggest to the Americans that the *Littorios* go to the US to be fitted for the Pacific Warfare and to be used there by them. I would also suggest to the President that after the war the ships be ceded to us because: first we had the main part of the war against them; secondly we have had heavy losses in capital units; and thirdly we have discontinued building capital units in order to

Italia (left) and *Vittorio Veneto* (right) at Augusta after returning from Egypt in 1947. *(T Marconi)*

further current short term operations. I am sure such a proposal will be received in a most friendly spirit …'[9]

A week later the First Lord replied to Churchill: 'We have not felt able to advise on the ultimate fate of the *Littorios* because we should first like to have them thoroughly examined in an allied dockyard port. We believe this should be done in an American port.' Churchill kept agitating. On 7 April 1944 the First Lord responded to a further enquiry about what resource would be required to fit the *Littorios* for war against Japan. The answer was nine months in a good dockyard, 1,300 men and £700,000 per ship.

Churchill duly proposed to President Roosevelt in March 1944 that the UK might wish to keep both ships after the war as compensation for UK losses in the Mediterranean, and to make good the battleships whose laying down had been suspended during the war. On 29 August 1944 First Lord A V Alexander minuted that he had agreed with First Sea Lord Cunningham that the twelve battleships envisaged for the post-war Royal Navy would be four *King George Vs*, *Vanguard*, two *Nelsons*, two *Littorios*, *Renown* and two *Queen Elizabeths*.[10] Roosevelt appears to have played this issue long. In due course the USA asserted a claim to one of the Italian ships.

The First Lord of the Admiralty set out a memorandum on the disposal of the Italian battleships for Cabinet on 11 July 1945.[11] He recalled that the Russian demand for one battleship, one cruiser and eight

Vittorio Veneto and *Italia* at La Spezia, late 1948 or 1949. Minimum destruction has been undertaken with funnels gone and gun barrels sawn off. *(Erminio Bagnasco)*

destroyers as a share of the Italian fleet had been made in October 1943 and agreed with Stalin at the Tehran conference (28 November– 1 December 1943). The Combined Chiefs of Staff had objected to the immediate transfer of Italian ships because they felt it would seriously prejudice Italian co-operation as co-belligerents in the war against Germany, where the UK was relying on Italian help on communications and dockyards to sustain the Italian campaign. The Prime Minister had personally suggested the transfer of *Royal Sovereign*, UK destroyers and a US cruiser as a loan to meet the Russian demands. This meant the Russians still had an unsatisfied mortgage on the Italian fleet for one battleship, one cruiser, eight destroyers and four submarines. France and Greece claimed some smaller vessels, and the USA had made no claims. Politically, the Admiralty suggested, France and Greece would want to see Italy substantially disarmed, the Royal Navy would want total suppression of the Italian submarine fleet, but Italy, and its navy in particular, had played an important role as co-belligerents against the Axis powers. The need was to find a solution that met the various Allied claims for ships, removed Italy as the largest Mediterranean navy, but did not permanently estrange that country.

The solution proposed was to meet the Soviet claim in full, but using an older *Cavour*-class battleship. 'We do not as things have turned out, require either of the two *Littorio*-class battleships – one of which is damaged – for the Pacific War. The question of adding those ships to our post-war seagoing fleet requires careful consideration as they have certain drawbacks.' These included lower fuel endurance than British ships, lighter construction, inadequate distilling equipment and difficulty in spares and ammunition supply. Major alterations and modernisation would be needed to make the ships compatible for operation in the Royal Navy. But: 'The ships would prove useful to us in any event for training and other purposes. The main consideration is that such powerful ships should not be in unreliable, particularly Russian, hands.'

The memorandum concluded that the UK should claim both of the modern ships (or one if the United States also wanted one) in order to prevent them falling into unreliable hands. 'We should persist in this claim through the treaty negotiations until the Russian claim is satisfied by a *Cavour*. Once the peace treaty was signed we should appropriate the ships, unless ultimately it was considered necessary to be more lenient with the Italian fleet.' So, at this early point it seems that the Admiralty, while wanting the ships, was prepared to consider leaving the *Littorios* in Italian hands, but only once it was sure they could not go to Russia. As to *Royal Sovereign*, apart from a sentimental wish to recover her, the Admiralty saw no practical advantage. She and the other old vessels on loan would be placed in reserve on their return and find their way to the scrapyard. 'Accordingly the Admiralty would not object to these British ships being left with the Russians if we could thereby secure some countervailing advantage.'

In essence this plan worked. The UK made its claim, and in December 1946 at a foreign ministers meeting in New York, Mr Molotov for the Soviet Union agreed the overall treaty texts. The division of the Italian fleet would see the two *Littorios* going one each to the US and UK, and *Giulio Cesare* to Russia; and the USSR would return the US and UK ships then on loan. Italy would be permitted to keep just *Duilio* and *Andrea Doria*. This deal was reflected explicitly in the final peace treaty and its accompanying protocols. The treaty between the Allies and Italy was signed in February 1947 and ratified in September. Annex XIII A specified that Italy was to keep only two old battleships. Annex XIII B stated that the other three active battleships were allocated to the victorious Allies. A four-power Naval Commission of the Allies (also including France) then agreed how to divide up the spoils and reconfirmed the Tehran principle that one Italian battleship would go to the Soviet Union. *Vittorio Veneto* went to UK, *Italia* to the USA and the far older and less capable *Cesare* was selected for the Soviet Union. The two *Littorios* were allowed back to Italy from their hideaway in the Great Bitter Lake in February 1947 after signature of the treaty and were based at Augusta in Sicily while their ultimate fate was decided.

However, political opinion in Italy regarded the surrender of their modern battleships as harsh recompense for the assistance given to the Allied cause after September 1943. In June 1946 Admiral Sir Algernon Willis, Commander-in-Chief Mediterranean, had written to First Sea Lord worried about losing control of the *Littorios* in the Great Bitter Lakes, and suggesting that they be moved to Malta to reduce the risks of the crews scuttling them in the event that they were allocated to the United Nations and thence the UK and USA.[12] There was no scuttle, but, although the Treaty was explicit that they would not have them, soon after its signature the Italians began to press for the return of the ships. They preferred scrapping them to turning the ships over to another power, especially France, which had requested one or both. Failure to save *Italia* from transfer to the USA prompted the resignation of Admiral de Courten as Italian Navy Minister on 14 July 1947 (and later as Chief of the General Staff). But by this stage the British Admiralty showed a renewed determination to keep *Vittorio Veneto*.[13] Their case was set out in a telegram to the British Defence Staff in Washington DC: 'The Admiralty are still unwilling to return *Vittorio Veneto* to the Italians. During Treaty negotiations strenuous efforts were made to secure the battleship for our own share and arguments consistently used were that we needed it for ourselves. We are unwilling to take actions now which would show such arguments were false. Moreover they do in fact still apply. *Vittorio Veneto* is still required by Admiralty, although proposed use will not be decided until there has been a chance of inspecting the ship ...' The next document on the file is unreferenced but is probably a Foreign Office appreciation, noting that the USA position is that they will return their allocation of ships including *Italia* to Italy and are pressing the UK to do the same. 'The Soviets made strong claims during the treaty negotiations to receive one or both of *Vittorio Veneto* and *Italia* but without success. It is necessary to emphasise the reasons for which we insisted the *Vittorio Veneto* be denied to Russia. The immediate political impression of such a ship sailing under the Russian flag through the Mediterranean, through the Turkish straits and into the Black Sea would be deplorable ... there is no doubt that she would be considered to have entirely altered the balance of power in the Black Sea, particularly vis a vis the Turks.' The concern was that the return of *Vittorio Veneto* to Italy would allow the Russians to reopen the Treaty negotiations and make a prior claim on her. However, the US position concerning *Italia* had already opened that possibility. An annex to this document summarises the material characteristics of the three battleships under discussion. *Italia* is described as having severe underwater damage dating from the German bombing in 1943, and could only steam at 17 knots. *Cesare* was rated in poor condition and laid up with only 20 per cent of her crew.[14]

A briefing note dated 3 October 1947 for the First Lord's meeting to discuss Admiralty concerns with the Foreign Secretary Ernest Bevin gives some insight into what they planned to do with *Vittorio Veneto*. 'We have laid down a refitting programme to prepare the ship for use as a controlled target; owing to the cuts [see above] it will not be possible to use her for this purpose. The most she could be used for would be ship target trials ... If we return the ship [to Italy] the Russians would consider themselves justified in reopening the whole question of allocation of Italian ships and claim one at least of the battleships in place of the ancient *Cesare* with which they were fobbed off. If they succeed the effect on Turkey and the Eastern Mediterranean would be deplorable.' The First Lord was advised to agree to the handing back only if the Foreign Secretary was completely confident he could resist Russian demands to reopen the allocation.

Count Sforza, the Italian Foreign Minister, visited Britain at the end of October 1947 to make representations to Bevin, who minuted Prime Minister Attlee on 29 October: 'As I had expected in my first talk with the Italian Foreign Minister he at once raised the question of the Italian battleship ... Count Sforza represented to me the very great sentimental importance which is attached by the Italian people to this point, and the bitterness which would be caused if we stood by our treaty rights.'[15]

The Count went on to point out the scale of Italian Navy losses during co-belligerency, which he put at sixty-five ships, including two battleships [presumably he referred to *Roma* sunk by the Germans and *Cavour*, ultimately sunk by the Allies], and over 3,000 men. It seemed to the Italian people unjust that their navy, which had played the most significant role of all their armed forces in the co-belligerent period, should be penalised so heavily by the treaty. Bevin confessed to being impressed by the Count's arguments. 'I think he is as anxious as I am to restore really friendly relations between the two countries. You will, I feel sure, agree this is an important objective and that to reach it we must be prepared to make some concessions.' Bevin also pointed out that the USA had agreed to hand back its allocation of ships to Italy, and was pressing the UK to do the same.

But there were difficulties: 'The Admiralty are opposed to returning the battleship for both professional and sentimental reasons. Above all there is the scrap value of the battleship to the United Kingdom in our present steel drive.' He estimated the salvage at 20,000 tons of steel, 7,000 more of armour plate, as well as non-ferrous metals. The dire economic position meant that the Italian fleet was as valuable a raw material asset to the UK as it was a political or naval one. Nonetheless, Bevin concluded that the political advantages were in favour of giving *Vittorio Veneto* back. He sought authority to tell Count Sforza that the UK Government would hand back its allocation of Italian ships, but only for scrapping, sinking or conversion to non-military use; and to try to reach a separate agreement with Italy for it to let the UK have an equivalent amount of scrap as that which would be generated by the battleship, at no greater cost than the UK Government would have paid to scrap her itself.

In order to get an answer to Sforza before he left the UK, Clement Attlee agreed to a snap discussion of the issue at Cabinet the very next day, and the Economic Policy Committee met on 30 October 1947.[16] Bevin reiterated his conversation with Sforza and his proposal to return the ship.

Lord Hall spoke for the Admiralty, and pointed out that the overall British claim had already been reduced to three tiny motor torpedo boats and *Vittorio Veneto*. 'If the Foreign Secretary's proposal were accepted the Italian Government would be left in possession of two very modern battleships. This was a situation which caused the Admiralty very great anxiety since they felt the Italian Government would be under as strong a pressure to refuse to carry out the Treaty requirements for scrapping of these ships as they were to resist handing them over to the Allied powers. The French and Turkish Governments would be greatly disturbed at a decision to leave a second modern battleship in Italian hands. It had also to be remembered that the French Navy possessed two powerful and modern battleships. In view of political developments on the Continent account should be taken of the possibility that in certain circumstances these four battleships might pass into hostile hands. This would create a menacing situation in the Mediterranean. The Admiralty had not reached any decision regarding the disposal of *Vittorio Veneto* after its transfer to the UK under the terms of the Peace Treaty, but there was a possibility that after thorough examination a proposal might be put forward for her conversion for use as a unit of the Royal Navy. This could be done at a cost of between £1 and £1 ½ millions, which would be substantially less than the cost of modernising *Nelson* and *Rodney*.'

The Minister of Defence, A V Alexander, supported the views of the First Lord of the Admiralty. 'Having regard to the losses which the Royal Navy had suffered in the Mediterranean during the war as a result of the Italian intervention there would be a good deal of criticism if the *Vittorio Veneto* were now handed back to the Italian Government.'

Notwithstanding the political and emotional arguments of the defence establishment, and its possible desire to incorporate the ship into the Royal Navy (implausible as that sounded when set against the parallel staff work noted above to reduce the Navy to just five modern battleships), these views did not hold sway. The minutes record that the general view of the Committee was that in present circumstances the overriding consideration must be the political objective of preventing Italy aligning herself with the communist bloc. The Committee therefore invited the Foreign Secretary to inform Sforza that the UK Government were prepared to leave the *Vittorio Veneto* in Italian hands, on the conditions, first, that the scrapping of the vessel would begin within a prescribed period and proceed at a prescribed rate, and that if these conditions were not fulfilled the UK Government would reassert their full rights in respect of the vessel under the treaty; and second, that satisfactory arrangements were made for the sale of the scrap equivalent of the *Vittorio Veneto* to the UK Government. The Minister of Defence was additionally invited to raise with the Commander-in-Chief of United States Naval Forces in Europe the question of whether the United States Government were prepared to take appropriate measures to ensure that the Italian Government would not fail to scrap the battleship allocated to the USA under the peace treaty (*Italia*).

The next day Bevin reported back to Cabinet on a further discussion with Count Sforza. Alongside the announcement of the return of the ships it was proposed to include in an exchange of letters with Italy an undertaking that *Vittorio Veneto* would be scrapped, and that an equivalent amount of scrap should be sold by Italy to the UK at cost price within twelve months. The Committee agreed that this was a good deal as it would probably secure the scrap metal in a shorter period than it would take to scrap the battleship itself.

So, the surprisingly persistent Churchillian dream of incorporating the *Littorio* class into the Royal Navy finally expired more than four years after the Italian surrender, under the twin pressures of United Kingdom economic stringency and fears that appropriating the battleships would alienate Italy from the West. But there were still twists and turns to play out. By October 1947 both the USA and the UK had agreed to return their ships to Italy. The former was motivated by a desire to make the scrap available to boost the recovery of the Italian economy. There was a provision in the Treaty that they should be scrapped by 15 June 1948. But the strategic fears about the battleship balance of power in the Mediterranean were roused once again as evidence mounted that the Italians were trying to retain the ships rather than scrap them. Velicogna says that the Italian Navy tried to save *Italia* by issuing a covert order to slow the demilitarisation process and preserve as much of her equipment as possible, and that eventually these efforts provoked the ire of the Allied Naval Armistice Commission, which ordered the destruction of the 15in guns.[17] US diplomatic sources indicate that the effort to retain the *Littorios* probably had some wider support in Italy.

On 21 January 1948 the US ambassador in Rome was reporting that the Four Power Naval Commission were concerned about the absence of arrangements to supervise the scrapping, and that the Italians would not meet the 15 June deadline. An interim list of measures to achieve 'minimum destruction' of hull, machinery, armament and electrical systems was agreed by Italy with a deadline of 15 April. On 15 March Ambassador Dunn reported that dismantling of *Vittorio Veneto* and *Italia* was proceeding very slowly. By 12 April his information was that Italy would shortly ask for a general revision of the naval clauses of the Treaty, but he expected the French to vigorously oppose such action, in particular the retention by Italy of any modern battleships. Two weeks later he said that he had received several indications that Italy was seriously thinking of trying to avoid scrapping the ships. He expected France, the UK and Russia would all refuse to entertain the idea, the last now motivated by disappointment that the Italian General Election on 18 April had dashed immediate hopes of a communist government and returned the pro-Western Christian Democrats with a decisive majority.

On 15 May the State Department told Dunn that the Italian embassy in Washington D.C. had made informal approaches about substituting the new battleships for *Duilio* and *Andrea Doria* in the Italian Navy. They were clear that the US would oppose such a move, expecting the other Allied powers to do likewise, and felt there was no genuine justification for a request to retain *Vittorio Veneto* and *Italia*. The message seemed to hit home with the Italian Government. By 18 May Count Sforza had told Dunn that he was disturbed to learn that the Defence Ministry had apparently been responsible for a failure to initiate the 'minimum destruction' agreed upon. Italian Prime Minister de Gasperi had issued strict orders that the work begin immediately.[18]

The two ships had been laid up at La Spezia since October 1947 since ratification of the Peace Treaty. *Vittorio Veneto* was deleted from the Italian Navy List in February 1948 and *Italia* in June. Although the Italian stalling meant that the nine-month deadline set in the Treaty had been missed, by 3 August 1948 Dunn was reporting to Washington that 'minimum destruction', including the cutting off of their 15in gun barrels, had been achieved. Smith suggests that the UK and USA were still arguing about their fate even at this date, and that it was Stalin who insisted that the ships be made completely non-operational, a demand to which the UK and USA meekly submitted.[19] However, this analysis does not square with the evidence in the UK and US archives. *Vittorio Veneto* and *Littorio* were gradually scrapped at La Spezia, the former gone by 1950, the latter, according to Smith, lingering as late as 1960, although Velicogna says 1954.

Returning to the ultimate fate of the five ships for which scrapping decisions had been made in January 1948, *Queen Elizabeth* was sold on 7 July 1948 to British Iron and Steel Corporation (Salvage) Ltd and allocated by them to Arnott & Young, and scrapped at Dalmuir. The hulk came down to Troon on 13 April 1949 drawing 9ft 6in forward and 11ft 6in aft. Demolition was completed on 31 October 1950.[20]

Valiant had continued her wartime repair and refit at Devonport until August 1946. In hindsight this appears to be one of the more wasteful decisions of the post-war era, although it made sense against the plan still then extant to hold ten battleships in the post-war fleet. *Valiant*'s logs for January to April 1946 show her completing the refit, shuttling between No. 5 Basin and No. 10 Dock. They show the minor indignities of being in dockyard hands. There were regular failures of the electrical system and lighting. On 8 April the ship's soap and tobacco store was broken into during the night, and on 16 April there was a fire on the bridge. They also show the churning of what was still a substantial crew. In four months 281

Rodney being manoeuvred into Inverkeithing, March 1948. *(MTSC)*

Opposite above: *Rodney* alongside at Thomas W Ward, Inverkeithing, March 1948. *(MTSC)*

Opposite below: *Rodney* being demolished, August 1948. *(MTSC)*

men joined the ship, 121 left for other appointments and 190 left specifically for demobilisation.[21] But, despite the expense of the refit, she never rejoined the fleet, and instead was allocated to *Imperieuse* at Devonport. She was sold to British Iron & Steel Corporation (Salvage) Ltd on 19 March 1948 and also allocated by them to Arnott & Young for demolition at Cairnryan, where she arrived on 12 August 1948. The hulk came up to Troon on 10 March 1950 and demolition was completed on 10 April 1951.

Renown also became part of *Imperieuse* at Devonport, in Category C reserve from October 1946. She was eventually sold to BISCO and allocated to Metal Industries on 19 March 1948. She paid off in June 1948, and arrived at Faslane for breaking up on 8 August 1948. The hulk was beached at Faslane on 9 December 1950, becoming the first job to use the specially constructed beaching ground.

Rodney, as noted in the Cabinet debate about her fate at the end of 1947, was in a very poor state after her strenuous service and lack of refit during the war, and had had to be dry-docked at Rosyth because she was leaking so extensively. She was allocated to Thomas W Ward at Inverkeithing for dismantling, possibly because a longer tow to a west coast breaker might have been problematic, and made her final 4-mile journey there on 26 March 1948.

Nelson followed a less direct route to the same scrapyard. The Air Ministry had first expressed an interest in undertaking bombing trials

against a modern battleship on 15 January 1945. Specifically, they wanted to bomb against modern standard 6in armoured deck protection. The Admiralty supported the idea in principle. On 22 February 1945 the Admiralty Director of Scientific Research minuted: 'The design and selection of bombs for air attack on heavily armoured warships is a subject on which there is much speculation, little agreed doctrine, and the greatest waste of effort in operations ... No full scale trials have been done against a battleship for ten years ... The need for provision of a capital ship as a bombing trials target thus has DSR's fullest support, as indeed it had the fullest backing of the Aircraft Anti-Ship Committee, the authoritative Admiralty/Air Ministry body on this subject.' The overall requirements for the trials were extremely ambitious and included the need to establish the effectiveness of triple bottom and circular side protection systems as used by the Italian battleships. This could only have been achieved had the UK got hold of *Vittorio Veneto*. They also aimed to establish where main armament magazines should be positioned, and heavy ship vulnerability to heavy shells and underwater explosions. At this stage there would still have been an expectation that these lessons could be worked into the final design of *Lion* and *Temeraire*.[22]

On 2 February 1945 Lord Cherwell, fresh from submitting his memorandum on battleship obsolescence to the Cabinet (Chapter Three), witnessed the complete obliteration of a 1/20th scale model of a modern battleship with a simulated 6in deck by a simulated 6-ton Tallboy bomb (the type that had sunk the *Tirpitz*). This led to enthusiasm at the highest level for a one-third-scale simulation trial by placing 2in of deck armour on a surplus sloop, HMS *Folkestone*, and dropping a suitably scaled bomb on her. On 18 May the First Lord, Alexander, minuted: 'I should be glad to know whether the results of the trials will be available in time to influence the design of *Lion* and *Temaraire*.' In June 1945 the Director of Naval Construction noted the scale of ambition of the trials programme and suggested that a Ship Target Trials Committee be set up to manage them. In early 1946 this committee decided to spare *Folkestone* and move instead to a full-scale ship trial in 1947. The difficulty was that there were still no suitable ships to spare.

The Committee's eye initially fell on *Warspite*, which had thinner decks anyway, but was at that stage still potentially required for the post-war fleet. After her approval for scrapping there was a further brief debate towards the end of 1946 about whether she should be used for these trials, but the Admiralty argued successfully that as she had by then already been promised by direct tender to Metal Industries, rather than via the Ministry of Supply/British Iron & Steel Corporation (Salvage) Ltd arrangements, and that as the Metal Industries tender was significantly better than the BISCO prices, the deal should stand. The Italian ships were also postulated for the trials, but the *Cavours* also lacked enough deck armour and 'It is understood that other ideas are entertained for the *Littorio* class' (which did satisfy the deck armour requirement and, in the case of the 'Considerably damaged' *Italia* might not find other uses). By October 1947 they too had been ruled out by the wider considerations noted above. It was therefore not until the Cabinet's January 1948 scrapping decision that suitable surplus ships with 6in decks were finally available. It was *Nelson*'s lot to be selected.

The trial was designated Operation Bronte.[23] It took place in the Firth of Forth off Inchkeith Island between 4 June and 23 September 1948. *Nelson*, which had been in reserve in the Forth since December 1947, was prepared for the trial in Rosyth dockyard and fitted with extra damage control equipment. At the end of May she was towed out and anchored a mile east of Inchkeith. The objective was to test *Nelson*'s deck protection (which was about the same as that of the five modern British ships and that envisaged for *Lion* and *Temeraire*) and to test the efficiency of the bombs used, in particular the new 2,000lb armour-piercing Mk IV. Highly skilled Royal Navy pilots were hand-picked to fly the Barracuda Mark III aircraft in dive-bombing runs.[24]

The trial had four phases, starting with 1,000lb Mark III bombs dropped from 3,000ft (one hit), then from 4,000ft (two hits) and 5,000ft (one hit with a striking velocity of 727ft per second). The report says: 'In none of these hits was the armour more than dented.' None of these bombs penetrated the deck armour. In phases three and four the 2,000lb Mk IV bombs were used, and the objective was to ascertain the striking velocity required to perforate a given thickness of armour. Again there were four hits. Those from 2,000 and 4,000ft saw the bomb rebounding from the 6in deck, but one from 3,750ft scooped the deck armour and one from 5,500ft, with a striking velocity of 760ft per second, finally perforated the armour. Splinters from this last hit penetrated through the bottom of the ship, and the holes had to be patched by divers before the trials could continue.

Phase three increased the height of release to 8,000ft, to increase the terminal velocity and determine the optimum time delay for the fuze. The first thirty-nine bombs dropped from this altitude all missed. Release height was lowered to 6,000ft and, to some relief as only sixty of the specially modified bombs were available, *Nelson* was finally hit by drop No. 42 on 15 September. This hit a heavily armoured barbette and exploded immediately into large splinters that did significant damage to the upper deck, but did not penetrate the armoured deck. The bombs were then modified with a smaller bursting charge to reduce the risk that their explosion might actually sink a battleship already destined for scrapping and make recovery of the trials data by forensic examination of the damage after each hit impossible. In the final phase *Nelson* was hit twice more. One of these bombs broke up on the armour. The other, on 22 September, did penetrate the main 6¼in deck armour and carried on out through the bottom of the ship.

According to Burt, the conclusions drawn from the test were that bombs needed to be dropped from 5,000ft or higher to be effective against this scale of armour protection; and that although it had not been an easy task (with twelve hits out of 104 bombs dropped), the fact that the armour had been pierced proved that battleships were vulnerable to this type of attack, and that their days were numbered.[25] It could instead be argued that the vulnerability of modern battleships to such large weapons was already clear from wartime experience, for example with FX1400, and that the more telling point was that even with wartime experience, crack bomber crews, perfect conditions, low release heights and an undefended stationary target, accuracy in this form of attack seemed little improved from the very first efforts of Billy Mitchell over a quarter of a century before to sink a battleship with bombs. Six years of warfare at sea had rather tended to confirm that the aerial or submarine torpedo and the guided weapon, not the bomb, was the main threat to capital ships. The 1951 report of the trials, although unaccountably three years delayed, did confirm the general effectiveness of the bombs, but also that the armour arrangements in *Nelson* were effective and behaved as expected under such a bombardment.

In any event, as intended because of her scrap value to the nation, *Nelson*, although holed, still floated. She was soon towed back to Rosyth,

Nelson leaves Rosyth for Inverkeithing, 15 March 1949. Scrapping of the 16in guns has already begun. *(MTSC)*

Nelson arrives at Inverkeithing, seen from *Revenge*.
(MTSC)

Nelson is moved to the beaching ground, March 1950. Revenge in background. (MTSC)

where the dry dock was drained so that the underwater damage could be photographed, but there was no work done to repair her. Then finally she was towed the very few miles to Thomas W Ward & Co. at Inverkeithing, where she arrived on 15 March 1949 to join *Rodney* and *Revenge*.

Thomas Ward kept an excellent photographic record of the scrapping of these ships. *Nelson*'s 16in guns were rapidly removed, and indeed had been cut short to begin the scrapping process while she was still at Rosyth. *Nelson*'s control top was toppled on 31 August 1949. Demolition was completed by October 1950, with 33,340 tons of scrap being realised.[26]

This left just one of the UK's First World War battleships: *Royal Sovereign*. As noted above, the agreement with the Soviet Union to transfer warships to assist her war effort was originally made at the Tehran

Nelson beached, March 1950. (MTSC)

Conference in 1943, and the Russians asked for one Italian battleship, one cruiser and eight destroyers. As Churchill explained to the House of Commons on 5 June 1945: 'The question arose of how to meet the very reasonable and natural request of Soviet Russia. His Majesty's Government did not wish to see Italy at that moment deprived of its navy which was an essential part of the national life we are resolved to preserve.' Leaving aside the merits of this argument – in practice there was a significant surplus of Italian ships once the Soviet request for one battleship had been satisfied, and the modern *Littorios* were kept cloistered well away from Italian national life in the Great Bitter Lake – the answer, suggested by the Prime Minister himself, was to loan *Royal Sovereign* instead of an Italian ship.

After the agreement about the disposal of the Italian battleships in 1947, it became evident that it would take some time to refit *Cesare* for her new role with the USSR, as required by the terms of the Treaty, so the Four-Power Naval Commission supervising this transfer agreed that *Royal Sovereign* would remain under the Soviet flag until *Cesare* arrived in Russia. The Russians eventually agreed to moderate the requirement that *Cesare* be refitted, but the Italians were now stalling on the transfer arrangements in the vain hope that the USSR would follow the UK and US lead and renounce its claim on her and the other thirty-two ships due to be handed over. They did not.[27]

As the Cold War deepened, concerns rose. Having signed her away when Prime Minister, Churchill in opposition became agitated. He asked his successor as Prime Minister, Clement Attlee, in a foreign affairs debate on 28 January 1948 whether or not the ship was to be returned to this country. Attlee said: 'I can see no reason why we, in return for such help to Russia and Italy, should leave our ships in Russian hands. We are entitled to get these ships back, and the scrap would be extremely useful to us at the present moment.'

Following some last-minute delays co-ordinating the simultaneous departures of the Russian and the Italian ship, the *Arkangelsk*, as *Royal Sovereign* was now called, finally sailed from Murmansk at the end of January 1949, and steamed under the Forth Bridge back up to Rosyth, whence she had set off five years before. There, on 4 February, a transfer ceremony took place in the Firth of Forth, and the Russian crew duly marched off to board an accommodation ship lying alongside for their trip back to Russia. All seemed to have gone well, and the Pathé News team recorded the battleship steaming up the Firth of Forth and Russians taking part in various civic receptions. But, in the increasingly frigid atmosphere of the Cold War – this was right in the middle of the Berlin airlift – some found cause to carp.

On 8 March 1949 Lord Ailwyn rose in the House of Lords to ask His Majesty's Government whether they had any comments to make on the circumstances surrounding the handover. He thundered: 'I must ask your Lordships' indulgence if I mince no words. The time has passed it seems to me, for being mealy mouthed in matters affecting the dignity of this country ... The *Royal Sovereign* was due to be handed back to the Royal Navy during a five day period between 24 and 29 January ... The five days go by and she fails to put in an appearance. So far as I am aware there was a complete absence of explanation, apologies or regrets.' He went on to criticise the Russian failure to fire a salute; to refuse traditional British hospitality, but find time to attend the Scottish USSR Society Reception; to refuse access to the ship by the media, and to refuse to make any speech in response to the civil and friendly speech by the British admiral. Ailwyn continued: 'Does the Russian Commodore respond? Does he thank the British admiral for his good wishes? Does he acknowledge the hospitality which has been offered to him? Does he tender the thanks of his country for the loan of *Royal Sovereign* and the other British vessels? He remains completely silent … The melancholy fact remains that what could and should have been a memorable, pleasant, colourful and perhaps even an historic occasion became a sombre, colourless event of shabbiness and gloom. The transfer was effected in sullen silence.'

Lord Hall, still First Lord of the Admiralty, was having none of it. His response confirmed that the late arrival was in accordance with the four-power agreement. The British had removed the saluting guns in the war, as they had on all ships. The Russians had accepted official hospitality. Sentiments expressed privately by the Russians to the British admiral had been warm. 'With regard to the facilities for the press the Russian Commodore indicated that his regulations allowed him no latitude at all in this respect on board a Russian warship … I take the view that the outcome of the re-transfer of the *Royal Sovereign* and other ships may reasonably be pronounced a distinct success.'[28] The press may not have been allowed aboard for the ceremony itself, but British Pathé got some good close-ups of the battleship steaming up the Forth and were able to film the ceremony from an adjacent vessel.

A storm in a teacup maybe, but aspects of the transfer were certainly bizarre. Almost nothing is known of *Royal Sovereign*'s four years of

Royal Sovereign takes *Nelson's* place inboard of *Revenge*, 6 March 1950. *(MTSC)*

service in the Soviet Northern Fleet. Peter C Smith says that she undertook two trial voyages in June 1945, a longer circuit of the White Sea in July, two short trips in 1946, and that she ran aground in 1947.[29] The Admiralty had a fairly reliable report from July 1948 that she was lying off Rosta in an unpainted and unkempt condition with a list of 5 degrees, although her condition on return seems to have been significantly better than that.[30] On her return the British found that the Russians had loaded all the ship's guns with live ammunition. Whether this was a contingency against some sneak attack that they felt the Royal Navy would perpetrate on its own returning fleet, or merely reflected standard Russian seagoing practice, or sloppiness, we cannot speculate. The last seems more likely as it was found that some of the 15in ammunition was rusted into place in the breaches, where it had obviously been for some years. In general the ship was found to be serviceable, but filthy. It mattered not, because, despite her brief recommissioning as a Royal Navy vessel, *Royal Sovereign* was already destined to join her sisters on the scrap heap. She was immediately sold to BISCO and also allocated to Thomas W Ward. She moved back under the Forth Bridge to join *Nelson*, *Rodney* and *Revenge* at Inverkeithing on 5 April 1949.

She remained anchored off shore for nearly a year while *Nelson* and *Rodney* were dismantled. During this period the forward 15in turrets were removed, before she joined *Revenge* at the jetty on 6 March 1950.

One substantial memento of her, and of *Revenge*, survives. The engineer designing Britain's first steerable radio telescope for Sir Bernard Lovell was Charles Husband. He decided that the rack and pinion training mechanism from their 15in turrets could be put to work in the construction of the new 250ft radio telescope dish at Jodrell Bank, Cheshire. Their slow rates of movement and angular precision were ideal for controlling the elevation of the big dish antenna. Husband found the Admiralty Gunnery Establishment at Teddington very helpful with practical advice on the mechanical limitations associated with the driving of heavy gun turrets by electrical and hydraulic means. The methods of automatic angular control used in naval gunnery provided a close analogy to the movements required for the large telescope.

He agreed at an early stage of the design procedure to earmark two complete 27ft diameter internal racks and their driving pinions from the hydraulically operated 15in gun turrets. An inspection of the racks was made at Inverkeithing; they were found to be in perfect condition and were subsequently purchased at a nominal price. It was a happy coincidence that the strength of the teeth on the racks corresponded, with a reasonable factor of safety, to the anticipated maximum torque caused by wind loading on the telescope dish. The racks were disassembled for transport to Jodrell Bank, and reassembled there in the machine shop. During the

Royal Sovereign's control top is toppled by Ward's. *(MTSC)*

operation of the telescope Husband opined: 'There has so far been no reason to regret the incorporation of this high class second hand material in the driving system.'[31]

A Central Office of Information film from 1957 entitled 'The Inquisitive Giant' features footage of Lovell and Husband discussing the

Jodrell Bank radio telescope, incorporating the 15in rack and pinion mechanisms from *Revenge* and *Royal Sovereign*. (Alamy)

telescope, and of the battleship rack and pinions being reassembled in the project workshop. Interestingly, the film script credits the idea for using the turret training mechanism to Professor P M S Blackett, then a colleague of Lovell's at Manchester University. This has a certain plausibility as Blackett was an ex-Royal Navy gunnery officer, and veteran of Jutland.

As the scrapping of the older British ships was completed, the Royal Navy retained in service now just the five modern vessels. However, their fate was also being debated as 1948 came to a close. The results of the Cabinet discussions on Defence in late 1947 that led to the various reductions including the scrapping of the five older battleships had still left fundamental structural and affordability questions hanging over UK Defence. Expenditure was still projected at £830 million per year and the Chancellor of the Exchequer requested another bite at the cherry, to see what could be done for £700 million. This was carried out via an independent team led by a civil servant, Mr Edmund Harwood from the Ministry of Food, although at the time Civilian Director of the Imperial Defence College. The naval representative on Harwood's team was Rear Admiral C E Lambe, who was air minded, having commanded the carrier *Illustrious* in the British Pacific Fleet. Nor was he any slouch, going on to become First Sea Lord. The Harwood Committee sat from December 1948 and reported in February 1949. It spoke unpopular truths about what might be afforded for a Defence budget limit of £700 million. Paragraph 8a says: 'The preponderance of US naval strength calls for a complementary rather than a competitive Royal Navy confined to tasks which are essentially a domestic responsibility. As a result ... the cut recommended in the present size of the Royal Navy, and particularly in its numbers of larger ships, is greater than the equivalent cuts in the other two services.'

Royal Navy manpower was proposed to drop from the planned 147,000 to just 90,000 by 1953, and the projected Navy budget would be £167 million, gradually skewed towards new construction. The fleet would have just one mobile carrier task force, and a front-line air strength of 200 by 1952 (at the time of the report it was about 168). The number of carriers overall would fall from fourteen to twelve, and seven of those would be in reserve. 'No battleships would be retained, and the number of cruisers would be considerably reduced.' (From twenty-three to twelve.) Paragraph 122 of Harwood's report says:

> the following tasks must be performed by allied naval vessels or not at all.

Home Waters
Cover against the small surface threat to Atlantic shipping ...

Paragraph 138 says:

> We do not foresee a need for the four *King George V* class and *Vanguard* except a) as possible platforms for new weapons such as heavy G.A.P (Guided anti-aircraft Projectiles); b) Royal Tours ... If Russia started to build battleships we believe that an increase in naval air strength would be the proper reply ... To keep the ships in reserve must be costly, we estimate £1 million per annum for the five ships.[32]

This was too radical for the Admiralty, as indeed the entire report proved for the Chiefs of Staff collectively. The First Sea Lord rubbished the proposals as incapable of supporting the political intent of the Western Union. During April and May 1949 the Admiralty prepared its response. A draft memorandum by First Sea Lord for the Chiefs of Staff Committee noted that the wartime fleet planned before the Harwood review proposals was already less than the fleet assessed to be required at the end of 1948 by eight light fleet carriers, five cruisers and fifty-six escorts, 'and that it is proposed to forego any modernisation of the 14in battleships until guided weapons are in supply'. These reductions were made possible by relying on the US Navy for half the naval force required for defence of sea communications in the North Atlantic and Mediterranean, and all defence requirements in the South Atlantic and Pacific, with Australia and New Zealand taking full responsibility for the Indian Ocean. Costs would come down from the present £300 million to £225 million, and manpower from 150,000 to 125,000. On battleships he noted: 'The present proposal is that these should be retained in reserve instead of being scrapped. No-one can say what heavy ships the enemy might have by 1957 and the battleships might be regarded as an essential insurance.'[33]

In a paper dated 20 April 1949 the Assistant Chief of the Naval Staff tried to be slightly more radical and proposed a 'Restricted Fleet'. Its tasks would be preventing enemy minelaying, minesweeping and protecting convoys against submarine, air and surface attack. The last would require surface cover to neutralise the surface forces available to Russia, and an air striking capability. Convoy protection would fall to a new class of 5in gunned light cruisers. Guided weapons development was noted as very fluid, and the long-range anti-aircraft weapon of the Seaslug type would need to be carried on a special guided weapons ship. Guided weapons as an operational reality were still a very long way off. Aircraft carriers were required as 'the backbone of the task forces which will protect our shipping against surface attack and provide our share of the offensive war against enemy ships and bases'.

Under the heading 'Battleships', Assistant Chief of the Naval Staff said: 'I think it can be assumed that we shall never be able to afford the luxury of battleships for any task other than to neutralise those of the enemy. Our prospective enemy has no modern battleships though there are two in Europe, *Richelieu* and *Jean Bart*, which might conceivably go communist and come under Russian control. The battleship threat cannot therefore be regarded as serious and is certainly not one against which we can afford to over insure. I do not however consider we should scrap our battleships. The possibility that the Russians might acquire or even build them cannot be overlooked. We might then at some future date be faced with the need to provide from our own resources some heavy surface cover to neutralise them. The risk of leaving this task to light cruisers and aircraft carriers would be great and might be unacceptable. Nevertheless I do not consider that in our present financial straits we should spend money providing against a threat which does not at the moment exist. I suggest therefore that our battleships be placed in "cold storage" and that no more money be spent on them. The five which we possess give us a more than sufficient lead over the Russians or any other conceivable enemy, and constitute an asset which has considerable political and moral force whether they are in commission or not. Plans for modernising their A.A. armament will need to be prepared and kept up to date. Meanwhile the ships will be there, a massive reserve, ready to be called forward, modernised and brought into service should the need ever arise.'

The very same day as this paper, First Sea Lord, now Sir Bruce Fraser, had articulated the need for the battleship as he saw it when questioned at a press conference in Greenwich on 20 April 1949 held to publicise Exercise Trident. This was a very detailed week-long seminar exploring the lessons of the Second World War and applying them to the Navy's role in a future war set in 1957. It was assumed that five battleships would still exist at that point, and that two would be available in short order with *Vanguard* joining four carriers in the striking fleet attacking Soviet targets in the far north.[34] Fraser said: 'We think in the Navy we must have battleships, and we must continue to have battleships whether we keep them in commission or not, or whether we keep any in commission at the moment; we must keep one or two. There has always been a demand for the strongest and heaviest and most powerful things that we have. I keep on pointing out to the Army that they are now building 'battleship' tanks because they are stronger and faster and larger than anything else. In addition to that of course, in the future it is probable that the battleship may be the only platform on which you can mount the weapons of the future, like guided missiles. When every armed landing has taken place there has always been the cry for battleships so we intend to keep the battleship because we think it will be of the greatest value.'[35]

The record of the Sea Lords meeting on 2 and 3 May 1949 states their near agreement with the proposal for a war readiness fleet of one active and four reserve battleships, with one of those to be active in the Training Squadron in peacetime. There were to be three active and three reserve fleet carriers and four active and two reserve light fleet carriers.[36]

First Sea Lord's commentary on Harwood's proposals, produced for the Standing Committee of Service Ministers on 11 July 1949, recognised the need to reduce the number of cruisers 'but we regard the figure of twelve mentioned by Harwood as impossibly low – even after full allowance is made for American help ... so reduced a number of cruisers would not give anything like a minimum level of security. NB. Note that the Russians may have thirty-three cruisers by 1957, most of them armed with heavier guns than ours. The use of some of these as ocean raiders points to the need not only for an adequate number of cruisers to oppose them, but also to the retention of the battleships to deal with any concentration of Russian cruisers.'

Pulling all the single service ministry opinions on Harwood together, the Ministry of Defence memorandum dated 27 June 1949 for the same meeting observed first that Harwood's proposals would probably actually cost well in excess of his £700 million per year estimate, and also that they were inadequate to meet the country's need to support NATO and the WEU, win the Cold War, support the United States defence effort and protect the dominions. Over £800 million, or around 8 per cent of national income versus the current 9 per cent, might be adequate to achieve these aims, with total service manpower of between 600,000 and 650,000.[37]

Ironically, given his earlier drive for economy, it was Defence Minister Alexander who led the many voices in the defence establishment that rejected the Harwood prescription and the so-called 'Restricted Fleet'. Although Harwood had first reported on 28 February, the hostile reception from the Chiefs of Staff and further work meant that the Cabinet Defence Committee did not discuss Harwood until 21 June and 5 July 1949. Even then, despite Alexander's attempts to square the circle to match commitments to resources, Harwood was parked as a result of this discussion, and a further working group set up under Sir Harold Parker, Permanent Secretary at the Ministry of Defence. This came up with revised proposals, including fewer front-line naval aircraft than Harwood's original, battleships retained and cruisers reduced only to eighteen. The modified Harwood template came back to the Defence Committee no fewer than four times between 19 October and 25 November 1949.[38] The presence of battleships, mainly in reserve, was apparently accepted. Retention of the five modern battleships was included as a plank in the argument that the Navy needed to sustain readiness, operations and refits to win the Cold War in the here and now instead of resourcing a new fleet for ten years into the future. The Royal Navy fought off attempts to reduce cruiser numbers and rely on the USA, arguing that cruisers were a more affordable response to the 1957 projected threat from Russia than extra aircraft carriers. Stafford Cripps, now fighting the Chancellor of the Exchequer's corner, warned of dire consequences for social services and increases in taxation if the revised bid for £830 million per year could not be cut to £760 million. In the end Attlee settled on £780 million, justifying the increase because of the need to fund additional commitments to support the Western Union and accepting that supplementary estimates were very likely to be needed to meet the actual cost of planned forces.

The upshot was that the Royal Navy's last five battleships survived in the fleet, although the need to economise further on their running costs was even then also under parallel consideration. In April 1949 *King George V* and *Anson*, together with the aircraft carrier *Victorious*, formed the Training Squadron. *Duke of York* was flagship of the Home Fleet, *Vanguard* was in the Mediterranean and *Howe* was undergoing a long refit at Devonport. None of the ships was in reserve, which was in relative terms a considerable achievement, given that by that date the US Navy was only maintaining a single battleship in commission.

However, this pattern of active employment was about to end abruptly, overshadowed as it was by yet another looming manning crisis in the Royal Navy. First Lord of the Admiralty Lord Hall submitted a paper to the Cabinet Defence Committee in mid-1949 arguing that it was preferable to place four out of five battleships in reserve in order to release their manpower to run as many as possible of the fleet's destroyers, escorts and minesweepers. The trigger for the proposal, he explained, was the temporary shortfall in manpower consequent on the heavy release of national servicemen. This shortfall would reach 3,000 by October 1949, and while it was expected to right itself as early as April 1950, Hall said: 'I should certainly hesitate to contemplate bringing back into commission battleships from reserve at any time in the relatively near future, that is while we shall still be hard pressed in the classes of vessel that for manning purposes must be accorded a higher priority.'[39]

In detail, to execute this proposal *Vanguard* would replace *Anson* in the Training Squadron, but remain available for Special Duties (her possible role as a Royal Yacht for visits to the Dominions). After a refit *Duke of York* would go into Category C reserve, meaning she would have a caretaker crew and be at six months' notice to rejoin the active fleet after mobilisation. She would be based at Portsmouth as flagship of Commander Reserve Fleet. *Howe* would be placed in Category A, or 'operational', reserve, at Devonport (meaning that the ship was fit for full operational service and required within three months of mobilisation, if possible to be maintained at only thirty days' notice). The caretaker crew was to be 163.[40] *Anson* would be reduced to Category C reserve in the Firth of Forth, and *King George V* would be laid up on the Clyde, also

Category C. The Category C ships were required to be preserved for future employment, but would not be commissioned until after the immediate post-mobilisation fleet expansion had taken effect.

The caretaker crew for a *King George V*-class battleship at Category C reserve was officially ninety according to the ship's book, but the manpower calculations used to underpin these proposals assumed between 150 and 170 men per ship. The placing of the *King George V* class into reserve combined with the reallocation of *Vanguard* to the Training Squadron, with a lower complement, would therefore save about 2,700 men, and, crucially, despite the net loss of one battleship in the Training Squadron, would not prevent delivery of the numbers who needed to be trained afloat. The manpower projection saw the number of men crewing battleships in peacetime declining from 4,060 in April 1949 (2.7 per cent of naval manpower) to 1,357 by August 1950 (1.1 per cent). The Admiralty Director of Plans confirmed on 12 April 1949 that this new arrangement satisfied the requirements of UK national war plans, which specified one battleship available on D-Day (*Vanguard*) and one at D plus three months (*Howe*).

The steering brief for the Prime Minister at the meeting of the Cabinet Defence Committee in early July 1949 to discuss these proposals noted: 'It seems hardly likely that the Committee will wish to dispute the First Lord's decision to place four out of five battleships in reserve, at this stage while the future size and shape of the navy and of the other two Services is still under discussion. HMG will be well placed to bring the ships back into commission, leave them in reserve, or even break them up – in accordance with whatever decision is reached about the role of battleships in the future.' This was a reference to the parallel debate about affordability of defence, and discussion of the Harwood report.

The Committee duly agreed, and also agreed that a press communiqué should be issued explaining the changes. This was reported in sober but unprotesting tones by *The Times* on 14 July 1949. The naval correspondent, no doubt suitably back-briefed, opined that the decision was not unexpected in the light of manning difficulties.

While the papers show unanimity in the Admiralty about the main decision, shortly after this announcement there was a further internal debate about how to manage the reserve battleships.[41] In August the Director of Plans proposed to maintain the 14in armament of just two of the ships soon to be in reserve, and to allow the guns of the other two to deteriorate as they (the guns) were not required for future plans. In September he further proposed to also place *Howe* in Category C reserve instead of Category A to save more manpower. He noted that present war plans required only two battleships, and to keep *Vanguard* and two 14in ships in such a state that they could be brought forward was sufficient for the Navy's needs. A debate about whether there was sufficient manpower or money to dehumidify fully the 14in turrets of the two spare ships led to the Director of the Tactical and Staff Duties Division suggesting that if this investment could not be undertaken, why not save even more expense and throw the ships away now?

The Head of Military Branch responded on 14 November 1949 that rapid deterioration of the 14in armament was not an argument for scrapping the two unmaintained ships because 'it is believed that they may possibly be used for other purposes, e.g. as launching platforms for guided weapons'. Director of Plans confirmed on 24 November that: 'It is Board policy to retain these ships until guided weapons are in supply … It is the hulls we require for the purpose of carrying guided weapons, and not the main armament at present in existence'. The Controller of the Navy explained, on 7 December, agreeing 'that the 14in guns on two ships should be allowed to rot away appears absolutely sound. The only use foreseen for these latter two battleships is as guided weapons ships in the distant future. Should they ever be converted, the 14in turrets, directors etc would have to be removed in toto'. The Vice Chief of the Naval Staff endorsed this position to First Sea Lord on 12 December: 'This proposal saves money and manpower and leaves three battleships for the surface role and two available for adaptation to guided missiles, in which case the main armament would not be required.'

There was then a further debate sparked by the First Sea Lord about whether it was possible to run *Howe* in the Training Squadron while *Vanguard* undertook a planned refit for five months in early 1951. VCNS, Vice Admiral Sir George Creasey, reported back to First Sea Lord on 11 January 1950: 'I consider the price to be paid for *Howe* to relieve *Vanguard* in the Training Squadron to be prohibitive.' Also, for *Howe*: 'I do not believe we can afford the difference between Cat C and Cat A.' The particular pinch point was engine room ratings. *Howe*, seagoing in the Training Squadron, would require a net extra 234 ratings, which would mean a corresponding reduction of one cruiser and three destroyers in the active fleet. Putting *Howe* into Category A reserve, with its requirement for full preservation, would also require a surge of 584 men for six months to carry out the work to reduce her to reserve, and ninety-one additional caretakers indefinitely, again at a penalty of being unable to run one cruiser and three destroyers. If *Howe* and *Vanguard* were running together, and if *Vanguard* was on a Royal Tour, the penalty would rise by three cruisers and a further destroyer. The conclusion, which First Sea Lord agreed, was that because of acute manpower challenges, *Howe* should go to Category C reserve; the potential absence of a battleship in the North Atlantic if *Vanguard* was away or in refit when war broke out should be accepted; and that at a pinch the Training Squadron could manage for a short period with just one aircraft carrier.[42]

So it was agreed that *Howe* should also reduce to Category C reserve, and the First Lord so minuted the Prime Minister on 7 February 1950. He noted that if *Vanguard* was away from the UK on the outbreak of an emergency, there would be no battleship available in the North Atlantic, but this was acceptable as no battleship was required in the area during the first three months of a war. (Note that this represented a change from the requirement for one to be ready at D-Day in early 1949.) Present war plans required only three battleships, but the other two *King George Vs* were also being retained 'Because they are comparatively modern ships and because there is the possibility of their being rearmed at a future date with a new type of weapon.'[43]

So, as 1949 faded into 1950, the *King George V* class were gradually wound down into reserve, still required, but seemingly increasingly at the margin of UK defence thinking, and with their future hanging either on the outbreak of a hot war, or on the delivery of a new, as yet experimental, weapon.

CHAPTER NINE

Stalin's Oceanic Navy – Soviet Battleship Ambitions

THE MAIN DRIVER for US and European policy during the period after 1945 rapidly became the tension and rivalry between the West and the Soviet Union. The de facto division of Europe was soon manifested through new flashpoints, and a Soviet policy best described as aggrandising and confrontational. Building up the relatively small and backward Soviet Navy played a big part in their ambition, and Joseph Stalin was closely and personally involved in the process. At the Eighteenth Party Congress in 1939, A F Tevosian of the Shipbuilding Commissariat said there was 'not a single plan of a naval vessel, of a naval gun, or of a great or small problem in general which did not pass through the hands of Comrade Stalin'.[1]

To put the post-war activity in context it is helpful to outline what Soviet Russia had been attempting over the previous decade. In the late 1930s Stalin, largely untrammelled by the Naval Treaties that had bound other powers, had aspired to build a Soviet battle fleet. Had its full scope been realised it would have been so formidable as to upset all balance of naval power in Europe and the Far East. The Soviets reached out to the West for assistance. In late 1935 the Italian Ansaldo Yard at Genoa provided the Soviet Navy with a 42,000-ton battleship design, very similar to the *Littorio* class then just beginning construction. This evolved into Soviet Project 23, and the *Sovietsky Soyuz* class of ships. The plans, notionally a response to the much more modest new battleship construction programme in Germany, underwent a number of iterations.[2]

The first possible programme to build an oceanic fleet was considered by the Council of Labour and Defence on 27 May 1936. It called for eight 35,000-ton battleships and eighteen 26,000-ton 12in gunned battlecruisers. On 26 June 1936 the Politburo approved eight plus sixteen, for a total of twenty-four de facto battleships (I include all 12in cruisers in these totals). They would be supported by twenty cruisers, 182 destroyers and 344 submarines. The hoped-for expansion ignited a debate about the purpose and priority of a big ocean navy in Russia, and Stalin called a conference at the end of 1936 to debate this option versus a more modest cruiser and submarine-based navy focussed on coastal defence and favoured by many naval professionals. The big navy party won, although dissenting voices were never entirely silenced. Admiral N G Kuznetsov, who was to be appointed People's Commissar of the Navy in April 1939, said in his memoirs that: 'We had no common point of view on the military doctrine … The naval doctrine was only in Stalin's head.' Kuznetsov himself seems to have eventually favoured a cruiser-based navy, with a leavening of aircraft carriers and a strong submarine arm. However, for the moment, he acquiesced in the battleship policy.

By May 1937 the Soviet Navy was arguing for the planned battleships to be in the 55,000–57,000-ton class, which would outmatch ships restricted by the naval treaties. The USSR was barely knocked off its stride by the bilateral Anglo–Soviet naval treaty signed on 17 July that theoretically limited both sides to 35,000-ton ships, to match the *King George Vs* being built under the London Treaty restrictions. The Soviets extracted a concession that allowed them 16in guns – they never contemplated plans for less – and for the qualitative limits not to apply in the Pacific where Japanese secrecy about their own plans was a big, and genuine, worry. Not long after, the official limit was raised to 45,000 tons as the escalator clause of the 1930 London Naval Treaty was invoked by the other powers, but the Soviets had always continued to plan larger ships still. In September 1937 Chief of Naval Staff Viktorev submitted more detailed plans for a Pacific Fleet of eight battleships, a Baltic fleet of eight, a Black Sea fleet of five and a Northern Fleet of two. This totalled twenty-three battleships, as well as just two aircraft carriers. This was converted into a shipbuilding proposal by Commissar P A Smirnov in February 1938, by then modified to fifteen battleships and ten battlecruisers. Kuznetsov inherited this programme a year later and only altered it modestly to the extent of extending implementation to cover a period of ten years. McLaughlin says this proposal never got Government approval.

By late 1938 strategic thinking had evolved to see the Japanese in the Pacific as the greatest threat to Soviet interests, and the intent was to base fifteen battleships in the Far East, although a more realistic plan envisaged a build up to six battleships and two battlecruisers by 1947. Over all its fleets, by August 1939 the USSR envisaged fifteen ships of the Project 23 class complemented by sixteen Project 69 battlecruisers. It would have been substantially the largest big-gun navy in the world, but even with the necessary resources, organisation and unified political will, and assuming the laying down of three or four ships each year, it would have taken at least twelve years to complete. The urgency to get something done was also illustrated by the extensive negotiations with Gibbs and Cox naval architects in the USA to build a 45,000-ton battleship for the Soviet Union in the United States, plus technical assistance with a second ship, a copy to be built in Russia. Stalin became personally involved to move this idea along and President Roosevelt himself approved the project, although again, nothing came of it.

The design for Project 23 had moved way beyond Ansaldo's 42,000-tonner. At over 60,000 tons full load (McLaughlin estimates 67,000 tons) with nine 16in guns and an unprecedented 16¾in main armour belt, it would have made these the largest and best-armoured battleships in the world with the exception, just, of the still secret Japanese *Yamato* class. The Soviet Council of Work and Defence authorised the construction of four battleships on 21 January 1938.[3] Meanwhile, one of the fruits of the Molotov–Ribbentrop Soviet–German Pact of 1939, following the crushing of Poland, was to have been material assistance from Germany to the Soviet Union on the Project 69 battlecruiser, which was briefly redesigned to mount 15in turrets to be sourced from Germany and originally intended for German battlecruisers.[4] In the event the Germans moved very slowly to provide this assistance, and no substantive help had been provided by the point of their invasion of the USSR in June 1941. By late 1940, even as the first four ships slowly began to rise on the slipways, the Soviet plan had contracted to ten battleships and eight battlecruisers overall, later modified again in 1944 under Kuznetzov's modernising influence to nine battleships, twelve battlecruisers and six aircraft carriers.

Soviet naval ambition was one thing, but delivering it, even on a much reduced scale, proved all but impossible because of the reality of her shaky, purge-ridden economy and the inherent backwardness and fragility of her heavy engineering and shipbuilding infrastructure. First the existing building slips at Leningrad and Nikolayev in the Black Sea had to be expanded to accommodate the enormous designs. A massive new purpose-built facility was also constructed at Molotovsk near Arkhangelsk in the Arctic. This was a covered facility sufficiently large to construct two of these ships simultaneously. If nothing else the creation of Molotovsk proved that the will to build battleships and generate the necessary infrastructure was definitely a priority. But the cumulative drag of a fearful bureaucracy, constant design changes and manufactured materiel shortcomings meant that only the first four Project 23 battleships were eventually laid down, and only the one at Leningrad had substantially progressed by the time of the German invasion in June 1941.[5]

One of these ships, *Sovietskaya Byelorossiya*, had to be broken up in 1940 at Molotovsk because it was discovered that 70,000 rivets used in her construction were faulty. Had she ever gone to sea, her bottom would literally have fallen out. The decision was made not to restart her immediately because the severely limited industrial capacity was by then required for Army projects. At the same time as the four battleships were progressing, there seem to have been also two 34,000-ton Project 69 battlecruisers with a designed 12in main armament under construction, one at the Marti shipyard in Leningrad (named *Kronstadt)* and one at Nikolayev (named *Sevastopol*).[6]

Project 23 –
Sovietsky Soyuz
on the building
ways in June
1944. *(NARA)*

Besides the rivet quality control issue, there was a series of further setbacks in the supply of armour, ordnance and machinery. Many of the most specialised forgings and parts as well as the turbines and even 12in main armament for the battlecruisers had to be ordered abroad from Italy, France, Switzerland and Germany because industrial capacity and quality were so low in the Soviet Union. Between January and April 1938, 160 out of 187 forgings produced at the Soviet shipbuilding works were rejected as defective. Four turbines delivered from Brown Boveri of Switzerland for *Sovietsky Soyuz* were to be copied at the Kharkhovsky Turbo-generator works, with eighteen to outfit the remaining ships in the programme to be delivered by 1942, but not one of these copies was ever completed.[7] The construction programme called for 10,000 tons of armour in 1939, but only 1,800 were delivered. Little wonder then that, by decree, work on the three remaining ships stopped altogether in July 1941 and priority was given to the urgent defence of Leningrad and Moscow against the rapidly advancing Germans, and thereafter to land and air force requirements to defeat the Nazi occupation.

After hostilities were over it seemed that Stalin was intent on carrying through the pre-war plan to have a fleet of heavy ships. On 7 September 1945, with the war over, the Politburo again reviewed naval plans. Kuznetsov, now Chief of Staff, despite his personal scepticism proposed four new battleships and four battlecruisers for the post-war fleet, but Stalin preferred a greater emphasis on the latter, armed with 12in guns.

Josef Stalin (front row right) with Admiral Kuznetzov (back far right) at the Yalta Conference, February 1945. *(Alamy)*

'Rowdy ships' he called them, intended to be faster than any better armed ship, and better-armed than any faster one. The final decision reached at this meeting was to complete *Sovietskaya Rossiya* at Molotovsk; to build two new design Project 24 battleships on an even grander scale – 73,000 tons, nine 16in guns, and capable of 30 knots – and to build seven new Project 82 battlecruisers. There would also be two new aircraft carriers. McLaughlin has a slightly different take on plans at this stage. He says that on 27 November 1945 the Council of People's Commissars approved by decree the two project 24 battleships to be laid down in 1955, preceded by four Project 82 battlecruisers to be in service by January 1956, with two more to follow later. This decree remained in force, guiding the design and shipbuilding agencies until after Stalin's death.[8]

So in late 1945 Stalin wanted to finish at least one Project 23 battleship. But there seems to have been little remaining support for this class in the Soviet Navy or Politburo. Although *Sovietskaya Rossiya* was 're-enrolled' in the fleet on 19 January 1946, a special commission chaired by the deputy minister of Ship Building, I Nosenko, was set up to review the class. It decided *Sovietskaya Ukraina*'s 13,000 tons at Sevastopol was beyond salvage, and, while noting the feasibility of completing *Sovietsky Soyuz*, with 15,818 tons of construction still undamaged on the slipway, it criticised shortcomings in the design compared to foreign contemporaries, and noted the three years or so it would take to update the design to make it effective. It also noted the disadvantages of operating just one of this class of ship. It stopped short of contradicting Stalin outright and recommending that all be scrapped, but eventually he seemingly acquiesced in the dismantling of the three Project 23 battleships and two Project 69 battlecruiser hulls probably still in existence from the pre-war programmes. The decree scrapping *Sovietskaya Ukraina* and *Sovietskaya Rossiya* was dated 27 March 1947, and that for *Sovietsky Soyuz* 29 May 1948.[9]

The evidence for the carrying through of these decisions and for the ultimate fate of the remnants is fragmentary and conflicting. Various Western naval attaché reports suggest that *Sovietsky Soyuz* at the Baltic shipyard, Leningrad, had not been worked on between June 1941 and June 1947. US Navy interrogation of returning German prisoners of war in 1948–49 suggested that she had by then been dismantled, although the keel plates were recycled into the structure of the cruiser *Sverdlov*. By May 1949 the UK Naval Attaché to Moscow reported that the large slipway where *Sovietsky Soyuz* had been laid down was apparently empty. But in August 1949 the US Naval Attaché reported seeing separate battleship hull sections with distinctive tubular Pugliese-style underwater protection systems (a technology borrowed from Italian constructors) both at this slipway and at the adjacent Marti shipyard, corresponding to the possible continued existence of both *Sovietsky Soyuz* and *Kronstadt*.[10] McLaughlin says that one section of the *Sovietsky Soyuz* hull was launched intact for experiments in underwater protection, which may have confused observers on the ground. By October 1949, however, there was no evidence of a battleship hull at the Baltic Yard.

Sovietskaya Ukraina was still on the slipway at Nikolayev in May 1946, although apparently scrapped by 1947. According to a former Soviet naval officer, the hull was finally scrapped at Kamyshin Bay, Sevastopol, beginning in 1956.[11] The precise fate of *Sovietskaya Rossiya* at Molotovsk is unknown, up to the issuing of the 27 March 1947 decree. Rowher and Makonov simply say that the plan to renew her building 'was never really started'.

As for the fate of fast battlecruisers laid down at the Marti yard, Leningrad, and at Nikolayev in 1938–39, the Leningrad hull (*Kronstadt*) was judged 5 per cent complete when the US Naval Attaché visited in 1944. By 26 June 1947 he assessed the hull as two-thirds complete with work in progress. By contrast, the UK Attaché in May 1949 observed no ships at the yard beyond the keel-laying stage, although the US Attaché, visiting again in August that year, saw his Pugliese stern section, noted above. This hull was twice observed in 1950, but its ultimate fate remains a mystery. A second part-built hull, *Sevastopol*, was apparently at Nikolayev as late as June 1949.[12]

Although both the pre-war projects had been abandoned, and the hulls apparently dismantled, the Soviets, or more accurately Stalin in person, still wanted big ships and battleships. Project 24 super battleship design work continued between December 1945 and March 1950, and plans (Variant 13) for an 80,000-ton monster ship, but still armed with nine 16in guns and capable of 30 knots, were presented to Stalin on 4 March 1950. Armour was to be up to 9.6in thick across the decks and 16 to 17.7in for the main belt. The ship was intended to outmatch the *Iowas*, whose armour characteristics were at that point still secret and believed to be greater than they actually were. Project 24's purpose was described as 'destruction of surface ships of all types, near or far from its own coasts …' This project, like its predecessors, fell victim to its overambition and protracted internal debate. Outline plans had escalated up to 100,000 tons, but provoked a reaction where some officers preferred a much smaller battleship so two or three could be afforded for the cost of one Project 24 monster. The Naval Construction Bureau and Ship Building Ministry met to discuss the alternative concepts in April 1951. They decided against a 73,000-ton option but had before them a range of other smaller possibilities between 34,000 and 45,000 tons full load, with up to 18in guns. The issues were referred to the deputy Chairman of the Council of Ministers, N A Bulganin, but he covered his back by referring the issue back for a further joint study by the Ministry and the Navy. There had been no further progress on Project 24 by the time Stalin died.[13]

Probably reflecting Stalin's personal enthusiasm, the new battlecruiser Project 82 seems to have made better progress in the early 1950s. This was notwithstanding the continued opposition of Kuznetsov, who favoured a smaller 8.8in gunned cruiser alternative. He paid the price with dismissal in February 1946 and demotion three ranks with a sort of internal exile in the Far Eastern Fleet. There was a wider purge of senior naval officers. The new Commander-in-Chief of Naval Forces, Admiral I S Iumashev, kowtowed to Stalin and backed Project 82. Configuration and designs for the ship also changed repeatedly as the project gestated, being modified after the design for a 35,000-ton ship was approved by the Council of Ministers on 25 March 1950 to incorporate more armour and better sea-keeping characteristics. In its final form submitted for approval on 14 June 1951 the ship was a very fast battlecruiser type of 36,000 tons, 41,600 full load. It was to be armed with a new design of 12in gun with a very long barrel of 61 calibres, as against typical Western guns of 40 to 50 calibres.[14] This would give a projected range of 58,000 yards, compared with the maximum of about 43,000 for conventional Western battleship guns. It was also designed for an implausibly high rate of fire of over three rounds per minute. One barrel for this gun was eventually manufactured by December 1953. The ship was intended specifically to outfight NATO cruisers protecting carrier groups. German naval architects captured in 1945 were allegedly employed in its design.

Stalin made changes to the design in 1949 to focus on increased speed and it was finally approved by him at the Council of Ministers on 25 March 1950, to be laid down in the autumn of 1951 with completion projected for 1954–55. Further modifications saw the final design incorporate more armour and better sea-keeping characteristics. The first ship, *Stalingrad*, was eventually begun at Nikolayev in December 1951. According to Garzke and Dulin, it was about 60 per cent 'ready for launching' in 1953. A second hull called *Moskva* was laid down in September 1952 at the Baltic shipyard, Leningrad, and a third, possibly a modified design to mount cruise missiles, at Molotovsk in early 1953. An earlier proposal to mount ballistic missiles was dropped because the available technology was too unwieldy and no stabilised launching platform could be devised to guarantee the necessary accuracy. So at this point there was a genuine prospect that, despite their purges, internal disagreements, delays and industrial backwardness, the Soviet machine might have delivered the ships, and Western navies would have faced very fast, modern, large and well-armed battlecruisers, possibly with guided weapons, from the mid to late 1950s. The only effective surface ship counter to them would have been the US, UK and French battleships.

But Project 82's vulnerability to continuing industrial difficulties meant that building proceeded slowly. *Stalingrad* was only 19 per cent complete by January 1953, *Moskva* 7 per cent and the third ship maybe 2 per cent. The ships then fell victim to internal Communist party machinations and the preferences of the Soviet Navy, especially the rehabilitated Kuznetzov, after Stalin died on 5 March 1953. The Project 82 ships were quickly cancelled on 18 March by the Ministry of Transport and Heavy Machinery. When Khrushchev secured his hold on power by 1956 he proclaimed a nuclear- and rocket-based 'revolution in military affairs' that led to deep cuts in conventional military spending, the deferment of any big-ship navy plans for a generation and inter alia the scrapping of Russia's older dreadnoughts. The hulk of *Stalingrad* was designated for surface target trials in June 1953, and a 500ft central section was modified and launched on 16 April 1954. It finally left Nikolayev in May 1955, but ran aground near Sevastopol while under tow in high winds. Salvage proved difficult and it was not refloated until July 1956. It was expended by the Soviet Navy as a target for SSN-1 surface-to-surface missiles fired from the modified cruiser *Admiral Nakhimov* in December 1956 – ironically the very missiles that the class would probably have ended up deploying had it been built – and then in subsequent weapons testing. Final scrapping probably followed in 1962. *Moskva* and the third ship had meanwhile been dismantled on the slipways.[15]

It is not easy to untangle the truth about Soviet plans and their delivery between 1938 and 1953. Information is fragmentary, secrecy abounded, and modern Western sources are not always consistent. There is very little contemporary evidence about UK knowledge of the Soviet programmes, although some files from that era still remain closed at the National Archives. In early 1946 the UK Joint Intelligence Committee believed that: 'Russia intended to construct a large modern navy and mercantile marine that will be commensurate with her status as a first class power.'[16] And the Admiralty Naval Intelligence Directorate said that Russia's 'declared intention to build a large ocean-going fleet stands', although battleship construction had been put back for years.[17] But by October 1946 the Joint Intelligence Committee suggested: 'It is most unlikely that Russia will embark on a programme of large battleship building as she probably considers this type of ship will be out of date by the time she is able to build any.'[18] In September 1948 the MoD Joint

Sverdlov in 1955. (NHHC)

Intelligence Bureau noted that 'two battleships have been lying partially completed at yards at Leningrad and Nikolayev since before the war but there is no prospect of their being finished'.[19] Subsequent intelligence reports from Moscow note the focus on large cruiser construction (the *Sverdlov* class) and submarine fleet expansion, but there is no inkling of knowledge of the Project 24 or Project 82 work.[20]

But stripping back to basics, it is clear that the Soviet Union continued after the war to plan for and attempt to build a new big-gun navy on a substantial scale, and well after the end of similar projects in the West. Western battleship planning and the retention of battleships in their navies after 1945 had at least half an eye to this possibility, noting the continued existence of older Russian ships and the formidable potential of the new cruisers, although I have not found evidence that the existence of Project 24 and project 82 was specifically acknowledged or addressed in the West. Ultimately, despite laying down nine keels, including the only three begun after 1945, the Soviet Navy failed to complete a single modern battleship. The great 'what if?' of battleship history after 1945 would be 'What if Stalin had lived?' In the event the Soviet Navy of the 1950s focussed much more effort on building up submarine forces, and settled for cruisers as their heaviest surface units. But even here the drive for size was evident. The fourteen cruisers of the *Sverdlov* class that were eventually built through the 1950s were, at 16,600 tons (the Admiralty estimated up to 20,000 tons), much larger than any European cruisers, and matched for tonnage only by a few of the very largest US cruisers. The *Sverdlovs* constituted a threat against which it was felt that a Western battleship backstop was justified to counter them, at least into the late 1950s. The First Lord of the Admiralty reported to Cabinet after the 1953 visit to Spithead by *Sverdlov* that she was bigger, more powerful and likely to be much faster than Royal Navy cruisers and 'she would be an unpleasant threat loose on the trade routes and would take a great deal of bringing to book'.[21] Had Stalin lived to the late 1950s it is likely that the Soviet Navy could have added to the *Sverdlovs* at least two or three 12in-gunned or missile-armed battlecruisers, magnifying the threat to the NATO lines of communication and the Atlantic Striking Fleet.

Secrecy about Soviet intentions was pervasive, and even well after the fall of the USSR it was difficult to tease out all the threads, but secrecy was also combined with some Maskirovka – the art of military deception – to produce some public perceptions that the Soviet Union was not only working on new rocket-armed battleships, for which there was some basis in fact, but had even got so far as commissioning one. *Jane's Fighting Ships* and its French equivalent *Les Flottes de Combat* both published plans, rough estimate dimensions and characteristics of a Soviet heavy ship derived from Project 23 designs, in their editions from 1948 to 1953. These showed the vessels not only with the heaviest-calibre guns, but also with domed emplacements designed to fire rocket-propelled guided missiles. This was possibly a window into the shadowy design world of late-era projects 24 and 82. Although Project 24 got no further than outline sketches and 82 got no further than the slipway, the Soviet Union allowed to be circulated in 1953 documents purporting to be submarine and aircraft recognition cribs for a class of ship described as 'Heavy Naval Unit *Sovietskaya Byelorossiya*'. In reality, no such ships existed, and the diagram, on closer examination, was an unsubtle direct reprint of the original *Jane's* speculation. [22] The Soviets did not deploy an anti-ship missile afloat until the late 1950s.

Notwithstanding the failure of the newer programmes, the Soviet Union remained keen to have the older battleships in its order of battle. McLaughlin attributes this apparent anomaly to a coherent strategy where Kuznetzov realised that building the new ships was easier than preparing the sailors and officers for them. The older battleship fleet, including hoped-for reparations from Italy, was needed as the training ground for the big ship, big gun sailors of the putative oceanic fleet. *Giulio Cesare*, following refurbishment at Taranto, survived a sabotage attempt at Augusta, Sicily, in December 1948, was stricken from the Italian Navy list on 15 December that year and transferred to Russia at Vlore (Valona), in Albania, on 6 February 1949, the timing synchronised to that of the return of *Royal Sovereign* to the UK at the opposite end of Europe. It had originally been intended to sail *Cesare* to Odessa in the Black Sea for transfer on 15 January 1949. Turkey, amidst general concerns about the impact of the Italian war prizes on the balance of naval power, decided to exercise her rights under the 1936 Montreux Convention to bar passage of the Italian ship through the Turkish Straits, even under a mercantile flag. The Four Power Commission therefore agreed to the Soviet suggestion to make the transfer at Vlore, as the Convention did not ban the transit of Soviet capital ships through the Straits.[23]

Cesare sailed to Albania not under her name, but designated as 'Z11' and flying the Italian Merchant Marine flag. The transfer was untrusting. The Italian crew were removed from their posts immediately and confined to the fo'c'sle under guard. All were removed from the ship within three days. Russia carried out a thorough search for hidden explosive devices. The Russian assessment on handover was that armament, main machinery, hull and lower bulkhead condition was 'satisfactory', upper bulkheads and water-tight doors unsatisfactory; and piping, internal communications, auxiliary machinery, firefighting and diesel generators poor or non-operational. Assimilation of the ship into the Soviet Navy was further hampered by the lack of any Italian-speaking crew members,

Novorossiysk (ex-Giulio Cesare) at Sevastopol *c.* 1950.

and two Russian junior officers with only rudimentary Italian language skills only arrived one month later. Under the circumstances the Soviet Navy did quite well to sail her through the challenging waters of the Dardanelles without incident. She arrived at Sevastopol on 26 February to join the Black Sea Fleet and was renamed *Novorossiysk*. In August 1949 she is reported to have taken part in squadron manoeuvres as flagship of the Black Sea Fleet, but McLaughlin notes that she was in dockyard hands on eight separate occasions between 1949 and 1955.

The *Gangut* class all remained in service too, with the exception of *Frunze*, which was gradually scrapped at Leningrad between 1944 and 1949. Even she was potentially to be rehabilitated. The Soviets ran a 'Project 27' that envisaged melding the undamaged bow of *Frunze* with the largely undamaged stern of the bombed *Petropavlovsk* to create a single, modernised, seagoing *Gangut*-class battleship. Kuznetsov was unconvinced and recommended this project be cancelled on 31 October 1946. Formal cancellation was not received until 29 June 1948.[24] However, two of *Petropavlovsk*'s 12in turrets and their guns were instead used to rebuild the Maksim Gorky coast defence battery No. 30 at Sevastopol in the Crimea and, amazingly, remained in service until 1997 when they were eighty-five years old.[25]

CHAPTER TEN

Conflict in Korea

HOWEVER FANTASTIC THE speculation about Soviet battleships became, the attention the issue got reflected the new reality of the post-war world. The Iron Curtain had descended over Europe. The Soviet Union was committed to hold its Eastern European gains, and to spread communism and communist influence elsewhere where opportunity existed. The Berlin blockade had been faced down in 1948–49. China fell to the communists in 1949. The West faced up to the newly perceived threats to liberal democracy by creating first the Western Union in 1948 and then in April 1949 the North Atlantic Treaty Organisation. Against this developing background of confrontation in a new bi-polar world, the North Koreans under Kim-il-Sung invaded the Western-backed republic in the south of the Korean peninsula.

On 25 June 1950, the day of the invasion, the number of battleships remaining in existence was forty-four (excluding those in the process of being scrapped). Four were to fight again in Korea. Survivors at the outbreak of the Korean War were:

UK: *King George V* in reserve at Gare Loch; *Duke of York* reducing to reserve at Portsmouth; *Anson* reducing to reserve at Devonport; *Howe* in reserve at Devonport; and *Vanguard* as flagship of the Training Squadron at Portland.

USA: *Texas* – State memorial at San Jacinto, Texas; *Mississippi* – Operational Development Force gunnery trials and training ship, based at Norfolk, Virginia; *Colorado, Maryland, West Virginia* – Pacific Fleet Reserve, Bremerton, Washington; *Tennessee, California* – Atlantic Fleet reserve, Philadelphia Navy Yard; *Washington, North Carolina* – Atlantic Fleet Reserve, Bayonne, New Jersey; *South Dakota, Indiana* – Atlantic Fleet Reserve, Philadelphia; *Alabama, Massachusetts* – Pacific Fleet Reserve, Bremerton; *Iowa, Wisconsin* – Pacific Fleet Reserve, Bremerton; *New Jersey* – Atlantic Fleet Reserve, Philadelphia; *Missouri* – In commission, Atlantic Fleet, visiting New York City; *Kentucky* – still incomplete at Norfolk Navy Yard; *Illinois* – still incomplete at Philadelphia Naval Shipyard; *Alaska, Guam* – Atlantic Fleet Reserve, Bayonne, New Jersey; *Hawaii* – still incomplete, Camden, New Jersey.

FRANCE: *Paris* – accommodation ship, Brest; *Lorraine* – training ship, Brest; *Bretagne* – hulk at Mers-el-Kébir, Algeria; *Dunkerque* – hulk at Toulon; *Strasbourg* – experimental hulk, Toulon; *Richelieu* – in reserve, Brest; *Jean Bart* – in commission, incomplete, visiting Casablanca, Morocco.

ITALY: *Andrea Doria* – Mediterranean Fleet flagship; *Caio Duilio* – Mediterranean Fleet.

RUSSIA: *Sevastopol, Novorossiysk* – Black Sea Fleet, Sevastopol; *Oktyabrskaya Revolutsiya* – 8th Fleet, Tallinn, Baltic; *Petropavlovsk* – training ship, Leningrad; (plus plans for the new *Stalingrad* class.)

TURKEY: *Yavuz* – largely inactive, Istanbul, Gölcük and Izmir.

BRAZIL: *Minas Gerais* – Flagship, Rio de Janeiro; *Sao Paulo* – training ship, Rio de Janeiro.

ARGENTINA: *Rivadavia, Moreno* – Puerto Belgrano battleship dock.

CHILE: *Almirante Latorre* – in commission, Talcahuano.

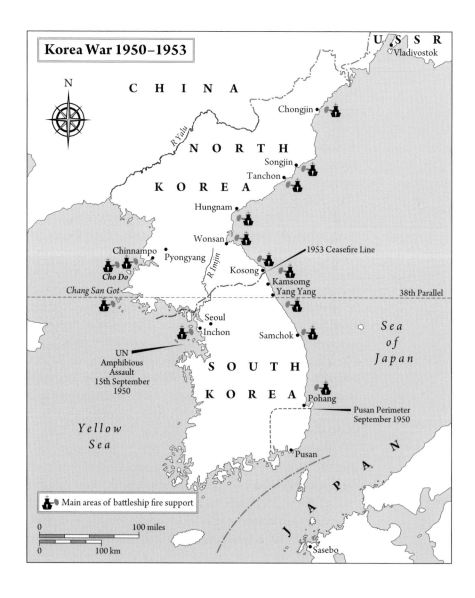

On 25 June 1950, after a number of armed clashes, North Korean forces crossed the 38th parallel. This marked the demarcation dividing the Stalinist north of the Korean peninsula from the Republic of Korea set up in the south in 1945 with United States backing following the ejection of the Japanese colonisers. Tensions had been evident throughout the five years since the defeat of Japan. Both sides saw the de facto division of the peninsula as an ad hoc and temporary arrangement. Both governments claimed legitimacy over the whole of Korea. This was the most serious international conflict since the Second World War. It came hard on the heels of the communist victory over the Nationalist Government in mainland China the previous October, and against the backdrop of a deepening Cold War and the evidence of Stalin's global aspirations. It was also the first occasion when the United Nations Organisation Security Council set out to impose its mandate by force. In the absence of a Soviet veto, because they were boycotting the UN at that time, the Security Council authorised the dispatch of UN forces to Korea by Resolution No. 83 on 27 June. In August the United States Congress approved the appropriation of $12 billion for military action in Korea, doubling the planned military expenditure for the fiscal year 1949–50.

The UN-backed Republic of Korea (ROK) forces quickly came under intense pressure from the Northern armies and retreated through the summer of 1950 into the small defensive perimeter around the port of Pusan in the far south of South Korea. There they held out, being steadily reinforced by US troops, initially from the occupation force in Japan and eventually from the US itself. Meanwhile, UN Commander General Douglas MacArthur exploited the flexibility offered by modest but locally overwhelming naval power; air superiority; and some materiel and experience still fresh from the Allied successes in island hopping the Pacific in 1945, to plan and launch the much admired counter-stroke of an amphibious landing at Inchon. This was well behind the enemy lines on the west coast near the 38th parallel and the Southern capital at Seoul. The attack took place with 40,000 troops as early as 15 September, with the war still only twelve weeks old. Seoul was recaptured quickly, and a drive into the north saw the northern capital Pyongyang fall to UN forces on 19 October. MacArthur's troops were soon closing in on the Yalu river, North Korea's border with China. Chinese Premier Chou Enlai, having been urged on by Stalin since early August, committed the People's Liberation Army across the Yalu on 19 October, and their first counter-offensive began on 25 October. The UN was once again forced back and fighting stabilised around Seoul and the 38th parallel from January 1951 onwards.

Although the contraction in US armed forces since 1945, and particularly the severe budget cuts by Secretary for Defense Louis Johnson in 1949, had left large gaps in its ability to respond quickly, the United

States Navy mobilised its available 7th Fleet resources based in Japan and was in action with one aircraft carrier and modest surface forces within days. Early on in the conflict a substantial proportion of the UN response was provided by the British Far Eastern Fleet, which happened to be visiting Japan at the outbreak of the war. There was no significant North Korean anti-ship threat other than from mines, but given the extensive seaward flanks of the Korean peninsula, and the concentration of population centres and road and rail communications near the coast, the UN commanders quickly recognised the potential for shore bombardment to support their hard-pressed ground forces. The only immediately available US cruiser, *Juneau*, and four destroyers were in action shelling North Korean troop columns as early as 29 June, just four days after the war began. But it was clear that much more firepower would be needed, both to provide more range and impact than could be achieved by these 5in guns and also to deal with the increasingly well-protected targets that became favoured by North Korea and the Chinese. So the battleships and heavy 8in gunned cruisers were called up by the United States, and also 6in cruisers by the UK.

The US heavy cruisers *Helena* and *Toledo*, then part of the active US Pacific Fleet, were ordered across the Pacific on 29 June and sailed from the USA on 5 July. The aircraft carrier *Philippines Sea* and two escort carriers left the next day. The first 6in gun bombardment of North Korean targets was by HMS *Jamaica* from the British Far Eastern Fleet on 5 July. By 18 July the carriers HMS *Triumph* and USS *Valley Forge* were providing air strikes in support of the initial US reinforcements at Pohang on the east coast. The first 8in cruiser bombardments were by *Toledo* in support of the 1st US Cavalry Division at Pusan on 27 July.

Missouri was by then the only US battleship in commission. It is claimed that even she only avoided relegation to reserve in 1949 because President Truman, from Missouri State, whose daughter had launched her, had an excessive fondness for the ship, and that he had overruled the original mothballing decision of Defense Secretary Johnson. *Missouri*, recovered and fully repaired from her January grounding, was serving in the Atlantic Fleet and was in New York City with a ship full of midshipmen on a training cruise when the war broke out. She was rapidly retasked and mobilised for war service at Norfolk, Virginia, and deployed on 19 August 1950. In appearance and capability, she was essentially as she had finished the Pacific War. Minor modifications included a new SPS6 air search radar, an SG6 surface search radar, some enhanced communications and some electronic warfare equipment.[1] She was also carrying helicopters on the quarter deck for spotting the fall of her shot. The original OSU2 Kingfisher and SC-1 Seahawk floatplanes had been removed by 1948. At least, she was carrying helicopters until, in his haste to sail her from Norfolk, Admiral Holloway, commanding Battleships and Cruisers Atlantic, directed her into an Atlantic hurricane off the Florida coast. She passed within 117 miles of the eye, and was maintaining 25 knots through mountainous seas. Both HO3S-1 helicopters were washed overboard, and there was also serious damage to exposed fittings on the weather deck. One 40mm mounting was destroyed, along with six boats. A 24in searchlight was torn from its mounting on the flag bridge. Later, the ship's track was diverted to avoid a storm of similar intensity in the Pacific and fresh helicopters came aboard.[2]

Missouri transited the Panama Canal and arrived off Kyushu, Japan, on 14 September, where she became flagship of Rear Admiral Allan Smith. The next day, the day of the Inchon landings, she bombarded Samchok on the east coast of Korea as part of a diversionary manoeuvre to draw DPRK forces away from the Inchon beachhead. She fired fifty-two 16in shells in this first bombardment, destroying one and damaging a second railway bridge. Her helicopters spotted the fall of shot, the first time this had been done. This mission was followed up with a 298-projectile bombardment around Pohang on 17 September, obliterating the North Korean positions on the north bank of the Hyung San river, helping ROK forces cross it and capture that city as part of the Pusan perimeter. A US Army observer commented: 'I didn't know it could be done. The *Missouri*'s fire was really demoralising to those Red troops. We practically walked across that river standing up.'[3]

There were some problems as she got into her work. Accurate positioning of the ship to calculate initial range was difficult because available charts were poor. Radio communications with the airborne and ground-based army spotters were initially unreliable. One shell exploded prematurely only 50ft after leaving the muzzle, attributed to a faulty fuze. That may have been a lucky escape for the ship, but fortunately proved an isolated incident. Showing the flexibility of naval power, *Missouri* sailed to the west of the peninsula and reached Inchon on 19 September, four days after the landings. The next day she was pushed as far up the Han river as her 35ft draft allowed, in the hope that she could fire on the road between Seoul and Wonsan up which the North Korean Army was retreating. She fired eleven 16in ranging shots, but by then the front line was already over 28 miles away and the fighting had passed beyond the range at which even she could participate.

Missouri then had a quiet few weeks acting as escort to the only US carrier in Korean waters at the time, *Valley Forge*. Options to use her for bombardment in the next phase of the war during the UN advance on the west coast were constrained by the very shallow island-dotted waters of the Yellow Sea. There were no such constraints on the east coast, where the deep water of the Sea of Japan was close inshore. MacArthur, while pressing on to Pyongyang and beyond in the west, was also contemplating another amphibious coup de main at Wonsan, some way north of the 38th parallel on the east coast. *Missouri* escorted *Valley Forge* to support this operation. On 12 October 1950 she undertook bombardment missions on the east coast at Chongjin and Tanchon, considerably north of Wonsan. The former was less than 50 miles from the Russian border, and about the same distance to China. Results were reportedly excellent, with the iron works, warehouses, docks, rolling stock and marshalling yards all destroyed by ninety-six 16in shells. The operation was the first joint effort of the war, with Commonwealth cruisers and destroyers also involved, and top cover protection being flown from *Valley Forge*. The next day *Missouri* ranged over a 120-mile stretch of coast south of Chongjin firing at five separate coastal targets as part of the UN advance. The Wonsan landings were delayed by the unforeseen North Korean deployment of Soviet mines and the inadequacy of the available minesweeping forces after five years of post-war neglect. The landings eventually took place on 21 October, although they were unopposed as the ROK forces had already made up all the ground from Pusan via the overland route to reach the port. But the battleships were to get to know Wonsan and its approaches very well over the following thirty-two months.

By this stage of the war the Chinese had intervened to prop up the flagging Northern forces, and the Wonsan invasion force soon came under heavy communist pressure in the hills north of the port. *Missouri*'s next mission, now from 5 November as flagship of the 7th Fleet under Vice Admiral A D Struble, was again to screen the carrier force in the Sea of Japan and east of Wonsan as their aircraft met the threat of the Chinese-backed counter-attack in the hills. By the end of December she became heavily engaged in the defence of the port of Hungnam on the northern east coast, where the retreating UN forces had become besieged by the rapidly advancing Chinese forces. To cover the successful evacuation of the US Xth Corps, she fired 162 rounds of 16in, as well as 699 rounds of her 5in secondary battery, between 23 and 24 December in a saturation barrage to prevent the enemy forces from threatening the final withdrawal. Other US Navy ships also fired 2,932 8in shells from three cruisers and 18,637 5in shells to cover the Hungnam withdrawal. *Missouri* suffered casualties on this mission as her spotter helicopter crashed at sea on 21 December and the crew of three were lost.

Although she did not fire during most of January, *Missouri* carried out more bombardments in early 1951. Between 30 January and 1 February on the east coast she fired on Kamsong and Kojong as part of another amphibious feint code-named Operation Ascendant. This involved firing 382 16in and 3,002 5in shells. Twelve crewmen suffered minor injuries handling the 5in ammunition to keep up the rate of fire.[4]

By 9 February she was back on the west coast at Inchon for another feint, and the port, lost to the second communist advance, was recaptured by the UN forces the next day. Thereafter, the priority for fire support became the destruction of the east coast road and rail communications, particularly the railway bringing reinforcements and supplies for the communist forces. *Missouri* returned to the east and carried out thirty-nine separate missions over two months, firing 1,991 more rounds of 16in artillery. Battle damage reports credited her with twenty road and rail bridges destroyed, some 70 per cent of the targets she engaged. These included the vital Tanchon railway bridges, tunnels and causeways, where the railway was directly next to the ocean. *Missouri* destroyed them on 22–23 February, expending 213 shells to knock out the three bridges. She put 400 shells into the Chongjin railway line from 14 to 16 March. This proved a tough target and ten direct hits with high-explosive shells on the causeway caused only superficial damage. *Missouri* therefore moved from the normal firing position, which was outside the 100 fathom line to avoid the moored mine risk, close to the 50 fathom line, and switched to armour-piercing shells at 10,000 yards range. Further direct hits generated a landslide down the mountain and the railway was destroyed.[5] *Missouri*'s final bombardment was on Wonsan port itself, now back in communist hands. The suppression of Wonsan was to last as long as the war itself.

Later analysis suggests that it took an average of sixty 16in shells to destroy one bridge. Overall during this January to March period the UN forces fired 18,000 shells of 6in calibre and above, of which *Missouri* contributed 1,610 16in, three-quarters of them directed at the road and rail system. There were also persistent air strikes from the carriers against the North Korean communications. The overall result was over 100 bridges destroyed and the railway line cut in over 200 places.[6]

Missouri left the Korean theatre on 19 March. She had fired 2,895 rounds of 16in and 8,043 rounds of 5in ammunition, and steamed 62,000 miles.[7] If her guns had been new when she deployed this would still have allowed her about 600–800 more firings before the barrel linings wore down to such an extent that her accuracy would diminish unacceptably. As she had been in continuous commission since 1945 she was probably carrying the same guns as she had finished the war with, so additional wear is likely. The reasons for withdrawing her at precisely that point bear scrutiny, because she had been heavily engaged and her battleship successor, *New Jersey*, did not reach Japan until 17 May 1951. There was thus a two-month gap in battleship coverage, when only 8in cruisers and smaller ships were available for fire support. This coincided with the communist spring offensive, which once more put the UN forces under considerable pressure and forced extensive retreats, including the loss of Seoul once again. Nevertheless, *Missouri* sailed back to the USA, arriving on 27 April 1951 at Norfolk, Virginia, after eight and a half months away. It was the length of this deployment and its impact on crew morale that was probably the constraining factor on keeping her in Korea, rather than the wear on the guns. After her return to the USA, *Missouri* nonetheless undertook two midshipman training cruises in the Atlantic before going into Norfolk Navy Yard in September 1951 for an overhaul that included gun relining, which lasted until March 1952.

The other *Iowa*-class battleships had all gone into reserve well before the outbreak of the war. It became evident very early on in the conflict that the US would need to recall reserve manpower and to reactivate many units of the reserve fleet in order to sustain the Korean War effort. President Truman authorised the activation of reserves on 19 July 1950. Regular enlistments were also extended for twelve months involuntarily. Reactivating the ships proved challenging because the care and maintenance teams and already trained reservists who would normally do much of the training for the recalled crews had in many cases been sent to the Far East themselves in the early waves of reinforcement. Nevertheless, reactivation of battleships, carriers, cruisers, escorts, minesweepers and amphibious shipping all proceeded through 1950 and 1951. For the larger ships the preservation measures described in Chapter Three had been largely effective. Work commenced aboard *New Jersey* on 26 September 1950. During October the crew, mainly recalled reservists, began to arrive. The formal recommissioning ceremony was on 21 November 1950 at Bayonne, New Jersey, following which there was a period in the dockyard. Inevitably there were some defects to rectify. One side effect of dehumidification was that machinery gaskets had dried up and needed replacing. The same happened to some of the electrical insulation. But in general the ship was in good shape. A shakedown cruise in the Caribbean in the New Year saw her ready to deploy from Norfolk on 16 April 1951. She would have passed *Missouri* on her return journey somewhere near the Panama Canal.

New Jersey's first deployment to Korea was as busy as *Missouri*'s. She became flagship of the 7th Fleet under Vice Admiral Harold Martin at Sasebo, Japan, on 17 May 1951. She was in action off Wonsan as early as 20 May. During that first bombardment she set herself on fire as a 16in discharge ignited fittings on deck and some 40mm ammunition exploded. It took seventeen minutes to extinguish the blaze. The next day at 0930 she was hit by a shore battery on number one turret. Although the damage was superficial, one of her crew, R H Osterwind, was killed, and two others wounded.

While the hazard of artillery fire from ashore continued and intensified as the communists brought in more and more guns to defend the coast, and there were many near misses on the battleships over the next two years, a more potent threat during 1951 remained mines. The destroyer *Walke* was severely damaged and twenty-five of her crew killed by a mine strike around this time. The mines were moored close inshore and deployed by sampan, and they necessitated regular sweeping of the corridors used by the gunnery support ships. Floating mines were also deliberately set adrift to cross the Sea of Japan on the southerly currents. Over 300 of these washed up on Japanese shores in 1951 but, using helicopters to spot for them, there were no other major casualties from this cause among the UN fleet. *New Jersey's* six months in the theatre saw her effort directed less at the railway line to the Russian border and more in support of the UN ground forces on the front line, as well as in sustaining what became known as the sieges of Wonsan and Songjin. The ports were behind the new front line, but strongly garrisoned by the communists, and the UN siege was maintained by regularly cutting the supply routes to the towns and destroying the facilities within them using naval bombardments.

Between 23 and 30 May *New Jersey* bombarded Yang Yang and Kamsong. A helicopter based on the ship was lost on 24 May while searching for a downed pilot. In June she carried out three shoots at Wonsan, where she was again nearly hit by shore battery fire on 28 June. Chief of Naval Operations Admiral Forrest Sherman was aboard her to witness those operations. From 4 to 12 July she fired in support of the ROK 1st Division attack on Kamsong, then she demolished the five 5in gun emplacements at Wonsan on 18 July, which had targeted the US destroyers with over 500 shells on the previous day. She was back supporting the Kamsong front from 17 to 29 August, firing 483 16in shells to drive off counter-attacks on Xth Corps. The Commander of Xth Corps stated that the battleship's intervention was decisive and future fire support by *New Jersey* was anticipated with keen interest.[8]

An intermission in operations between late July and mid-August was caused by Number 3 main engine failing on 16 July because it lost lubricating oil pressure. The resulting damage to the turbines was severe enough to require a three-week period with the Repair Ship *Ajax*, as oil seals, bearings and carbon packing for the turbine were replaced.[9] The fact that she could be repaired in theatre was testament to the extent to which US Navy logistics had geared up for the war by that stage; and the fact that this was the only significant breakdown suffered by the class on operations between 1945 and 1992 was testament to the *Iowa* class's resilience and reliability. On 30 August *New Jersey* went north again and bombarded Chongjin with spotting provided by helicopter. Then it was back to Kamsong in September and October, where the advance of the US Xth Corps had reached the upper stretches on the Soyang river. Although this was on the western side of the Korean peninsula watershed, the battleship was able to fire over 2,000 foot hills at ranges of between 11 and 16 miles in support of the US 1st Marine Division.

New Jersey bombards Hungnam, 5 October 1951. (NARA)

On 1 October 1951 *New Jersey* hosted a conference between General Omar Bradley, Chairman of the US Joint Chiefs of Staff, and Lt General Matthew Ridgeway, the UN Commander-in-Chief Far East. In the first week of October she also ranged up the east coast to bombard targets at Hungnam, Hambong, Tanchon and Songjin.

On 16 October she undertook a joint bombardment of Kojo Island at Wonsan with HMS *Belfast*. In the first week of November she went to the far north and took on Chongjin and Iowon, under tactical command of Rear Admiral Scott-Moncrieff RN, and with Australian spotters flying from the carrier HMAS *Sydney*. *New Jersey* rounded off her tour of duty with her only deployment to the west coast, firing on communist troop concentrations at the Chang San Got peninsula and Yellow Sea islands.

On 12 November 1951 she fired her final bombardment and 3,000th 16in round of the deployment. The ten weeks of operation between September and departure were rated as consistently excellent shooting. Nor was it just the gunners who excelled. One of her helicopter pilots, Lieutenant (Junior Grade) Tuffanelli, was commended for rescuing under fire a pilot from the carrier *Bon Homme Richard*, shot down 10 miles inland south of Wonson. Back in July he had to fly a doctor to attend the crash of another helicopter, which had been carrying 8th Army commander General James Van Fleet away from the ship, but had hit a mountain in fog. Fortunately no one was seriously injured. *New Jersey* was relieved on station by *Wisconsin*, and was back in Norfolk, Virginia, on 20 December 1951. But she would return.

Wisconsin had begun reactivation in early 1951 and was formally recommissioned on 3 March. However, she did not depart from New York until 25 October 1951, a gap of nearly eight month, partly due to undertaking midshipman training cruises to Cuba and Europe before

New Jersey fires a broadside off the Korean coast, 10 November 1951. *(NARA)*

sailing for the Far East. Still she was on station at Yokosuka as flagship of the 7th fleet (still Vice Admiral Harold Martin) by 21 November 1951, ensuring almost seamless battleship presence in the Far East as *New Jersey* departed. *Wisconsin*'s crew included a Divisional officer, Lieutenant Commander E R Zumwalt, who would go on to great things and, as Chief of Naval Operations, play a decisive role in the fate of the battleships in the 1970s. *Wisconsin*'s first bombardment was at Kosong on 2 December. She was in fire support of the front line at Kanmung from 3 to 14 December, before bombarding Kojo. She re-ammunitioned at Sasebo from 15 to 17 December, but was back at the gun line by 18 December and Wonsan on the 20 December. She probably registered a first for a battleship on 28 December when Cardinal Francis Spellman, archbishop of New York and outspoken anti-communist, was helicoptered onto the ship at sea off the east coast to say mass for the Roman Catholic members of the crew.

As 1952 dawned *Wisconsin* continued on the gun line in support of the 1st US Marine Division and 1st ROK Corps. Her average ranges for January were 16 miles, and ten shells were fired at the 48th Chinese Division. Captives from that unit said that their political officers were explaining the size of the 16in shell holes to their troops by attributing them to atomic artillery.[10] At the end of January and into early February she returned to the siege of Wonsan, bombarding the islands of Kojo and Hodo Pando. Then she put 300 shells into Kosong in a snowstorm, destroying an estimated 50 per cent of the town. After a resupply in Japan, she bombarded Songjin on 15 March.

Here her captain probably became rather overconfident and closed

Wisconsin at sea on 8 February 1952 with snow and a Sikorsky HO3-S1 helicopter on her aft deck. *(NARA)*

The destroyer *Buck* (left) and heavy cruiser *St Paul* (right) flank *Wisconsin* on 22 February 1952. *(NARA)*

the shore to engage a train with 40mm batteries. Although successful, she paid the price as she became the second battleship of the war to be hit by a shore battery. A 152mm shell struck a starboard 40mm gun shield and made a hole 24 × 30in in the starboard side of 02 deck amidships at frame 144. Damage was minimal, although three of the crew were injured. Retribution was swift and complete, as she destroyed the gun battery responsible with 16in gunfire.[11] It was her final bombardment of the war. She was back in Japan by 19 March and relieved by *Iowa* on 1 April 1952. She reached the continental USA at Long Beach on 19 April 1952.

Iowa's reactivation commenced on 14 July 1951. She was commissioned on 25 August, but did not sail for Korea until early March 1952, a six-month work-up period. This was as eventful as *Missouri*'s preparations. She was ordered to undertake machinery trials at 20 knots in the narrow and current-ridden confines of San Francisco Bay. The orders were queried but flatly confirmed so Captain Smedburg did as he was told and circled Alcatraz Island. This was a rare treat for the prisoners, but nearly ended in disaster as currents swept her within feet of grounding on the Rock. Admiral of the Fleet Chester Nimitz, Pacific Fleet

Wisconsin firing at the east coast railway, March 1952. *(NARA)*

Commander during the Second World War, had retired to a house overlooking the scene of this manoeuvre and felt sufficiently outraged by what he had witnessed to ring up Captain Smedburg the next day and berate him for taking the risk.[12]

Iowa became 7th Fleet flagship (now under Vice Admiral Robert P Briscoe) on 1 April 1952, and was in action at Wonsan, Suwon Dan and Kojo on 8 and 9 April. On 13 April her firing in support of 1st ROK Corps was estimated to have killed 100 of the enemy and destroyed six guns. In her first nine days of firing she expended 549 16in and 1,486 5in shells. She went north on 20 April to fire at the railway at Tanchon. The communists were repairing the line continuously, requiring periodic repeat bombardments to suppress it. On this occasion *Iowa* closed four tunnels and sailed on to Kosong. She went north again in May to Chongjin and Songjin, the bombardment of Chongjin on 25 May taking her further north than any operation since November 1950, a mere 48 miles from Russia. In a joint air and sea bombardment, 200 aircraft dropped 230 tons of bombs and *Iowa* fired 202 shells weighing 192 tons. The shoot lasted all day and targets destroyed included the iron works, brick works, sugar

factory, gas storage, power station, three transformers, radio tower and dockside cranes. Russian aircraft were detected by the task force, but no intervention took place. *Iowa* then resumed the siege of Wonsan.

In June the pattern was much the same, but also featured a visit to the west coast to repeat *Wisconsin*'s shelling of troops on the offshore islands of Cho Do and Sok Cho. Smedburg carried out these last two operations at anchor to improve accuracy, but this was considered too risky by the chain of command, and thenceforth, as before, battleships had to keep moving while shooting. On 1 June and 16 July her helicopter rescued downed pilots from the carrier *Princeton*. And on 28 August she stood by the mined and seriously damaged destroyer *Thompson* rendering assistance. On 23 September General Mark Clark, the new UN Commander-in-Chief Far East, observed *Iowa* bombarding Wonsan. Two days later she was in action against a moving train. During October 1952 her tour of duty culminated in forty-three missions against fixed targets and twenty-seven firings on the gun line in direct support of the front-line troops.

Vice Admiral Joseph J Clark had taken over Command of the 7th Fleet. He disliked using the battleship as his flagship and found the

Iowa fires her 16in guns off Korea, mid-1952. *(NARA)*

bombardment work tedious, preferring to spend his time visiting the carriers. When he was aboard *Iowa* his cabin was severely affected by blast from firing of the ship's forward 16in turrets. He ordered that all shots should be from the aft turret, and caused much grumbling among Iowa's gun crews as they had to manhandle the 1-ton projectiles from the forward magazines down the length of the ship to reach the stern turret.[13] All told *Iowa* fired 16,689 rounds in Korea, probably around 3,000 of 16in and the remainder 5in.

Iowa was in turn replaced by *Missouri*, which had set off for her second tour of the war from Norfolk on 11 September 1952. She reached Yokosuka on 17 October and became flagship of the 7th Fleet on 19 October when, notwithstanding his disillusionment with *Iowa*, Vice Admiral Clark came aboard. *Missouri* was on the gun line and suppressing the east coast communications between 25 October and 2 January 1953, before a brief visit to Inchon and thence to Japan. On 21 December she lost her spotter helicopter at sea off Hungnam and the crew of three were killed. By the end of January she was back in Korean waters, repeating the bombardments of Wonsan, Kojo, Tanchon and Hungnam. Her final bombardment was on 25 March 1953. Sadly her captain, Warner J Edsall, suffered a fatal heart attack while bringing the ship back to Sasebo on completion of her deployment. Among those to witness *Missouri*'s impact on the ground during this deployment was Lt Col R D Heinl, US Marine Corps, who would go on to be a major advocate for retaining and reviving the ships for amphibious fire support roles in the 1960s and '70s.[14]

New Jersey had set off from Norfolk on 5 March 1953 for her second tour of duty in Korea. She reached Yokosuka on 5 April, was the flagship of the 7th Fleet (still Vice Admiral Clark) the next day and back on bombardment duty up in the north at Chongjin by 12 April. She was lucky on that trip as a floating mine was spotted in her bow wave. Fortunately it passed down the ship's side and was then taken under fire and sunk by the destroyer *Laws*. Her pattern of operations was similar to that of her predecessors, alternating between close support of the gun line, forays to the northern targets to suppress the railway and port facilities on the east coast, and a lot of work around Wonsan. Her bombardment at Wonsan on 1 May was particularly effective, destroying eleven enemy gun batteries. On 25 May she transferred to the west coast to take on artillery emplacements at Chinampo harbour and Sok Cho and Cho Do islands. As the prolonged armistice negotiations at Panmunjom dragged towards their eventual conclusion there was a final intensification of fighting around Wonsan and Kosong, where *New Jersey* provided direct support to UN forces under severe pressure on 6 June following the communist capture of an important ROK position on Anchor Hill. She carried out an all-day bombardment of Wonsan on 24 June, and similar prolonged firing on 11 and 12 July. She was firing for thirteen days in support of the gun line during June and July, and also conducted bombardments to the north. Her final bombardment of the war was on its penultimate day, 26 July, once again directed at long-suffering Wonsan.

After long, drawn-out negotiations, the armistice was at last signed on 27 July 1953, with thirteen of *New Jersey*'s crew among the UN delegation, bringing to an end more than three years of conflict. She left Korean waters briefly for a rest and recreation trip to Hong Kong on 20 August, but she was back in Korea by 16 September. There she was visited by South Korean president Syngman Rhee, where the ship's and the US Navy's role in preserving the democratic republic in the southern half of the peninsula was recognised by his conferring the Korean Presidential Unit Citation to the Commander-in-Chief of the 7th Fleet. *New Jersey* then left for home and arrived in late October.

The amount of naval fire support delivered by UN forces during the Korean War was comparable to the total Second World War effort. More than 1 million rounds of 5in and larger ammunition were fired altogether, 414,000 in 24,000 separate missions between May 1951 and March 1952 alone. Numerically the vast majority of these were by destroyers or cruisers, but the battleships played a very significant role, using not just their 16in guns but also their secondary batteries. Burr and Muir both give the figure for the total number of 16in shells fired in the Korean War as 20,424, an average of 3,400 for each of the six battleship deployments. Commander-in-Chief Pacific's post-war analysis opined that this had been excellent value for money at a total cost of $27.6 million in ammunition expended, with disproportionate damage inflicted, especially on hardened targets. The 16in fire was very favourably rated for effect, range, accuracy, and all-weather capability.[15] Analysis showed that overall 20 per cent of battleship missions were at ranges exceeding 30,000 yards. They conducted fire support missions often at ranges that were challenging for the five 8in-gunned cruisers that were also used regularly for similar missions, and well beyond the range of any lighter guns. There were a total of 423 missions in support of 1st US Marine Division between December 1950 and March 1951. *Missouri* conducted ninety-eight of these against hardened targets such as bunkers at an average range of 32,500 yards. The average range for the 8in cruisers targets was 20,000 yards.

In his immediate post-war analysis, the US Commander of the fire support Task Force 95 said: 'Five inch had little or no effect on coastal defence battery positions unless a direct hit was secured on the aperture … On the other hand gunfire of heavier calibre from battleships and cruisers had a much greater effect. On occasion batteries were permanently silenced … in other cases they were placed out of action for long periods.' *New Jersey*, in action in September and October 1951 in support of the

1st ROK Corps and US 1st Marine Division, fired 1,945 16in rounds. The 1st Marine Division, whose front line was 9 miles inland, estimated 3,600 enemy casualties from this fire. On 24 September they reported many bunkers destroyed on Hills 1190 and 951. On 2 October they reported twenty-five bunkers definitely destroyed and forty-nine estimated destroyed with 600 enemy casualties from 136 16in rounds on Hills 802 and 951.

From the middle of 1951 the battleships alternated operations between direct support of ground forces and bombardment against the crucial railway down the east coast that supplied the communist front line, together with its increasingly extensive defences, eventually amounting to more than 1,500 artillery pieces. In March 1951 *Missouri* conducted thirty-nine missions firing 1,167 rounds and destroying twenty bridges on the railway, some 70 per cent of the targets engaged. *New Jersey* between May and November that year undertook sixty-five missions, firing 767 rounds and destroying twenty-nine bridges (60 per cent of targets). On 24–25 April 1953 she fired 148 rounds and destroyed five bridges and five tunnels. On 27 May 1952 *Iowa* fired ninety-six rounds and destroyed all her five bridge and four tunnel targets. Spotting the fall of fire at long ranges remained a challenge through the war. When helicopters, carried aboard the battleships, were available to do that job bombardments became more effective. In the anti-bridge missions listed above an average of 3.6 salvos was needed to register the first hit using helicopters to spot the shells, and 6.1 using aircraft. Helicopters could not always be used because of the weather, and for the inland targets they were vulnerable to fire from the ground (although none seems to have been lost to this cause). The US analysis estimated that despite the resilient communist efforts to repair and defend it, this persistent assault on the east coast railway corridor reduced its cargo-carrying capacity by over 80 per cent from 3,000 to 500 tons per day, with commensurate atrophying of the communist effort at the front line.

As an example of the counter-battery fire, *New Jersey* put 115 rounds of 16in into the Hodo Pando artillery emplacement on 5 May 1953, and silenced it until 27 May. The Twikotchwi battery had fired 389 rounds at UN forces in May until *New Jersey* silenced it on 24 May. It did not fire again until 12 July. With Hodo Pando active again, she put 164 rounds into it on 11–12 July and it remained silenced until the ceasefire.[16] Many contemporary reports, especially those of the US Marine Corps, were in no doubt of the effectiveness of battleship gunfire support, its accuracy and sustainability when compared to air strikes, and its ability to engage at ranges well beyond those of lighter ships. Unsurprisingly, these lessons reflected very closely the outcome and impact of shore bombardment missions in the war against Japan. They still echo down the years in the prolonged US Navy debate about guns at sea and Littoral Combat Support.

The UK Government, in conjunction with the Commonwealth, decided to make a significant contribution to the United Nations forces in Korea. The Chiefs of Staff agreed that the one light carrier, two cruisers, two destroyers and three frigates that were coincidentally in Japanese waters at the time was the right level of force to place at the disposal of the US Naval Commander of UN forces, and the US Chief of Naval Operations endorsed that view.[17] A Royal Navy contingent was thus maintained, consisting of one or two light carriers, with six cruisers also involved at various times, and destroyers and frigates as escorts or in other direct support roles, often gunnery support to troops. It would have been possible for the UK to send *Vanguard*, which was in commission in Home Waters in the Training Squadron at the outbreak of the war, and as flagship of the Home Fleet from September 1950. However, I have found no evidence that this was ever contemplated. The *King George Vs* were all only just going into reserve in mid-1950, so could also have been deployed after relatively short reactivations. There were also still (just) British 8in-gunned cruisers available at that juncture as well, four ships surviving until 1951.

In the event the UK Government opted for the more economical option of 6in gunned cruisers to act as flagship, carrier escort and in shore bombardment roles, for which they were used extensively. Finding the crew to raise *Vanguard* to her war complement, which would have required about 1,000 men above her Training Squadron complement of 600, or to recommission one of the reserve battleships alongside her, which would have needed slightly more, was probably beyond the means of a navy still in the midst of a severe short-term manning crisis. Priority was instead given to increasing manning in the existing Far East Fleet. Its ships and those being sent to reinforce them required an additional 1,300 men to bring them up to war complements.[18] There was no surface threat for battleships to counter, and cruisers delivered the bulk of shore bombardment missions. There are also hints in the First Sea Lord's papers that the Government and Admiralty were assuming in late 1950, on the basis of General MacArthur's confidence about progress of the war at that point, that the Korean conflict would not last much longer. The focus of war planning was turning much more to the increased risk posed by an awakening Soviet threat closer to home, against which *Vanguard* and the *King George Vs* would still potentially have a part to play.

CHAPTER ELEVEN

Cold War – Rearming and Deterring in the Early 1950s

Sao Paulo midships close-up in 1921, showing the casemates for the 3.5in guns, which were probably the cause of her loss thirty years later. (© National Maritime Museum, Greenwich, London)

BATTLESHIPS REMAINED ACTIVE for much of the 1950s as the Western powers, now organised under the NATO umbrella, regularly exercised deterrence by demonstrating a forward presence in the North Atlantic, North Sea and Mediterranean. Elsewhere in the world, however, time was running out for some very old ships.

South America

This was particularly true in South America, where the three rival battleship navies still kept up their guard. However, as the decade wore on they elected to retrench with surplus Second World War light cruisers available from the US and the UK, and eventually small surplus aircraft carriers, too.

In Brazil, *Sao Paulo* was stricken from the active duty fleet on 22 August 1947, but remained in use as a training ship until August 1951. She had lain in Rio de Janeiro harbour since 1946, and had last been in dry dock in November 1948. She was then sold on 24 August 1951 to the British Iron and Steel Corporation (Salvage) Ltd (BISCO) for scrapping in the UK by Metal Industries at Faslane. BISCO hired the Ensign Rigging Company to provide a 'Runner crew' for the voyage. Mr W Painter, the managing director of Ensign Rigging, went to Rio to prepare the ship. Nearly 4,000 man hours of effort was expended making *Sao Paulo* ready for the voyage. Most of this was devoted to installing timber shoring to block the gunports for the original secondary armament of 3.5in guns.

The guns themselves were long removed, but their empty casemates, seven on each side, represented a vulnerability to seaworthiness as they were located low down in the ship's sides, below the main weather deck. A seaworthiness certificate was obtained from Mr Authur Polono Russi, the Bureau Veritas Surveyor in charge of Rio de Janeiro District. BISCO also contracted with Metal Industries Ltd for two tugs: the Admiralty ocean rescue tug *Bustler*, leased out to Metal Industries; and *Dextrous*, sub-contracted for the tow from the Overseas Towage and Salvage Company Ltd. *Bustler*, it will be recalled, was one of the tugs that had failed to tow *Warspite* to Faslane in 1947. The runner crew who would travel aboard the battleship was to be nine men under Mr Painter, but one, a Mr de Vos, was injured as the ship was about to leave and had to be taken ashore to hospital. He had a fortunate escape.

The tugs took *Sao Paulo* out of Rio de Janeiro on 20 September 1951. It was a slow voyage at an average speed of 4 knots. All went well for six weeks. Two minor difficulties with the trim of the ship and the alignment of the forward 12in turret, which had slewed off centre, were successfully corrected by the runner crew. The flotilla survived strong north-easterly winds on 19 and 20 October. But *Sao Paulo* had only reached a position just north of the Azores by 4 November when a north-westerly gale struck, requiring the ships to heave to, head to wind. Mr Painter reported to the tugs that his inspection of the ship had found that all was sound at around 1400, but at 1730 that evening the battleship seemed to sheer off suddenly to starboard, and both tow lines to the tugs snapped. The weather was now exceptionally bad with Force 12 winds and mountainous seas. The tugs were unable to maintain contact as darkness fell, and *Sao Paulo* disappeared towards the south-east. The tugs began a search the next morning, although *Dextrous* had to run for port because of heavy weather damage. *Bustler*, which was equipped with radar, searched until 19 November, and a third tug, *Turmoil*, until the next day.

British, Portuguese and American planes also scoured the Atlantic for over a week, without result. Master Signaller R V Wilks was among the crew of RAF Shackleton VP256 of No. 224 Squadron Royal Air Force, based at Gibraltar and flown by Pilot Officer Pollington. The Shackleton was brand new in service and had the ASV Mark 13 radar installed. M/Sig Wilks's logbook shows the plane left Gibraltar at 0500 on 7 November, to 'search for Brazilian BB Sao Paulo lost while being towed to UK'. They scoured the search area before landing at Lagens airfield in the Azores over thirteen hours later. They spent nearly seven hours airborne on 8 November continuing the search, seven and a half hours the following day, and nearly eight hours on 10 November before returning to Gibraltar that evening.[1] It was all to no avail. The ship and her crew were never seen again.

Because *Sao Paulo* had belonged to a British company, been under tow by British tugs and was in the charge of a British citizen, the UK Board of Trade held a formal investigation into the circumstances of her loss. This did not take place until 4 to 8 October 1954, mainly because of a prolonged delay in obtaining relevant information from the Brazilian authorities about *Sao Paulo*'s material state at the start of the final voyage. Correspondence shows increasing frustration at the British Ministry of Transport through 1953 and early 1954 at the delay in starting the inquiry and in particular with the failure by the British Embassy in Brazil to obtain necessary evidence from the Industrial Department of the Naval Arsenal of Rio de Janeiro concerning the blocking of the gunports with timber. The Board of Trade was particularly keen to get copies of any drawings showing how the timber shoring was installed, but could not obtain any.[2]

The inquiry under Mr Justice Hayward found, starkly but inevitably, that *Sao Paulo* sank and that all hands were drowned. As to the cause, it discovered that the ship had lost the original steel covers for nine or ten of her secondary armament gunports, which, being below the upper deck constituted a potential vulnerability in heavy seas. However, the gunports had been sealed for the voyage with timber and the last report from the towing crew on the day of her loss indicated that they were sound. The court concluded: 'Due to the lack of signals or messages from the ship at the material time and the failure to find the wreck, the direct cause of the casualty is unknown, but the court finds that she probably foundered or capsized before foundering, due to a combination of very high beam seas and very heavy pressure on her high upperworks, quite possibly aided by breakage of the temporary closing of secondary armament gunports and possibly other closures.' This probably happened pretty soon after the tow was parted. The arrangements for the voyage, the tugs and the towing were all felt to be satisfactory, and no blame was attached to anyone by the court.[3] The Metal Industries Board had already decided that in future they would avoid open-water towing during the winter months.[4]

After the Second World War *Sao Paulo*'s sister, *Minas Gerais*, remained largely inactive. She was decommissioned on 16 May 1952, but still used as headquarters for the Commander-in-Chief of the Brazilian Navy until 17 December. She was eventually sold to the Italian shipbreaking company SA Cantiere Navale de Santa Maria in Genoa in 1953. She began her final voyage on 1 March 1954 and reached Genoa on 22 April, fortunately without incident.

In Argentina, *Rivadavia* had been largely inactive after her 1945 Caribbean cruise, although she conducted some seagoing evolutions in 1947. She was moored alongside the battleship dock at Puerto Belgrano from 1948, largely inoperable by 1951 and disarmed and unmanned by 1952, but remained in service being cannibalised for spare equipment. She was finally listed for disposal on 18 October 1956 and stricken from the Navy list on 1 February 1957. On 30 May that year she was sold to another Italian shipbreaking company, Azienda Ricupiere e Demolizione Marittime Spa. of Genoa, for $2,280,000. But still she lingered, and did not start her final tow with the tugs *Zwarte Zee* and *Ost Zee* until 3 April 1959, arriving at Savona on 23 May before moving on to Genoa for dismantling.

Her sister, *Moreno*, was active as part of the Battle Squadron until 1949, when she was placed in reserve also at Puerto Belgrano and thereafter used as a stationary accommodation ship. She enjoyed one last brief period of excitement when she was used as a prison ship to hold Peronist sympathisers during the Revolucion Libertadora in 1955, in which the Argentine Military overthrew the President, Juan Peron. *Moreno* was sold on 11 January 1957 to Yawata Iron and Steel Company in Japan for $2,469,660. On 12 May she was saluted by the assembled Argentine fleet as she was towed from Puerto Belgrano by the Dutch ocean tugs *Clyde* and *Ocean*. It was, at the time, the longest tow in history, taking ninety-six days to reach the breakers via the Panama Canal.

Moreno in 1947. *(Alamy)*

Chile's *Almirante Latorre* thus became by just a few weeks the last South American dreadnought. Unlike Brazil and Argentina, Chile

Latorre in 1948.
(Alamy)

continued to maintain and invest in its battleship as a seagoing concern. She was active until at least 1951. Updates between 1946 and 1948 saw the fitting of war surplus US radars and the creation of a Combat Information Centre, as well as upgrading of the water mains and other firefighting equipment.[5] There is a snippet of evidence in a letter from UK Rear Admiral William Tennant, Commander-in-Chief American and West Indies station, sent to the First Sea Lord on 5 April 1947 reporting on his recent South American cruise aboard HMS *Sheffield*, that suggests there may have been commercial prospects at that point for British firms to refit *Latorre* more extensively.[6] The Chilean Navy did continue to pursue this possibility seriously over the next few years. They still viewed their battleship as the centrepiece of a fleet designed to deter the re-equipping Argentine Navy, although they also purchased two surplus *Brooklyn*-class cruisers from the USA in 1951 to match Argentina's equivalent purchase.

In May and June 1950 a party from Vickers-Armstrongs Ltd, her original builders, visited Talcahuano to assess the modifications that would be needed to keep her active for the next ten years. The British Embassy feared that the parallel acquisition of the two *Brooklyns* would absorb the available funds,[7] but a contract for £1.2 million was indeed signed by Chile and Vickers-Armstrongs on 23 August 1951 (British Embassy records say 17 October 1951). This was to carry out the work, which would have included overhauling the machinery and new radars and fitting an updated anti-aircraft battery of twelve 4in and 40mm Bofors guns, at Talcahuano in Chile. Once feasibility studies began, however, it became clear that work of that scope could not be done in Chile, and the extra expense of getting

Latorre back to the UK to complete it meant that the project became unaffordable. It was eventually cancelled in 1953, but the Chileans honoured its spirit by paying £300,000 compensation and using the other £900,000 to order, in 1955, two new destroyers from Vickers-Armstrongs.[8] In informing the Prime Minister of the destroyer sale on 12 November 1954, J P L Thomas, First Lord of the Admiralty, still described the Chilean order of battle as including one battleship '(to be modernised)', but this is unlikely to reflect real Chilean Navy intentions by that date.[9]

Meanwhile, *Latorre*'s seagoing career had ended when an accidental explosion in the engine room, caused by the bursting of a corroded steam pipe, killed three of the crew. The date of this incident is a bit of a mystery. Published sources say 11 March 1951, but this pre-dates the refurbishment contract, and is not compatible with the British Naval Attaché's annual report for 1951, dated 14 February 1952, which states: 'The battleship *Almirante Latorre*, flagship of the squadron, has done a considerable amount of sea time during the year and carried out a very successful full calibre 14in shoot which was witnessed by the Minister of Defence and high-ranking officers of the Navy, Army and Air Force.' No accident is mentioned, nor is *Latorre* specifically referenced in his earlier reports.[10] I therefore suggest that the accident and subsequent immobilisation of the ship took place in 1952 or 1953. In any case, thereafter she was moored at the naval base at Talcahuano, and used mainly as an oil fuel storage hulk. She went into reserve in early 1954, but was still maintained and was dry-docked on more than one occasion. She was finally decommissioned only in October 1958, and sold to Mitsubishi Heavy Industries in Japan for $881,110.

On 29 May 1959, seven weeks after *Rivadavia* had left Puerto Belgrano, and one day shy of forty-three years since she had raised steam to go to fight the Battle of Jutland, *Almirante Latorre*, that battle's last dreadnought, was saluted by the assembled Chilean fleet and towed from Talcahuano by the tug *Cambrian Salvor*. She reached Yokohama by the end of August 1959, although scrapping did not begin immediately. The hull remained in existence for a number of years thereafter until finally scrapped. It seems that part of her fabric even found its way into the Japanese museum battleship *Mikasa*, which was then undergoing restoration at Yokohama. Some reports suggest that *Latorre* might have provided the majority of *Mikasa*'s new superstructure.[11] Thus passed the last of the long-lived South American dreadnoughts. One of *Latorre*'s original 6in guns (when serving with the Grand Fleet as HMS *Canada)* still survives, redeployed aboard the Monitor M33 and now preserved in the Historic Dockyard at Portsmouth.

United Kingdom

Vanguard, while rarely far from the centre of the size and shape debate in Whitehall, was more active in general during the early 1950s than had been the *King George Vs* in the 1940s. We left her at Portland at the outbreak of the Korean War. As President Truman deployed *Missouri* to Korea, *Vanguard* took trainees on a summer cruise to Gourock and Ballachulish in Scotland, then Bangor, Northern Ireland, between 5 and 27 July 1950. She had a week at Cowes at the end of that month, then went back to Portland, where on 6 August there was a double christening aboard, of Victoria Joan Langley-Smith and Anthony Russell Brenton. On 18 August she got a new captain, D H Hill-Thompson, and by 15 September she was on her way to Gibraltar once again, in company with the carrier *Vengeance* and the Home Fleet.

Three weeks at Gibraltar were followed by a venture to West Africa, specifically the Cape Verde islands, then a Portuguese possession. There on 22 October at Saint Vincent there was another double christening aboard of Robert John Simpson and Derek Vincent Thompson, although it is hardly conceivable that at such an out of the way location they were

Vanguard under way, seen from a carrier. (NHHC)

offspring of the ship's officers. The return trip was via Funchal, Gibraltar and Lisbon, with all the usual formalities, until she regained Portsmouth on 7 December 1950.[12]

By January 1951 she was flying the flag of Commander-in-Chief Home Fleet, Admiral Sir Philip Vian, and on 19 January was off to Gibraltar again, conducting Bofors firings on the way. While moored alongside at Gibraltar on 10 February she was hit astern by the carrier *Indomitable* as the latter came in to her berth. Damage to both ships was fortunately negligible. On 15 February *Vanguard* went up to Genoa as she had in 1949, then on 20 February to Villefranche for a week, where 1,004 visitors came aboard. On the way back to Gibraltar there were more Bofors firings. She sailed from Gibraltar on 10 March and was back at Plymouth by 14 March, where she was de-ammunitioned then scraped clean at No. 10 dock until 17 April. She went to sea on 5 May and travelled up the Channel via Cawsand Bay to Dover to fire the Royal Salute there on 8 May to greet the arrival in the UK of King Frederick and Queen Ingrid of Denmark (for his appointment as Knight Companion of the Order of the Garter).

Vanguard with awning spread at Portland. *(NHHC)*

She returned to Portland the same evening and became flagship of the Training Squadron again. John Duncan Willis McDonald was christened aboard on 19 May. *Vanguard* spent the summer on the south coast, visiting Bournemouth and Eastbourne in June. From there she deployed to Loch Ewe on 3 July, then Scapa Flow on 4 July for exercises with the Home Fleet, with the Commander-in-Chief embarked in *Indefatigable*. She sailed south again on 19 July and was back at Portland by 21 July. Thence to Devonport on 16 September, entering No. 10 dock for a short refit on 26 September.[13] While 1951 was a relatively quiet year for the ship, she was much busier in 1952 and 1953.

The refit cost £476,000, £61,000 over budget.[14] While alongside at Devonport on 7 February 1952 she half-masted her colours together with *Howe*, moored adjacent to her, to mark the death of King George VI.

Vanguard went to sea for trials at the end of February 1952 and once more followed the familiar route to Gibraltar in March, where she undertook three days of 5.25in and one day of Bofors firing. On 25 March she set off back to Portsmouth in company with the Home Fleet, the Commander-in-Chief, now Admiral Sir George Creasy, flying his flag in *Indomitable* for this voyage. By 16 May, however, he was back aboard *Vanguard* for an intense series of manoeuvres that reflected the new tensions of the Cold War. She proceeded to Portland and then on 12 June via the Straits of Dover to Rosyth. On the way up the North Sea she was subjected to mock attacks by US Air Force Thunderjets. The new NATO partnerships were also underscored by the arrival during the passage of the Royal Netherlands Navy Aircraft Carrier *Karel Doorman* (previously HMS *Venerable*). On 19 June *Karel Doorman* conducted flying operations,

while *Vanguard* was attacked again 'without warning' by aircraft from *Illustrious*. Her destroyer screen closed to within 1,000 yards to provide a close escort, and her Bofors crews were closed up to exercise defence against the attack. She spent 21 to 26 June at Rosyth, then sailed back across the North Sea for a visit to Rotterdam, which included hosting Queen Juliana of the Netherlands and Prince Bernhard aboard for dinner on 1 July. After dinner they were taken on a tour of the harbour in the Commander-in-Chief's barge to view the illuminated battleship. *Vanguard* then went back down the English Channel to visit Torquay and Weymouth, before spending most of July and August regrouping and with the crew on summer leave at Portsmouth.

Then the serious business began. *Vanguard* sailed to Invergordon on 22 August. During her time there she undertook 5.25in gun firings in the North Sea on 1 and 2 September. On 7 September she sailed for Greenock, where she rendezvoused on 9 September with the US carrier *Franklin D Roosevelt*. This was the start of Exercise Mainbrace, the first full-scale NATO maritime exercise of the Cold War to be held in the vital sea area of the North Atlantic. Mainbrace had begun being planned during the incumbency of Dwight D Eisenhower as the first Supreme Commander

Europe. By the time it was carried out between 13 and 25 September, Ike had been replaced by General Matthew Ridgeway, who commanded jointly with US Navy Admiral Lynde McCormick, NATO Supreme Commander Atlantic. Theatre Commander was Admiral Sir Patrick Brind RN, since 1951 Commander-in-Chief of Allied Forces Northern Europe.

The scenario was designed to demonstrate to the Soviets that Norway and Denmark could rely on NATO maritime forces to push reinforcements into the Baltic and Arctic regions in the event of Soviet aggression. The forward Allied forces, including *Vanguard* and *Franklin D Roosevelt*, were to carry out offensive operations against a 'Red' force simulated by other Allied ships, conducting anti-air, anti-submarine, and anti-surface warfare, and then to rendezvous with a convoy of reinforcements sailing from the United States escorted by *Wisconsin*. This force would deploy US Marines

Sunset ceremony aboard *Vanguard* in the Clyde estuary before Exercise Mainbrace, 12 September 1952. *(NHHC)*

to land in Denmark. It was a massive undertaking, and 80,000 men, more than 200 ships and 1,000 aircraft took part. There were ten aircraft carriers from three nations (US, UK and Canada), two battleships, six cruisers and ninety-six escorts. France, Denmark, Norway, Portugal, the Netherlands and Belgium also provided forces.

Wisconsin, carrying the afloat Commander US Vice-Admiral Felix Stump, Commander of the US 2nd Fleet, and the US Navy carriers *Wasp* and *Midway* arrived at Greenock on 10 September.

The press came aboard *Vanguard* to witness the exercise. It was noteworthy for the high speed at which operations were conducted. *Vanguard*'s log shows she was averaging 20 knots for a number of days after sailing on 13 September. There was also some atrocious weather with very low visibility on 14 September, then Force 8 gales and Force 9–10 on

Vanguard taking part in exercise Mainbrace, 19 September 1952 . *(NHHC)*

17 September. Through all this, flying operations went on, but were severely restricted. *Vanguard* was refuelled at sea on 19 September and herself refuelled destroyers the next day.

Her role in the exercise was low key. She played no part in interception of the cruiser *Quebec*, playing the role of a Russian raider, which dominated the early phase of the exercise as the task force moved into north Norwegian waters. The interception was left to a surface action group of US and UK cruisers, later supported by *Wisconsin*. An initial attempt to stop the raider using air strikes on 15 September failed due to worsening weather. At 2100 the raider was spotted on radar to the southwest of the task force and *Wisconsin* was ordered out of the formation at 27 knots to support the cruisers. *Columbus and Wisconsin* opened fire and *Quebec* was judged sunk at 2252. A second raider encountered later during the southern phase of the exercise was also dealt with by cruisers without battleship or aircraft involvement.

The Commander-in-Chief of the Home Fleet, analysing the exercise

The threat to NATO convoys to Europe: *Sverdlov* operating in the North Atlantic in 1959. *(NHHC)*

lessons, concluded that this experience showed the necessity of a balanced force to include surface action groups.[15] The *Wisconsin* group was encountered by *Vanguard* again on 23 September as the exercise drew to a close, and early that morning *Vanguard* was operating her helicopter and transferring correspondence to and from *Wisconsin*. On 24 September she returned to Rosyth in accordance with her exercise instructions.

Despite inevitable teething trouble, Mainbrace was reckoned a significant success at the operational level and served political notice of Allied determination on the Soviet Union. Many of the American ships showed their flexibility and endurance by going on to participate during November in the equivalent SACEUR/SACLANT exercises in the Eastern Mediterranean, code-named Longstop. *Vanguard*, however, stayed on duty in northern waters. She went first from Rosyth direct to Oslo to reinforce the messages of solidarity with Norway. King Haakon came aboard on 27 September and Crown Prince Olaf two days after. She returned to Rosyth on 4 October and was mock-attacked by Thunderjets, Sea Hornets and Sea Furies on the way. The First Lord of the Admiralty, James P L Thomas, later to be Viscount Cilcennin, went up to Scotland to visit her between 6 and 8 October. She then spent four weeks based at Invergordon presiding over the Home Fleet. On 6 November she left Invergordon at 1200 and conducted a brief 15in firing in the North Sea from 1543 to 1555. Then on 12 November she returned to Rosyth for five days until 17 November, when she led the Home Fleet north again, this time a very long way north.

Jan Mayen Island was sighted on 20 November, a Force 10 gale endured the next day, and on 22 November, still in Force 9 to 10 winds, she recorded the furthest north of her career at the edge of the Arctic ice at 72 degrees 45 minutes North. Having turned about, she undertook some gunnery exercises on 24 November, firing 5.25in broadsides with *Eagle* as the target, and what the log rather alarmingly describes as 'blind 15in firings on merchantman'. At 2140 on 25 November, still north of the Arctic Circle, she stopped for an hour because of a suspected man overboard. However, once the ship's company were mustered, all were found present and correct, so on she went. The next morning there was a small fire in the 5.25in armament store, extinguished after twelve minutes. The last major evolution of this voyage was also a sign of the new times, as the log records her going to damage control state one (the highest) and closing down the ship, relying only on internal ventilation for a few minutes, to simulate defensive measures against atomic attack fallout. On 1 December 1952, after three gruelling months in northern waters, she moored at Portsmouth's South Railway Jetty.

The pace was maintained during 1953. She sailed, flying the flag of Commander-in-Chief Home Fleet, from Portsmouth to Gibraltar on

20 January, accompanied by the French gunboats (also called submarine chasers) *La Ruse* and *Emporte*. On 28 January she was dry-docked at Gibraltar for four weeks, although during this time she hosted both the Governor of Gibraltar and on 12 February the Spanish Civil Governor of Algeciras, Senor General de Division Don Antonio Barroso Sanchez-Guerra. It was the first such high-level contact since the Spanish Civil War.[16] The battleship then emerged from dock to participate in the combined fleet exercise Crossbar. On 2 March the log records her firing 5.25in starshell and Bofors against attacking Sea Furies, and also 'opened fire on destroyers'

Vanguard stars in the Coronation Review Brochure, June 1953. *(Alamy)*

CORONATION REVIEW OF THE FLEET

BY HER MAJESTY THE QUEEN AT SPITHEAD ON MONDAY, 15TH JUNE 1953

OFFICIAL SOUVENIR PROGRAMME PRICE 2/-

Published under the Authority of the Commander-in-Chief Portsmouth

during a simulated night encounter. There were more mock air attacks on the formation on 4 and 5 March, before returning to Gibraltar. Crossbar was rather fraught, with numerous air accidents following a fatal explosion aboard *Indomitable* on 3 February. The voyage back to the UK was nonetheless punctuated by more NATO exercises with *Eagle* and *Indomitable*, plus participation from French, Dutch and Portuguese ships. A courtesy call at Brest allowed the Commander-in-Chief to meet French Admiral Robert, Commander Bay of Biscay, and there were 374 attendees at a children's party. *Vanguard* was back in Portsmouth on 24 March, where a forty-gun salute was fired two days later to mark the death of Queen Mary. In early April she hosted Navy Days, and then sailed to Portland on 8 May. She visited Southend from 1 June, but returned to Portland on 5 June for a final sprucing up before an important day.

On 15 June 1953 *Vanguard* was centre stage at, arguably, the apogee of her career, as flagship of the Home Fleet for Queen Elizabeth II's Coronation Fleet Review at Spithead.

At the equivalent event for her father in 1937 there had been ten Royal Navy battleships and four aircraft carriers, plus four battleships from overseas. But in 1953 *Vanguard* was the only battleship, with six carriers (although four of them were soon to precede her to the scrapyards). Overseas powers sent cruisers. While the USA's *Baltimore*, as key NATO ally, was given pride of place at the head of the line of foreign ships, *Sverdlov* herself was only a couple of places back, well within view of *Vanguard*. One is tempted to regard this as no coincidence – the Soviet cruiser on her first overseas outing gun barrel to gun barrel with her designated 'killer'?[17]

Vanguard dressed ship to begin the day. The band went to Review Stations at 1440, and the Royal Salute was fired at 1516. HM The Queen, on board the stand-in Royal Yacht HMS *Surprise*, passed between *Vanguard* and *Baltimore* at 1521, and *Vanguard* cheered ship at 1533. After the Review *Surprise* anchored near *Vanguard* for the Fleet Air Arm flypast of 300 aircraft. The Queen transferred to *Vanguard* for dinner at 2025 and to witness the lighting up of the fleet at 2230 and the final fireworks at 2245. She departed at 2325. The BBC deployed more than 170 personnel to cover the event, six of them aboard *Vanguard*. The UK radio audience was estimated at up to 12 million, and the television audience at up to 10 million, with a further 20 million worldwide.[18]

A further chapter in the *Vanguard* story was nearly written for June 1953 immediately after the Review. On 17 June Vice Chief of the Naval Staff wrote to apprise First Sea Lord that Prime Minister Churchill was minded to travel to Bermuda in *Vanguard* for a planned tripartite conference with the new US President Eisenhower and French President Auriol, to take stock of the world after the death of Stalin and the imminent end of the Korean conflict. It would have been a grand gesture, a throwback to his use of *Prince of Wales* to impress Roosevelt at the Atlantic Charter conference at Newfoundland in August 1941. The Navy put planning in full swing. Commander-in-Chief Home Fleet, Admiral Sir George Creasy, said he planned to stay aboard for the trip, but there was still plenty of accommodation for Churchill's party of forty. He sent a private note in parallel to the First Sea Lord assuring him that he could make the Prime Minister very comfortable and that the Downing Street staff could be accommodated in spite of the fact that the inclusion of fifteen 'females' was 'a slight shock'. He requested an early announcement so that the remainder of the ship's 1953 programme could be managed.

On 21 June a signal from the Admiralty to *Vanguard* confirmed that the Prime Minister would embark from Portsmouth on 30 June, to arrive at Bermuda for the beginning of the conference on 8 July. On 22 June *Vanguard* was diverted from Portrush, Northern Ireland, where she had sailed after the Coronation Review, back to Portsmouth to undertake the mission. The Admiralty even planned to use the week that Churchill would be captive aboard her for Creasy to brief him on their perspective of the 1953 Defence Review and the threat posed by *Sverdlovs*, on which the Prime Minister was regarded at that point as unsound. It all came to nothing very suddenly. Even as *Vanguard* was on her way south, Churchill suffered his debilitating stroke on the evening of 23 June. Although he chaired Cabinet the next day, and his condition was kept secret, described as 'exhaustion', he was recuperating at Chartwell by the weekend. On 27 June the Admiralty signalled to Creasy 'Bermuda conference postponed. Arrangements for use of *Vanguard* cancelled'. The conference was reinstated after his partial recovery in December, but Churchill flew instead, and there is no evidence that *Vanguard* was considered as an option for the later trip.[19]

Instead the programme resumed. Having rushed to Portsmouth for the Prime Minister, she returned to northern waters, visiting Oban on 30 June and Loch Ewe on 8 July. She had only 870 visitors at these locations, but 6,500 at Falmouth between 16 and 20 July. There were dummy attacks by Meteors, Vampires and Seahawks in the Western Approaches as she made her way south. On 20 July she set sail for Portsmouth via ASW exercises the following day. At Portsmouth she was the star attraction for Navy Days, and 48,175 visitors were logged between 1 and 4 August. She took on ammunition on 17 August and sailed for Invergordon on 2 September. A series of exercises took place over the following two weeks with the carrier *Eagle* and other Home Fleet units. Then it was time for NATO exercise Mariner. In a sign of things to come, the Commander-in-Chief and his staff left the ship on 20–21 September to fight this exercise from a shore base and *Vanguard* sortied for Mariner without them on 22 September.

She sailed north, then west. The exercise was held mainly in the waters south of Iceland and was similar in scope and scale to Mainbrace. The weather was even worse than the previous year.

On 24 September flying operations were interrupted by the death of Firefly pilot Lieutenant Commander Keogh from *Eagle*. *Vanguard* half-masted her colours for his funeral aboard HMS *Crossbow* at 1630. Flying was cancelled the next day and on 26 September it was too rough to refuel the destroyers. Regular submarine contacts and air raid warnings punctuated the following days. As with Mainbrace, a raider was on the loose, this time played by HMS *Swiftsure*. On 27 September *Vanguard* was in company with the US cruiser *Des Moines* in Force 10 gales. Speed was increased to 24 knots and at 1052 she was 'detached with *Macon* and *Des Moines* to intercept raider', the decision being made to send the ships ahead unescorted due to the problems the destroyers were having keeping up. The next day she steamed at over 20 knots most of the time and at 1245 altered course to intercept the 'enemy' cruiser, which had been detected by air reconnaissance and was now within 85 miles of the main task force.

Vanguard ploughing through rough seas, Exercise Mariner, September 1953. (Imperial War Museum)

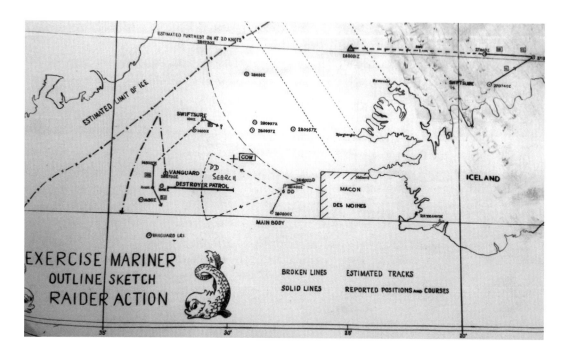

A sketch chart showing the raider phase of Exercise Mariner. *Vanguard*'s track is to the left, intercepting the raider (*Swiftsure*), which has moved from north of Iceland to threaten the NATO task force. *(National Archives)*

The cruisers were detached to protect the fleet's replenishment group, which was potentially under threat. *Vanguard*'s search was complicated by numerous radar contacts from icebergs and trawlers. Once again the attempted air strike on the raider by Skyraider dive bombers from USS *Bennington* failed, this time because they attacked *Vanguard* in error. She fired back, and for exercise purposes judged herself as undamaged. *Swiftsure* was detected by radar at 15 miles range, and at 1521 the log finally confirmed that 'Skunk' (the code name for the enemy) was in main armament range. At 1555 *Vanguard* changed course to open A arcs and engaged with 15in and 5.25in guns at 12 miles range.

On 30 September at 0430 Task Force 218, a US formation led by *Iowa* was sighted and *Vanguard* took station on her for the remainder of the day, including more high-speed operations. At 2300 she had to take over from *Iowa* as air defence co-ordinator for the whole formation because both *Iowa*'s and *Des Moines*'s radar aerials were unable to turn due to the high winds. 1 October saw more Force 10 gales and the starboard whaler was smashed by breaking seas at 0825. Later *Vanguard* joined with *Eagle*, but the ships remained 6 miles apart in an atomic defence formation. There was much 'enemy' air activity as Bomber Command tried to overcome the weather to launch various attacks and feints to achieve success with a simulated atomic bomb. It was judged ineffective. The British and American squadrons parted company at 1500, and *Vanguard* returned to Greenock at high speed. There was a further simulated atomic attack on 2 October, when the photo-flash bomb was detected 4,000 yards south of *Eagle*. All the heavy ships were judged to have avoided damage.[20]

Sir George Creasy came back aboard on 4 October. A further week of exercises followed based on Invergordon, including 5.25in and Bofors firings on 16 October. The Home Fleet then sailed north around Scotland and undertook a further set of exercises from 21 to 23 October off the west coast. This included further simulated atomic attacks. On 22 October the log notes at 0930 'conned ship from armoured bridge – atomic attack expected', and at 1020 'observed burst astern of *Eagle*'. The next day at 1030: 'attacked by enemy aircraft. Atomic attack-ship sunk (exercise only)', and at 1100: 'Atomic attack ship sunk'.

Vanguard returned via Portland to Portsmouth on 26 October, where she de-ammunitioned and spent a quiet winter alongside the Middle Slip Jetty until 21 January 1954, when she made the familiar visit to

Vanguard refuelling from the Royal Fleet Auxiliary tanker Wave Victor on 30 September 1953, while also operating with a US helicopter. (Imperial War Museum)

Gibraltar with Commander-in-Chief Home Fleet. She had another scraping and painting in No. 1 dock there between 26 January and late February. On 15 March she left for Exercise Touchline with the Mediterranean fleet, alongside *Implacable* and *Indefatigable*. This included the usual anti-submarine and anti-aircraft evolutions including the firing of 5.25in starshell, and on 17 March she practised defence at damage control state one against a simulated atomic explosion 1½ miles distant. But there was to be no extended Mediterranean cruise this time.

Back in Gibraltar by 19 March, on 27 March she undertook a macabre if vital duty. At 1100 Crane Lighter 21 was alongside the quarterdeck and the battleship embarked the wreckage of Comet G-ALYP. The aircraft had crashed into the sea near Elba on 10 January 1954 after taking off from Rome, killing all thirty-five aboard. Its wreckage had been found by Royal Navy ships based at Malta and raised by the Royal Fleet Auxiliary *Sea Salvor*. On 2 April *Vanguard* delivered the Comet wreckage to a lighter at Portsmouth, whence it made its way to the Royal Aircraft Establishment at Farnborough for the forensic investigations that eventually helped pinpoint the structural weaknesses that had contributed to three fatal Comet crashes in quick succession.

In May 1954 *Vanguard* sailed from Portsmouth flying the flag of Commander-in-Chief Home Fleet for the final time. She visited Brixham and Portland before heading north to Rosyth and Invergordon once more, then on to Scapa Flow between 19 and 29 June. She crossed the North Sea and made the visits so important to underpin Western solidarity in the northern area, to Oslo, Kristiansand, and Helsingborg in Sweden, while the Commander-in-Chief took part in meetings with NATO Commander-in-Chief North. At Helsingborg the King of Sweden, Gustaf VI Adolf, visited on 11 July and the same day the son of the Defence Attaché, Jochaim Roger Spollin, was baptised aboard; so far as the logs confirm the last child to be baptised on a British battleship. *Vanguard* returned to Portland, then Portsmouth on 21 July. She then went to Devonport for her refit in September 1954.[21]

Vanguard's operations in the 1950s need to be viewed in the context of evolving UK defence policy. The rising evidence of tensions in Europe starting with the communist takeover in Prague in 1948, a Soviet and communist world challenge and a naval build-up on their part, and the formation of the North Atlantic Treaty Organisation (NATO) in spring 1949 together had a profound influence on United Kingdom defence policies and spending in the final years of the Attlee Government. The Harwood-era arguments about whether defence should spend annually £830 million, £780 million, or £700 million, even though barely a year old, melted away in the face of this complete reappraisal of the UK's priorities. Initially, however, prospects looked poor for the Royal Navy, as Attlee's reshuffle after his narrow February 1950 election victory had brought the anti-Navy and specifically anti-carrier left-winger Emmanuel Shinwell into the Ministry of Defence. At this juncture the Royal Navy was only able to deploy one operational squadron of twelve Firebrand aircraft in the anti-ship strike role. Shinwell was opposed to funding a replacement type.

There was a newly framed debate about what the Royal Navy's role was to become as part of a NATO response to Soviet aggression. Specifically, did it need strike carriers of its own to take the fight to Russia in the early stages of the war while America got its act together? Or was the Atlantic Striking Fleet essentially a United States entity, with the Royal Navy confined to defensive roles, primarily anti-submarine and fighter escort to convoys? In May 1950 the UK produced a Global Strategy paper that threatened the Royal Navy's place in the service hierarchy and its share of the resources. The paper proposed that more resources were devoted to trying to hold back the Russians on the Continent of Europe using land forces, and that more air forces would be needed to support that role, and for direct protection of the UK. After the outbreak of war in Korea, the timeframe to achieve an overall war posture for the UK's armed forces was shortened from previous assumptions of 1957 to 1954 and the Prime Minister agreed to spend an average of £1,130 million on defence per year from 1951 to 1954 to achieve this. This was simultaneously unaffordable – it was projected that over this period £550 million would be needed in US Foreign Military Aid to balance the UK books – and insufficient to meet the United Kingdom Chiefs of Staffs' full rearmament plans, by at least another £300 million per year. Those plans were themselves probably inadequate to meet NATO's Medium Term Defence Plan, which had just been formulated for the first time by a meeting of the Defence Committee in Washington DC in October 1950.[22] Attlee then increased his planned expenditure further after a December 1950 visit to Washington convinced him more needed to be done to demonstrate to both the US and European partners that the UK was bearing its share of the burden. His defence plans increased to £1.6 billion per year and by 1954 would have absorbed an eye-watering 14 per cent of GDP.

The naval new construction and modernisation programme had been very heavily constrained from 1945 onwards. Besides the shelving of battleships *Lion* and *Temeraire*, carrier construction was severely curtailed. Only *Ark Royal* and *Eagle* of all the planned new fleet carriers ever made it to a much-delayed completion. Only one of the six wartime fleet carriers, *Victorious*, was ever modernised, and that turned out to be an expensive eight-year project management disaster. This was despite the Admiralty Plans Directorate noting as early as 1948 that these ships could not operate the projected modern aircraft. There was also growing evidence from exercises with the Light Fleet Carriers in 1948 that they struggled to operate most aircraft in poor weather, in even moderate seas or (before steam catapults) in calm conditions, too.[23]

A 1948 template for the proposed 1955 fleet also noted the suspension of the cruisers *Lion* (not to be confused with the earlier planned battleship – while battleship *Lion* was still a gleam in the eye the cruiser was originally named *Defence*), *Tiger* and *Blake* since 1945, and said that 'from 1954 it will be necessary to lay down two cruisers per year as replacements for overage ships'.[24] But the three *Lions*, eventually finished around 1960, were the last British cruisers. The 1949 new construction programme was only £3,612,000, and that for 1951 was only £3,228,000. Total construction expenditure on these and all previous approved programmes only averaged £10–12 million per year before rearmament. There was a supplementary programme of £7,604,000 in 1950–51 after the outbreak of hostilities in Korea, but that all went on investment in home defence, minesweeping and anti-submarine escorts in response to new perceptions of the shape of the Russian threat to the UK homeland and lines of communication, and also in response to the shortfalls in those areas evaluated against NATO war planning requirements.

Looking in more detail at the Admiralty input to this rearmament process, at the end of 1949 the Admiralty's Director of Plans produced a paper showing shipbuilding requirements in the event of a war with the Soviet Union beginning on 1 January 1950. He assumed that two UK battleships would be deployed in the North Atlantic by D plus six months, and that neither would be lost to enemy action in the first eighteen months. There would also be three US battleships deployed in the Mediterranean, and the opposition would be the three old Soviet battleships of the *Gangut* class. He also assumed that in such a war the UK would lose one aircraft carrier and five cruisers in action. However, such was the nature of the threat and the low availability of ships in other categories that he concluded that all naval new construction should consist of escorts, submarines and mine warfare vessels.[25]

The analysis was much the same nine months later when, on 11 October 1950, the Director of Plans responded to a call from the Ministry of Defence to identify naval deficiencies needed to prepare for a war. The tabled deficiencies did not mention battleships. All anti-aircraft improvements required were for carriers, cruisers and below. The need to invest particularly heavily in minesweeping and ocean escorts was evident. The total British forces required to meet the recently agreed NATO Medium Term Plan (R51/294/1) were tabulated. Across all the Alliance nations that plan called for two battleships, thirty-one carriers and twenty-nine cruisers to be available in 1954. It required no UK battleships at D plus six months (although *Vanguard* was assumed to be available, so in fact represented a surplus). NATO also required fewer UK cruisers (fifteen instead of the eighteen available) and fewer fleet destroyers (fifty-three instead of sixty-two available). By contrast, in 1954 the UK would be deficient by three aircraft carriers (six instead of the nine required), and over 60 per cent of the front-line carrier aircraft requirement (210 versus 530 required). There was also an assessed shortfall of a staggering 158 escort vessels and 481 mine warfare vessels. This analysis clearly showed the developing worry about keeping the Atlantic lines of communication protected from submarines and countering the Soviet mining threat to the UK base. The Government duly decided that the new construction and modernisation programme from 1951 to 1954 would be focussed on frigates, submarines, mine warfare, conversion of surplus fleet destroyers to convoy escorts, the modernisation of six carriers and painfully slow expansion of the Fleet Air Arm front line (but still only expecting to meet 50 per cent of NATO's requirement for naval air by 1957). Manpower would need to rise from a planned 124,000 in 1952 to 130,000 in 1954 to support the programme.[26]

There was no room for any battleship modernisation, nor even for holding *Howe* at Category A reserve to meet the national (not NATO) requirement for a battleship at three months' readiness or to replace *Vanguard* in the Training Squadron (see above). This would have required just thirty more chief engine room artificers (CERA) and chief/petty officer stoker/mechanics (CPOSM), a particular pinch point, at a time when the Navy was striving and struggling to get the Far East Fleet up to its war complement for Korea. Indeed, it was noted shortly afterwards that 1,400 CERA and CPOSM were expected to leave the Navy in the eighteen months from June 1950 to December 1951, and that consequently further immobilisation of running ships was viewed as imminent, despite the suspension of planned releases and the call up of some reservists.[27]

Although the naval estimates rose significantly from their 1950–51 level, these rearmament aspirations were only partially carried through into the Royal Navy programmes of the 1950s. The General Election in October 1951 returned the Conservatives, with Churchill initially reprising his wartime role as Defence Minister, although he soon relinquished this to Field Marshal Lord Alexander of Tunis (not to be confused with Albert V Alexander of the previous administration). More influential in making the running during the early defence deliberations of the Conservative Government was Chancellor of the Exchequer R A Butler, who rapidly decided that Attlee's scale of rearmament could not be afforded, and that defence resources, particularly the steel-consuming industries, needed to be diverted to an exports drive to generate foreign exchange and avert a balance of payments crisis. A series of re-examinations of defence policy and global strategy took place against this background, which resulted in the notion that the UK would have to continue to fight a 'broken-backed war' after an initial nuclear exchange. This implied the need for a navy of three components: a ready fleet to survive and fight a six-week intensive war, a reserve of ships to be brought forward to sustain supply lines for a prolonged period thereafter, and further units, including *Vanguard* and extra cruisers, to be active in the peacetime fleet to maintain a world power presence and cold war deterrence. The starting point for this tussle over defence policy was the paper on Global Strategy DO(52)26 from July 1952, which identified a requirement to defend the North Atlantic Lines of communication against nuclear, submarine and 'attack on allied sea routes by large cruisers'. By 1955, at D plus three months it was proposed to have mobilised one battleship and five carriers, against a NATO requirement of one and six. In September 1952 the Chiefs of Staff articulated the continuing requirement for one battleship to be available through to at least 1958 to meet the Lisbon NATO force goal, and preserved this under all potential options for cuts being proposed by Butler. Four battleships were also intended to remain in reserve under all these proposals.[28] But, for defence as a whole this 'broken-backed' strategy would still cost about £200 to £300 million more each year than Butler considered affordable.

The result was a 'Radical Review' of defence that lasted most of 1953 and rumbled into 1954. Not surprisingly it exposed deep differences of view. On 16 June 1953 Churchill chaired a meeting where the challenge to the Navy came from a combination of Butler, Duncan Sandys, the Minister of Supply, and Lord Cherwell, back at Churchill's side as Paymaster General once again. To meet the priorities identified from the global strategy would require a Navy of 130,000 men in 1955 and £400 million. Butler would only countenance £360 million and was increasingly dominant in discussions, eventually chairing the Defence Policy Committee discussion on 17 July, as Churchill was sidelined by his stroke. As a precursor to that session, the Chiefs of Staff met on 10 July. The Admiralty Director of Plans, Captain D E Holland-Martin, briefed the First Sea Lord: '*Vanguard* is likely to come under fire. You may consider it a wise tactical move to agree to show her as a possible sacrifice. Her present complement is 1,250, which with training and administrative backing would mean a saving of the order of 2,000 men.' This, he asserted, would mean scrapping her as manpower was not available to put her into reserve.

The briefing notes for the First Sea Lord's meetings in June and July 1953 now increasingly bear the stamp of a service that was on the defensive in a potentially existential struggle. The emphasis on the first six weeks of warfare forced the Admiralty to focus on the initial Royal

Navy contribution to the Atlantic Striking Fleet, which it was argued would require two strike carriers, four cruisers and some destroyers to provide the 'Covering Force' of the Atlantic Striking Fleet to match the Russian cruisers. There was no mention of *Vanguard* in this context, but in his final response to the Chiefs of Staff on 10 July, the First Sea Lord found room for her in his requirements, referring to a directive issued by the Prime Minister concerning her current peacetime commitments. The First Sea Lord listed the immediate Striking Fleet contribution as three carriers, four cruisers and ninety-one escorts, but also required in parallel one battleship, an additional carrier and nine more cruisers as 'overseas forces necessary to maintain our position as a world power'. Furthermore, the *King George Vs* (and more ships in other categories) were also needed at six months' notice, 'when they might well play a valuable part in the war at sea', reflecting the Admiralty belief in the need to prepare for an enduring phase of broken-backed war.[29]

Vice Chief of the Naval Staff and the Director of Naval Intelligence spent three hours briefing the hostile Duncan Sandys on 11 July. They thought they had landed some punches but Sandys was universally sceptical about the Navy's underpinning assumptions, being particularly hostile to the argument for cruisers. He also asked about the cost of upkeep of the *King George Vs* but seemed reassured that it was negligible, consisting of a few 'Shipkeepers'. Nevertheless, a Sea Lords meeting on 27 July 1953 to discuss new construction decided to focus it on modernisation of carriers and particularly angled decking. 'It was decided that the docking of the battleships [i.e. the periodic docking of the *King George Vs*] now due should be deferred.' The three suspended cruisers were, finally, to be finished, and a second guided weapons ship added to the future programme. The possibility of scrapping the battleships and older cruisers and the savings thus realised were to be examined in the next costing exercise.[30]

Battleships had now moved perilously close to the margins of the Navy thinking in these pressured times, but the argument to retain some again won out on this occasion. First Lord of the Admiralty J P L Thomas offered Butler a compromise plan on 31 August 1953, but it would still involve cutting two-thirds of the Royal Marine Commandos, scrapping all reserve ships that would need refitting to bring back into service (including the old fleet carriers and *King George Vs*) and decommissioning *Vanguard*.[31] This was despite Thomas's personal view: '*Vanguard* alone may not have a fighting value as decisive as the rest of the active fleet in the opening stages of a war but I have come to the conclusion that despite the heavy cost of keeping her in commission she has a value for prestige purposes that makes it important to retain her if this can be contrived without the sacrifice of even more important things.'[32]

At this juncture in late 1953 the Admiralty came under renewed and quite sustained pressure from the Ministries of Supply, Air and Defence to justify even the very existence of a Fleet Air Arm and its four fleet and eight light fleet carriers. Cruiser expenditure was also criticised again and the battleships were proposed for scrapping (again). Duncan Sandys was once more the main protagonist. On 9 November 1953 the First Sea Lord explained the role of aircraft carriers: 'The main function of our fleet carriers may be summarised as a contribution to the "Striking Fleet". The Atlantic Striking Fleet consists of British and American battleships, carriers, cruisers and destroyers. Its role is analogous to that of the Grand Fleet and the British Home Fleet, namely the offensive force for Atlantic and Northern waters.'[33] A meeting in the Ministry of Defence chaired by Defence Minister Lord Alexander of Tunis on 10 November heard that the Navy felt unable to manage its commitments if held to Butler's strict expenditure limit of £360 million per year. For £9 million extra in 1955–66, £12 million in 1956–57 and £20 million in 1957–58, 'the more disastrous consequences of a strict limitation on naval votes to £360 million could be avoided. For example, the two commandos could be retained, and *Vanguard* could be kept in commission.' And carrier strike in support of NATO commitments could also be delivered.

The outcome of this first hard-fought round of the Radical Review was indeed a decision to manage on £369 million per year. The gain of £9 million against Butler's baseline was felt to be enough to save the Commandos and *Vanguard*. Her costs at this juncture were estimated to be £1.6 million annually. In the event all five battleships were retained, the marginal costs of the *King George Vs* continuing in reserve offset by some reduction in frigate conversions. This apparent reversal of priority occurred not least because Churchill, now back functioning, took a strong stand in favour of the battleships. Thomas had sent him a memorandum on 15 September explaining that the radical review limitations would lead to the scrapping of all the *King George Vs* and three fleet carriers, saving £1 million a year. Three days later Churchill responded:

> I cannot agree to this proposal which involves the scrapping of all the battleships in the Navy except *Vanguard* for the sake of saving £1 million out of the estimate exceeding £335M [sic – actually £360 million]. It is hardly possible to conceive such a penny wise pound foolish policy. These powerful battleships carry guns as heavy as any in general use. If properly mothballed they form an irreplaceable reserve should a prolonged war come. When the ace is out the King is the highest card. All experience shows the prudence of keeping such vessels at a comparatively small cost as a safeguard against mortal peril. The reduction in our prestige of having but a single

battleship and no material reserve would have an unfortunate effect abroad alike with friends or potential foes … I am deeply distressed that such a proposal should have been made.[34]

Thomas did not give up and pressed for discussion at Cabinet. The Admiralty was behind him. The staffing of the response to Churchill's memorandum emphasised that the four ships had no immediate wartime role and would need extensive modernisation, especially to anti-aircraft armament, to be fit for war service. They also required expensive storage for the 14in ammunition reserve, still held globally, and were certainly of less priority than the ships of the active fleet that Churchill viewed as of 'dubious fighting value'.[35] Churchill chaired the Cabinet Defence Committee on 10 October 1953 and was again critical of the Admiralty's willingness to sacrifice the older reserve ships. 'In the broken-backed warfare that is likely to succeed the first atomic phase of a future war, these ships would be able to fulfil a valuable role. The more modern vessels on either side might well be lost and the situation might easily arise where the older ships might be able to hold their own against anything left in active service on the enemy side.' He felt that the extra marginal costs, around £1 million, should instead be absorbed by cutting manpower.[36]

The Admiralty argument for running *Vanguard* was certainly based on prestige, presence and deterrence, but was also underpinned by their assessment around this time that there were only two available squadrons of Firebrand carrier strike aircraft, and that they might well not be sufficient to stop the *Sverdlovs*. *Vanguard* and the Royal Navy's remaining 6in cruisers were more reliable *Sverdlov* killers than the Fleet Air Arm. In the longer term a modern carrier strike force armed with a new jet aircraft based on the Staff Requirement NA 39, later to evolve into the Buccaneer, might eventually fulfil this role and that of tactical nuclear attack, but they were still years off.

The focus on *Vanguard* and what to do with her amidst these pressures was thus considerable. She was much in demand. Commander-in-Chief Mediterranean, Lord Louis Mountbatten, had written to the First Sea Lord on 14 November 1952 requesting a large flagship particularly for visits to Turkey because face counted in their culture and the size of ship was one of the most important things in this respect. 'The effect of *Vanguard* in the Mediterranean for the two summer cruises of 1949 was most marked.' In response the Director of Plans advised First Sea Lord that *Vanguard* could not be spared in 1953, because she was already committed to the Coronation Fleet Review in May and then NATO exercise Mariner in the North Atlantic. 'It is desirable from the point of view of prestige that *Vanguard* who is already committed, should take part in "Mariner" though her presence is not of great importance operationally.' Mountbatten was offered the fleet carrier *Indomitable* instead, but for the longer term Director of Plans recommended that *Vanguard* should become Mediterranean Fleet flagship, and Commander-in-Chief Home Fleet should get the Depot Ship *Woolwich* in her place.[37]

These sentiments about *Vanguard* were reinforced a year later in a note from the Admiralty Director of Operations to the First Sea Lord on 4 December 1953 as the debate over the future of the Royal Navy role intensified:

> my own experience of the ship, both as a private ship and as a fleet flagship, has convinced me beyond all doubt that *Vanguard* has a very real value to the Navy and also to the country out of all proportion to the cost of keeping her going ... first the undoubted value to C-in-C Home Fleet in his dealings with SACLANT [NATO's Supreme Allied Commander Atlantic] in exercising his peacetime command from a modern battleship, and of having *Vanguard* under command in NATO exercises. I have myself observed the impression that she creates upon American officers ... Second the extremely heartening effect of *Vanguard* upon our lesser allies which was noticeable last year during visits to Rotterdam and Oslo ... Third, the pride which the navy and even more the public feel in the ship, which I am sure is a very good thing for the navy ...
>
> ... if *Vanguard* were paid off I think that would be taken as an admission of a parlous naval state, a sign that we could not maintain the status of a first class naval power, and would seriously weaken our naval influence in future dealings with the Americans and other NATO powers. I think it would dishearten our friends and encourage our enemies. I am very doubtful whether any talk about our naval strength in other types of ships would convince the public or our allies that *Vanguard*'s retirement was not a sad sign of the times.
>
> I also suggest that events in MAINBRACE and MARINER have produced evidence of the importance of *Vanguard*'s role in war. In MAINBRACE a strong carrier task force found itself unpleasantly close to an enemy coast and unable to put up an effective air strike owing to bad weather, and I think that it was generally felt then that had a powerful enemy surface force been encountered in these conditions, the carriers would not have been in a happy position without a battleship. In MARINER this year I think it is right to say that without *Vanguard* the enemy raiding cruiser would not have been brought to action.
>
> ... it will be a profound pity if we lose *Vanguard*. Once paid off into reserve we can never look to have her going again in

peacetime, even though a future government might have some second thoughts about all this.[38]

The operational argument in favour of retaining battleships was also reflected in the post-exercise reporting for Mariner. *Vanguard*'s own report dated 11 October 1953 by Captain Robert Ewing was highly critical of the small contribution that shore- and ship-based aircraft had made to the surface engagement. It said: 'The results obtained in the search for the enemy raider proved beyond doubt that there is still a need for heavy ships which can steam far and fast in bad weather when conditions do not permit flying and restrict the operation of lighter surface forces.' Vice Admiral J A Hughes-Hallett, commander of the Heavy Squadron during the exercise, wrote that: 'A carrier task force is neither a sure nor an economical way of denying the Denmark Straits or the Bear Island passage to Russian cruisers especially in winter. It would be cheaper and more effective to rely on battleships carrying helicopters for long range radar reconnaissance.' However, the evidence did not convince the Commander-in-Chief. Sir George Creasy's own report commented that: 'Flag Officer Heavy Squadron advances the interesting if grandiose concept of the use of converted battleships in the North Atlantic in war. I doubt if this is practicable. Apart from the cost in money and manpower it is unlikely ever to be acceptable to employ such ships in the area without a screen ... which we cannot afford. Shore based strike and AEW [airborne early warning] aircraft should prove more an economic and flexible weapon than the converted battleship.'[39]

The Radical Review arguments rumbled over into 1954. In January Sandys proposed a compromise cutting £66 million from carrier strike and reducing the planned Fleet Air Arm front line from 250 to 160 aircraft with no provision for anti-surface ship or shore strike roles. It would be only an anti-submarine convoy defence force of six carriers. Thomas countered to the Prime Minister on 22 February that provision of two strike carriers with modern strike aircraft to NATO was of supreme importance. The Navy's final word in this stage of the debate was a 'Navy of the Future' paper for the Defence Minister in March 1954. It argued that the Navy of 1965 should include fourteen aircraft carriers supporting strike as well as anti-submarine warfare convoy defence functions (down from seventeen in 1954), seven battleships and cruisers (down from thirty-one) and four guided weapons ships including conversion of existing hulls for ballistic missiles. The latter were not specified but logically the *King George Vs* must have been at least in the frame for this role, as envisaged a few years previously.[40]

There followed a short hiatus, as Churchill sat on the fence, before a second round of the Radical Review was launched to assess the impact of the Hydrogen bomb (first tested by the US in November 1952 – the UK had decided to build one on 16 June 1954); and to manage within a new reduced ceiling of £1,500 million per year for defence as a whole. This time the Admiralty once again put its weight behind preservation of the carriers and its proposed cuts included the scrapping of the reserve ships and keeping *Vanguard* in reserve. A new Ministerial Committee under Lord Swinton that was appointed to look at this challenge was felt by the Admiralty to be pro-RAF and anti-carrier. Swinton's Committee considered the Fleet Air Arm unaffordable and increasingly constrained by land-based enemy air power.

The argument was articulated by the Naval Staff as early as September 1954 as *Vanguard* began her refit:

> For both manpower and financial reasons in order to keep *Vanguard* in commission two 6in cruisers would have to be taken out of the active fleet and placed in reserve. For peacetime and cold war purposes the value of having a battleship in commission is great. It is an impressive representation of naval might and unsurpassed for the training of young officers and men. On the other hand our 6in cruisers are not unimpressive and the alternative of keeping two of these cruisers in commission instead of *Vanguard* would allow greater flexibility in meeting our peacetime commitments all over the world. Nevertheless, balancing cold war and hot war requirements the Admiralty consider that the number of cruisers cannot be further reduced and for this reason regretfully conclude that *Vanguard* must go into reserve.[41]

On 25 September 1954 Thomas again wrote to Churchill, asking for confirmation of the earlier decision that *Vanguard* should join the reserve fleet after her refit. He noted that the new defence policy placed greater emphasis on retention of the United Kingdom's symbols of world power 'and it might be held that a battleship in commission is one which we ought not now to abandon'. However, manpower constraints made it 'more than ever difficult' to retain her in commission. Defence Minister Alexander weighed in, sincerely trusting that there would be no question of reopening the earlier decision, and Foreign Secretary Anthony Eden agreed, saying he saw 'no reason why the withdrawal from commission of the last British battleship should have an adverse effect on our prestige'. Churchill, having earlier sought information on the relative costs of *Vanguard* and cruisers, disagreed and minuted the Cabinet Secretary on 27 September that: 'It should be taken as settled that the *Vanguard* should be kept in commission, that the *Iron Dukes* [sic] will not be broken up but will remain in their mothballs.' He proposed reductions in cruisers to compensate.[42] Swinton eventually conformed to this directive, dissenting from the Admiralty view. His Committee presented its conclusions to Cabinet in November 1954 – that the number of cruisers in commission should be reduced from ten to eight and the manpower saved should be used to retain *Vanguard* in commission 'for prestige purposes and for having a vessel superior to the latest Russian cruiser'.[43] This was confirmed at the seventh meeting of Swinton's Committee at the end of 1954.[44]

So, in the end the Navy once again got its cake and ate it. A fierce rearguard action saved the large carriers, helped no doubt by Sandys being removed from the fray at a crucial juncture to run the Housing portfolio. And the Naval Estimates in 1955–56, presented in Command Paper 9396, confirmed that, while the old fleet carriers would be scrapped as they could not operate new aircraft, *Vanguard*, by then under refit, would return to commission at the end of 1955 with three of her four 15in turrets and 50 per cent of her secondary armament operational. Furthermore, the *King George Vs* would remain available in the reserve.

These debates reflect growing doubts and scrutiny of the affordability, but also the purpose of the battleships. *Vanguard* was both an important peacetime presence and a deterrent if in commission, but also a *Sverdlov* cruiser killer in war, and a possible guided weapons ship conversion. The *King George Vs* were impossible to commission in under six months given other manpower priorities for the mobilised fleet, but might still be useful as traditional battleships to back up *Vanguard* in a long war, and still had some potential as missile ship conversions, although it is striking that none of the Ministerial level correspondence from 1953 onwards refers to this alternative possibility. Five still new-ish battleships was clearly enough for the UK's needs, and more than enough for the emerging NATO force goals, so there could be no question of spending additional scarce resources on them, or on cruisers, at a time when the national and NATO priority for the UK needed to be the creation of a coherent carrier strike force out of a chaos of old, small and part-built ships and inadequate numbers of obsolescent aircraft types, combined with a build-up of escort capability. The battleships kept coming under scrutiny in these size and shape arguments, and kept surviving. While they may have been on the margins of priorities, they were also on the margins as regards cost, absorbing maybe 0.5 per cent of the Royal Navy budget during the period 1950–55, so still represented a good-value contribution to active deterrence and a wider insurance policy.

Manpower challenges aside, if the UK's battleships were to have a longer-term future, it would likely be as guided weapons platforms. What was the reality that British battleships in the 1950s, explicitly held in reserve for such a purpose, could actually be rearmed with guided weapons? In practice guided weapons development was sporadic and very slow.

Before the end of the Second World War the Admiralty Gunnery Department was already working up the aspiration to replace heavy guns with guided weapons. On 6 April 1945 they sent out across the Admiralty the Naval Staff Target for three types of future anti-ship weapon. 'X' was a cruise missile designed to strike a target underwater, with a range of 30,000 yards and an accuracy three times that expected from 16in artillery. Only a few hits would be needed to sink an enemy battleship. 'Y' was a ballistic homing missile to strike the decks of ships. It would be more difficult to counter and was seen as complementary to 'X'. Range was up to 45,000 yards and hitting power equal to a 16in shell. 'Z' was a cruise missile of 20,000 yards range, designed to deliver a homing torpedo with a minimum range of 4,000 yards, with a warhead of at least 1,000lb. These could possibly be controlled by aircraft to achieve greater ranges.[45]

I have found no evidence of the precise fate of these Staff Targets. However, it is clear from the subsequent development of guided weapons in the Royal Navy that none came close to getting off the drawing board. The Cabinet Defence Committee noted guided weapon issues periodically in the 1940s and while paying lip service to their priority within defence planning, in practice devoted very little resource to research and development (R&D). Shortages of scientists and facilities persisted. By early 1947 around 50 per cent of R&D effort was already going into Britain's atomic bomb programme, and in 1949 only £1.5 million out of an R&D budget of £51 million was being spent on guided weapons.[46] Following initial prioritisation decisions by the Ministry of Supply in 1947, Research and Development effort became focussed quite early on an extended-range air defence missile, which was eventually to become Seaslug. In 1948 this system was having to fight its corner in R&D priorities with a projected much longer-ranged, ground-based air defence system called 'Red Heathen'. The Admiralty could not accept that guided weapons for defence of the fleet would not be in the top priority for defence Research & Development, and won its case. Nevertheless, there was unease about the pace of progress, with the First Sea Lord underlining in November 1948 that this was a matter of great importance.[47] The response from the Assistant Chief of the Naval Staff was that Seaslug languished under control of the Ministry of Supply and their work at Farnborough was hampered by that establishment's perceived priority being aircraft development. Sir Ben Lockspeiser (later to become the first President of CERN, the European Organisation for Nuclear Research) was in charge at Farnborough and was seen as a particular blocker for Seaslug. The First Sea Lord wrote to the First Lord saying he would press for a greater priority for the naval missile. Seaslug was eventually endorsed by the Defence Procurement and Research Committee and Cabinet in August 1949 as a joint Army and Royal Navy system with a designed range of 30,000 yards. The first test firings of a missile were in 1949, but even then the Ship Design Policy Committee were not envisaging the system being deployable before 1958.

It had initially been hoped to satisfy the Seaslug requirement with a vertically launched missile weighing about 1,800lb, but this proved beyond the limits of available technology. By 1949 Sea Slug had emerged as a very unwieldy liquid-fuelled missile with four wrap-around solid fuel boosters, launched from a trainable launcher to fly down a radar beam to its target. This was very much how it appeared when finally deployed into service in 1962 aboard the large guided missile destroyers of the County class. There were further delays in development, including a gap of three years in test firings after 1950 because of the Conservative Government's reprioritisation of Attlee's rearmament plans. The Navy briefly considered buying the US Terrier system instead, which was then being tested aboard the battleship *Mississippi*, but opted against reliance on foreign supply. Terrier would have been easier to retrofit to existing ships, as the US Navy later did extensively, but it had less range than Seaslug and by no stretch of the imagination could it double in the anti-surface role. In 1953 the Soviet surface threat from large 6in-gunned *Sverdlov* cruisers caused the revival of a requirement for a surface-to-surface missile that could outrange their guns. A variant of Seaslug called Blue Slug was suggested, but it was judged to lack hitting power against *Sverdlov*s: 'One hit has no appreciable chance of sinking the ship.' A nuclear variant was being considered by 1955, but was abandoned in 1956.[48]

In the meantime, during debate about the size and shape of the future fleet in 1953 discussion was focussed on a new 5in-gunned small cruiser of 5,000 tons armed with new rapid-fire guns, but no missiles, which was designed to defeat Soviet large cruisers in combination, or to deter them if deployed singly as a convoy escort. The Deputy Chief of Naval Staff opposed this small cruiser concept and minuted on 9 May 1953 that: 'Our current 6in cruisers will gradually wear out and will require replacement for cold war duties and as the ultimate arbiter on the surface and also for A.A. defence of the striking fleet by Guided Weapon ships of the 10–18,000 ton class. We can't afford many but we should do what we can.' However, his doubts about guided weapons in the here and now were reflected in further proposals to build a trickle of *Lion*-class 6in-gunned cruisers at the rate they could be afforded, with guns until the time came to change over this size of hull to a fleet guided weapons ship capable of both anti-aircraft and surface action. He speculated that the change might not be until the period 1965–70. 'Guns have got about as far as they can go, and the gunnery world should be told by the Admiralty Board to get cracking as talent becomes available, on guided weapons, launchers and GW control.'[49]

The platform to take Seaslug to sea was meanwhile emerging through a number of designs in the late 1940s and into the '50s. Conversion projects considered in the period 1949 to 1951 included *Vanguard*, the fleet carrier *Formidable* or a *Majestic*-class light fleet carrier.[50] Clearly size was the main driver rather than any obvious compatibility of a particular hull type with the missile system. Battleships were still in the frame in April 1954 when the Director of the Gunnery Division in the Admiralty was noting that a decision was needed that year on the ship that would take Seaslug to sea in 1960. He assumed that the ship would be a slow convoy escort cruiser of around 10,000 tons. Contemporary US plans to convert gun cruisers to carry guided missiles were noted, but he did not favour following that path as it was sub-optimal when compared to a purpose-built platform. Meanwhile:

> The question of converting the after end of *Vanguard* or *King George V* is now under investigation by DNC [Director of Naval Construction] ... If such a conversion were planned before 1962, it would be necessary to use development equipment which would otherwise be fitted in the first of the new convoy escort ships, as some of the required equipment cannot be available from production before 1962 ... If any other existing ships are to be converted the hulls chosen will require to be preserved until 1963 ... Although the time required for a conversion, say *Vanguard*, could be expected to be sensibly shorter than that required to build a new ship, the effort and cost of the former would be a substantial part of that for the latter, and the short remaining life might balance any saving ... it will be preferable from a ship building standpoint and also from the viewpoint of technical departments if a new ship could be proceeded with in the first instance. The expense of operating a conversion such as the *Vanguard*, and her potential as a fleet flagship, may militate against her employment for all the tactical investigations inevitably required of the first operational GW ship.[51]

Examination of battleships as Seaslug carriers seems to have evaporated around this point.

So, a new ship it was to be. In November 1954 design GW25C presented to the Sea Lords required four 6in guns to meet the *Sverdlov* threat, and one twin Seaslug launcher, but it was 645ft long and came in at 18,300 tons, with a crew of 1,300. By 1957 it was essentially unchanged, a little less hungry on manpower with a complement of 1,100, but marginally larger at 18,450 tons. This monster was promptly cancelled by Duncan Sandys in the 1957 Defence Review. Had it survived as a concept, notwithstanding Director of Gunnery's 1954 analysis it would probably have been cheaper and quicker to put the system to sea in the five remaining battleships or in the 6in gunned cruisers. But even the battleships would have needed extensive rebuilding because the size and launching limitations of Seaslug would have probably prevented the use of existing main armament barbettes and magazine spaces for storage. These would have worked well for any vertically launched system, but Seaslug had to be trained near the horizontal to acquire its radar guidance beam. As it turned out, the experimental ship for Seaslug development was HMS *Girdle Ness*, a *Beachy Head*-class landing craft repair ship of around 9,000 tons. It took over three years to convert her between February 1953 and July 1956. This involved complete removal of the superstructure and gutting of much of the forward hull in order to accommodate the Seaslug launcher and magazine.[52]

There was one other strand of thinking in the 1950s that might also have involved using the battleships. From January 1954 the Royal Navy was struggling with a tasking from the Defence Research Policy Committee (DRPC) to investigate a ballistic rocket with a projected range of 1,000 nautical miles. On 1 February 1954 the Admiralty Director of Plans was assuming a 'submersible launching ship' based on advice from the Director of Operational Research that 'substantial invulnerability at little cost can only be achieved by making the launching ship submersible'. Director of Naval Ordnance raised another issue in January. If the long-range ballistic weapon was needed, and was a strategic [i.e. an atomic] weapon, was it right for the Royal Navy to act in a strategic role? Would the Navy not be better and fully employed during war in keeping the sea lanes open? He suggested converting merchant ships to carry the ballistic missile 'and keep the *KGV* hulls for conversion to a purely tactical weapon of the Seaslug type, for use, for example on the Atlantic lifeline'. The draft of a paper for the DRPC preferred the submersible option for the long-range weapon, but left open the idea of an interim surface option: 'Some types of existing surface ships will be suitable for conversion, both as test ships and interim operational ships.' This must have meant the battleships, or possibly cruisers, even if it did not say so.[53]

The discussion rumbled on into 1955. In April the Director of Naval Ordnance was envisaging the requirement being satisfied by a missile (presumably with a nuclear warhead, although the papers do not say so) accurate to between 250 and 3,000 yards at 750 miles range, but it would be 90ft long, 8ft in diameter and weigh 70 tons. 'This will call for innovative and revolutionary ship design,' he said, with understatement. Such a missile would protrude well above the upperworks of all existing ships and would require fuelling of its liquid propellant rocket motors shortly before launch: 'uninviting but not insuperable'. The Director of Tactics, Ship Requirements and Staff Duties supported the idea but reverted to the preference for a submersible to reduce vulnerability, and suggested conversion of an existing submarine in the first instance.[54]

Despite the enormous size of the projected missile, and the absence of any existing submarine remotely capable of handling its size and dangerous logistics, these papers do not mention the obvious battleship platform as a deployment possibility. Despite the preference for submerged invulnerability, practically speaking at this point in missile technology development only a battleship or a carrier could conceivably have been adapted to carry such a large weapon remotely safely. The concept of a UK developed sea-based ballistic missile died away in the face of the technological challenge and expense, and the priority accorded by the 1957 defence review to the V-bomber force to carry the United Kingdom's nuclear deterrent. It was not until half a decade later that United States technology had advanced sufficiently to allow the melding of solid fuel propellant, improved range and accuracy and miniaturisation to create the Polaris missile that, at 16 tons and just 33ft in length, could feasibly be carried in a new generation of ballistic missile submarines. From 1968 onwards it was to arm the Royal Navy's invulnerable ballistic missile submarines.

As a commentary on the desultory progress towards guided weapons in the Royal Navy, it is worth comparing the US and Soviet achievements. The Regulus anti-surface cruise missile system was in service aboard a handful of US carriers, destroyers and submarines from 1954, but while it had an impressive range of more than 200 miles, its radio guidance arrangements were highly problematic and easily jammable, and it was no less unwieldy than Seaslug, 6 tons in weight, over 30ft long and with a wingspan of 14ft. In practice it was only useful to deliver a nuclear payload, which it was eventually modified to carry. But it was not a popular system and never widely deployed. The Soviet Navy also fielded a system on destroyers from 1955 onwards (SS-N-1), of similar dimensions but with a much shorter range of 25 miles. The bulk of their development effort in this era went into missiles to be launched from aircraft, and increasingly into their land-based ballistic missile programme.

No viable surface-to-surface missile system was ever developed by the United Kingdom. So long as they existed, and indeed until the Royal Navy deployed the French Exocet system aboard its frigates in the 1980s, the UK could not deliver a surface-to-surface weapon more accurately, more potently or at greater range than with the 15in battleship guns originally designed in 1911.

Jane's Fighting Ships continued to pay attention to the potential of battleships as missile carriers in its editorials during the 1950s, but these also reflected the rapid changes of emphasis taking place in technology and the planning world. The 1953–54 edition of *Jane's* reiterated an earlier view that atomic missiles are big ship weapons, but said that it was not expected that any more battleships or destroyers of a conventional type would be built. It noted that the battleship was really a super cruiser with the same speed, better protection, better gun power and heavier anti-aircraft armament, but expensive to build, maintain and crew. Limited resources meant the UK could do better with cruisers than by keeping battleships in commission.

The 1954–55 edition made reference in the light of guided missile developments to a new type of battleship armed with large missiles 'and sufficiently heavily armoured to give protection against similar weapons used by the enemy'. By 1955–56 the editor considered the technological situation too confused to predict future ship shapes with any accuracy – but the offensive strength of the British fleet was based on the fast battle group centred on the carrier. In 1956–57 he noted the fitting of Terrier missiles to USS *Mississippi*, and asserted that the US Navy considered the battleship the best type of ship for using atomic ballistic missiles. However, only a year later *Jane's* completely changed its tune. The nuclear submarine would be the new capital ship, to replace the aircraft carrier, never mind the battleship, because it had a greater chance of survival in combat, and required no support from other types of vessel and little maintenance. By 1958–59 *Jane's* noted that battleships were rapidly becoming extinct. The emphasis on submarine war was very marked in new construction. Aircraft carriers were too expensive. But the publication also noted that the USA was an exception and that it still clung on to the very old battleships of the *California* and *West Virginia* classes. In fact, even as this was published, those ships were very soon for the scrapyard.

CHAPTER TWELVE

End of the Line?
The Late 1950s and '60s

THE HIGHER TENSIONS of the Cold War meant that there was a need to sustain a strong Western maritime presence in both the North Atlantic and the Mediterranean. The fleets needed to be exercised regularly to show that the new and untested NATO Alliance had the will, and real capability, to underpin its deterrent effect. This meant that even during the Korean War, and after the armistice in 1953, the USA maintained a larger peacetime navy than before 1950, and deployed it overseas far more than had been the case in the 1940s. Although *Missouri* did not venture far from the USA after her two Korea deployments before beginning deactivation in September 1954, the remainder of the *Iowa* class stayed

Mississippi test firing a Terrier anti-aircraft missile, 1953–55. *(NARA)*

active and deployed through the 1950s. Altogether, including the Korean War, between 1950 and 1957 the US battleships made twenty-six major deployments overseas, including thirteen to northern Europe and four to the Mediterranean.

United States of America

In fact, during most of this period the USA was operating five battleships. *Mississippi* was also still active and underwent a second major reconfiguration in 1952, during which she lost her final 14in turret and acquired two firing platforms in X and Y positions aft for the sea trials of the RIM-2 Terrier guided missile. She launched the US Navy into the age of the guided missile warship when she successfully launched the first Terrier from a ship on 28 January 1953 off Cape Cod.

Terrier test firings continued through to mid-1955. *Mississippi* also assisted with the final evaluation of the Petrel radar homing missile in February 1956. She was decommissioned at Norfolk, Virginia, on 2 September 1956 and sold for scrapping to the Bethlehem Steel Corporation on 28 November 1956.[1] The *Herald Press* ran an

Mississippi departs for the last time from Hampton Roads, bound for the scrapyard, 6 December 1956. (NARA)

unsentimental article on 13 December 1956 under the headline 'She's Had It' showing the ship at her final destination, the Patapsco scrapyard in Baltimore, where she was cut up during 1957.

After her return from Korea in November 1952 *Iowa* was overhauled at Norfolk over the winter, then spent spring 1953 training in the Caribbean. She took midshipmen under training to Europe in July 1953, and then repeated *Wisconsin*'s role in the previous year's Mainbrace NATO exercises by taking part in Exercise Mariner in September as flagship of the 2nd Fleet under Vice Admiral E T Woolfidge. As it had been during Mainbrace in 1952, the weather for parts of this exercise was very poor, and when *Iowa* was in company with *Vanguard* there were opportunities to see which ship stood up to the conditions better. The British view was that *Vanguard* rolled less (15 degrees as opposed to 26 for *Iowa*) and was the steadier gun platform. The US had always known that the *Iowas*, with their long fo'c'sles and fine lines, were wet ships, and this confirmed the fact. For the next year *Iowa* operated around Norfolk, Virginia, and the Caribbean. In June 1954 she took midshipmen to Guantanamo, Cuba. On the way to that assignment, for just a few hours on 7 June off Norfolk, Virginia, Battleship Division 2 under Rear Admiral R E Kirby, flying his flag in *Missouri*, brought the four ships together for a few hours. It was the only occasion in their seventy-five years of existence that all the *Iowas* were together manoeuvring at sea.

In September 1954 *Iowa* became flagship of Battleship-Cruiser Force, US Atlantic Fleet. From January to April 1955 she made an extended cruise to the Mediterranean as the first battleship assigned to the 6th Fleet. Ports of call included Gibraltar, Mers-el-Kébir, Genoa,

A unique occasion: The four *Iowa*s together on 7 June 1954 off Virginia Capes. *(NARA)*

Iowa at sea during the 1950s. (Author's collection)

Naples, Istanbul, Athens, Cannes and Barcelona. Another midshipman training cruise followed in the summer of 1955, after which she was overhauled for four months in Norfolk, including relining of the 16in guns. They had fired 8,279 rounds during her twelve years of existence. She spent 1956 doing training cruises and exercises off the east coast and in the Caribbean, and deploying with midshipmen to northern waters in June, visiting Copenhagen and Portsmouth. On 4 January 1957 she left Norfolk for another stint with the 6th Fleet.

Spring 1957 saw a midshipmen's cruise to South America. She took part in an International Naval Review off Hampton Roads near Norfolk on 13 June 1957. This echoed a similar event held in 1907 to mark the 300th anniversary of the founding of the first colony at nearby Jamestown in 1607.

Then on 3 September she sailed for Scotland to take part in the NATO exercise Strikeback. She returned to Norfolk on 28 September, and departed on 22 October bound for the Philadelphia Naval Shipyard, and deactivation. She decommissioned into the Atlantic Fleet reserve on 24 February 1958 after seven years active since her Korean War recommissioning.

New Jersey stayed in Japan following the Korean ceasefire until relieved as flagship of the 7th Fleet by *Wisconsin* on 14 October 1953. She set off the next day and reached Norfolk on 14 November. As part of the Atlantic Fleet she spent 1954 and 1955 undertaking training and exercises on the east coast and in the Caribbean, with summer cruises to Europe both years. In Valencia, Spain, more than 400 of her midshipmen were struck down with gastro-enteritis. She also visited the UK with stops at Portsmouth and Weymouth. Then on 7 September 1955 she changed scene, leaving Norfolk for a tour of duty with the 6th Fleet in the

Iowa and *Wisconsin* in company with the heavy cruisers *Boston* and *Albany,* 3 August 1957. *(NARA)*

Wisconsin returning from Korea, in floating dock AFDB-1 at Guam, 5 April 1952. *(NHHC)*

Mediterranean. Ports of call included Gibraltar, Valencia, Cannes, Istanbul, Souda Bay, Crete and Barcelona. She came back to Norfolk on 17 January 1956, but was soon undertaking her spring exercise schedule and took midshipmen under training to northern Europe during the summer. Just four weeks after returning she set off again on 27 August 1956 as flagship of Vice Admiral Charles Wellborn Junior commanding the 2nd Fleet. Having called at Lisbon, she took part in the NATO exercises off Scotland and Norway. Her stop at Greenock included a dance for the enlisted men at the local women's prison, followed by a tour of the ship for 'fifty unwanted children'. *New Jersey* went on to visit Norway, where Crown Price Olaf was a guest. She returned to Norfolk on 14 October and was then transferred to the New York Naval Shipyard, where inactivation work began on 14 December. She was decommissioned and placed back in the Atlantic Fleet Reserve at Bayonne on 21 August 1957, having been active for nearly seven years, longer than during her first commission.

Wisconsin began her journey back from Korea on 1 April 1952. She came via Guam, where she was raised in the floating dock on 4 and 5 April, the first time an *Iowa*-class battleship had used that type of dock and the heaviest load then lifted by a floating dock. She reached Long Beach in April and Norfolk in May. In June she took her midshipmen to Greenock, Brest and Guantanamo Bay, Cuba. Having dropped them back in the USA, she recrossed the Atlantic on 25 August for the North Atlantic and NATO exercise Mainbrace, alongside *Vanguard*, as described above. Back in the USA, she was overhauled at Norfolk during the winter and spent spring 1953 on the east coast and in the Caribbean, before going down to Rio de Janeiro via Cuba and Trinidad with midshipmen over the summer.

After a brief overhaul in August, she left Norfolk on 9 September bound for the Far East. Although the Korean armistice had come into force and was holding, US naval force levels were maintained at much higher levels than before the war. A battleship remained on station. On 12 October *Wisconsin* relieved *New Jersey* as 7th Fleet flagship. She visited a number of Japanese ports and spent Christmas at Hong Kong. She ceased to be 7th fleet flagship on 1 April 1954 and reached Norfolk on 4 May 1954. The familiar pattern of training cruises and exercises resumed: Greenock, Brest and Guantanamo Bay in July, the Caribbean and Atlantic coast, and NATO exercise Springboard; before repeating the pattern pretty closely during 1955, taking in Denmark, then Haiti, Mexico and Colombia. Winter 1955–56 was spent around the Caribbean. She returned to Norfolk on 31 March 1956.

The next few weeks were spent exercising locally. Off the Virginia Capes on 6 May 1956 she was taking part in anti-aircraft gunnery exercises in a heavy fog. A man was reported overboard from the carrier *Coral Sea* and the destroyer *Eaton* cut across the formation at 27 knots to try to effect a rescue. She had no working radar and encountered *Wisconsin* doing 20 knots. In the low visibility a collision was inevitable. *Wisconsin* ploughed into *Eaton* head on, causing severe damage to the destroyer, including destruction of both 5in forward mountings. *Wisconsin* secured to *Eaton* while the damage was assessed and contained. *Wisconsin* returned to Norfolk with a heavily damaged bow. Despite the disparity in their sizes, *Wisconsin* being some twenty times the displacement of the destroyer, there had just been time for avoiding action to make it a glancing blow, and *Eaton* survived with just one minor casualty and also made her own way back to Norfolk.

On 14 May the battleship went into the dry dock at Norfolk Naval Shipyard. Repairs were expedited by the decision to simply cut off the

Wisconsin after her collision with *Eaton*, with damaged bow, May 1956. *(NHHC)*

mangled portion of *Wisconsin*'s bow and graft onto her a 68ft-long section from the bow of the uncompleted, but still languishing, *Kentucky*, which was at Newport News Shipbuilding and Dry Dock Corporation on the opposite side of Hampton Roads. The new bow was transported by barge across the bay and was attached by the shipyard in just sixteen days.

Kentucky's bow is transported from Newport News to repair *Wisconsin* in May or June 1956. *(NARA)*

This meant that *Wisconsin* was back in action by 28 June 1956 and available to undertake the summer midshipmen's cruise as scheduled. She called at Barcelona, Greenock and Guantanamo Bay.

In autumn that year she took part in Atlantic Fleet exercises, and then was overhauled at Norfolk from November to January 1957. In January and February she was in the Caribbean as flagship of battleship Division Two, and the exercises included a shore bombardment off the isle of Culebra, Puerto Rico. In April 1957 she arrived at Gibraltar and went on to the Aegean Sea and Turkey to take part in the NATO exercise Red Pivot.

She also visited Naples and Valencia, returning to Norfolk on 27 May. Here she joined *Iowa* at the Hampton Roads Review on 12 June. The two battleships were moored at the head of the line. The UK's star turn at this event was the new aircraft carrier *Ark Royal*, which had finally joined the fleet. During the summer *Wisconsin* went through the Caribbean and Panama Canal to South America, as far south as Valparaiso on another midshipman training cruise. After further operations in the Caribbean and off the east coast, she crossed the Atlantic along with *Iowa* for the NATO exercise Strikeback from 3 to 12 September, based on the Clyde, and visited Brest before returning to Norfolk on 22 October 1957. Strikeback was the first occasion the US had deployed nuclear-powered submarines, *Nautilus*

Cold War close encounter: Soviet tanker *Komsomol* crosses the bows of *Wisconsin*, probably on Exercise Red Pivot, April–May 1957. *(NHHC)*

and *Seawolf*, in such manoeuvres, and it was the last deterrent contribution of the 1950s for the battleships. On 4 November 1957 *Wisconsin* departed from Norfolk with a large group of guests aboard to mark the retirement of the US fleet's last active battleship. She reached New York on 6 November, then crossed the harbour to Bayonne, New Jersey, where she began deactivation. She went out of commission at Bayonne into the Atlantic Fleet Reserve on 8 March 1958. It was the first time since 1895 that the USA did not have a single battleship in commission.[2]

However, although in reserve, these ships were still very much viewed as potential assets and were far from out of the minds of US Navy planners. Their potential for adaptation to new ways of warfare was first shown from late 1954 when first *New Jersey*, then *Iowa* and *Wisconsin*, had their No. 2 magazines modified to carry a new nuclear version of the 16in shell, designated Mark 23 and also known as 'Katie'. This weapon came out of an original US Army project for 8in atomic artillery and was an air-burst weapon with a yield of about 20 kilotons. The 16in weapon had been successfully tested at Los Alamos in 1954. The modification to the ships allowed the segregation and securing of up to ten live and nine practice shells and their nuclear warheads in No. 2 turret main magazine. *Wisconsin* is reported to have fired just one practice round in 1957[3] but details of where, when and indeed how many live rounds were actually carried during the final active months of the class are still not available. *Missouri* was not modified because she had already begun deactivation when the Mark 23 programme began. With all four ships in mothballs by 1958, and tactical nuclear warfare at sea moving into a new focus on anti-submarine warfare, the Mark 23 was soon scrapped between 1961 and 1962.[4]

In June 1958 the US Navy Bureau of Ships conducted a study on converting the *Iowas* into guided missile ships. *Mississippi*'s trials had finished successfully and Terrier was a going concern, as was a longer-range derivative called Talos, and a shorter-range missile, Tartar. Some of the Second World War heavy and light cruisers were being partially converted to carry these weapons. The *Iowa*-class conversion would have removed the entire 16in armament and replaced it with two twin Talos launchers, two twin Tartar, an ASROC anti-submarine guided missile launcher and just four Regulus II missiles to provide the long-range anti-surface striking power. The configuration suggests that their role would have been as flagships and escorts to carrier striking forces, echoing the roles that the unmodernised ships had played during the NATO exercises of the 1950s. The estimated cost of $193 million per ship was considered prohibitive, so a partial conversion was proposed instead that would have kept the forward 16in turrets and installed one Talos, one Tartar and ASROC, but now with six Regulus. Although the estimated cost had dropped to $84 million per ship, this proposal never got approval in the US system.

Four years passed before the Navy, and particularly the US Marine Corps, tried to get support for a new proposal to reconfigure and reactivate the class as shore bombardment and amphibious assault ships. They were considered a potent and self-contained option. The forward 16in turrets would remain for fire support, but with the aft 16in turret and 5in guns removed there would be space for a helicopter landing deck, hangar and capacity for embarking twenty helicopters, sixteen landing craft and a Marine Assault battalion. This was rather good value at only an estimated $15–20 million per ship, although that low figure for an extensive conversion does sound fairly implausible set against later projected 1960s reactivation costs. But again the project was never authorised.[5]

Although the other modern reserve fleet battleships (excluding the *Iowas*) were not considered for reactivation in the Korean War, there had been interest in their potential in the US Navy hierarchy. In 1952 the Bureau of Ships drew up class improvement plans for all ten modern battleships then in service or reserve, including the *Iowas*, *North Carolinas* and *South Dakotas*. Based on Korean War experience and the advent of jet aircraft, these plans focussed mainly on anti-aircraft capability, replacing all 40mm mountings with the much longer-range automated 3in twin Mk 33 gun mounting and new fire control systems. Some initial work was done on *Iowa* and *New Jersey* fire control from 1955, but they never got the new guns and the plans for the other classes of ship remained unused.[6]

More ambitiously, on 26 July 1954 the Chairman of the US Navy Ships Characteristics Board requested a preliminary design study of both the *Washingtons* and *South Dakotas*, with a view to increasing their speed to a target of 31 knots so that they were better suited for modern high-speed fleet operations (they were notionally capable of 27 as originally designed). The requirement for extra speed presumably envisaged operations with the carrier battle groups, as a close escort, rather than independent operations or a bombardment role, for which the extra speed would not have been needed. With the main armoured belt removed to lighten the ships, the required power for 31 knots was still 216,000 shp. As the existing power plant generated only 115,000 in the case of the *Washingtons*, and 130,000 in the case of the *South Dakotas*, there was a need to remove the aft 16in turret and magazines as well to fit in the necessary additional machinery. Modifications to the propellers and hull shape would also have been necessary. The cost was estimated at only $40 million per ship, which does not sound a very realistic figure considering the scale of the work envisaged. The upshot was that while the conversion was considered technically feasible, the project was abandoned.[7]

Alaska and *Guam* were also the subject of another US Navy Bureau of Ships study for potential conversion into fully fledged guided missile heavy ships to parallel the proposals made for the *Iowa* class in June 1958. The plan mirrored that for the *Iowas*. It envisaged complete replacement of the main 12in gun armament with two long-range Talos anti-aircraft missiles, two medium-range Terrier anti-aircraft missiles, an ASROC anti-submarine missile system and four Regulus II long-range, nuclear-capable, anti-surface missiles. The cost was estimated at $160 million per ship, which was judged too high, so a partial conversion where only the aft turret would be removed and the number of Talos and Terrier mountings reduced to one each, was also proposed, at $82 million per ship. The project did not proceed.[8]

The almost completed *Hawaii* was also the subject of studies to convert her to other uses. Initially, way back in September 1946 she was considered for a scheme called CB(SW) (where SW presumably stands for special weapons, or surface weapons) for use in the test and development of guided missiles. In this configuration she would retain only sixteen of the new 3in Mark 33 anti-aircraft guns and have missile launch decks in place of the three 12in turrets forward and aft. There would be no armour. The timing of the scheme makes it likely that this was an alternative to using *Mississippi* for missile trials, with the option of then bringing the newer ship into fleet service. Again, it was never authorised, and when *Hawaii* was 85 per cent complete as a conventional battlecruiser, construction halted on 16 April 1947. She was mothballed, with her main armament remaining in place.

A different conversion of *Hawaii* to a large tactical command ship was proposed in August 1951, which would redesignate her as CBC-1. Main armament would be reduced to 5in dual-purpose guns for self-defence, with a major investment in enhanced communications. This conversion was indeed authorised in 1952, but no contracts were awarded and it was abandoned by September 1954. The heavy cruiser *Northampton* was converted to the command ship role instead and served until 1970.

Instead of conversions, this period saw the scrapping of all the other US battleships that had remained inactive since the Pacific war, after a ten-year hiatus in such activity. New pressure on the defence budget meant that the whole reserve fleet was pared back significantly. Between 1958 and 1962 the United States scrapped or sold sixteen battleships, fifty-three aircraft carriers, nine heavy cruisers and twenty-one light cruisers. The older battleships went first. Forty-year-old veterans *Tennessee* and *California* were stricken from the Naval Vessel Register on 1 March 1959 and sold to Bethlehem Steel on 10 July. They reached Baltimore for

Hawaii under construction, Camden, New Jersey, 8 January 1947. *(NHHC)*

scrapping on 26 July 1959. From the Pacific Reserve Fleet, *Colorado* and *Maryland* went to Seattle and Oakland respectively in the same timeframe. *West Virginia* was also sold on 24 August 1959 for $781,290 to Union Metals and Alloy Corporation of New York, but she lingered a further eighteen months before leaving Puget Sound on 3 January 1961 to make the short journey to the Todd shipyard for torching. Her mast was rescued

311

by funds raised by University of West Virginia students and is preserved on the campus at Morgantown, West Virginia, where it was dedicated as a memorial on 11 May 1963.

North Carolina was eventually stricken from the Navy List on 1 June 1960 and purchased by the state of North Carolina for $250,000. She was dedicated as a war memorial near Wilmington in the Cape Fear River on 3 October 1961 (see Chapter Fifteen). *Washington* was stricken from the Navy list on the same day as her sister. She was sold for scrap on 24 May 1961. *South Dakota* and her three sister ships were all stricken on 1 June 1962. She was sold to the Lipsett division of Luria Brothers on 25 October 1962 for $466,425 for scrap. *Indiana* was sold for $418,387 on 6 September 1963 and scrapped in 1964. *Massachusetts* was made available to the State of Massachusetts and became a state memorial moored at Fall River on 4 June 1965 (see Chapter Fifteen). *Alabama* was eventually sold to the State of Alabama on 16 June 1964. She left Bremerton on 2 July 1964 bound for her final mooring at Mobile, Alabama (see Chapter Fifteen).

Alaska was stricken from the Navy List on 1 June 1960 and sold to the Lipsett division of Luria Brothers for scrapping at New York in July 1961. *Guam* too was stricken from the Navy list on 1 June 1960 and sold to the Boston Metal Company, which scrapped her at Baltimore, Maryland, from 10 July 1961. *Hawaii* was finally scrapped in the same timeframe as her sisters, at Baltimore from January 1960.

Also finally scrapped as part of this clear out was the 22 per cent complete hull of *Illinois*, inexplicably retained in limbo for over thirteen years on her slipway at Philadelphia Navy Yard and finally broken up

Hawaii is towed to the scrapyard, 20 June 1959. (NHHC)

The end of *Kentucky* – towed to Baltimore for scrapping on 31 October 1958. *(NHHC)*

there from September 1958. *Kentucky* too was finally disposed of. Construction had been continued until August 1946, then suspended while she was considered by the Ship Characteristics Board for conversion as an 'anti-aircraft battleship', known as project 19. Armament was to have been a mix of then undefined anti-aircraft missiles and 8in 55-calibre guns in triple or quadruple mountings. This was stillborn, but construction resumed in August 1948, allowing her to be launched. She was included in the plans to convert the *Iowa* class to missile ships in the 1950s, and the Ship Characteristics Board had also suggested in 1955 that she become a missile battleship. Two projects were postulated, the first for full conversion to Talos, Tartar and vertical-launched Jupiter missiles in silos; and the second from 1957 with two 16in turrets retained, but new 5in and 3in guns, Talos, Terrier or Tartar, and at least eight Regulus II long-range, anti-surface missiles, as well as Polaris silos. This was initially projected to cost $130 million but had escalated to nearer $200 million the following year when Polaris was being considered instead of Regulus.[9] The $200 million request got as far as the initial budget submission, but failed to pass scrutiny so, again, nothing came of it.

 Kentucky had been progressively cannibalised during this period, losing her bow to *Wisconsin* after the accident in 1956 and having her four main engines removed in 1958 and installed, two each, in the new

313

Fast Combat Support Ships *Sacramento* and *Camden*. These 54,000-ton, 800ft monsters continued in service for forty more years, driven at up to 27 knots by the *Iowa*-class power plant, until they were decommissioned in 2004. The experience of their crews, using the last 600 psi machinery then in commission in the US Navy, was invaluable in getting the *Iowa*s recommissioned in the 1980s. The rest of *Kentucky* was sold to the Boston Metals Co. on 30 October 1958 for $1,176,006. She was towed to Baltimore with the mangled bow of *Wisconsin*, her own uninstalled conning tower and various loose 5in mountings scattered over her upper deck, and scrapped there from November 1958 onwards.

Europe

The European powers also disposed of most of their remaining battleships during the 1950s, although a few survived into the following decade. Although largely inactive, *Caio Duilio* and *Andrea Doria* remained on the Italian Navy list well beyond the demise of their modern *Littorio* ships, and went to sea until 1956. As in the 1940s, they spent most of their time between Augusta, Syracuse and Taranto. While the British Admiralty was still prepared to count them as potential adversaries in late 1949 (see Chapter Seven), and had sent a technical team to analyse their gunnery

Duilio at La Spezia in 1954. *(Erminio Bagnasco)*

Andrea Doria leaves Taranto for the last time, 28 April 1960. *(USMM)*

capabilities in June 1946,[10] Admiral Sir Arthur Power, Commander-in-Chief of the Mediterranean Fleet, was more scathing. On 20 March 1950 he wrote to the First Sea Lord, reporting discussions with the Italian Navy, who wanted to borrow scarce Royal Navy submarines to do anti-submarine exercises. He felt they needed their own submarines (banned under the peace treaty). 'Would it be possible to let them have two submarines without tubes on condition they scrapped their useless battleships and put the money saved into anti-submarine units?'[11]

However, Italy felt the ships still had a value. *Duilio* was the fleet flagship between 1 May 1947 and 10 November 1949, in which capacity she had both visited Malta in June 1949 and hosted *Vanguard* at Taranto the following month. She was inactive at La Spezia from 1953. *Andrea Doria* took over as flagship in October 1949 until 9 December 1950, although she was in refit at Taranto for much of that period. She became flagship again between 9 March 1951 and May 1953. She remained in service as a training and gunnery ship at Taranto until 16 September 1956. The two ships were finally stricken on 15 September (*Duilio*) and 1 November 1956 (*Andrea Doria*). The former was scrapped in 1957, the latter not until 1961.[12]

Before the old Italian ships reached the end of their service, their Soviet sister suffered a violent end. *Novorossiysk* spent a prolonged period under refit or repair at Sevastopol until late 1954, receiving new radars, 37mm anti-aircraft guns and new, indigenously built turbines, the Kharkhov factory having finally got its act together. The hull survey undertaken then indicated that she was fit for another ten to fifteen years of service. From May 1955 she was employed as a seagoing training ship, and once again as flagship of the Black Sea squadron. She made many trips to sea over these months and on the evening of 28 October 1955 she returned from a typical cruise in the Black Sea. She anchored, moored fore and aft to her usual buoys in the Sevastopol battleship moorings, which were only around 100m from the shore beside the marine hospital. The captain, Kukhta, and many senior officers went ashore for the night.

At 0130 on 29 October 1955 *Novorossiysk* became, in all probability, the final battleship casualty of the Second World War when she detonated an old German influence mine on the seabed of Sevastopol harbour. Older Western sources blamed an internal explosion, but it now seems clear from the Soviets' own hastily convened Commission of Inquiry that the cause was detonation of an RMH or LMB type of German mine with around 700kg of high explosive. Despite a number of sweeps and diver inspections of the seabed over the eleven intervening years, the Russians had never properly cleared the harbour of wartime ordnance, and a further search after the sinking found thirteen (some sources say nineteen) more unexploded German mines in the harbour, several of them within 50m of *Novorossiysk*'s mooring.

Other much later and exotic theories for her loss blamed, variously NATO or KGB sabotage to foment political moves against the Soviet Navy hierarchy. There was also the notion of a covert attack by former members of Italy's underwater commandos led by Second World War hero and unreconstructed fascist Prince Junio Valerio Borghese to revenge the indignity of the terms of the peace treaty and the enforced handover of *Giulio Cesare*. Aside from their inherent political and logistic implausibility, these ideas were never entertained by the Soviet Union at the time. In fact, the Russians had arguably been very lucky that the 144 previous occasions when *Novorossiysk* or *Sevastopol* had used the same mooring since 1944 had not generated a similar catastrophe.

The explosion was under the starboard side just forward of the forward turret and ruptured the hull for 75ft. The hole was 150 sq m in extent, and the explosion's force penetrated up through all her decks and punctured the fo'c'sle deck forward of the turret. Soon the whole fore part of the ship was flooded with around 3,500 tons of water and she began to list to starboard. Damage control was hindered by loss of electrical power and the absence of the senior officers ashore. By 0240 the fo'c'sle was underwater. From 0200 attempts were made to move her closer to the shore, but she was still anchored by the bow, so these were restricted to pulling the stern around, a process still under way when she sank. The Fleet Commander, Vice Admiral V A Parkhomenko, arrived at 0210 to supervise attempts to save her, supported by no fewer than two other vice admirals and four rear admirals plus twenty-eight other senior officers. [13]

More helpfully, damage control parties also began arriving from other ships. Despite their efforts, the water spread steadily aft and a new list to port became progressively worse as buoyancy decreased. By 0400 the list was 18 degrees and with around 7,000 tons of water aboard she capsized at around 0415, then remained afloat upside down for some while until she settled to the harbour bottom. There was no systematic evacuation and around 1,000 of the crew were still gathered on the quarterdeck when she capsized. There were 609 fatalities from a total crew of 1,600, swollen as it was by a new draft of recruits and naval academy cadets who were also aboard. A number of men were trapped in the upturned hull, of whom seven were rescued through a hole cut in the ship's bottom five hours later, while two very lucky ones were led out by divers more than two days afterwards. Others survived trapped beyond this point, but their knocking on the hull had ceased by 1 November.

Subsequent enquiries were highly critical of the failure to save more of the men. The Squadron Commander, Rear Admiral N I Nikolskiy, twice asked permission to remove sailors not engaged in damage control to boats standing by the stricken battleship, but was refused by Parkhomenko, who testified that up to the last minute he was hoping to save the ship. There was also criticism of the absence of adequate technical documentation aboard to assist with damage control. Salvage of the capsized ship began in the following summer by sealing the hull and blowing compressed air in. It took nine months to make these preparations, and the hull was successfully raised on 4 May 1957. On 14 May it was towed to Cossack Bay, where it was, apparently, turned upright, and dismantled, with the scrap metal being recycled through the Zaporozhstal Factory.[14]

The investigation into the sinking was headed by Deputy Chairman of the Council of Ministers and Minister of the Shipbuilding Industry V Malyshev, who, ironically, had reviewed the drawings of *Giulio Cesare* back in 1946 and recommended to Stalin refusing her transfer. He was given a very tight timeframe for his work, and reported to the Central Committee of the Communist Party as soon as 17 November. They approved his report blaming the German mine. The investigation criticised Vice Admiral Parkhomenko for failing to save the battleship and the heavy loss of life. Parkhomenko was severely reprimanded and removed from his post on 8 December 1955. A number of other senior officers were also removed and punished by reductions in rank, including those responsible for the seaward defence of the naval base, which was, serendipitously, found to be severely lacking. The junior officers and sailors who were at the heart of the damage control efforts were praised, but their efforts were negated by the 'criminally reckless, unqualified and indecisive command'. The highest-ranking victim may have been Kuznetsov, who was removed in 1956 after falling out with Red Army head Marshal Zhukov, reportedly citing the loss of the battleship as a pretext.

Of the other three ex-Tsarist ships that were *Novorossiysk*'s battleship contemporaries in the Soviet Navy, *Oktyabrskaya Revolutsiya* had remained in commission in the Baltic serving with the 8th Fleet at Tallinn. She was relegated to a training role only, and reclassified as a 'school battleship' after 24 July 1954, then stricken on 17 February 1956, before being broken up at Kronstadt from 1956 to 1959. *Petropavlovsk* never went to sea after the war and was reclassified as a stationary school training ship on 28 November 1950, renamed *Volkhov*. She was stricken on 4 September 1953 and scrapped thereafter. *Sevastopol* continued in active service in the Black Sea despite her complete obsolescence until 24 July 1954, then as a 'training battleship' until 17 February 1956, when she was towed to Kamyshin Bay for dismantling over the following two years. The investigation into the loss of *Novorossiysk* shows that *Sevastopol* was genuinely active during the post-war period. She used the mooring where *Novorossiysk* perished on 134 separate occasions over a decade, a level of activity that compares rather favourably with the number of movements recorded in their logs by most of the British training battleships during the 1940s.

United Kingdom

In the UK we left the *King George V* class settling into reserve in 1949–50. The surviving records for their reserve service are very sparse. This is probably not a great loss to posterity, for the few ships' logs that exist, for *Howe* during early 1951 and the first half of 1952, show that there was not a lot of significance to record.[15] The logs for these years in Category C reserve are now completed only in pencil, not ink; they are often rough and difficult to read; and often completed by an able seaman as opposed to the officer of the watch or navigating officer when the ships were in commission. In 1951 *Howe* is berthed at *Imperieuse*'s moorings in Devonport (although *Imperieuse* itself had paid off in 1948) and she is still being used for training, as the log records 'Hands' and 'Trainees' activity separately. On 21 February 1951 for example, ninety-two stoker trainees joined the ship from HMS *Raleigh*. The Senior Officer Reserve Fleet (SORF) Plymouth is based aboard her, as well as her captain, although in rank the latter is now only a lieutenant commander. The log records, as in earlier days, the daily cycle of the ship's existence, the comings and goings of senior officers and guests, and the arrival and departure of other ships from her vicinity. The date 17 March was a red-letter day as she was visited by the Flag Officer Commanding the Reserve Fleet, the Commander-in-Chief of the Home Fleet and the Admiral Superintendent of Devonport. Sadly the log does not record why they all came on the one day.

By January 1952 *Howe* is still at the same moorings, SORF

Plymouth is still aboard and there are still men under training. But there is a new entry in the logs that betokens the next stage of her life: 'Hands employed preservation of ship', or 'general clean ship'. On 5 February she is moved, to No. 6/7 Wharf at Devonport, moored next to *Vanguard*. While there, she fired a fifty-six-gun salute on 15 February to mark the funeral of King George VI and held a two minutes' silence. Britain's last battleship sailor king, veteran of Jutland, had died at Sandringham on 6 February. On 25 February *Howe* moved again, to Number 8 wharf, where she remained in reserve well beyond 30 June 1952, although that is the last surviving entry in her log. The hands are still scrubbing the decks, SORF is still coming aboard every day, visitors are still calling, ratings are still being drafted, divers are down between 1000 and 1155 on the port quarter for examination of the underwater fittings, and the Confidential Books are still being mustered and found correct. That is the last first-hand evidence we have of life aboard a *King George V*-class battleship.

The ship's books do, however, provide a little more detail for the final years. We know that *King George V* was transferred to the administration of Flag Officer Commanding Reserve Forces (FOCRF) on 6 September 1949 for reduction to Category C reserve. This process of preservation happened at Portsmouth, and would, notionally, have involved a reduced crew of 592. The same principles were followed as in the USA, but whether they were as thorough or effective was not to be put to the test as there was never a need to recommission the ships. It is likely that *King George V* and *Anson* were more thoroughly preserved than *Duke of York* and *Howe*, because FOCRF later noted the latter two as among a number of Category II reserve fleet ships not properly reduced to reserve or dehumidified as a result of the crews being reduced or removed well before their pre-reserve refits were completed.[16] It took the 592 men nearly seven months to cocoon her, a process that completed on 27 March 1950 when she was accepted into Category C reserve, administered by Senior Officer Reserve Forces Portsmouth. Her caretaker crew at this juncture was authorised to be 163. She was towed to Gare Loch on 14 June 1950 to be laid up there.

However, she was not completely neglected. She was docked at the Gladstone Dock, Liverpool, between 29 June and 10 August 1955, and a full examination of the wear on her propeller shafts was carried out on 1 July. The next major step in reduction of her readiness was placing her in Extended Reserve on 16 December 1955, which reduced the crew to just eighty-six.[17] The costs of maintenance dropped dramatically at this point by about 90 per cent, to an estimated £46,000 per year for all four ships, most of which was spent on *King George V*.[18] The precise timing of this decision is confusing, because First Lord J P L Thomas did not seek Cabinet approval until February 1956 when he offered options to Cabinet, saying: 'there is no good naval reason for keeping these ships.' However, there was some fear of a public backlash if they were scrapped 'before our guided weapons cruisers are laid down to replace them' and in particular from the recently retired Churchill, replaced as Prime Minister by Eden in April 1955. So keeping them in reserve but not spending money on maintenance seemed a pragmatic compromise.[19] Treasury officials noted the decision was made because the value of the ships as a deterrent and their potential value in war had fallen so low that the 'heavy outlay of money and manpower in maintaining them is no longer justifiable'. Keeping the ships in extended reserve meant accepting that they would deteriorate and might be scrapped in a few years. Although the £50,000 per year cost was viewed as unnecessary, it was not worth making a fuss over. The Chancellor of the Exchequer, however, pressed to keep the scrapping option under review.[20]

Three *King George Vs* in reserve at Gare Loch, 1957. *(Alamy)*

The axe finally fell in the Duncan Sandys Defence review of April 1957. *King George V* was sold to BISCO and allocated to Arnott and Young for demolition in January 1958. She left Gare Loch on 20 January to be towed up the Clyde to Dalmuir for dismantling. By 19 May 1959 her

35,000 tons had been reduced to maybe 8,000, and the hulk, drawing 9ft 4in forward and 8ft aft, made its final journey back down the Clyde to Troon, where demolition was completed on 5 February 1960.[21] On 2 March 1960 Parliament was told that her scrapping had realised about £500,000.[22]

Anson was transferred to the administration of Flag Officer Commanding Reserve Forces on 10 November 1949 at Devonport. It took nearly ten months to prepare her for laying up, including a docking at No. 10 Dock in Devonport between 28 April and 22 May 1950. She was accepted into Category C Reserve on 2 August 1950 and was also towed up to Gare Loch. Her final docking at Liverpool was between 6 September and 7 October 1952, when her bottom was painted. The condition of the ship's bottom was recorded as: 'mussels excessive, soft bodied marine forms and tubeworm where mussel clusters are slight'. *Anson* too went to extended reserve in December 1955, and was sold off via BISCO in 1957 to Ship Breaking Industries, the new entity within the Metal Industries operation now running the Faslane facility. So her final journey was an even shorter one up Gare Loch on 17 December 1957.[23] *Anson* yielded 33,673 tons of scrap material.[24]

Duke of York had been in refit in Portsmouth after her stint as Home Fleet flagship. The docking lasted from 11 May to 30 September 1949, during which period the decision to reduce her to reserve was made (see Chapter Seven). Nevertheless, the refit ended up costing £264,000, although this was £32,000 below the allocated budget. The work included refurbishment of the main armament, replacement of all the sixteen 5.25in gun barrels and refurbishment of the boilers and all diesel generators, as well as work on the bathrooms. She remained in Portsmouth as flagship of the Flag Officer Commanding the Reserve Fleet (FOCRF), who hoisted his flag on 20 June while she was still in dock. The ship's book says: 'This unit will be an independent unit of the reserve fleet … to reduce to Cat C or as near as practicable on completion of refit.' The extra demands of having the Flag Officer aboard meant that despite the head start given by the dockyard work, it took nearly another year to get the ship prepared for the reserve. She formally entered Category C on 1 August 1950. FOCRF remained aboard thereafter until he transferred his flag to the rather less spacious accommodation of the small cruiser *Dido* at 0800 on 28 August 1951.[25]

Duke of York left Spithead on 3 September under tow of three tugs, *Jaunty*, *Saucy* and *Envoy*. The interim destination was to be Gladstone Dock for a pre-laying up scraping and painting. It was the battleship that was to be saucy, as the voyage was interrupted near its end on 7 September at 10 pm by a collision in the River Mersey with the brand new Wallasey Corporation ferry/cruise ship *Royal Iris*. The latter was nearing the end of a three-hour cruise organised by the Merseyside branch of the

Amalgamated Engineering Union. They got more than they bargained for as the ferry was carried against the side of the battleship by the flood tide. More than sixty people were injured and some hospitalised.[26] *Royal Iris* went on to become an icon of Merseyside, cruising among others with The Beatles, and still exists. *Duke of York* anchored for a number of days (not because of the collision), and eventually entered the dock on 24 September, leaving Liverpool on 6 November 1951. She continued her journey north and arrived at Gare Loch to join her two sisters on 10 November. There the three of them spent the next six years together until placed on the disposal list on 30 April 1957. *Duke of York* was the last to go, following *Anson* to Faslane on 18 February 1958.

Howe remained at Devonport. She came under command of FOCRF on 21 June 1949, a day after *Duke of York*, and the original intention was to hold her at Category A reserve. This was soon rescinded to Category C and she reached that point probably in early 1950, although the ship's book is not specific.[27] She was docked at No. 10 Dock in Devonport between 8 and 27 September 1950, and again between 24 June and 21 July 1953, on which occasion her bottom was described as having 'very heavy covering of Mussels, Barnacles, Polyzoa and soft bodied forms. Heavy deposits of slime.' Extended reserve status duly followed in December 1955. The ship's cover also has a snippet showing how the ships were still tended, even in this state of near suspended animation. Senior Officer Reserve Forces Plymouth reports on a 'Boiler Wear and Waste Test' on 9 April 1956. Y1 and Y2 boilers had not been steamed since their renewal in the 1949 refit. 'The delay in carrying out this test was due to the ship being unmaintained between May 1954 and January 1955 and again for a short period from June 1955 due to manpower situation.' There are also references to annual relining of the boilers.[28] *Howe* was joined at Plymouth by *Vanguard* in December 1955 after the latter's refit, and the two were moored together for nearly a year until *Vanguard* was towed to Portsmouth on 26 October 1956. *Howe* was disposed of at the same time as her sisters, but not taken from Devonport under tow to the shipbreakers until over a year later, on 27 May 1958. She was the last *King George V* to be allocated to the breakers, this time to Thomas W Ward. She was towed to Inverkeithing and arrived there on 2 June, although her final voyage was delayed by three days due to running aground in the Forth estuary. She was floated off and came alongside on 5 June to begin demolition.

The high hopes for *Vanguard* expressed in the 1955 Naval Estimates gradually fell victim to further austerity and changes in policy and personality soon thereafter. In February 1955 the ship's book noted an intention to commission at Portsmouth for general service in January 1956, with a two-year commission expected to involve one year abroad

Howe showing lots of freeboard, grounded off Inverkeithing, 3 June 1958. *(MTSC)*

(presumably the Mediterranean), six months at home and six months refitting.[29] The new First Sea Lord was Mountbatten, who had craved *Vanguard* for his Mediterranean command in 1953. Now, however, he considered that the Navy needed to focus resources on the active fleet and slim down the still substantial reserve. It was at this juncture that the *King George Vs* went into extended reserve and that *Vanguard* was also eventually relegated to the reserve alongside *Howe* at Devonport.

On 24 August 1955 First Lord of the Admiralty Thomas wrote to the Prime Minister that the current position was agreement that *Vanguard* would be commissioned at the end of the refit, and she would be ready in January 1956. However, a fresh manning crisis was in train due to failures to achieve recruiting and re-engagement targets. Fifteen ships were having to be withdrawn from the active fleet up to April 1957 to meet this challenge, and the Admiralty also needed to commission the newly converted Seaslug trials ship *Girdle Ness*. She alone would require more radio electrical ratings than the battleship. Thomas concluded: 'We believe the weight of argument is now overwhelmingly against commissioning *Vanguard*. It has long been agreed that her contribution in cold or limited war is only her prestige value. In global war her value particularly against *Sverdlovs* is undoubted, but she would still be available in reserve for this

role.' The cost of the refit, £700,000, could be justified politically by the need to get her ready for operational reserve.[30]

Prime Minister Eden wanted a Defence Committee discussion on the issue, and on 26 August 1955 it was agreed not to commission *Vanguard*. However, Eden recalled earlier debates and was anxious not to arouse Churchill's hostility. He wrote to his predecessor on 28 August, explaining the change of heart. Churchill was not acquiescing quietly. He responded three days later, arguing that *Vanguard* could be kept in commission for four or five years with a complement of under 1,000 'as a moveable command post', and that the skilled ratings needed for radio work would not be needed by her until some weeks after any outbreak of war. Thomas was adamant that this could not work. There was also a shortage of engine room ratings, which commissioning *Vanguard* would exacerbate. The radio ratings would indeed be needed in peacetime if she was to be a 'command post', i.e. a flagship. And a reduced ship's company as Churchill suggested would mean a deterioration in her appearance, with a deplorable impact on morale and no gain in prestige. More than 1,000 men would be needed to man her. Eden concurred and responded to Churchill on 5 September: 'I too would like to keep *Vanguard* in commission if it could be done, but I fear we are beaten by the manpower problem.' A press release explaining the decision and the need to prioritise *Girdle Ness* and other small ships of particular value to the fleet went out on 12 September, and *The Times* reported, without rancour, the following day under the headline: '*Vanguard* to go into reserve – Releasing men for rocket test ship'.[31] Thus, in a strange irony, the ship that might herself have been the rocket-armed heavy ship of the future was sacrificed to the immediate needs of the guided missile programme.

Although she was officially to be held at Category A reserve for operational readiness within thirty days, her close-range anti-aircraft armament was now removed. Her total cost at this state of reserve was now about £700,000 per year.[32] She transferred to Portsmouth under tow on 26 October 1956. In her new home she was flagship of the reserve fleet and also carried out various training functions. Although her readiness was now ebbing away, she still survived the 1957 Defence Review. This came rapidly in the aftermath of the Suez fiasco. Duncan Sandys became the Minister of Defence, but with wider powers than his predecessors, foreshadowing the creation of the unified Ministry of Defence seven years later. The ability of the Admiralty to plough its own furrow was diminished and the appointment of the Earl of Selkirk as First Lord was made conditional on his acceptance of this shift in power. Sandys used those powers to push through in a very short time a radical defence review that underlined the need for nuclear forces, ultimately rocket based, and nuclear deterrence. The Navy kept its carriers, but there would be fewer of them focussed more on the anti-submarine warfare role in war and as mobile airbases in peacetime as overseas stations shut down. There would be much less emphasis on large ships, with numbers restricted to a minimum.

An early draft of the White Paper from mid-March said: 'Since there is no foreseeable use for battleships HMS *Vanguard* and the four older battleships now in reserve will be scrapped.' But the Admiralty Board on 14 March recorded: 'While there would be no objection to the announcement of a decision to scrap the *King George* V class battleships, no reference should be made to HMS *Vanguard* since she was declared to NATO and proper discussion with NATO authorities would be required before she too could be scrapped.' Hence, the first draft of the

White Paper considered by Cabinet on 18 March 1957, said: 'The number of cruisers in the active fleet will be reduced and replaced by ships of the *Tiger* class and guided weapon vessels. The four older battleships now in reserve will be scrapped. The future of HMS *Vanguard* will be discussed with NATO.' No dissenting voices were recorded, and the next draft dated 26 March said: 'The nine cruisers in the active fleet will be reduced to three … A considerable number of ships now in reserve, including battleships, will be scrapped.' The final drafts in late March and on 1 April left out the reduced number of cruisers to be retained but confirmed the fate of the battleships: '… the number of large ships will be restricted to the minimum … the cruisers in the active fleet will be reduced … A considerable number of ships now in the reserve, including battleships, will be disposed of or scrapped.'[33]

Vanguard had lost her placeholder in the text, and was potentially as vulnerable as other reserve ships, but she had not lost her unique status. So while the *King George Vs* were on the disposals list less than a month after the White Paper (Command 124) was presented to Parliament on 4 April 1957, Sandys and Prime Minister MacMillan hesitated to bring down the curtain on *Vanguard*, although they also failed to endorse her. It is clear from the Admiralty papers that there was no doubt about her ultimate fate. Mountbatten's principal concern in the debates on the White Paper concerned the future level of naval manpower, and it was only the technicality of the NATO declaration that saved her at this juncture.[34] The Parliamentary debate on Command 124 did not touch on the future of battleships.

The reality was that *Vanguard*'s role as flagship of the reserve fleet, accommodation for up to 1,000 ratings and her declaration and potential to be allocated to NATO if needed still gave her a lingering purpose, and her cost, reduced to only £230,000 during 1957–58, was maybe too small to attract hostility from those seeking immediate efficiencies, although this was a matter of sensitivity. On 13 February 1958 the Admiralty Board agreed to scrap sixty ships in extended reserve, and the Civil Lord pointed out that retention of *Vanguard* in reserve might provoke serious (presumably Parliamentary) criticism. The Board agreed to review the ship's future again with particular regard to her manpower requirement.[35] On 23 April 1958 the Parliamentary Secretary to the Admiralty, James Allan, told Sir A V Harvey that the battleship's future was being reconsidered, that she remained a short notice for sea, presently required a crew of 136 and that she had burned about 3,000 tons of oil fuel over the previous six months. But by 23 July that year he announced the end of the commitment at high readiness in operational reserve to meet Treaty obligations. '*Vanguard* will now come to a lower state of readiness but continue as training accommodation and Reserve Fleet Headquarters until satisfactory alternative arrangements can be made.' The newspapers interpreted this as a scrapping announcement.[36] She was formally reduced to Category C reserve in 1958. Although the new Minister, Ian Orr-Ewing, still felt able to congratulate the crew on maintaining her at what he described as a 'high state of readiness' on 10 March 1959,[37] by August 1959 her sands were running out. The indigenous ballistic missile project, which she might have carried, was dead, and decisions were about to be taken that would provide the UK with a submarine-launched nuclear deterrent. Little had changed in terms of the Navy's ability to kill *Sverdlovs* since 1954, other than that there were more of them to kill, and the Buccaneer S2 strike aircraft did not enter service to perform this role effectively until the mid-1960s. Admiral of the Fleet Viscount Cunningham of Hyndhope, although a critic of *Vanguard* when in office, noted in the 1958 Debate on the Naval Estimates that the Royal Navy now had nothing that could catch or match the *Sverdlovs*.[38]

Nonetheless, the Admiralty Committee on Estimates recommended that if no positive function could be found for her, *Vanguard* should be disposed of. And so it was. Her approval for scrapping was noted in the ship's cover on 12 February 1960, and announced in the Statement on the Naval Estimates on 24 February 1960. Orr-Ewing explained to a grumpy Emmanuel Shinwell that the money spent on her upkeep, £1.71 million since 1951, was justified by the part the ship played supporting the UK's naval alliances and that until 1958 *Vanguard* 'was considered by NATO as a very useful warship'. It was the cessation of the NATO declaration that ultimately sealed her fate.[39] She was paid off for disposal on 7 June 1960, and the white ensign was lowered for the last time on a British battleship.

Unusually the Admiralty sought tenders directly from shipbreakers, as well as from BISCO. Metal Industries bid £480,000 and its board authorised a fixed price deal with BISCO at 110 shillings per ton plus commission for non-ferrous metals if BISCO should get her. They duly did, paying £550,000. Henry G Pound, the new owner of Cairnryan military port, had it reported in the *Glasgow Daily Herald* on 2 June 1960 that he would be bidding at £400,000 to scrap her there, and planned to mobilise the local MP in support. This caused a stir at Metal Industries, who considered the Cairnryan facility unsuitable and planned to mobilise their own Faslane MPs if need be.[40] However, the deal with BISCO duly went through in their favour.

But when the time came for her to make the journey to Faslane in the wake of so many of her kind, like *Warspite* she baulked at the voyage. Her tugs lost control of her at the narrow mouth of Portsmouth harbour as she tried to exit on 4 August 1960. She veered to port and grounded just off the Still and West public house.

Patrons and others gathered for the historic occasion enjoyed an unexpected spectacle as the tugs struggled for an hour to free her. Pathé

Vanguard aground at the mouth of Portsmouth Harbour, 4 August 1960. (Author's collection)

had a film crew aboard for the historic occasion and their footage shows her veering off course some way before the harbour entrance, then tugs desperately reversing engines to hold her back. But she was not to escape her fate, and soon she was backed off and the voyage resumed. Pathé recorded a serene passage with three ocean tugs pulling her through calm seas and thick fog. One of the tugs is *Bustler*, of *Warspite* and *Sao Paulo* fame. Although at one point she had to come alongside the battleship to clear a snagged line, on this occasion *Bustler* did not lose her charge.[41] *Vanguard* reached Ship Breaking Industries, amid much sentiment, on 9 August 1960. The torches were soon at work with 2,075 tons removed by 1 October and a further 2,267 tons four weeks later. The tugs *Flying Duck* and *Flying Buzzard* towed her to the beaching ground on 2 April 1962, by which stage she was drawing just 4ft 11in forward and 10ft 3in aft, weights deliberately skewed so that her keel matched the slope of the beach. She was gone by the end of 1962, although Ship Breaking Industries were still removing her scrap from the yard well into 1963.[42]

France

The French battleships were generally less active than *Vanguard*, but *Jean Bart* had one brief operational flourish. After emerging from her long refit at Brest, from summer 1952 *Richelieu* was base ported in Toulon as a training ship. She hosted Rear Admiral Champion, the Flag Officer for training in the Mediterranean, and the gunnery school. Sorties for gunnery training and occasional visits to the Riviera and Algeria became rarer, averaging four days per month. She had received relined guns in No. 2 turret and four new guns for No. 1 turret. One was newly manufactured, but the other three had been made before 1940 and were originally destined for *Jean Bart*. They had been seized by the Germans during the war. One was installed in a shore battery in Norway, one in Normandy and one at the Krupp proving ground at Meppen, Germany. But they were only to fire once more, nine rounds each in the post-refit proving trials. *Richelieu*'s main armament was silent thereafter.

Richelieu was again in dock and scraped between 1 October 1953 and 15 February 1954, before resuming her earlier pattern of operations

329

as the flagship of the Groupe des Écoles Sud. At the end of January 1956 *Richelieu* and *Jean Bart* briefly manoeuvred together off Toulon. It was the only time in their existence that they did so. *Richelieu* returned to Brest, and just a few months later on 1 June 1956 went into reserve there. Light anti-aircraft guns were removed and the main and secondary armaments preserved via dehumidification. The French Navy still thought of her as potentially operational, although her active life was confined to becoming the base for the Reserve Officers School and the Navigation School. After a decade alongside in these roles, she was finally stricken on 30 September 1967 (some sources say 16 January 1968) and became designated as Hulk Q432. Shipbreaking Industries were interested in breaking up *Richelieu* and inspected her at Brest between 30 May and 5 June 1968, noting that she was offered less the four guns from A turret with an estimated displacement of 37,500 tons. They bid £686,000 for the hulk, but were well short of the winning bid, which they estimated at £800,000.[43] She was sold to Cantieri Navale Santa Maria of Genoa and on 25 August 1968, just as *New Jersey* was showing there was still life in the battleship, the Dutch tug *Red Sea* took *Richelieu*/Q432 in tow bound for La Spezia, where she arrived on 8 September. By the end of 1969 she had been completely dismantled.[44]

Five of her 15in guns survive today. One remains on display by Penfeld river dockside, near Recouvrance Bridge at the naval arsenal in Brest; one is at Gâvres; one at the École Navale Lanevoc Poulmic; and one at the manufacturing site at Ruelle. A final weapon went to be scrapped but was removed from the ship at La Spezia and used by the Italian Navy

Jean Bart at New York, July 1955. *(NARA)*

for projectile tests in the late 1960s. It remains on display at the naval arsenal there.[45]

Jean Bart spent the early part of the 1950s completing the fitting of the modern anti-aircraft mountings, then on continuing trials of the anti-aircraft armament. The 100mm mountings were starting to come on stream from July 1952, but director-controlled firing trials were not completed until October 1954. The 57mm mountings took even longer, with firing trials lasting through 1955 and 1956. *Jean Bart* was exercising from Brest, with a brief visit to Le Havre in June 1953, where 10,000 visitors came aboard. Further firing trials took place in October and November 1954, and she was docked in April 1955.

On 1 May 1955 she was finally declared ready for active service, and her first job was to take President of the Republic René Coty for a state visit to Denmark and Oslo. In July she crossed the Atlantic to Newport, Rhode Island, New York and Hampton Roads to take part in the 175th anniversary celebrations of the landing of the Comte de Rochambeau in America to support the War of Independence. Further exercises around Brest followed in the summer. Then on 1 October 1955 she left Brest for the last time. Via Oran and Arzew in Algeria (by then gripped by the revolt against French colonial rule, although *Jean Bart* played no part in that conflict), she reached Toulon on 17 October. She became the flagship of the Groupe des Écoles Sud taking, over that role from *Richelieu* on 21 October. The period 1955–56 was spent at Toulon or taking part in exercises locally, plus one French Mediterranean Fleet exercise, Ajax II, and the annual cruise to Algeria in June 1956.

Although she had finally been completed, *Jean Bart* was already operating in a state of semi-preservation over this period, with much of the 15in and 6in armament in care and maintenance, without operational crews. In view of the deteriorating situation in Egypt, L'État Major Général de Marine decided on 8 July 1956 to remove *Jean Bart* from the Groupe des Écoles Sud and bring her back to active duty as a command and fire support vessel. This was easier said than done. The crew was increased from 757 to 1,280 personnel, but this was still only sufficient to man one of the 15in turrets and one of the 6in turrets, plus around 50 per cent of the 100mm and 57mm mountings. Less than half her armament could be made operational at Toulon with the available crew and time. She was worked up during August to October, including gunnery practice on 7 September.

Jean Bart sailed from Toulon on 24 October 1956 for Operation Musketeer, the Anglo–French seizure of the Suez Canal from General Nasser, who had recently nationalised it. She went via Algiers, where soldiers from Commando Hubert and the 1st Parachute Regiment of the French Foreign Legion were embarked from 29 to 31 October. *Jean Bart* convoyed them at a speed of 25 knots to Limassol in Cyprus, where on 4 November they were transferred to amphibious shipping for the assault on the canal. *Jean Bart* then joined the intervention force, which for France also consisted of the carriers *Arromanches* and *La Fayette*, a cruiser, four fleet destroyers and an anti-submarine group. Although she was designed to command such operations, she did not do so on this occasion. Vice Admiral Pierre Barjot (he of the 1945 debates about *Jean Bart's* possible conversion to an aircraft carrier) commanded the French contingent from the cruiser *Georges Leygues*.

The Royal Navy also had the 6in cruisers *Jamaica* and *Ceylon* ready to provide fire support for the amphibious assault. But on 3 November UK Defence Minister Anthony Head and Chief of the Imperial General Staff Sir Gerald Templar arrived in Cyprus for a conference with UK Commander on the spot General Keightley and his French counterpart, Barjot. They placed severe last-minute restrictions on the military planning, including that the operation was to be confined to the Canal Zone, and that civilian casualties were to be minimised by confining the naval gunfire support to 4.5in guns and below. On 6 November the two governments went further and tried to forbid a bombardment of any kind to cover the assault. The commanders on the spot countermanded this instruction, fearing it could increase casualties in the assault force, and a small-calibre gunfire support mission did take place. *Jamaica* and *Ceylon* did not fire any 6in shells on 6 November, but *Jean Bart* was also deployed off Port Said covering the landings and did fire just four rounds of 15in. Whether she broke the embargo briefly because of confusion, or in response to a particular targeting request, is unclear. Nor is it clear if she fired her 100mm battery. No sources confirm this. In view of the new constraints and the military success gained so rapidly by the landing forces, there was no need to keep *Jean Bart* at Port Said, and she left the next day, sailing back to Toulon. However, her captain, Digard, became a casualty of the invasion when he was injured by stepping on a mine while briefly ashore.[46]

After some time in dock to repair the boilers, she resumed her former Groupe des Écoles Sud training duties on 1 December 1956. But time was already running out for the ship. There were occasional sorties in 1957, but the last one was between 11 and 19 July, in the course of which all of her armament was test-fired, the last occasion that a French battleship fired her guns. Back in Toulon, she went to Special Reserve Category A on 1 August 1957. She was used as an accommodation ship, with her reserve status downgraded to B on 1 January 1961. She lingered in that role a surprisingly long time. Despite the tortuous journey towards a modern anti-aircraft battery, which had only reached fruition in 1956, the French Navy was already considering a further modernisation of her anti-aircraft battery using new single 100mm turrets in 1957–58, to replace all the 100mm twin and 57mm turrets. Just a year later thinking had moved on to various projects for conversion to a guided missile battleship, some suppressing the 15in battery altogether, some only elements of the secondary batteries and one using US Terrier missiles.[47] In common with the contemporary plans to convert US battleships, none of this tinkering got close to serious implementation. Finally, in 1964 France was looking for a command ship for her South Pacific nuclear testing programme at Mururoa Atoll in French Polynesia and *Jean Bart* was considered, but ruled too expensive to convert and sail to the Pacific. The large cruiser *De Grasse* had sufficient capacity for the necessary technical staff and communications and was sent instead.

Jean Bart was not stricken until 10 February 1970, when she became hulk Q466. There was a proposal to turn her into a museum, but the funds to preserve her could not be raised.[48] She was instead sold in Paris on 21 May to Société des Chantiers Navals Varios les Abeilles, and was towed away by them on 24 June 1970 for demolition at Brégaillon.[49]

Turkey

The demise of the French ships left just one European dreadnought – Turkey's *Yavuz*. This extraordinary relic of a bygone age had fought her last battles for the Ottoman Empire against Imperial Russia during the First World War, but she remained active in the Turkish Navy into the NATO era, by some distance the last coal-burning battleship. She took part in annual fleet manoeuvres in the Aegean Sea until 1950 and was decommissioned into reserve on 20 December 1952. She was allocated the hull number B-70 when Turkey joined NATO on 18 February 1952. Although stricken from the active fleet on 14 November 1954, she remained at Gölcük on the Sea of Marmara as Headquarters of Battlefleet Command and Headquarters of Mine Fleet Command until 1960. An offer to sell her back to (West) Germany in 1963 for preservation as a museum ship was declined. Some sources say that the Germans made an offer to purchase in 1962 but that this was refused.

Awareness of her historic significance was raised by Aubrey Houston Bowden, who visited the ship in the mid-1960s and mounted a campaign to try to save her. He reckoned she was in excellent condition save some cosmetic problems with planking and paintwork, and her historic interest was enhanced by her almost mint condition, with virtually no modifications since she had been built.

He and others set out the case in *Warship International* magazine in autumn 1969. The Turkish Government was looking to sell her for scrap, but had put an unrealistic reserve price of $5million on her. The Turkish public and military were keen, but preservation in Turkey was unlikely because of the nation's financial position. Germany probably had the

Yavuz at Gölcük, Turkey, in August 1966. *(Author's collection)*

money, but the political mood was against military memorials. The UK was focussed on saving *Warrior* and the US was not interested in foreign vessels. A number of imaginative collaborative schemes were proposed, but no traction could be found for them.[50] *Yavuz* remained at Gölcük for a further four years, but was eventually sold to the Mechanical and Chemical Industry Corporation for scrapping. A farewell ceremony and parade was held on the quayside at Gölcük on 7 June 1973 when she finally sailed for the breakers. Demolition lasted until 1976, but her foremast was preserved at the Turkish naval academy and her propellers are at Gölcük and at the Turkish Maritime Museum at Istanbul.[51]

CHAPTER THIRTEEN

Vietnam, 1967–69

ALTHOUGH NOT IN commission for a decade, *New Jersey* was selected to be reactivated in 1967 because the US Navy and the US Marine Corps felt the need for heavy fire support in the escalating Vietnam War. The United States had become steadily more embroiled in that conflict after the French defeat in 1954, following which Vietnam had, like Korea, split into a notionally democratic South and a communist North backed

by the communist superpowers. A policy of embedding United States advisers to support the South Vietnamese Government, Army and Navy gradually evolved into greater and greater combat support. By the mid-1960s this had become 500,000 boots on the ground, which included 38,000 US Navy personnel by September 1968. The stakes were increasingly high. The USA, guided by Defense Secretary Robert McNamara, saw the threat of progressive communist takeover in South East Asia as vital ground in the Cold War struggle. Ho Chi Minh saw the unification of Vietnam under a socialist one-party state as non-negotiable, and received plenty of help from China and Russia to back his ambitions and support the growing insurgency of the indigenous South Vietnamese communists, the Viet Cong. By 1967 the Viet Cong were infiltrating the South along its whole length by land, and to a much lesser extent by sea thanks to the US Navy presence off shore and on the river estuaries. Supported by the involvement of the North Vietnamese Army, the Viet Cong were able to launch all-arms conventional assaults in the demilitarised zone around the 17th parallel (see map) and to besiege the US–South Vietnamese strongholds at Hue and Da Nang, capturing the former for a period in the massive Tet offensive in February and March 1968.

Fire support for the Vietnamese, US and other allied combat forces, and interdiction of supply routes, had become as integral to the US plan of campaign in Vietnam as they were during the Korean War. Vietnam was even better suited to naval intervention than Korea, with the country barely 60 miles wide for much of its length, and with population and infrastructure particularly heavily concentrated within gunfire range of the coast around the Demilitarized Zone just north of Hue. As in Korea, there was an advantage to delivering some of this fire support using aircraft, and some using naval gunfire. Aircraft could reach well inland, including eventually into neighbouring Cambodia and Laos, to try to cut off communist troops and supplies travelling to South Vietnam through those countries. By 1968 there were usually three aircraft carriers stationed in the Gulf of Tonkin, delivering between 5,000 and 6,000 strike missions per month. However, the price was much higher than it had been in Korea as North Vietnam had more extensive and more sophisticated air defences provided to her by China and Russia. A total of 130 US aircraft were lost in combat between the end of 1968 and 1971 alone, and there were also very severe accidents aboard *Oriskany* and *Forrestal* in 1968 that put both carriers out of action. For targets near the coast, and for rapid concentrations of fire in tactical emergencies, the naval fire support gun line was as important as air strikes. A force of cruisers and destroyers plus specialised rocket firing ships delivered 250,000 rounds of ordnance in 1966, 500,000 in 1967 and 900,000 in 1968. Twenty-two ships were deployed to help defeat the Tet offensive and recapture Hue, including two guided missile cruisers with only limited gun armament.

Remembering Korea, and with the requirement for support on the increase, the US Navy brought more of their 8in heavy cruisers out of reserve, but also began to think in terms of a battleship. Initial calls for reactivation of the *Iowa* came as early as November 1964 from the Marine Corps. The Bureau of Naval Weapons conducted a survey of fire support tasks for Vietnam and concluded that 80 per cent of the targets against which the Navy's aviators were then being tasked were within 16in gun range. The predictable clash between air-minded and not so air-minded hierarchies took place once again. Battleship reactivation seems to have been opposed in particular by the Chief of Naval Operations, Admiral David L MacDonald, and by Vice Admiral Roy L Johnson commanding the Pacific Fleet from 1965 to 1967, who argued (without the facts supporting them) that 8in guns had the same range as 16in, and that there were no reserve stocks of 16in projectiles.[1]

However, the sheer cost-effectiveness of a battleship solution gradually gained ground in the Pentagon. Analysis of the three years of air attacks from the carriers between 1965 and 1967 on the notorious Thanh Hoa bridge, near the 20th parallel and defended by five North Vietnamese Army air defence regiments, showed that 700 sorties dropping 1,500 tons of inaccurate ordnance had achieved only intermittent success in damaging it, but at the cost of fifty aircraft shot down and pilots lost or captured. Planes cost around $2million and pilot training $1million per head, so the bridge had absorbed well over $150 million of resources, let alone weighing the human and political costs. And yet the bridge still stood. *New Jersey* could destroy the bridge in an hour with maybe 100 shells, and repeat the mission as required at minimal risk, and with a total refurbishment cost to bring her back into commission initially estimated at just $25 million.[2] Senator Richard Russell led Congressional calls to bring back the battleship with support from General Wallace M Greene, the Commandant of the US Marine Corps, whose units would be the direct beneficiaries of her fire support on the ground. There were also vocal opponents. Congressman William E Minshall bizarrely warned that *New Jersey* should not be risked because of the potential that the North Vietnamese might pull off a propaganda coup by capturing her.[3]

On 31 May 1967 Secretary for Defense McNamara authorised work to look at the reactivation of a battleship. The studies were favourable and on 1 August 1967, the day after Admiral MacDonald's retirement, McNamara decided to recommission one ship for employment in the Pacific Fleet to augment the naval Gunfire Support Force in South East Asia. *New Jersey* got the nod for reactivation ahead of her sister ships because *Iowa*'s electronics installation was more primitive and considered outdated; *Missouri* still (allegedly) had a speed restriction imposed after her 1950 grounding in Chesapeake Bay (although that did not prevent her doing two tours of duty in Korea and remaining in commission thereafter, so it seems a flimsy rationale based on rumour if used in 1967); and *Wisconsin* had been damaged by a fire in her last inactivation overhaul and would have required more expensive repairs than *New Jersey*.[4] Sumrall says it was because *New* Jersey had been re-gunned in the late 1950s and had the best life remaining in her 16in gun battery.

Work on *New Jersey* began at Puget Sound Navy Yard in late 1967. It was to be an austere modernisation, with the total cost eventually

New Jersey working up for her Vietnam deployment, 1968. *(NARA)*

authorised at $21.5 million. Congress had also suggested even more austere options: a 16in battery only with no 5in guns reactivated; no main machinery with the ship to be an artillery hulk towed along the Vietnamese coast; or a refurbishment of only half the main machinery for basic mobility at low speeds. In the end the Philadelphia Naval Shipyard submitted that a full refurbishment of guns and machinery could be done for $24 million and give seven years of operational life, and that argument won the day. The remaining 20mm and 40mm anti-aircraft guns were all removed, although four of their tubs were retained, painted white and used as swimming pools during the deployment. A fog foam firefighting system was installed in the engine room and air conditioning in the living spaces. She received modern communications, SPS 10 and SPS 12 search radars, an electronic countermeasures suite including Zuni 5in rockets firing chaff, and modern HF, VHF and UHF communications and the Naval Tactical Data System. The electronic countermeasures were given priority following an incident off Israel in June 1967 when the destroyer *Eliat* became the victim of an Egyptian-operated, Russian-built Styx, the first vessel lost to a ship-launched anti-ship weapon, highlighting this new threat to surface warships. During her work-up trials off San Clemente, California, on 17 July 1968 *New Jersey* practised using the countermeasures and managed to break the radar lock of an F-4 Phantom aircraft simulating a cruise missile attack.[5]

Refurbishment of the main machinery was largely trouble free, but valves and seals often had to be replaced and all four propellers were found to be cracked and needed replacing. *Iowa* and *Wisconsin* were raided for some of these parts to avoid delay while new stocks were manufactured to be back fitted to them. Elements of the rangefinders were sourced from Picatinny Arsenal in New Jersey State, Hawthorne, Nevada, and from a pile of parts originally intended for *Kentucky* and *Illinois* still held at Washington DC Navy Yard.[6] The helicopter pad was upgraded, and Hueys as well as drones (modified DASH – Drone Anti-Submarine Helicopter, known as 'Snoopy') with line-of-sight TV camera links to the range keeper aboard the battleship were carried on the deployment, to be used for spotting the fall of shot. There was also a new target designation system with a Mark 48 Shore Bombardment Computer and two new Mk 34 fire control directors.

The Mark 48 was an important step forward in accuracy, because for the first time it combined radar and rangefinder data to track known navigational reference points and fix precisely the ship's own position before the target data was plotted and the computer produced a firing solution.[7] The main and secondary gun batteries were unchanged, but the 16in shells were now fired with a 'Swedish Additive' of titanium dioxide and wax inserted among the powder bags. This substantially reduced wear

New Jersey practises aerial resupply from a UH-46A helicopter, 24 July 1968. *(NARA)*

on the gun barrel rifling, and vastly extended the effective life of the 16in guns. In Korea they had been rated for about 350 effective full charges (called ESR in the USA), but the additive reduced wear to about one quarter of the previous rate. The guns were ultimately rated for 1,500 rounds, with the principal determinant of failure becoming the mechanical stress on the gun rather than wear on the barrel rifling.[8] This dramatic improvement was reflected in *New Jersey*'s performance in Vietnam, where she was able to fire twice as many rounds in a six-month deployment as she had in Korea, without rifle wear becoming a consideration in her effectiveness.

After engineering trials between 26 and 28 March 1968, *New Jersey*

recommissioned on 6 April under command of Captain J Edward Snyder. The ceremony at Philadelphia Naval Yard was attended by Paul R Ignatius, Secretary of the Navy, and Admiral T H Moorer, Chief of Naval Operations. She commenced loading ammunition on 10 April and commenced sea trials on 15 April, as the deck log puts it 'headed fair down Delaware River'. The President of the Board of Inspection and Survey was aboard to witness her work up to 20 knots. The full-power trials the following day saw her reach 31.9 knots, although she had to slow down at 2156 due to an overheated spring bearing on No. 1 shaft. On 17 April she fired eighteen 16in practice rounds at full charge. Back in Philadelphia there was a brief hiatus in preparations on 7 May as the ship was evacuated between 1235 and 1435 while she was searched for a reported bomb on board. Nothing was found by the search. The Brazilian Ambassador Vasco Leitao da Cunha and his Naval Attaché were unlikely visitors on 10 May. Shakedown cruises based at Norfolk, Virginia, followed from 17 May featuring operations with helicopters and surface gunfire calibration for both 16in and 5in batteries, witnessed by media representatives who arrived by helicopter. She was under way for Panama on 29 May and transited the Canal on 4 June. During the voyage to Long Beach she fired 5in 'windows' shells, another countermeasure to anti-ship guided weapons. From 17 June, operating out of Long Beach, she undertook shore bombardment training at San Clemente island, but also refuelling at sea, more helicopter operations and anti-aircraft drills.

Six weeks of intensive work-up activity completed at San Diego on 2 August, where she stayed until the end of the month while the crew got some leave. Final deployment preparations included taking on fuel, 515 rounds of 16in and 4,250 rounds of 5in ammunition.[9]

According to the *Guinness Book of Records*, during her work-up *New Jersey* broke the world speed record for a battleship: 35.2 knots, maintained for a six-hour period with 207 revolutions per minute. This is unlikely to have been at full load displacement, and compared to the 33 knots for which her 212,000 shp had been designed. Ironically, considering their reputation as the fastest battleships ever built, none of the *Iowas* ever ran a formal measured mile, so no claims can be directly comparable to *Vanguard*'s figures or *Jean Bart*'s (see above). Intriguingly, there is also no mention of this achievement or such a full-power trial in the deck log for this period. Sources say that the achievement occurred off the Virginia Capes on 27 March 1968,[10] during engineering trials and before the ship was commissioned, and before Captain Snyder formally took command and the deck log was commenced. The sources are authoritative,[11] but such an ambitious trial on only her second day at sea seems odd, and is also difficult to square with the details in the deck log for 15 and 16 April, which describe a rather cautious stepped build-up in speed before going to full power on the evening of 16 April. But the class was undoubtedly quick. Captain Smedburg recalled getting *Iowa* to 33 knots in operations off Korea, and regularly transited between missions on that deployment at 28 to 30 knots. *Iowa* could still mange 32 knots when recommissioned in 1985.[12]

On 5 September 1968 *New Jersey* was ready to leave Long Beach, California, and a US battleship deployed for the first time in over eleven years. She crossed the Pacific via Pearl Harbor and Subic Bay in the Philippines. Her crew was much reduced from her Second World War complement thanks to modernisation and removal of the anti-aircraft armament, but also to strict limitations placed on the complement by the

US Navy itself, which was struggling to man the expanding fleet. The approved total was 1,556 (Sumrall says 1,626), compared to around 2,750 authorised in the Second World War and 2,500 in Korea. As one example of the constraints, for the first time in US history a major warship was deployed on operations without a Marines detachment. The mystique of a battleship for her crew was undimmed. *New Jersey* achieved an 80.7 per cent re-enlistment rate after her first deployment, during the most unpopular war in US history.[13] Public and international interest in the deployment was intense. The Russians had as much of a stake as anyone, and two Tu-95 'Bear' long-range reconnaissance aircraft greeted her in the western Pacific, making three low-level passes near the ship.[14]

New Jersey's tour of duty coincided with the peak effort of Naval

New Jersey replenishes at sea off Vietnam, taking on 16in powder, 4 October 1968. *(NARA)*

Gunfire Support in Vietnam, but also, paradoxically, with the first signs of indecision within President Lyndon Johnson's Administration about the conduct of the war, and the beginning of de-escalation. Days before the battleship recommissioned the President had ordered the cessation of offensive operations north of the 19th parallel, which took the Thanh Hoa bridge and many other strategic targets, which *New Jersey* would have been particularly well suited to destroy, off the target list. She nevertheless showed her versatility and flexibility. She started operations near the Demilitarised Zone (DMZ) at 0734 on 30 September with twenty-nine 16in rounds fired at People's Army of Vietnam targets from turret two. There were three more 16in firings that day and two 5in. A number of operations in this area followed before on 7 October at the mouth of the Song Giang river she sank eleven waterborne logistics craft bringing supplies for the Viet Cong. Over 300 16in rounds had been fired by the time of her first replenishment at sea, ninety-six rounds from the stores ship *Mount Katami* on 6 October.

She then sallied into the Gulf of Tonkin between 12 and 14 October to bombard the well-fortified Vinh caves, before engaging artillery positions on Hun Mon island. On 12 October the log recorded her furthest foray north to 18 degrees, 44 minutes. This turned out to be her only visit to the North, as on 1 November 1968 the Johnson Administration further de-escalated and ordered a complete ban on attacking targets in North Vietnam. On 16 October *New Jersey* was back near the DMZ firing in support of 3rd US Marine Division, then 173rd Airborne Brigade. Her fire was returned on 23 October near Cap Lay north of Da Nang, but there were no hits on the ship. She remained near Da Nang supporting 1st US Marine Division. On 29 October she engaged a target 4 miles south of Cap Lay and demolished the mountain top on which the enemy artillery had been positioned.

On 4 November she moved a long way south to support the II Corps area around Phan Thiet. The most concentrated bombardment of the deployment took place at Quang Ngai south of Da Nang between 25 and 27 November, during the course of which she destroyed 182 structures and fifty-four bunkers. On 28 November she was near Hue supporting 101st US Airborne Division and between 2 and 8 December back at Da Nang with the 3rd US Marine Division again.

Rest and replenishment at Singapore were followed by support of the 47th Republic of Vietnam Regiment at Tuy Hoa on 26 December, then over one month's operations around the DMZ and Da Nang supporting the 1st US Marine Division, up until 10 February. This included an operation in thick coastal fog on 8 January 1969, where the Mark 48 computer showed its value, as she was able to destroy a bunker complex despite being shrouded from the shore herself, and with the target quite

New Jersey firing towards the end of her Vietnam deployment, 14 March 1969. *(NARA)*

invisible to the ship. She then moved a little south to fire with the Korean Marine Brigade, and 3rd US Marines once again. On 22 February it was back to the DMZ for three weeks of varied bombardments, then well to the south to support 9th Korean Infantry Division at Cam Ranh Bay on 20 March.

A week of firing around Phan Thiet and Tuy Hoa followed, before she finished the deployment where she had begun, with the 3rd US Marines at Con Thien, firing an observed mission in the evening of 31 March at bunkers 3 miles north-east of the town. Observers reported seven bunkers destroyed. She fired further during the night, a total of forty-nine 16in and 815 5in, and left the gun line at 0600 on 1 April 1969.[15]

Over her six months in South East Asia *New Jersey* fired 5,866 16in rounds at the enemy, and 14,891 5in. Much of the 5in firing took place at night. The total fired during the whole deployment, including shakedown, was 6,200 16in, which compared with 771 fired during the Second World War, and 6,671 during her entire career from 1945 to 1957, including the two tours in Korea. She spent 120 days actually on the gun line, with the longest continuous period at sea being forty-seven days. The US Navy's official analysis 'Operational History of Fast Battleships; World War II, Korea and Vietnam' provided the following assessment of her effectiveness:

	16in gunfire	5in gunfire
Structures destroyed	439	56
Structures damaged	259	92
Bunkers destroyed	596	59
Bunkers damaged	250	73
Artillery sites neutralised	19	2
Machine Gun/mortar sites	35	6
Secondary explosions	130	46
Roads interdicted	26	-
Metres of trench destroyed	1,925	-
Cave and tunnel complexes	75	-
Enemy killed	153	17
Troop movements halted	12	-
Craft sunk	-	9

This makes a total of more than 2,000 targets engaged over 120 days, averaging seventeen targets per day. The preponderance of damage caused by the 16in guns is striking. Her positive impact on the troops she was supporting was immense and widely praised by both senior commanders and those in the front line. An eyewitness from 3rd US Marine Division who had been unable to advance against a large bunker complex told how: 'We heard what first sounded like a subway train moving through a tunnel – a big rushing noise then – bang!' When his unit went back to the target area they found it obliterated. 'It was like something had come along with a big eraser and wiped everything clean. And they were big heavily fortified bunkers, targets our own artillery couldn't reach.'[16] *New Jersey* was also credited with hits creating 200-yard diameter clearings in forest, big enough to be used by large troop-carrying helicopters, and defoliating areas half a mile across.

It was not all plain sailing. *New Jersey* registered occasional 'wild shots' up to 1,100 yards over or short of her targets. From December 1968 a Mark 25 radar was installed to measure the muzzle velocity of each shot to help correct for this anomaly. It was noted that this problem was less prevalent when firing using reduced charges, so wherever possible this approach was adopted for all but the longer-range targets. Nevertheless, there was a steady deterioration in muzzle velocity consistency, and hence accuracy, measured from the Second World War onwards. In 1943–45 cordite powder manufactured to a specification of plus/minus 10ft per second (fps) of muzzle velocity actually achieved plus/minus 5 fps in action. In Korea this worsened to plus/minus 14 fps, and in Vietnam to plus/minus 20 fps. By the time she was firing on Lebanon in 1983–84 it was plus/minus 32ft per second. The problem was traced to inconsistency and deterioration in certain lots of powder manufactured in 1945, and was eventually cured only by remixing and rebagging all the powder to achieve consistent ballistic performance. The original plus/minus 10 fps specification was again being achieved once this programme was complete.

New Jersey briefly stopped over in Japan on her way home, and set off back across the Pacific from Yokosuka on 9 April 1969. However, she was to have one last excitement when her journey was interrupted at 0803 on 15 April. Out of the blue, the North Koreans shot down an unarmed American EC-121 Constellation electronic surveillance plane well out in international waters over the Sea of Japan. Thirty-two US Service personnel were killed, the largest loss of life in any Cold War incident. In response *New Jersey* was ordered back to Japan, sailing at 25 knots and arriving at Sasebo on 22 April. She immediately set sail as part of the hastily assembled response to the crisis, designated Task Force 71, to patrol in the Sea of Japan. Altogether the US collected four aircraft carriers, one battleship, three cruisers and twenty-one destroyers for this show of force. The Nixon administration, new in power and still finding its feet, considered what military options were available. The National Security Council and Joint Chiefs of Staff included shore bombardment of North Korean targets among their suggestions, and the presence of *New Jersey*, the Fire Support heavy cruiser *St Paul* and eleven all-gun destroyers among the ships of Task Force 71 shows this was taken as a serious possibility. It offered the option of striking coastal targets with less risk of further US losses than if air strikes had been used as an alternative. It was certainly taken seriously enough for *New Jersey* to embark 837 tons of ammunition from USS *Paricutin* at sea on 24 April, including 474 16in projectiles and 5,153 5in. She spent the next two days steaming independently off the east coast of Japan awaiting developments. In the end, however, Nixon and National Security Adviser Henry Kissinger sensibly elected to de-escalate matters, and no action was taken beyond ostentatiously resuming the regular EC-121 flights, now with a fighter escort. *New Jersey* once again headed for home at 0015 on 27 April and reached Long Beach on 5 May 1969 after a deployment of eight months and three days.

The crew, basking in the afterglow of a US Navy Unit commendation for 'Exceptionally Meritorious Service', immediately began preparations for a second deployment to Vietnam. They completed the gunfire qualification exercises and other work-up preparations at San Clemente in June, and sailed to San Francisco then Tacoma, Washington, before returning to Long Beach by 1 August. However, matters were to turn out otherwise. Taken in the round, the events of 1968–69 persuaded the new Nixon Government that the war was not going well. Combined with growing domestic pressure to end it, and concern about escalating costs, a decision was made to withdraw gradually from South East Asia. The pace of Vietnamisation of the anti-communist struggle was accelerated, and diplomatic talks with North Vietnam began in Paris. The US wanted to negotiate from a position of strength, so 1969 to 1971 saw a major effort to push the enemy's main forces out of border areas, enhance the Republic of Vietnam's presence in Viet Cong strongholds within the South, and consolidate control of major population centres. *New Jersey* had played her role in the beginning of that process, but as 1969 progressed it was assessed that the anti-infiltration campaign was succeeding, and there was less combat activity in coastal areas, with most action shifting inland to the Cambodian border in 1970 and Laos in 1971. The fourteen Naval Gunfire Support ships of 1969 had dwindled to only three by 1971, and the number of rounds fired declined from the 1968 peak of 900,000 to 454,000 in 1969, 234,000 in 1970 and just 114,000 in 1971. In parallel the US Navy was required to make significant economies, and would fall in size from 692,000 personnel in June 1970 to just 602,000 two years later.

Expense was certainly the reason given by Nixon's Secretary for Defense Melvin Laird for the withdrawal of *New Jersey* from her planned second deployment, although lack of spare 16in gun barrel liners was also cited.[17] This latter excuse rings completely hollow as at least twenty-seven were ready to be transferred from the other reserve ships of the *Iowa* class, and a number of spares would also have been held ashore, as was confirmed during the 1980s reactivations. Nevertheless, on 22 August 1969 Laird announced a list of 100 ships that were to be deactivated as this rundown got into its stride. *New Jersey*, to the shock of her crew and disgust of her captain, was among them. The Under Secretary of the Navy, John Warner, also protested about the decision, but was overruled. It was also claimed, during a Senate debate on *New Jersey*'s next reactivation in 1981, that her withdrawal from a second Vietnam deployment just a fortnight before it was due to begin was directly linked to the effort to get the Paris peace talks started, and the fact that her presence on the gun line had been so effective that it was seen as intimidating and destabilising to the peace process. That same John Warner, now the Senator for Virginia,

and thus probably in the best position to know, said in 1981: 'it [cancellation of the further 1969 deployment] was ordered from the White House as it was impeding peace negotiations.'[18] Snyder was relieved of command on 27 August, and the ship was de-ammunitioned. Instead of Vietnam, *New Jersey* headed back to Puget Sound on 6 September, arriving on 9 September, and was decommissioned once again into the Pacific Reserve Fleet on 17 December 1969.

As things turned out she may still have had a handy role to play as the war played out its last agonies. The increasingly powerful communist forces launched a major Easter offensive in 1972. The 7th Fleet was back on the gun line in a big way, with fifteen to twenty ships delivering gunfire support each day to 1st Corps around Hue, and 117,000 rounds fired in June alone, more than during the whole of 1971. *New Jersey*'s erstwhile Captain Snyder, now an admiral, was summoned to the White House to discuss with staffers whether she could be reactivated and sailed for the gun line within thirty days. Snyder said such a timescale was impracticable.[19] The 8in gun cruiser *Newport News* was given the mission instead and was rushed back to Vietnam as an emergency stopgap. This naval gunfire support was judged to be a prime factor in the successful South Vietnamese defence of Hue. The US Navy went on to play a huge part in the next phase of the Nixon strategy, to blockade North Vietnam by sea and air in Operation Linebacker with the hope that this would exert positive pressure on the peace negotiations. On 16 April the heavy Cruiser *Oklahoma City* and three destroyers were bombarding Do Son peninsula guarding the entrance to North Vietnam's major port, Haiphong, and three heavy cruisers took part in a blockade of the North between May and September. But *New Jersey* was by then well and truly deactivated, and could not bring her firepower to bear.

CHAPTER FOURTEEN

Revival – The 600-Ship Navy

N*EW JERSEY* HAD gone out of commission and back into the Pacific
Reserve Fleet at the Puget Sound Navy Yard on 17 December 1969,
alongside *Missouri*. *Iowa* and *Wisconsin* were in the Atlantic Fleet Reserve
at Philadelphia Navy Yard, where I saw them together during a visit in
April 1980. After Vietnam, the *Iowa* were around twenty-five years old
and only one had had any significant modernisation since their
completion. They had outlasted their fellow US Navy battleships in service
by a decade, and were among only seven battleships now remaining in
fleets worldwide (excluding the four museum ships, see below). Although
many of their contemporary fighting ships – aircraft carriers, cruisers,
destroyers and other types from the 1945 fleet – remained commissioned
in the US Navy active fleets, there was informed speculation at that time
that the *Iowas*' days were numbered. One commentator wrote: 'There is
little likelihood that any of these "super dreadnoughts" will again see
active service ... It is expected that these ships will be stricken from the
Navy list and scrapped in the near future.'[1]

So the four ships settled into reserve, but there was little evidence
that the Navy was on the brink of scrapping them. Almost all the other
major surface combatants of their vintage did gradually disappear through
the 1970s and early '80s. All the US heavy cruisers, including those that
were with *New Jersey* in Vietnam, were also back in reserve by 1975 and
stricken by 1978, with the exception of *Des Moines* and *Salem*, which
continued in reserve until 1991. Only the five guided missile cruiser
conversions – *Boston*, *Canberra*, *Chicago*, *Columbus* and *Albany* –
remained in the active fleet until 1980. But deep in the Pentagon a faint
candle still burned for the *Iowas*. They were still recognised as
extraordinary ships, capable of considerable speed and massive endurance,
and immensely versatile.

A further decade passed, and still they persisted, despite attempts to
cull them. In 1972 it was proposed to scrap all but *New Jersey*, but the
US Marine Corps (USMC) fought a successful rearguard action, arguing
that the fire support requirement needed two ships for each Marines
deployment, to allow rotations, and as the Corps was tasked with two
simultaneous intervention missions, all four *Iowas* were still needed. The
sympathetic John Warner, now promoted to Secretary of the Navy, was
probably decisive in keeping them in being on that occasion. Potential
conversions to carry the Aegis anti-aircraft warfare system in 1973, or a

wider modernisation with Aegis, Sea Sparrow for self-defence and Harpoon missiles for anti-surface ship use were studied in 1975 but left unfulfilled.[2] Meanwhile, a further bid by Naval Sea Systems Command for their disposal in 1974 was also fought off by USMC, this time with support from Korean War battleship veteran and now Chief of Naval Operations, Admiral Elmo Zumwalt, who said he had always been an advocate for retaining the ships because their reactivation was one of the few options for quick restoration of guns to the fleet, or provision of platforms for new strike weapons.

The wheel of political and technological fortune now began to turn back in the battleships' favour. The Cold War intensified, and the Soviet Navy was now being developed at great pace by Admiral Gorshkov. While the demise of Stalin meant there was no remaining appetite to build new traditional battleships with a heavy gun armament and armour, the Soviet Union, having passed through Khrushchev's ballistic missile phase, resumed Stalin's ambition to build an ocean-going navy, and to build big. Much effort went on the submarine force, including as the maritime delivery platforms for ballistic missiles. But the complexity of supporting distant proxy states and power projection, as well as homeland defence and protecting the strategic submarine force, also drove the Politburo to build up the surface navy. The *Sverdlovs* were succeeded as the main surface presence of the fleet by the *Kynda*, *Kresta I* and *Kresta II* classes of guided missile destroyers. Displacement increased from 6,000 tons to 7,500 between the early and late 1960s. Unlike their NATO contemporaries, they were armed with SSN-3 'Shaddock' long-range (450 nautical miles) surface-to-surface missiles. In 1968 the *Moskva* class of hybrid missile/helicopter carriers at 18,000 tons broke new ground, giving the Soviet Navy for the first time a true modern capital ship. The *Moskvas* were mainly anti-submarine platforms. So were the *Kara*-class cruisers of the 1970s (9,700 tons), but the follow-on *Slava* class at 12,500 tons carried as their main armament sixteen SSN-12 'Sandbox' anti-ship missiles. The process reached its apogee with the nuclear-powered *Kirov*-class 'Battlecruiser' of 1980, which raised displacement to 28,000 tons full load and deployed twenty long-range SSN-19 'Shipwreck' anti-ship missiles in vertical launchers. At last after thirty-five years, the four *Kirov*-class ships manifested the idea of the future heavy ship with guided weapons that the British Admiralty had first mooted in early 1945.

The *Kirov*s, and their close successors the aircraft carrier/cruisers of the *Kiev* class, also focussed NATO, and especially United States, attention on what needed to be done to respond to the build-up of the Soviet surface navy, now clearly aspiring to be more than a coastal defence and anti-submarine force. The corresponding recent trajectory of US naval power was perceived by many in official Washington circles, and those commentating on the sidelines, as downwards, with the number of ships in commission dropping to 520[3] and the number of carrier groups dropping back to twelve by 1980. President Jimmy Carter, in office from January 1977, seemed determined to continue down this route, with a five-year plan refocussing the Navy mission from power projection to control of sea lines of communication, and further reducing to a planned 392 ships by 1985.

A lobby in the Pentagon and Congress was pressing for a change of direction, and Republican Presidential nominee Ronald Reagan was campaigning, and eventually elected in November 1980, on a ticket that emphasised the need to rebuild American global power to match Soviet assertiveness in the Cold War struggle. While this involved rearmament and renewal across all aspects of US Defense, there was a particular focus on forward projection of US power via the Navy. This eventually became characterised under the sound bite of the '600 ship Navy'. It involved a major programme to build new ships, as many of the 520 in commission were reaching the end of their lives in the 1980s. It also involved Ship Life Extension Programmes for older ships, especially the carriers, and the bringing of some older ships out of mothballs to be modernised. Because increasing the number of deployable carrier groups from twelve to the projected requirement for fifteen would take a decade, and because the US Navy sought to project power through not just carrier groups, but also through smaller Surface Action Groups that could add to US reach in the shorter term, the battleships came back into the picture.

Studies in the mid-1970s by Gibbs and Cox, the same naval architects who had provided some of their modern battleship ideas to Stalin in the 1930s, showed the potential of the *Iowa*-class ships to carry the latest self-contained and bolt-on weaponry, which did not require expensive structural alterations to the ships, specifically the Harpoon anti-ship missile, Sea Sparrow short-range air defence and the Phalanx autonomous, multi-barrelled, close-in weapons systems designed to bring down anti-ship cruise missiles. A 1977 inspection of the battleships' material condition found it excellent, but nevertheless recommended their disposal. This time the new Chief of Naval Operations, Admiral Thomas B Hayward, backed the Marines' pleas for retention.

The US Navy and the Marine Corps began lobbying at the turn of 1979–80 not merely for retention of four battleships in reserve, but for their reactivation. A seminal article appeared in the November 1979 proceedings of the US Navy Institute by ex-Navy pilot and defence analyst Charles F Myers entitled 'A Sea-based Interdiction System for Power Projection'. It compared the bombardment capability of a battleship and a carrier. His analysis was that a battleship could deliver more explosive, more accurately, quickly, cheaply and for longer than a carrier. He

resurrected the 1960s analysis of the Thanh Hoa bridge in North Vietnam
(see Chapter Thirteen above). Senior ranks in the US Navy were beginning
to back the idea and a head of steam began to build in Congress, where
Myers was lobbying intensively. This was also stoked by Hayward. The

CNO, faced with indifference to his proposals from Secretary for Defence Harold Brown, had already broken ranks with the Administration in late 1979 and was briefing Congress and media on his modernisation plans.

Hence, *Aviation Weekly and Space Technology* magazine reported on 22 January 1980 that the US Marine Corps was interested in de-mothballing an *Iowa*-class battleship, installing a vertical take-off and landing ski-jump on the aft deck and modifying the aft hull to take a hangar and storage deck below. The forward 16in turrets would be retained for offshore bombardment. By 8 March 1980 *Flight International* magazine was reporting that Admiral Hayward proposed taking all four battleships and an aircraft carrier out of mothballs and equipping them with cruise missiles and vertical take-off aircraft. Some of the battleship's 16in gun turrets would be replaced by Tomahawk cruise missile launchers. In addition, each vessel would carry several AV-8Bs (the US version of the Harrier jump jet). It speculated that *New Jersey* would be the easiest to restore, *Iowa* and *Wisconsin* having been cannibalised to restore *New Jersey*, and *Missouri* not fully restored after running aground in 1950. The US Navy was quoted as saying that each ship could be refurbished for $700 million.'[4]

Congressional hearings in early 1980 showed strong support for an increase to spending in response to world events, and that battleship reactivation should be part of that package. Representative Paul Trible, a Republican from Virginia on the House Armed Services Committee, backed an alternative to President Carter's low-key shipbuilding plan, which included reactivation of all four *Iowas*, plus the carrier *Oriskany*. Strom Thurmond in the Senate supported, asking for an extra $2.2 billion in total, including $294 million specifically for *New Jersey*. Supporters giving testimony included Admiral Hayward, who ranked the battleships ahead of a third new Aegis-equipped cruiser in his priorities (although behind *Oriskany*); Commandant of the Marine Corps, General Robert H Barrow, who was enthusiastic to see the 16in guns returned to service; and Deputy Secretary of Defense and recent Navy Secretary Graham Claytor, who had been impressed by the original arguments of Charles Myers. The House of Representatives Armed Service Committee eventually added $6.2 billion to the President's authorisation request to pay for a variety of equipment, including $560 million for the reactivation of *Oriskany* and *New Jersey*.

So, as the Defense appropriations process for that fiscal year 1981 got under way, and with pro- and anti-battleship protagonists squaring up, President Jimmy Carter himself got sucked into the debate about the battleships. Despite his time aboard *Wyoming* in the 1940s, he was not impressed by reactivation arguments. His political goal was to show he could present a trimmed Defense appropriation to balance the Federal budget as part of his re-election platform. His opposition ran to the extent of ordering Navy personnel to cease lobbying Congress for the battleships, and putting the legislators on notice that he would personally become involved to help defeat any legislation that was in favour of reactivation. Having taken evidence from all the Service Chiefs of Staff, the House Armed Services Committee rebuffed the President, and by a two to one majority authorised a record sum of $51.9 billion for equipment and research and development, including $598 million for conversion and reactivation of *New Jersey* and *Oriskany*. Note that despite its prominence in the debates and their reporting, this element represented barely 1 per cent of the overall package.

The White House and Defense Secretary Harold Brown then shifted their fire to the Senate, and objected to the Chairman of the Senate Armed Services Committee, Democrat John Stennis of Mississippi, that the extra request would require thousands of new crew members and aggravate current Navy manning problems, all for 1940s technology – although they simultaneously argued against brand new B-1 bombers and in favour of refurbishing 1950s technology B-52s as cruise missile carriers![5] Stennis and his Committee were in truculent mood. The Bill with the battleship provisions still in it passed them as well. It then also passed on the floor of the Senate in a debate on 1 July 1980, despite the efforts of Democrat Senators Dale Bumpers and John Chafee to introduce an amendment to prevent funding for the battleship, which lost by forty-one votes to fifty. Carter redoubled his efforts with attacks on the viability of the costings and the inability of the Navy to man the extra ships. At his Cabinet meeting on 25 July 1980 he indicated his willingness to become personally involved in lobbying Congressmen against the reactivation. The pressure told, and during August first the House Appropriations Defence Sub-committee on a tied vote, and then the Senate, thirty-nine to thirty-six, defeated the reactivation provision.

So Carter, using the byzantine ways of the United States appropriations process, eventually managed to block the US Navy's and Congress's efforts, but it availed him nought because he failed to get re-elected in November. Ronald Reagan took over in January 1981, and his platform was certainly conducive to greater defence spending to underpin a stronger forward presence in the Cold War. So the ball was already well and truly rolling in favour of reactivation before Reagan won the White House and the Navy quickly picked up the earlier momentum and harnessed it to the new political climate. Reagan himself was won over to the specifics of the battleship idea as President elect at a meeting with John Lehman and soon to be National Security Adviser Richard V Allen in November 1980. They proposed that the four *Iowas* provided the ideal focus around which to base four proposed Surface Action Groups as a quick route towards the 600-ship target. Thereafter, Lehman, who had been appointed Republican Secretary for the Navy by Reagan, took up the cudgels and won the bruising succession of battles that still had to be fought in Congress to secure funding for all four ships. Lehman explained the context: 'Our naval strategy is to go back into the highest threat areas, the Persian Gulf, Eastern Mediterranean, North Atlantic, and defeat the best the Soviets can throw at us. The battleship can increase our firepower and bolster our capability to keep fighting. That's what high threat warfare is all about.'[6] By 1988 the US Navy's Integrated Long Term Strategy had elaborated this 'in harm's way' approach to three distinct roles for the ships, as an integral part of carrier battle groups, as the core of battleship battle groups, and in the traditional amphibious operation fire support role.

Costs and timescales for refurbishment were indeed substantial, but much less than for building up carrier numbers and their air groups. Refurbishment of *New Jersey* cost only $326 million, less than a new frigate. *Iowa* was then estimated to require $417 million because of the longer time she had been in reserve and the lack of an interim update in the 1960s. The full programme for four ships was just $1.5 billion over five years. This was only 5 per cent of the initial increases in naval spending of $33 billion proposed by the new administration for the 600-ship Navy in a supplemental request to Fiscal Year 81 and an amended 1982 Defense Bill. These requests eventually passed both Houses of Congress by two to one majorities, but opponents of the battleship continued to resist. On 7 April 1981 the Senate debate on the Defense appropriations was graced by Senator Warner, arguing in favour of the battleships, and Senator John Chaffee of Rhode Island, also a previous Secretary for the Navy, arguing against.[7]

In November 1981 the Senate debated funding for *Iowa* again, and Dale Bumpers was still ridiculing the battleships capabilities: 'If 16in guns are so great, why have we not put one on a ship for the past 35 years?' Senator Jeremiah Denton of Alabama responded. As a Republican he could be expected to support additional spending, but he was also a former pilot who had been shot down in Vietnam in 1965 attacking the Thanh Hoa bridge and had spent seven years as a prisoner of war. He said: 'In Vietnam we lost hundreds of aircraft at a great cost in lives as well as dollars, that could have been saved had a battleship been on station. A battleship could have knocked out the Thanh Hoa bridge that I was bombing at the time I was shot down. We lost five planes in one day on that one target. I point out that the Thanh Hoa bridge was only twelve miles inland, well within reach of the 16in guns on the *Iowa* class battleships. There is a reason for those ships and thank God the Navy is coming forward and asking for them again.' It was a powerful intervention. A number of the senator's colleagues told him that they had changed their minds on the basis of his speech. The Appropriation Bill passed the Senate fifty-one to twenty-nine. Funds to complete *New Jersey* and long-lead items for *Iowa* were approved in Fiscal Year 1982, the balance of *Iowa* funding in FY83, *Missouri* and *Wisconsin* between FY84 and 88.

Still the debate over whether this was the right thing to do echoed around Congress and the press. The overall 600-ship Navy plan remained controversial. Some worried that it would inevitably spark a Soviet response and increase tensions rather than benefiting the West. Others saw the 1982 Falklands War between the UK and Argentina as a warning about the vulnerability of surface ships to missiles, and preferred to invest in submarine platforms. The revival of the forty-year-old battleships created sharp differences of view within this wider debate. There were hyperbolic claims, both for and against, about the *Iowas*' capabilities and vulnerability. Extensive correspondence about survivability against Exocet-type missiles was stimulated by the juxtaposition of the battleship revival with the Royal Navy's Falklands War experience. Ballistics authority Nathan Okun's detailed technical analysis published in *Aviation Week and Space Technology* on 6 September 1982 seemed to brook no argument. Exocets could not penetrate the battleship's side armour and could not dive on its deck armour. 'It would take a lot of Exocets – even supersonic Exocets – to put the *New Jersey* completely out of action.' But the debate was as much about politics and the budget as about military capability. Democrat senator Gary Hart of the Armed Services Committee said: 'The *Sheffield* and the *Belgrano* [both sunk in the Falklands war] have sent us a message. Will we listen? Pouring defense dollars into old battleships and new super-carriers is to invite naval and national suicide.' Senator James Exon added: 'Dreadnoughts may scare the hell out of some people, but not the Soviets. They know that a smart projectile or two would send those rust buckets to the bottom.'

There were even Republican doubters. Arizona Senator Barry Goldwater said: 'I love to see these fine old ships go through the water. I don't like to see them go to the bottom, which is where the *New Jersey* would go in a great big hurry in combat today.' The naysayers who saw the whole escapade as a massive and wasteful anachronism in the late twentieth century, and the ships as so many targets for Soviet submarine-launched missiles, were joined by those who saw the Reagan defence build-up and the 600-ship Navy as ultimately unaffordable. This debate continued after the approval of funds for *New Jersey*, in particular during Administration debates about matching naval and defence aspirations to pledges that there would be a balanced federal Budget in 1984. Democrat Senator Dale Bumpers, going down fighting, commented on a Centre for

Defence Information estimate that the four ships would conservatively cost $6 billion to reactivate: 'That's too much to pay for a romantic vision of a return to nineteenth century maritime power doctrines.'

There was undoubtedly an element of romance and of nostalgia. Chief of Naval Operations Thomas Hayward was an enthusiast: 'These ships are going to be very, very impressive,' he was quoted as saying. Many ex-battleship sailors, although long in the tooth by now, were inspired to rejoin the Navy and provided an essential leavening of experience in dealing with the older systems on the ships. Overall Navy manning worries were easing as pay had been increased and the US economy began to slow, encouraging more men to stay in. The mystique of the battleships was such that when a call for active duty volunteers was made in July 1982 to select the 800 personnel who would be the first and second increments to the crew of *New Jersey*, more than 4,000 requests to serve aboard her had been received by the end of August.

The work of reactivation had ultimately been authorised and got under way. Because Lehman had given a personal commitment to the Senate Armed Services Committee that $326 million would be a top price for *New Jersey* there was a great deal of early project momentum to deliver her on time and below budget, using the embedded project teams at the Long Beach Navy Yard.

New Jersey under tow from Bremerton, Washington, to Long Beach, California, to be reactivated, 2 August 1981. *(NARA)*

On 27 July 1981 *New Jersey* began an eleven-day tow from Puget Sound to Long Beach. Although three of the four ships had not been reactivated for thirty years, and not been in commission for twenty-five, the process was well understood and proven, and the time and trouble taken over earlier deactivation once again showed its benefits. The 16in guns and turrets in particular were largely trouble free to reactivate, with few major problems encountered because of the care with which they had been preserved when deactivated.[8] There were minor problems with the elevation mechanisms on two of *Iowa*'s guns, which oscillated instead of steadying on the required elevation – a problem inherited from the 1950s and easily solved by replacing some valves. The tendency of the corrosion-preventing compound in the hydraulic system to have hardened required flushing out and new filters to catch the residue. There was a need to replace only one major sub-component, the breech operating valves. Looking at the logistics to sustain the main armament, there were in 1981 still forty spare gun barrels in storage, and 21,000 shells.[9]

There were also plans to upgrade the capability of the artillery, in particular to fit the radar velocimeters as used by *New Jersey* in Vietnam, to measure 16in gun muzzle velocity and, in combination with remixed powder charges, to achieve consistent muzzle velocity and hence accuracy. There were also projects to achieve longer ranges with the existing guns. An improved High Charge round was test fired from *Iowa* and at the Dahlgren proving ground, reaching a range of 51,000 yards, about 9,000 more than had previously been possible. There was also work on a 13.65in sub-calibre round with a sabot designed to fire anti-personnel sub-munitions up to 70,000 yards, and a more speculative 11in sub-calibre round with a range of up to 100 nautical miles. All these projects were cancelled around 1991 when the battleships were again retired.[10]

Although the fundamentals of the ships in terms of their 16in guns and machinery remained much as they had been in 1945, their size and flexibility combined with the march of technology did allow them to be significantly upgraded in the 1980s. The most visible manifestations of this were the addition of three modern weapons systems to the upper decks: thirty-two BGM 109 Tomahawk cruise missiles in armoured box launchers; sixteen Harpoon anti-ship cruise missiles; and four Phalanx autonomous 20mm rotary cannon close-in weapon systems, reflecting the new concern about sea skimming anti-surface missiles, even then being demonstrated by the French Exocet missile in actual naval combat between the UK and Argentina in the South Atlantic. To make space and weight for these additions, all the 40mm guns were removed, and also the four aftermost 5in turrets. The Tomahawk in particular, with its range of 900 nautical miles, terrain-following Global Positioning System guidance and precision land-attack capability, gave the battleship back the range

BGM-109 Tomahawk missile firing from *Wisconsin* during Operation Desert Storm, January 1991. *(NHHC, US DOD)*

advantage that it had not enjoyed relative to aircraft carriers in Korea and Vietnam. *New Jersey* became the first ship to take Tomahawk to sea.

Just as significant as the weapons in the modern era were major upgrades in the electronic countermeasures, with the AN/SLQ32(V)3 system, Mark 137 SBROC chaff launchers, SLQ N1XU anti-torpedo decoys; and in the sensors, with state-of-the-art AN/SPS49 air search radar, and SPS 10 surface search. There were also new communications, including the Naval Tactical Data Systems Link 11 and Link 14, plus a New Combat Engagement Centre on 02 level, and Command and Control facilities. Additionally the ships were made compatible with the modern fleet logistics train by modifying the main engines to burn marine diesel instead of furnace fuel oil. One of the most complex modifications was the requirement to meet modern environmental regulations by treating all the ship's sewage on board rather than just pumping it over the side as had been acceptable in earlier years. From 1986 the ships could also operate the Pioneer drone from the quarterdeck, with dedicated refuelling facilities and a retractable net to recapture the returning machine over the fantail. Six of these aircraft were eventually carried on each ship.

The original plan was to conduct the upgrades in two stages. The simple bolt-on improvements described above were phase one, easily and cheaply achievable to get four new Surface Action Groups into the front line by 1988. Options for further phase one upgrades including Sea Sparrow short-range air defence missile, full Link 11 capability and fragment path barriers (as armour now seemed to be called) to protect against horizontal missile strikes were not in the end incorporated. More ambitious plans still harked back to the autonomous surface action concept of the 1960s and '70s, replacing the aft turrets with an expanded aviation facility to take not just Marines assault helicopters, but also AV-8B jump jets for close air support of amphibious operations. The boxed missiles would also be replaced by very large vertical-launch missile silos, which would provide greater anti-surface, anti-air, or land attack capabilities in flexible configurations as required. At the time that *New Jersey* and *Iowa* were beginning phase one conversion, there was speculation that *Missouri* and *Wisconsin* might be held back slightly and be refurbished directly to one of these more advanced configurations once the necessary design work was done. In the event the more ambitious ideas proved operationally controversial and ultimately unaffordable as the steam ran out on the Reagan military build-up.

Work on *New Jersey* progressed well. President Reagan attended the recommissioning ceremony on 28 February 1982, and she became the 514th ship of the expanding Navy on 28 January 1983, under command of Captain William Fogarty. Trials were run amid considerable publicity in late 1982. The first Harpoon firing by a battleship took place successfully on 23 March 1983, and the first Tomahawk firing by a battleship on 10 May 1983, when the missile, launched off the Pacific Coast, hit its target in Nevada, 500 miles away. A month later *New Jersey* was ready to deploy and joined the Pacific Fleet in the Philippines. Meanwhile, *Iowa* was towed from Philadelphia to Avondale Shipyard in New Orleans on 1 September 1982, and completed the overhaul at Ingalls Shipyard, Pascagoula, Mississippi. She did sea trials in December 1983, and was recommissioned ahead of schedule and within budget on 28 April 1984. *Missouri* was next, leaving Puget Sound on 14 May 1985 and recommissioning at San Francisco on 10 May 1986. *Wisconsin* followed *Iowa*'s track from Philadelphia to New Orleans and Pascagoula between 8 August 1986 and recommissioning on 22 October 1988.

Although the controversy about reviving the battleships never quite subsided, as it happened the geo-strategic challenges of the 1980s and early '90s, and the chosen United States response under the Reagan doctrine of forward defence, combined to allow the US Navy to use the battleships on deployments and live operations very much in line with the Surface Action Group concept, as battleship battle groups, combining the ships with an Aegis-equipped *Ticonderoga*-class cruiser for long-range air defence and a variety of destroyer types for closer air defence and anti-submarine protection.

New Jersey had a busy first year back in active service and demonstrating forward presence, first with the 7th Fleet in the Gulf of Siam in June and July and then on the other side of the Pacific off the coast of Guatemala in Central America as relations with Nicaragua's communist-backed Sandinista regime deteriorated. Her three weeks there in August and early September were uneventful. Next she was sent to the Mediterranean, and was on station off Lebanon from 24 September 1983. Lebanon, long a failing state, had become the site of a large Palestine Liberation Organisation presence that was inimical to Israel and backed by Syria. Following earlier clashes, Israel had invaded Lebanon on 6 June 1982. Reagan agreed to commit US Marines to a multinational force to police a ceasefire and allow Syrian and Israeli forces to withdraw. This process was frustrated by a developing civil war between Christian and Moslem factions in Lebanon. A year of internecine chaos and violence against the multinational force presence included the bombing of the US embassy and killing of US Marines at the airport, which had elicited an extensive naval bombardment of Shia positions by six US destroyers in May 1983. There was further naval gunfire support on 8 September just before *New Jersey* arrived. Then the US Marine barracks was suicide bombed by Shia militants linked to Iran on 23 October 1983. Some 299 US and French peacekeepers died.

Amidst this deteriorating situation, on 14 December 1983 16in guns fired in anger for the first time since 1 April 1969, the target being Syrian air defence assets that had just shot down two US Navy jets over the Beqaa Valley. Only eleven shells were fired on this occasion. Reagan decided to withdraw the US contingent from Lebanon on 7 February, but *New Jersey* was in action that day firing thirty-two 5in shells, and again the following day, on 8 February 1984 firing 270 shells into Syrian and Druze militia artillery positions threatening Beirut. Some of the shells hit a command post, killing the general commanding Syrian forces in Lebanon.[11] By the end of that week the US Marines had relocated offshore and amid growing policy disagreements within the US Administration, overall involvement in Lebanon was scaled back. However, *New Jersey* fired one more 16in bombardment of thirty-two shells on 26 February.

There were claims that some shots from the 8 February bombardment were 'wild' and landed in built-up areas, causing civilian casualties. The US Navy took this seriously enough for Lehman to set guidelines that all shots had to land within a circle error of probability no larger than the US Capitol Building.[12] *Iowa*, just becoming available after her refurbishment, was tasked to carry out gunnery trials to achieve this

New Jersey in action off Lebanon, 1984. *(NHHC)*

consistency. Wild shots were experienced and blamed on a combination of inaccurate muzzle velocity readings, inaccuracies in the range tables and in the ballistic cams in the (original 1940s) Mark 8 fire control computer as well as the inconsistent composition of the powder noted above. The solutions were new range tables, remixing the powder to improve consistency and installing a Doppler velocimeter on the middle barrel of each turret to make precision measurements of each round fired. Accuracy was much improved as a result. When *Iowa* tested the new system off Crete on 23 November 1987 she fired fifteen rounds at a range of 34,000 yards with an overall pattern size of 219 yards, eight shells within 150 yards, and a round-to-round variation of only 123 yards, which was considered a superb performance.[13] Compare that with the results achieved by *Richelieu* in 1952, with variations averaging 300m, shot to shot.

New Jersey spent 111 days at sea on her Mediterranean mission, but saw no more action in Lebanon, nor indeed in her subsequent deployments. She returned from Lebanon for a lengthy refit, then spent late 1985 and all of 1986 back in the Pacific conducting a series of fleet readiness exercises as the centrepiece of her own battle group. She was the only major US unit in South East Asia between May and October 1986, but also exercised her passage rites far to the north in the Sea of Okhotsk on 27 and 28 September, when unsurprisingly she was buzzed by a variety of

Soviet aircraft and shadowed by a *Kara*-class cruiser of the Soviet Pacific Fleet. This really was testing the forward deployment policy to its limits. *New Jersey* was back at Long Beach for another refit between December 1986 and November 1987. In 1988 she deployed across the Pacific again and operated near the coast of Korea before the opening of the Seoul Olympic Games, then went to Australia for the bicentennial celebrations. In 1989 she deployed to the Pacific for a final time, taking part in the international manoeuvres Pacifex 89 with allied navies. She then sailed through the Indian Ocean and into the Persian Gulf, then an area of high tension because of the threat posed by Iran to international shipping, where she stayed until the end of the year and returned to the USA for the last time in February 1990.

Iowa was carrying out trials in the Caribbean in May 1984, including 16in and 5in firings at the Vieques Island range, Puerto Rico, on 21 May. She spent June visiting Venezuela and Central America, before more 16in firing at Vieques Island on 1 July. She passed through the Panama Canal on 6 August and spent a fortnight off the Pacific coast of Nicaragua, as close as 13 miles, before returning to the Atlantic.

In 1985 she spent February in the Caribbean and undertook humanitarian projects in Costa Rica and Honduras, as well as exercising the Battleship Surface Action group concept. After a three-month dry docking at Norfolk, she took part in her first NATO exercise for nearly thirty years, Ocean Safari in August and September, convoying US reinforcements to Western Europe and rendezvousing with the aircraft carrier *America* battle group. The parallels with the scenarios for Mainbrace and Mariner in 1952–53 were striking, including deploying far north into the Arctic Circle. The old pattern of European port visits was then resumed at Le Havre, Copenhagen, Aarhus and Oslo. On

Iowa at Panama, August 1984. (Author's collection)

12 October however, she broke new ground as she very visibly manifested the Lehman doctrine of high threat deployments by entering the Baltic Sea and exercising for a week with NATO allied naval forces on the Russian doorstep, including 16in firings, before visiting Kiel on 18 October 1985. This was the only occasion that any NATO battleship went to the Baltic, and, together with *New Jersey*'s Sea of Okhotsk deployment, might be said to mark the symbolic high point of the Reagan doctrine.

Back in Norfolk by the end of the month for refit, *Iowa* then deployed afresh to the Caribbean in February 1986, and once again went through the Panama Canal for 'presence' operations off Central America from March. President and Nancy Reagan, as well as John Lehman, were hosted aboard for Independence Day celebrations and an international naval review and gathering of tall ships in New York to mark the one hundredth anniversary of the Statue of Liberty. *Iowa* led the US Navy contingent of eleven ships from the Atlantic Fleet under the Verrazano Narrows Bridge at noon on 4 July, then up the Hudson River to anchor off Hoboken. In August it was off to Europe again to undertake NATO exercise Northern Wedding. In September 1986 she visited the UK, where at Portsmouth I was one of thousands able to visit her at the South Railway Jetty.

The deployment to the UK also featured an exercise to support a US Marine assault on 5–6 September at Cape Wrath, north-west Scotland, when she fired nineteen 16in and thirty-two 5in shells over ten hours of fire support. I speculate that this might be the only occasion when the UK has been shelled by a United States battleship. *Iowa* continued to

Iowa at Portsmouth, September 1986. *(Author's collection)*

Bremerhaven in Germany. Other milestones of 1986 included the first Pioneer drone launch and recovery on 9 December, and firing the 1,000th 16in round of her latest commission on 14 December. The early part of 1987 was spent on the east coast and in the Caribbean undertaking a series of exercises, but in early September she left for the Mediterranean and the NATO exercise Display Determination, finishing off with the gunnery trials off Crete described above. She paid a port visit to Istanbul on 8 October. By the end of the month she was back in the North Sea for further NATO exercises testing forward deployment, and called at Trondheim, north Norway, on 30 October.

There was then a complete change of focus as she was directed back through the Mediterranean again, and through the Suez Canal on 25 November. After a brief stop at the US base of Diego Garcia in the Indian Ocean, she commenced Persian Gulf presence operations, Operation Earnest Will, and New Year's Day 1988 saw her south of the Straits of Hormuz as part of the international force that had been assembled to deter Iranian fast attack craft that had threatened to close the vital oil trade from the Persian Gulf. In the Gulf of Oman she escorted convoys through the southern Strait of Hormuz and protected the convoy assembly areas off Masirah and Muscat. That mission ended for *Iowa* on 20 February, and she came back through Suez, to reach Norfolk, Virginia, on 10 March 1988. The middle of 1988 was occupied with a refit at Norfolk, before further operations in the Caribbean and US East Coast. On 26 January 1989 she is credited with firing the longest ever conventional 16in round, hitting a target 23.4 nautical miles distant (46,800 yards) with her first shot. This was, however, the prelude to the darkest episode in the story of the ship.

The worst ever accident in a US Navy battleship took place on 19 April 1989 when there was a cordite fire and explosion in *Iowa*'s No. 2 turret during further target firing at the Vieques Island range. Some 500lb of propellant in the centre gun ignited before the gun breach was fully closed. The flash spread throughout the turret, killing all there. Video footage of the accident taken by a crewman on the bridge shows the violence of the combustion as it vents out of the turret. The flash went down into the powder handling room below, igniting all the charges in that compartment as well, and also killing all the occupants, in scenes eerily reminiscent of the experiences of the British and German battleship cordite fires in the First World War. Altogether forty-seven men died. Fortunately, and in contrast to the British experience at Jutland, the interlock systems in the handling room, which closed the scuttles to the lower compartments in the barbette and sealed off the powder magazine when those to the turret were open, worked. The fire was contained and eventually, after seventeen desperate minutes, extinguished. Some sources say that *Iowa*'s Captain Moosally ordered the flooding of the magazine. It would certainly have been a sensible precaution.

Tragic as this incident was in itself, unfortunately it was just the start of a long, tortured investigation process that raised serious doubts about the safety culture and wider judgement of the entire US Navy hierarchy. There were no eyewitness survivors as to the precise cause of the tragedy. The initial inquiry was established by Commander Naval Surface Forces Atlantic, and appointed Rear Admiral Richard Milligan, a former commanding officer of *New Jersey*, to undertake it. Milligan was aboard *Iowa* to start work the day after the accident, but already crucial forensic evidence had been destroyed as the bodies were recovered without any record being made of their positions in the turret, and much damaged material had simply been thrown overboard.

Milligan found that the centre gun (and the others where the powder did not catch fire) were firing an unauthorised, non-standard combination of a 2,700lb armour-piercing shell with five instead of the standard six bags of powder, and using D-846 type powder, which was clearly authorised for use only with the lighter 1,900lb high-explosive HC version of the 16in shell. He found that the *Iowa*'s 16in turrets were all significantly undermanned, and that of fifty-one turret crew positions that required trained and formally qualified personnel, only thirteen in turret two were manned with personnel at the required level. The sailor manning the rammer on the centre gun, later the focus of much attention, had never done a live shoot before. The investigation found that the rammer had been over-extended by 21in as it pushed the powder bags into the breech, which could have over-compressed the powder charges. Milligan summed up the issues as:

> lack of an effective and properly supervised assignment and qualifications process, and poor adherence to explosive safety regulations and ordnance safety. Whilst none of these factors have been determined to be the cause of the explosion, or provide an ignition source, they cast the proper operation of gunnery systems in USS *Iowa* in a very poor light and generate doubt.

Despite the wider evidence of widespread safety failings, Milligan in fact blamed the explosion on a deliberate act of sabotage by a crew member, the centre gun captain Gunners Mate Grade 2 Clayton Hartwig. Hartwig, it was claimed, had recently taken out a life insurance policy, named another crewmate as its beneficiary, possessed some publications explaining how to improvise explosive devices and had behaved erratically and morbidly in the weeks preceding the accident. A criminal investigation by the Naval Investigation Service was therefore blistered onto Milligan's.

Although not included in any formal evidence, widespread leaks from investigation sources alleged Hartwig's motivation was a failed homosexual relationship with another crew member. It was suggested that he had inserted a detonation device between the powder bags. Initial forensic evidence of foreign substance residues found in the gun lent credence to this theory, although the FBI had already discounted the significance of this finding by the time the Milligan report was endorsed by the US Navy hierarchy, including Chief of Naval Operations Admiral Carlisle Trost on 31 August 1989.

On 7 September Milligan and Vice CNO Admiral Edney briefed the press on the findings, blaming Hartwig for sabotage. The briefing stated that the *Iowa*-class ships were safe to operate and the 16in powder was stable and safe to use. The media reaction was very negative, with many including Hartwig's family accusing the Navy of scapegoating a dead man to cover up serious operational and safety deficiencies. The investigation was widely seen as inadequate and Congressional criticism culminated in November 1989 with Senator John Glenn (former US Marine pilot and Mercury spacecraft astronaut) requesting that the Government Accounting Office (GAO) conduct an independent review of the Navy findings. Captain Moosally of the *Iowa* muddied the waters when he testified on 11 December that he agreed the initial explosion was intentional but not that Hartwig was the culprit. The House Armed Services Committee issued a report in March 1990 entitled 'USS *Iowa* Tragedy: An Investigative Failure', which was highly critical of the Navy.

Meanwhile, investigations initiated in late 1989 by Congress and undertaken by Scandia Laboratories dismissed all the alien residue theories that underpinned the detonation device theory. It focussed instead on the stability of the powder under ramming and over-ramming conditions. In the eighteenth ramming test on 24 May 1990 the powder exploded. On 30 June Admiral Frank Kelso, Trost's replacement as CNO, ordered a second Navy investigation headed by Captain Joseph Miceli of Naval Sea Systems Command. Miceli, who was an ordnance specialist, was chosen despite having recognised conflicts of interest as he had already testified to the Milligan inquiry and had previously commanded the depot where the suspect powder in question had been stored and prepared for use. Miceli remained unconvinced by the Scandia work, and reaffirmed the initial inquiry finding that no accidental cause for the explosion could be found. This was despite the continuing Scandia over-ramming experiments, which had by now generated no fewer than five explosions of powder in the gun breach. Scandia's final report to the GAO in August 1991 left that body in no doubt that an over-ramming-generated explosion was a previously unrecognised safety problem. Admiral Kelso held a press conference on 17 October 1991 to draw a line under the second investigation. He said: '... despite the Scandia theory and almost two years of subsequent testing, a substantial body of scientific and expert evidence continue to support the initial investigation that no plausible accidental cause can be established.' But he went on to add that there was no clear and convincing proof that Hartwig was to blame and offered sincere regrets to his family.

So officially, a definitive cause of the explosion was not established, but the US Navy and Scandia Laboratories had between them identified a combination of inexperienced gun crew; incorrect loading of unauthorised propellant; over-ramming of the propellant into the breech; and also defects in the pellets in some of the powder bags. Modifications were made to *Missouri* and *Wisconsin*, by then the only two battleships remaining in commission, to limit the speed of the rammers and the distance they were able to travel into the breech, and the powder bags were redesigned to eliminate the suspect component.[14]

Although *Iowa*'s turret two was never repaired, the ship's programme was sustained through the remainder of 1989. During this final deployment starting on 7 June 1989 she steamed 31,000 miles, visited many old haunts including Kiel, Portsmouth again, Rota, Casablanca, Gibraltar, Marseilles, Antalya, Gaeta, Istanbul, Haifa, Alexandria, Ajaccio, Augusta, Naples and Palma, Majorca. The Mediterranean leg included the NATO exercise Display Determination and one last deployment for contingency operations off the Lebanese coast. On the return journey to Norfolk she fired her last 16in round, the 2,873rd of her final activation and 11,834th of her career.

Missouri began her stint in the 600-ship Navy by undertaking a three-month round the world cruise, the first time a US battleship had done this since President Theodore Roosevelt's Great White Fleet cruise of 1908. She went across the Pacific and became the first battleship to visit Sydney, Australia, for forty years, to take part in the fleet review to mark the seventy-fifth anniversary of the Royal Australian Navy. She then sailed to Diego Garcia, Suez, Istanbul from 11 to 14 November 1986 (reprising her 1946 visit), Lisbon and Panama, regaining Long Beach on 19 December. After a short refit, she deployed again to the northern Arabian Sea on 27 July 1987 to undertake Persian Gulf presence operations (see above) for over three months as the centrepiece of battle group Echo.

By this stage the very expensive Western warships operating in the Persian Gulf faced asymmetric threats from Boghammar speed boats manned by the Iranian Revolutionary Guard Corps. In common with other fleets, the US Navy took steps to defend against these, in *Missouri*'s case by fitting 40mm grenade launchers and 25mm chain guns. She returned to Long Beach in early 1988 via Diego Garcia, Australia and Hawaii. Later that year she took part in the RIMPAC exercises with

Canadian, Australian and Japanese ships, and visited Vancouver and Victoria in British Columbia. During her 1989 overhaul at Long Beach the music video of Cher's 'If I could turn back time' was filmed aboard the ship. Words, at this point, fail me. Just watch it on YouTube. The ship's photogenic qualities also commended her to director Andrew Davies for the 1992 Steven Seagal film *Under Siege* (Rotten Tomatoes website score 78 per cent). With all due respect to Seagal and co-star Tommy Lee Jones, the star of the film will always be the battleship, although *Alabama* in fact stood in for most of the close-up scenes. Following this cultural excitement, participation alongside *New Jersey* in Pacific Exercise 89, when they fired 16in guns simultaneously for the benefit of the accompanying aircraft carriers *Enterprise* and *Nimitz*, must have seemed thin gruel. Early 1990 saw *Missouri* repeating the RIMPAC exercise, but her planned western Pacific cruise for later that year fell victim to unfolding world events.

Wisconsin was reactivated from 1 August 1986, and re-commissioned on 22 October 1988 in front of a crowd of 12,000. She was assigned to the Atlantic Fleet and base ported at Norfolk, Virginia. Early 1989 saw her working up in the Atlantic and conducting 16in firing trials off Vieques Island from 8 to 14 April, as had her sister. Much of the rest of 1989 was spent alongside for more modifications and upgrades. On 19 January 1990 she went back to Guantanamo Bay for refresher training, then took part in naval gunfire support training (timely in view of what was soon to follow) and during June an Atlantic Fleet exercise in the Caribbean.[15]

Iowa was never fully repaired after her accident and went out of commission for the final time on 26 October 1990, well before the investigations into its cause had finally concluded. *New Jersey* followed in February 1991. Ironically, this was at exactly the time that their two sisters were in action once again, in the Gulf War of 1991. Saddam Hussein, dictator of Iraq, had invaded and occupied Kuwait in August 1990, claiming it as his nineteenth province. The United Nations was swift to condemn, and use of military force was mandated by the Security Council to remove the occupying Iraqi troops. A large coalition was assembled with major contributions from the United States, UK and France. Ground and air forces began to build up in Saudi Arabia, and a major coalition naval presence was assembled in the Persian Gulf, in the initial hope that this pressure on Saddam might make him back down. *Wisconsin* and *Missouri* were both assigned to the Persian Gulf Battle Group. *Missouri* sailed for Desert Storm on 13 November 1990 and passed through the Strait of Hormuz on 3 January 1991. *Wisconsin* had preceded her, coming on station on 23 August 1990 and playing her part to exert pressure on Saddam and reassure friendly nations in the Gulf by patrolling in the Gulf and visiting Muscat, Bahrain, Dubai and Abu Dhabi.

The new capabilities of these ships were shown to great effect, in combination with their original and well-tried weapons, once the combat phase began. On 17 January 1991 time ran out for Saddam, and *Wisconsin* used her command and control capabilities to act as Tomahawk Land Attack Commander for the Persian Gulf. She co-ordinated the launch of forty missiles, fired from across the fleet starting at 0140. *Wisconsin* fired seven herself, while *Missouri* fired eight. The targets were hundreds of miles away inland, namely Iraqi regime command and air defence centres around Baghdad. The next day *Wisconsin* fired sixteen more Tomahawks and *Missouri* thirteen. Altogether she directed the launching of 213 Tomahawks during this opening stage of the war.

Saddam, however, was not budging. The next operation would involve *Missouri* co-ordinating fire support for US troops who were to move into Kuwait. She began by firing on Iraqi bunkers with her 16in guns as early as 3 February, using the Pioneer drones for spotting. Further 16in firings took place on 6 and 7 February. Then she fired against Iraqi troops conducting a half-hearted invasion of Saudi Arabia, near Khafaji, on 11 February. On 24 February the coalition's own offensive took place and *Missouri* bombarded Iraqi coastal defences on Failaka Island as a feint to make the Iraqis believe that they faced an amphibious landing, instead of General Norman Schwarzkopf's left-hook attack launched well inland. Some 133 rounds of 16in were fired, and on this occasion ten Iraqi divisions were allegedly pinned in place by the threat, so it was generally reckoned a great success.

Iraq did fight back, and two Chinese-built Silkworm cruise missiles were fired at *Missouri* that day. Silkworm was a large missile, weighing around 2,000 kilos, and with a correspondingly large warhead. It was considerably larger than Exocet, which had had such an impact against destroyers in the Falklands, and had got congressmen hot under the collar. But the hotly debated question of battleship vulnerability to this form of attack was not to be put to the test. HMS *Gloucester*, the Royal Navy Type 42 destroyer acting as close escort to *Missouri*, shot down one Silkworm with its Sea Dart missile, and the other Silkworm crashed into the sea. There was minor damage and one minor injury aboard *Missouri* caused by stray Phalanx rounds from her US escorting destroyer *Jarrett* hitting the ship. The Silkworm battery was then silenced with fifty 16in shells from the battleship. *Wisconsin* came up to join *Missouri* on the gun line, and the much-reported incident took place where *Wisconsin* launched her drone, and, in anticipation of another 16in bombardment to follow, the Iraqi positions surrendered to the drone. It was all over in four days, with

Wisconsin fires a 16in broadside during her 1988–91 commission. *(NHHC)*

Iraq driven completely out of Kuwait at negligible loss to the coalition forces. A ceasefire took effect on 28 February.

Altogether during Operation Desert Storm *Missouri* fired 759 16in shells and twenty-eight Tomahawks, and *Wisconsin* 319 16in shells and twenty-four Tomahawks. There was also extensive expenditure of 5in and Phalanx ammunition. The two ships between them destroyed twenty-one of the floating mines that presented a constant challenge to the coalition warships. The changing nature of maritime warfare was reflected in the statistics for *Wisconsin*'s air operations. During the deployment she recorded 661 helicopter landings and her drones were airborne for 348 hours. To *Wisconsin* fell the task of firing the last battleship main battery salvo in history. She was decommissioned by September that year, and *Missouri* in March 1992.[16]

Was Reagan's reactivation of the battleships worth it? The cost was relatively tiny set against the overall defence spending of those years, and the anticipated budget for reactivation was generally achieved. The ships made a moderate military impact in the Lebanon, but arguably a greater political one. Using their missiles as well as guns, they proved highly effective in the Gulf War. Less easy to quantify, but powerful, was always the intangible but evident fact of their existence, off Central America, in the Arabian Sea, Persian Gulf and Indian Ocean, and as the backbone of forward-deployed NATO task forces exercising command of the sea in the Eastern Mediterranean, North Atlantic and Pacific, just as they had done thirty years and more previously. They were instantly recognisable across the globe, taking their place alongside carrier battle groups as highly visible and highly publicised manifestations of Western military power. The forays into the Baltic and Sea of Okhotsk were unmistakeable assertions of capability. Ultimately the debate about their contribution and effectiveness evaporates in arguments over what alternative force structure might have been provided (and how quickly) for the $1.5 billion and 6,000-odd sailors that this final battleship reactivation cost. What is not deniable is that they played a very visible part in deterrence as the Cold War climaxed in the collapse of the Soviet effort, and very soon after the collapse of the Soviet Union itself.

Following that break-up of the Soviet Union, and before the degree of instability ushered in by the new world order was evident, the demand for a peace dividend and a balanced US budget made it once more inevitable that the size of the US Navy must shrink. The 600-ship Navy had never quite been achieved – they got to 594 in 1989 – but the rapidly contracting power and influence of the main rival superpower meant a corresponding reduction in US Navy budgets and readiness was an appropriate reaction. As in the 1940s, '50s and '60s, the battleships, having done their bit, were once again deactivated. This was despite their continuing exceptional reliability and the US Navy's estimate in 1987 that they were still good for fifteen to twenty years of active service and were expected at that point to stay in use beyond the year 2000.[17]

The four battleships were not in commission, but were back in reserve, with the same care having been taken over their deactivation on the latest occasion as previously. They now began a new phase of uncertainty. Some in Congress wanted to keep them available for potential reactivation. Others felt that this time, finally, at nearly fifty years of age, they really had outlived their economic and military effectiveness and that new platforms needed to be found to project sea power in the twenty-first century. The Cold War dynamic of the Reagan years was gone, and with it the critical mass of professional opinion within the US Navy that had been so important in commending them to Presidents and Congress. So, in 1995 the Secretary for the Navy, John H Dalton, decided to strike them from the Naval Vessels Register, in effect saying that the requirement for them had ceased to exist. But Congress once again intervened and disagreed. It required that two of the ships be maintained in reserve until the US Navy could testify to Congress that it had naval gunfire support within the fleet that matched or exceeded the battleships' capabilities. The 1996 National Defense Authorisation Act therefore named *Wisconsin* and *New Jersey* to be maintained in the US Reserve Fleets as potential shore bombardment vessels. Later amendments substituted *Iowa* for *New Jersey*. It is mystifying why she was chosen ahead of the other two candidates given her still unrepaired No. 2 turret.

So the battleships remained in reserve for a further ten years, until in 2005 the Secretary for the Navy, now Gordon R. England, decided to try again to remove the ships from the Naval Vessel Register. The mitigation offered to meet the terms of the 1996 Act was a two-part plan, first to increase the range of existing 5in destroyer guns with an extended-range guided munition; and second to field the Advanced Gun System and in due course potentially an electro-magnetic rail gun on the new *Zumwalt*-class destroyers. Some in Congress were still not happy about the loss of the naval gunfire support capability that the battleships above all embodied, and the perceived failures to make it good through other programmes. So, despite the fact that they were now sixty-three years old and fifteen years out of commission, the National Defence Authorisation Act 2006 (Pub.L. 109-163) required that the two battleships, even if given over to preservation projects, still be maintained at a state of readiness so that they could be returned to active duty if needed. The specific requirements were that they not be altered in any way that impaired their military utility; that their condition be maintained through use of cathodic protection and dehumidification, and other preservation as required; that spare parts and unique equipment, for example 16in gun barrels and projectiles, be maintained to support possible reactivation; and that plans be maintained for potential rapid reactivation. These requirements were only finally abandoned under the terms of the National Defense Authorisation Act 2009.[18] Sixty-six years after entering service, the *Iowas* were finally, unambiguously, allowed to settle into retirement and their new incarnation as museum ships.

CHAPTER FIFTEEN

Preservation, Historic Ships and Relics

PRESERVATION OF WARSHIPS as museum ships began systematically early in the twentieth century. The USA preserved the wooden frigate *Constitution* and one of their earliest pre-dreadnought battleships, *Oregon* (BB3). She dated from 1890 and was a veteran of the Spanish–American War of 1898. She was decommissioned in 1919, and from 1921 a movement began in her home State to try to preserve her as a museum. This aspiration was realised in June 1925 when the ship, still officially on the Navy list with the title 'Relic', was loaned to the State of Oregon and moored at Portland as a floating museum. Sadly (for the historic ship enthusiast), when the Second World War broke out she was deemed a

The hulk of *Oregon* (centre, next to crane) at Guam, April 1952. *Wisconsin* is in AFDB-1. *(NHHC)*

valuable scrap asset and was towed to Kalama, Washington State, for dismantling in March 1943. Although the torches removed her superstructure (the mast is still preserved at Portland), she avoided her ultimate fate for thirteen more years because the US War Shipping Administration suddenly decided they needed her as an ammunition barge to serve at Guam in the later stages of the war.

The hulk remained marooned at Guam after the war, apart from a brief unplanned excursion of 500 miles when, in the glorious traditions of unruly decommissioned battleships, she broke adrift in a typhoon in November 1948 and went missing in the Pacific for three weeks. It was not until 1956 that she was finally sold for scrap and went to Kawasaki, Japan, to be broken up by Iwai Sanggo.

Japan herself had also preserved a battleship, the historic *Mikasa*, built by Vickers at Barrow in Furness from 1899 to 1902. She was Japanese flagship at the victorious battle of Tsushima against the Russians in 1905, and was decommissioned in 1923 following the Washington Naval Treaty. The signatories to the Treaty agreed that she could be preserved as a memorial, and despite vicissitudes during and after the Second World War she still survives, although now encased in concrete, at Yokosuka. So does her opponent at Tsushima, the Russian cruiser *Aurora* at St Petersburg, in her case because of her historic importance to the USSR following the ship's pivotal intervention on the Bolshevik side at Leningrad during the 1917 revolution.

In the UK there was no comparable sentiment before the Second World War. HMS *Victory* was an exception because of her association with Nelson and Trafalgar, and had been preserved with considerable difficulty, not without Royal intervention, and retained in commission in various guises by the Royal Navy (as she remains to this day). Other wooden ships of the line employed as hulks survived well into the twentieth century, although many were swept away by that unsentimental arch-reformer Admiral Jackie Fisher. Among the last of them were *Wellesley* dating from 1815, sunk by the Luftwaffe in the Thames Estuary on 24 September 1940; *Nile*, a two-decker from 1839, still being used as a cadet sail training ship when wrecked in the Menai Straits in 1953; and *Implacable*, earlier the French *Duguay-Trouin*, which had been built at Rochefort in 1800. She had survived as a boys' training ship, holiday accommodation and a coal hulk, but after the Second World War the cost of restoring her, £200,000, was simply too great. The French did not want her either, so she was scuttled in the English Channel on 2 December 1949, flying the flags of both nations. Her stern gallery was removed and now adorns the main hall of the National Maritime Museum in Greenwich, and her demise was controversial enough to spark the first beginnings of a concerted movement to preserve the UK's maritime heritage.

This was not enough to save the only other wooden battleship to outlast *Nile*, the *Cornwallis* of 1813, Napoleonic War veteran and flagship of the British Fleet in the first China War of 1842, which was 144 years old when her role as an accommodation hulk at HMS *Wildfire* in the Medway finally came to an end and she was broken up in 1957. A few historic British warships have survived through the accidents of their employment in auxiliary roles, most notably the splendid *Warrior* of 1860, first and last of all the British Ironclad battleships, many years an oil fuel depot jetty at Pembroke Dock, and now magnificently restored and resplendent at the Historic Dockyard in Portsmouth. But none of the twentieth-century dreadnoughts (or indeed the aircraft carriers) is among the United Kingdom's surviving ships.

Before the Second World War there was no obvious candidate, although there were some calls in the 1920s to save *Lion*, Beatty's flagship at Jutland. Battleships were then still very much part of the contemporary Navy. After the second war there was very little room for sentiment in the era of rationing, reconstruction, steel shortages and general austerity. This, remember, was when swathes of Britain's historic country houses also went to ruin because they simply could neither be afforded nor saved. Sources refer to campaigns to save some battleships, but there is precious little public evidence for more than plaintive, and usually retrospective, calls for what a few individuals felt should have been done. So, in the Parliamentary record there is only one single call for the saving of *Warspite*, and none, before her scrapping, for *Vanguard*, although by that stage it must have been evident that she would be the last of her line. Her ex-captain, now retired Admiral Sir Frederick Parham, did approach the Director of Naval Construction to ask if preservation at Devonport might be possible, but got a dusty and unsentimental answer that the cost, the same as keeping her in reserve, could not be justified as a use of public funds.[1] Neither of them seem to have considered the possibility of private initiatives, and despite the contemporary efforts getting under way in the United States, there was no evidence that such an initiative was seriously contemplated in the UK in 1960. It would take another decade before the cruiser *Belfast* (another of Parham's ships) could be saved for the nation by the Imperial War Museum and an independent trust.

There are fragments of UK battleships here and there, as noted in previous chapters. By far the most impressive are the two surviving 15in Mark 1N guns outside the front of the Imperial War Museum in Lambeth, resting together on a cradle, as they would have looked aboard the sixteen British battleships that carried them. This was a lucky rescue. The museum started to seek the guns after the sale of the monitor *Roberts* to Ward's. She was already being broken up at Inverkeithing in 1965 when the request was made. Ward's would not agree to forego their scrap value, and it was thought then that these were the last 15in guns in existence, but a final two were found at the Army Proof and Experimental Establishment at Shoeburyness, one complete, and one without a breech mechanism. It was possible to reconstruct this using a spare breech mechanism held at the depot at Woolwich. The guns, valued at £6,176, were gifted to the museum in 1967.[2] There is also a 14in gun from the *King George V* class outside Fort Nelson Royal Armouries Museum on top of Portsdown Hill, Hampshire.

France was even less able to afford the luxury of ship preservation than the UK and today has a much less enticing historic ship offer. The anti-aircraft cruiser *Colbert* was preserved at Bordeaux for some years, but proved controversial and uneconomic as a museum and function suite. She has now been scrapped. Other battleship nations did not generally see preservation as important (although we must make an honourable mention for Greece, which never possessed a dreadnought, but has preserved its largest ever warship, the armoured cruiser *Georgios Averof*). A prime candidate for saving would have been *Yavuz/Goeben*, but as noted above it proved impossible to preserve her, and she leaves behind as monuments just her propellers, at the Maritime Museum in Istanbul and at Gölcük on the Sea of Marmara where she had been based for much of the fifty-eight years of her existence.

This left the United States as the only nation with a culture and habit of ship preservation and the resources to rescue dreadnoughts. Eight US battleships survive to this day, the only representatives of the 175 dreadnought battleships that once existed. Although the US has also preserved five Second World War vintage aircraft carriers, nine destroyers and fifteen submarines, she has only two cruisers, one just post-war (*Salem*) and one an early guided missile ship conversion (*Little Rock*). The eight battleships represent by far the largest proportion of any United States warship type to be preserved.

Texas was the first State Memorial. From a historical perspective too, she was an excellent choice for preservation, with her First World War service with the Grand Fleet as well as her D-Day and Pacific War credentials. The Texas Legislature established a Battleship Texas Commission on 17 April 1947 to acquire and care for the ship. They raised an initial $225,000 to pay for the towing of the ship from her reserve fleet berth at Baltimore, and for the preparation of her new home by dredging a berth off the Houston Ship Channel at the San Jacinto State Park and Battlefield memorial. This was where the Republic of Texas was born after the decisive battle for independence against Mexico on 21 April 1836. On 17 March 1948 *Texas* began the tow from Baltimore. She arrived after five agonisingly slow weeks across the Atlantic and Gulf of

Texas at San Jacinto, April 1980. *(Author's collection)*

Mexico at San Jacinto on 20 April, and was formally turned over to the State of Texas on the following day, the 112th anniversary of the battle.

Although the mission was to preserve *Texas* as a permanent memorial to Texans who served in the Second World War, the Commission seems to have struggled from the beginning to deliver on that challenge. The funding and expertise was not sufficient to conduct the preventative maintenance required for a thirty-five-year-old ship that had suffered a great deal of hard usage in the war. Cumulative neglect resulted in cracks and gaps gradually opening up in the upper decks, and water intrusion. There was also steady insidious corrosion from the seawater of the ship channel, and valves on various vents open to the sea ultimately failed, leading to flooding of various tanks and bunkers, and wider corrosion. By 1968 the original wooden planking on the upper deck had rotted so badly that rainwater was leaking through into the ship and pooling in a number of compartments. The Commission decided that replacing the wooden deck would be prohibitively expensive, so they elected to remove what remained and coat the upper deck in concrete instead. She was in this anachronistic state when I visited her in April 1980. The concrete proved a false economy, as it cracked and rainwater again began to enter she ship from above, as well as accelerating corrosion of the upper deck by keeping it permanently damp. Although three local charities had contributed $50,000 to allow the Commission

Forward 14in turrets of *Texas*, San Jacinto, April 1980. *(Author's collection)*

to sandblast and paint the hull in 1971, this work did not touch the deck or address the underwater problems.

There was growing concern about neglect and lack of funding. *Texas* was designated as a US National Historic Landmark by the National Park Service in 1977, but her management remained with the original Commission. By 1983 the concerns over the Commission's period of stewardship had crystallised and the State Legislature abolished the organisation on 31 August, transferring the ship to the care of the Texas Parks and Wildlife Department. They remained responsible for her up to August 2020, when she was passed to the care of the Battleship Texas Foundation.

The new stewards quickly realised that a full survey was needed to assess the deterioration and generate a holistic plan to save the ship. The survey revealed the ship's watertight integrity badly compromised, with the hull open to the sea in many places and the standing rainwater adding to corrosion difficulties in many other compartments. Despite the urgency of major repairs in a dry dock, it took a further five years to raise the $15 million necessary to allow this. Finally, on 13 December 1988 she was manoeuvred from the San Jacinto berth by six tugs and began the 50-mile journey to the Todd shipyard in Galveston. She immediately started taking on water, with a serious leak just forward of the engine room. Five pumps operated continuously throughout the ten-hour transit, but even with them working flat out her draft increased by 20in, representing a net ingress of around 1,500 tons of water. It was a close thing. She was moved straight into the Todd company's floating dock at half past ten that night with only 6in of clearance between the sinking keel and the blocks in the dry dock. For nineteen months until mid-1990 she underwent major reconstruction and repairs at Todd's and then at Green Bayou. This included replacement of 170 tons of rusted metal from inside the hull, including structural beams and deck plates; seal-welding of 40,000 failed or failing rivets in the underwater hull; sand-blasting and repainting of the above water hull and superstructure; and removal of the concrete deck and its replacement with a new pine deck. Finally, ten quadruple 40mm anti-aircraft gun mountings removed in 1948 were installed to give her the same appearance that she had in 1945. *Texas* was back in her berth at San Jacinto on 26 July 1990 and reopened to the public on 8 September.

The Texas Parks and Wildlife Department (TPWD) stated: 'As a one of a kind artefact from the early 20th century, Battleship Texas is priceless.'[3] But preserving her against the continuing ravages of time remains a constant and expensive struggle, and despite the big refit at Todd's the outcome is still very much in the balance. The work at Todd's could address only the most serious and immediate repairs, but on the available budget could not extend to the full requirement. As a result, as soon as she was back in the water *Texas* once again began to corrode. TPWD spent a number of years evaluating a range of options to preserve her. In 2004 a Master Plan for the San Jacinto Battleground State Historic Site was approved, which included placing *Texas* in a permanent dry berth as the only realistic way to achieve lasting preservation. Still progress remained painfully slow and it was not until November 2007 that the voters of Texas approved a State Legislature proposal to vote a further $25 million to dry berth the ship. The Battleship Texas Foundation, now managing the ship on behalf of TPWD, raised the required $4 million in matching funds by 2009, and a contract was signed for the project with AECOM on 26 October 2010. A preliminary design was completed in 2010–11. The conditions of the grant include that the ship remains open for display at the current site. In practice, given the site's environmental and historic constraints, the funding seems insufficient to provide a dry berth at San Jacinto, and the long-term solution seems to remain unresolved.

Meanwhile, *Texas* started leaking again. In June 2010 she sank 2 to 3ft at her mooring because a pump had burned out and she took on over 400 tons of water, which then had to be pumped out. Again, on 9 June 2012, the ship's hull sprang new leaks with higher water inflow than anything seen in the past fifteen years. Ingress was up to 2,000 US gallons a minute (450 tons per hour). The ship was closed for emergency repairs, consisting of temporary patching of the hull and installation of additional pumps costing $2.3 million. On 12 June 2017, a 6 × 8in hole deep below the waterline caused further major flooding and a 6 degree list, which required fifteen hours of emergency pumping to restore equilibrium. The ship continues to take on water to this day and constant pumping is required. To address the problem it will be necessary to dock the ship again. In the meantime, corrosion and deterioration continues.

The outer plating was not the only problem. In October 2012 a need was identified for urgent internal structural repairs to stabilise the ship, essential whether her future was to remain in a wet dock or longer-term preservation in a dry dock. The work, by contractors Taylor Marine Construction, began in January 2014 and was completed in December 2018 at a cost of $45 million. This project improved structural stability at the ship's stern and under the engine rooms. The two reciprocating engines, each weighing 1,100 tons, were resting on frames that were 80 to 90 per cent disintegrated. The degraded frames were cut out and replaced, or reinforced with doubler frames alongside the originals. There were insufficient funds to begin with to complete all the work identified as necessary in 2012. A second phase from summer 2015 saw Taylor Marine improving the structural integrity of the Steering Gear Room, D-13 trimming tank, Aft Emergency Diesel Generator Room, Dynamo Condenser Room and various tanks, trunks and storerooms. Once again funds were insufficient to repair her degraded structure under the boiler rooms, so the contractor instead suspended the boilers from the upper structure to alleviate some of their weight on the ship's bottom frames. Unfortunately this and other emergency work used all of the $29 million (and more) originally allocated for the dry berth project.

The Battleship Texas Foundation is alive to the challenge and further steps are in hand to fund and undertake more preservation work. In 2019 the Texas Legislature voted a grant of another $35million to dock the ship. She is now being prepared for that docking and the fraught journey she must make to reach it. This was expected to happen between April and August 2020, but its start has now been pushed back to 2022. At the end of October 2021 it was announced that *Texas* will be towed to the Gulf Copper shipyard at Galveston, Texas, who have procured a floating dock to undertake the work. The choice of site minimises the length of the tow, to just 50 miles, and ensures that it is all in sheltered waters. Work has now completed to prepare her for the voyage. Instead of patching the leaks in the hull, the blister spaces adjacent to the hull plating have been filled with hardened foam, so the compartments cannot fill with water during the voyage. This expedient has reportedly reduced the rate of flooding from 20,000 gallons a minute to just 20. The 2022 dry dock work will focus on a complete replacement of the outer skin of the hull so that leakage, for a time, comes to an end. The Foundation, which signed a ninety-nine year memorandum of understanding with TPWD in 2019 to lease, manage and maintain the ship on behalf of the State of Texas, have also made the decision that when she emerges from repair she will not go back to San Jacinto, where visitor numbers are judged insufficient to sustain her upkeep in the long term. *Texas* has been closed to visitors since early 2019. Is she facing the end of the road? At this point it is too early to say. In March 2014 she celebrated her 100th birthday. How many more?[4]

North Carolina was the next ship to be preserved when she was stricken from the reserve fleet on 1 June 1960. Whereas *Texas* was saved by the efforts of her Legislature, *North Carolina*'s journey began as a grass roots movement in 1958 when an Army veteran, James S Craig of American Legion Post 10 at Wilmington, North Carolina, read in a newspaper that she might be scrapped. A resolution to save the ship was passed by his local American Legion Chapter in 1959, and the State Governor Terry Sandford got behind the campaign by appointing Hugh Morton as chairman of a Battleship Commission. A campaign began to raise funds from citizens across the whole state. It was spectacularly successful. Contributions ranged from the $100 pledged by naval veteran, Democrat Senator, and soon to be President, John F Kennedy down to donations of just 10 cents each from the spare change and lunch money of 700,000 out of the state's 1 million public schoolchildren. The amount raised was $330,000, enough to purchase the ship from the Federal Government, tow her from her resting place at Bayonne, New Jersey, and prepare a purpose-built berth opposite Wilmington, on the other bank of the Cape Fear River. She was handed over to the North Carolina

North Carolina arrives at Wilmington, NC, to begin her life as a museum ship, September 1961. *(NHHC)*

Commission at a ceremony at Bayonne on 14 September 1961, then made the tow to Wilmington.

Unsurprisingly in view of what we have already seen by way of battleships running amok, as she was making the final turn out of the river and into her berth the tugs lost control and her stern swung towards downtown Wilmington. She collided with a floating restaurant, the Fergus Ark. It was no match for 35,000 tons of battleship and was so severely damaged it had to close permanently.

The ship was dedicated as a memorial on 29 April 1962 by Admiral Arleigh Burke, ex-Chief of Naval Operations, in the presence of Governor Sandford and thousands of dignitaries and spectators. Sandford said: 'I pledge to you today … that no stone will be left unturned to the end that this will be the greatest World War II memorial in the United States.' The memorial inscription is on a bronze plaque at the bow and reads:

> In memoriam. The USS *North Carolina* Battleship Memorial Commemorates the Heroic Participation of the Men and Women of North Carolina in the Prosecution and Victory of the Second World War and Perpetuates the Memory of the More Than Ten Thousand North Carolinians Who Gave Their Lives in That War.[5]

North Carolina has not moved from her memorial park in nearly sixty years. In the mid-1980s the ship's systems were scavenged for some spare parts to help recommission the *Iowa*-class battleships. The removal of large items such as high-pressure air compressors has left large gaps in her machinery, and turret one is described as an empty shell. In 1986 she

North Carolina berthed at Wilmington, April 1980. *(Author's collection)*

joined *Texas* as a National Historic Landmark. She has not yet faced such dire challenges in her upkeep as has *Texas*, but she has had twenty-seven years less wear and tear to contend with. Her preservation is nevertheless still a challenge. She remains in the hands of the original Battleship Commission, eighteen individuals appointed by the Governor. No local, State or Federal money is involved in her administration and operation, which is paid for mainly by the visits of over 250,000 people per year. She has benefited from generous donations for upkeep, including one that has allowed the renewal of the deck with high-quality teak from Myanmar. There is an annual inspection by Navy engineers. Around 2001 they noted damage to the starboard bow, where the shell plating had corroded at the waterline as repeated wetting then exposure to oxygen by wave action accelerates degradation of the steel. The first round of repairs in 2011 involved Taylor Brothers Marine Construction building a small mobile coffer dam, which was placed against the ship to allow flexible access to small sections of the waterline for painting and reinforcement of the ship's skin.

Similar deterioration was evident along the entire waterline, with the hull plating described in a 2016 press release as 'wafer thin'. The Commission considered options to dry dock the ship at Norfolk or Charleston to make repairs, but at $35 million that was judged too expensive. Instead, a semi-permanent solution has been adopted with the construction between 2017 and 2018 by Orion Marine Group of a full cofferdam 1,900ft long stretching around the entire ship, topped by a visitor walkway. This cost only $15 million, provided by State funds. The cofferdam weighs over 2,000 tons and has a design life of forty years. It does not provide a dry berth, but periodic draining of the water inside it to a depth of around 10ft will allow planned maintenance on and reinforcement of the entire hull around the waterline.[6] While the situation

North Carolina, April 1980. (Author's collection)

is for the present much more encouraging than that for *Texas*, the Commission have as yet identified no solution to maintenance of the deep hull, of which the bottom approximately 25ft is now buried in Cape Fear River silt. They say that corrosion there is much less severe than at the waterline, but it will still inexorably be corroding. At some point, as her 100th anniversary approaches, *North Carolina* too will probably have to face that further battle with the ravages of time. At least she survived Hurricane Florence in September 2018. Press releases in 2020 describe the awarding of a contract to Atlantic Coast Industrial Marine Construction LLC to undertake hull plating repair work at the bows and another to improve the surrounds of the site, which are regularly subject to flooding. After a year of work this task is completed and the cofferdam was flooded to river level in July 2021. In September 2020 the battleship was a central part of celebrations to mark the seventy-fifth anniversary of the end of the Second World War and the announcement of Wilmington as the first World War II Heritage City.

Massachusetts and *Alabama* were the next ships to be saved. The US Navy struck all four of the class from the Naval Register on 1 June 1962. There were no takers for *South Dakota* or *Indiana* (although extensive memorabilia from the former have been preserved in a memorial at Sioux Falls, South Dakota), but both the littoral states got behind campaigns to preserve their ships.

Alabama began to be saved over breakfast on 1 May 1962 when Jimmie Morris, an employee of the Mobile Area Chamber of Commerce Tourist and Visitors Department, read in his local paper an article about the imminent scrapping of the ship and her sisters. He persuaded Stephens Croom, chairman of the Chamber's Committee for Preservation of Historic Landmarks, to start a campaign. With the support of other Chamber of Commerce associates, they quickly contacted the State Governor John Patterson, who agreed that she should be saved as a memorial. The State Legislature was immediately petitioned and lent its support. The Governor set up a fact-finding commission to report on the feasibility of bringing the ship to Mobile's deep water port. They reckoned it was feasible. *Alabama* now benefited from the patronage of one of the more colourful and controversial figures of US politics, new State Governor George C Wallace, himself a Second World War veteran. In between promoting racial segregation, being a leading Democrat, running for President and generally stirring up controversy, one of his earliest actions as Governor was to convene a meeting of twenty-two representatives of counties in summer 1963 at Montgomery to charge them to 'bring the *Alabama* home!' Wallace signed into law Alabama Senate Bill 152 on 12 September 1963, which set up a nineteen-member Battleship Commission. It was a State agency consisting exclusively of

Alabama residents serving eight-year terms, charged with the task to acquire, transport, berth, renovate, maintain and establish *Alabama* as a memorial to all Alabamians who served in the Second World War and Korea (since extended to all conflicts of the USA). Wallace was the first chairman, and the Commission convened on 21 November 1963.

Public fund raising was the only way ahead. As in North Carolina, State school children were at the vanguard, over a million of them contributing $100,000. One of the leaders of the fundraising campaign was Frank Samford of the Liberty National Life Insurance Company, who enlisted his agents and underwriters to collect donations as they crossed the State to collect monthly insurance premiums. By spring 1964 $800,000 had been raised, enough for purchase and towing from Bremerton, Washington, and the Navy signed *Alabama* over to the Commission on 16 June 1964. One of the provisions was that the ship could be pressed back into service if needed. Although *Alabama* never moved again under her own steam, she, together with *North Carolina* and *Massachusetts*, supplied over $270 million worth of parts, mainly from their engine rooms, to allow the 1980s modernisation of the *Iowas*. *Alabama* arrived at Mobile on 14 September 1964, where some cosmetic improvements began. Over 2,000 people attended the official opening of the memorial park by Governor Wallace on 9 January 1965.

Alabama berthed at Mobile, Alabama, April 1980. *(Author's collection)*

The Commission has managed to operate self-sufficiently since its inception by charging admission to the battleship. Fifteen million visitors have so far come. Funds also come from donations and occasional borrowing. The ship was added to the National Historic Landmark register in 1986. In the early 2000s there was a major fundraising effort to restore her. A total of 2,700,000 US gallons of contaminated water was removed from the hull in 1999. In 2001 the project completed a watertight coffer dam around the ship (the precursor of the *North Carolina* project), which would allow periodic access to the underwater hull for repairs. The restoration cost $15 million. *Alabama* suffered severely during the devastating Hurricane Katrina on 29–31 August 2005. Katrina's eye passed over Gulfport, within 50 miles of the ship, and the maximum storm surge in Mobile Bay was 16ft, the highest ever recorded. The family members of eighteen Park employees were using the ship as a hurricane shelter at the time, a regular practice dating back to Hurricane Camille in 1969. *Alabama* shifted at her anchorage and listed 8 degrees to port, towards her pier. This seems to have been due mainly to shifting of the silt in which she now rests, rather than flooding inside the ship. The concrete gangways giving access to the ship snapped, and the shelterers were temporarily marooned aboard. Total damage to the Park and particularly its aircraft collection was $4 million and *Alabama* did not reopen to visitors until 9 January 2006. She has remained a popular attraction since, the last published visitor numbers being 335,717 in 2017.[7]

Massachusetts was preserved initially thanks to the efforts of a number of Navy veterans who had served aboard her during the Second World War. Fundraising again encompassed the whole State, with the school children raising $50,000 in this case. She was transferred to a Memorial Committee on 8 June 1965, towed from Norfolk, Virginia, to Battleship Cove at Fall River, Massachusetts, and set up for public display on 14 August 1965. Some 250,000 visitors came in the first year, and she was soon recognised as the official memorial to Massachusetts citizens who had given their lives in the Second World War. More than 5 million visitors have been welcomed so far, and the Battleship Cove memorial park has been steadily expanded, both in terms of permanent exhibitions and other historic ships. In common with the other 1940s-built ships, *Massachusetts* was cannibalised by the US Navy to help get the *Iowas* back into service in the early 1980s, and was designated as a National Historic Landmark on 14 January 1986. The National Register of Historic Places Inventory Nomination Form states that after she was stricken from the inactive reserve list by the US Navy in 1962 some 5,000 tons of equipment was removed for use on other naval vessels. This must be a mistake, as 5,000 tons is one seventh of the ship's entire structure – possibly a typographical error instead of a more plausible 500 tons?

In November 1998 the Commonwealth of Massachusetts awarded a $10 million grant to the ship to allow her to be dry-docked for restoration work at Boston. She was towed the 300 miles around Cape Cod between 4 and 7 November, and entered dry dock number 3 at Boston for cleaning and inspection. She was also found to be corroding along the waterline, and had leaking rivets. Two outboard propellers were removed for access to repair the stern bosses, and instead of being replaced, they were themselves polished and coated for preservation and mounted ashore to allow visitors to see them. More than 100 tons of steel plating (108 plates) was added to reinforce her hull at the waterline and 2,000 rivets were welded to their adjacent plates. A number of the riveted seams were also repaired before 10,000 sq ft of the underwater hull was coated in Red Hand Epoxy protection. A total of 3,000 gallons of paint were applied in four coats to protect against erosion, electrolysis and marine growth deterioration. The work took four months and she was then towed back to Battleship Cove, arriving on 13 March 1999 with a twenty-one-gun salute and a reception by Fall River mayor Frederick Lambert, to reopen to visitors.[8]

Massachusetts at Battleship Cove, Fall River, Massachusetts, April 1980. *(Author's collection)*

Massachusetts,
April 1980.
(Author's
collection)

Three battleships had thus joined *Texas* as State memorials by the mid-1960s, but eventual preservation of the *Iowa* would be deferred for another forty years. *Missouri* had been partially open to visitors at Bremerton, Washington, since 1955 because of her importance as the site of the Japanese surrender and welcomed about 100,000 people a year there while still firmly part of the reserve fleet. After their last reactivation, there was little question that all four ships would find safe final berths given their cultural status as technological achievements and their headline roles in United States late twentieth-century history. Ironically, there was some uncertainty over their final disposal because some in Congress still felt they should be available for active deployment, as noted above. So *New Jersey*, having been in reserve for four years, and *Wisconsin* were initially struck from the Naval Vessel Register in January 1995. But Section 1011 of the National Defense Authorisation Act of 1996 required the US Navy to reinstate two of the class to the reserve fleet for potential reactivation and use in Marine Corps amphibious operations. *New Jersey* and *Wisconsin* were selected, but the National Defense Authorisation Act of 1999 instead nominated *Wisconsin* and *Iowa*, while also directing that *New Jersey* be struck and transferred to a not-for-profit entity located in the State of New Jersey. *New Jersey* is the only one of the four to have become a State memorial, and was struck from the Naval Register for the second and final time on 4 January 1999. In September 1999 she was towed from Bremerton, Washington, making her last transit of the Panama Canal, for restoration at Philadelphia Naval Shipyard prior to her donation as a museum ship.

There were two competing bids to host her, from the USS *New Jersey* Battleship Commission of Bayonne, and the Home Port Alliance of Camden. The US Navy reviewed both plans, and Secretary of the Navy Richard Danzig selected Camden in an announcement on 20 January 2000, stating: 'Applicants, with strong support from their respective localities worked extremely hard in developing comprehensive plans to operate and maintain the museum in a manner celebrating *New Jersey*'s rich history. The patriotic expressions and grass roots campaigns, coupled with the strong support from the public, local officials and members of Congress were both gratifying and impressive.' On 15 October 2001 *New Jersey* made the shortest of final journeys across the river from Philadelphia to the Camden Waterfront. She was added to the National Register of Historic Places in 2004.

The Home Port Alliance explains that: 'The mission of the battleship *New Jersey* Museum and memorial is to restore, preserve, exhibit and interpret the history of the USS *New Jersey* and her veterans.' In January 2019 it was looking to raise funds to preserve three spare 16in gun barrels still kept at Dahlgren, Virginia, for display at the ship and at other locations in the State.[9]

Iowa is today operated by the not-for-profit Pacific Battleship Center at the Los Angeles waterfront. The State of Iowa provided $3 million to help set up the museum, otherwise all running costs are met from admission fees or donations. The mission of the Pacific Battleship Centre, which opened on 7 July 2012, is 'to celebrate the American spirit through the preservation and interpretation of the battleship *Iowa*, to educate the public on the accomplishments and sacrifices of American patriots, and to engage our guests in unique and exciting ways that bring the ship to life by connecting the past with the future'. Her journey to Los Angeles was convoluted. She had spent four years in reserve at Norfolk before being struck from the Naval Register on 1 January 1995. She was towed to Newport, Rhode Island, to be part of the Naval Education and Training Centre on 24 September 1998, and was reinstated to the reserve fleet on 1 January 1999. This role might explain the anomaly of her featuring in the Defense Appropriations Act of that year in lieu of *New Jersey*, even though her readiness for fire support missions as mandated by Congress was much less. On 8 March 2001 she was towed again from Rhode Island, making a final transit of Panama, and was laid up in Pacific Reserve Fleet at Suisun Bay, San Francisco, from 21 April, until struck again from the Naval Register in 2005.

She was allocated for donation as a museum by the Federal Government on 1 March 2006. Various bids were made by groups based at Vallejo, Stockton and San Francisco, of which Vallejo proved the most robust, but the US Navy was concerned about the environmental impact of the proposal and the dredging that would be required to get her to the proposed berth. These concerns could not be mitigated, so *Iowa* languished for a further three years until the Port of Los Angeles Harbour Commission stepped in and applied on 21 November 2010 for the ship to be berthed at Pier 87. The final application by the Pacific Battleship Center was awarded to Los Angeles on 6 September 2011. On 27 October she began a tow to Richmond, California, in San Francisco Bay for external refurbishment, where she began to accept visitors. The painting and re-stepping of the mast were complete by 30 April 2012 and a formal handover from the Navy took place. She was due to sail on 20 May, but was held up for six days by bad weather. She finally passed under the Golden Gate Bridge towed by four tugs on 26 May and anchored off Los Angeles on 30 May. There, in a sign of the times, she had to be moored to have her hull scrubbed to remove any invasive species or contaminants. She entered the harbour on 2 June and was at Pier 87 by 9 June. The formal opening was on Independence Day. The 100,000 visitor mark was passed by 1 November 2012.[10]

Missouri was the last active battleship, decommissioned for the final time on 31 March 1992. She spent some years in reserve and was finally struck from the Naval Register in 1995. For some years the USS *Missouri* Memorial Association Inc., founded in Hawaii in 1994, had been working to bring her to Pearl Harbor in Hawaii. As the ship aboard which the Japanese surrender had been signed in 1945, the Association argued that she would, symbolically and physically, complement the *Arizona* memorial that marked the start of the Pacific War in 1941. The Association's mission is to preserve the battleship *Missouri* and share her story and place in history. She was allocated to the Association in 1996 and following formal transfer of ownership on 4 May 1998, she was towed from Bremerton and arrived off Waikiki on 21 June 1998. She opened to visitors moored at Battleship Row, a few hundred yards from *Arizona*, on 29 January 1999 after six months of repair and restoration. She is easily the most popular of the memorial battleships, having hosted over 9 million visitors up to 2019. All funding is by donation and admission fees, although the Department of Defense made a grant to assist with funding the ship's dry docking in 2009. On 19 April 2017 the US Navy signed a lease agreement with the Association for *Missouri* to remain berthed at Pier Foxtrot 5 in Pearl Harbor for the next twenty-five years until 31 December 2041. She

Wisconsin preserved at Nauticus, Norfolk, Virginia, 2014. (Ann Stephenson-Wright)

has recently undergone two major repair and preservation projects for the main superstructure in 2017 and the after superstructure in 2019, the latter designed to restore her drone radome and communications antennae to reflect her appearance in 1991 at the completion of her final mission.

Wisconsin was decommissioned on 30 September 1991 and put into reserve at Philadelphia. She was stricken from the register on 12 January 1995 and moved to Norfolk Navy Yard on 15 October 1996. On 12 February 1998 the provisions of the National Defense Authorisation Act 1996 (see above) required that she be restored to the Naval Register for possible reactivation in a shore bombardment role, but even while serving as a part of the reserve fleet, she was awarded to the National Maritime Center, Nauticus, also at Norfolk, Virginia – on 17 August 1999.

The US Navy paid for the $5,800,000 cost of moving the ship from her reserve berth and dredging the channel to allow her to berth upriver at Nauticus. Some 15ft of mud had to be removed from the river bed to allow her to get there. She made the short tow to her new berth on 7 December 2000, and was initially opened to the public (weather decks only) on 16 April 2001. *Wisconsin* was struck from the Naval Register again on 17 March 2006 (along with *Iowa*), but the continuing provisions of the National Defense Authorisation Act 2006 prevented formal transfer of ownership to the City of Norfolk until 14 December 2009. A ceremony to mark this acquisition was held on 16 April 2010, and her transition to historic artefact was completed when she was listed on the National Register of Historic Places on 28 March 2012. So the last US battleship to be completed became the last to be, hopefully, permanently preserved.[1]

Wisconsin at Nauticus, 2014. *(Ann Stephenson-Wright)*

Epilogue

THE BATTLESHIP STORY after 1945 can today be told with better hindsight and longer perspective than was accessible to earlier historians and commentators. The sources show that the leading world navies were initially keen where possible, manpower and budgets allowing, to operate battleships alongside aircraft carriers. They kept a beady eye on each other's battleship holdings, and the balance of battleship power. Large, fast gun-armed ships were seen as valuable assets, particularly among the navies who expected to fight in the challenging conditions of the North Atlantic and Arctic. The United States excepted, no navies had sufficient reliable carrier-borne strike assets to guarantee the safety of their fleets, convoys and operations against large surface ships until well into the 1960s.

Additionally, the battleships were likely to be the best protected type of ship when facing the threat of tactical nuclear weapons before the widespread deployment of the hydrogen bomb in the later 1950s. The size of battleship hulls and other characteristics of protection, speed and mobility also made them the obvious choice to carry the large and unwieldy first generation of sea-based anti-ship missiles. Eventually, however, the slow pace of missile development was overtaken by the hydrogen bomb and the need to focus on invulnerability as the prime requirement for a nuclear deterrent, which led to the first generation of operational ballistic missile carriers being submarines. This left the Second World War battleships without a mission except naval gunfire support to ground forces. The battleships showed their effectiveness in this role from 1950 to 1991. And then the wheel of technology turned again to give the battleship a second lease of life via modularised box-mounted surface-to-surface and land-attack missiles.

So the story of battleships after 1945 is more complex and convoluted than often previously described. Although it can now definitely be said that the dreadnoughts of the twentieth century will not see action again, Russian vessels of the *Kirov* class still exist. New large surface combatants for superpowers cannot be ruled out, although the US Navy's programme to replace the fire support capability of the *Iowas* with the *Zumwalt* class and the Advanced Gun System also seems to have faltered, after just three of a planned thirty-two ships. Once again, a combination of size, cost and technological difficulty has derailed an ambitious programme of big ship construction.

For now the story rests with those eight United States battleships of the twentieth century that survive to give this and future generations a glimpse of past wonders. Their story is not over. The harsh realities of economics, budgets and business plans, combined with the relentless erosion by weather, salt water and time, mean that their future, although secure measured in terms of a mere few decades, might not be so in the longer term. At the time of writing these issues for *Texas* are acute and immediate. Further chapters to this story will need to be written one day.

APPENDIX

The Royal Naval Armaments Depot Priddy's Hard Gun Logs

THE BRITISH BATTLESHIPS' navigational logs in the ADM 53 series at the National Archives, Kew, where they exist, seem to provide a pretty accurate record of when gunnery practice took place, if rarely showing exactly how many rounds were fired. The Royal Naval Armament Depot Priddy's Hard Gun Logs, all now held at Hampshire County Archives, Winchester, provide an additional insight into the management of battleship main armament before, during and in many cases well after the lives of the ships in which the guns were mounted. These logs record the service histories of each individual gun built for the Admiralty from about 1900. GL2 covers the 16in 45 calibre Mark 1 mounted on *Nelson* and *Rodney*. GL3 covers the 15in Mark 1 mounted on the *Queen Elizabeth* class, the *Revenge* class, *Renown* and *Vanguard*, and GL3 the 14in mark 7 mounted on the *King George V* class.

The logs record the life history of each gun, showing when and on which ship it was mounted, often for these large calibres in which turret and position, and how many effective full charges (efc) the gun had fired between periodic inspections for wear of the rifling, which was recorded at three points along each barrel to the nearest 1,000th of an inch. This led to the calculation of a 'Probable Remaining Life' (PRL) measured in efc, before the wear on the gun's rifling would become so severe that accuracy would suffer and the gun would need replacing and relining if it was to continue in service. An effective full charge was the full amount of explosive cordite propellant designed to throw the shell to maximum range, for these big guns about 400lb of cordite. During gunnery practice often only three-quarter or half charges of cordite were used to reduce wear on the barrel. A three-quarter charge caused only one quarter of the rifling wear of a full charge, and a half charge only one sixteenth of the wear. The cumulative number of full, three-quarter and half charge firings by each gun is therefore often expressed in sixteenths of an efc. The gun logs also record which spare or proof guns were kept ashore, where, and usually when the guns were finally scrapped.

Before the Second World War the gun logs for these large-calibre weapons are a very thorough record. They often record separately the number of full, three-quarter and half charges fired, and inspections are taking place for every battleship main armament gun every one to two years or so. The frequency of inspections drops off during the war, and post-war inspections are not as systematic as previously. The last inspection recorded in the logs is not necessarily an indication of when the gun was last fired, but it is suggestive of the Admiralty's expectation about whether the gun would need to be used again or require relining. The number of efc that could be expected of the guns varied from type to type, but was expected to be 270 efc for the 16in and 320–350 efc for the 15in. In practice no guns ever became completely worn out, even during the war. The logs show them being replaced and relined usually between 160 and 200 efc.

For the 16in Mark 1 there is no evidence for inspection of the guns in *Rodney* after the war. Two of *Nelson*'s, barrels S13 and S17, were inspected on 28 December 1945, the day before she deployed to Portland as flagship of the Home Fleet. PRL was estimated at 240 efc, only 27 and 17 2/16th efc respectively having been fired by them up to that point. There is no evidence from the ship's log that these guns were fired after the end of the war, although *Nelson* remained fully ammunitioned throughout 1946 and 1947, both as flagship of the Home Fleet and in the Training Squadron. Eighteen of these guns were scrapped with the ships in 1948–49. The sawn-off barrels are a very distinctive feature of the photographs of *Rodney* and *Nelson* taken by Thomas W Ward in 1948–49 at their scrapyard at Inverkeithing. The final spare 16in gun did not leave the armament depot at Crombie until 30 September 1950.

The 15in gun was the one most widely mounted in British battleships in the Second World War, and was also carried on big-gun monitors. Of 184 of these guns constructed before and during the First World War, 137 still existed on 1 September 1945. Most of these had been scrapped with the ships they were mounted on by 11 March 1951, when only *Vanguard*, the monitor *Roberts* and forty-four guns remained. Apart from the guns on *Vanguard*, the only (inconclusive) evidence in the gun logs for post-war 15in firings, is for *Queen Elizabeth* firing 8 efcs per gun at some point between 20 May 1945 and her last inspection on 11 September 1945. The ship's log for the period thereafter suggests it is very unlikely she fired again. *Vanguard* had five 15in gun inspections in her career: on 2 July 1946 after her work-up programme, 4 November 1949 after the intensive firing practices in the Mediterranean (Chapter Six), 16 January 1953 (X and Y turret guns only), 15 May 1953 (A and B turret guns only) and 24 December 1954 (A and B only). From these we can infer that each gun fired between 12 and 20 efc during her working up and trials. Only between 5 and 7 efcs per gun were fired between mid-1946 and the end of 1949, suggesting that much of the firing in the Mediterranean was at reduced charge, Only A and B turrets were fired thereafter, expending between a further 19 and 26 efc per gun up to the final inspection in

December 1954. This evidence reflects both the difficulty in manning her to full effectiveness, but also the determination to train her, exercise her and use her as a functioning battleship up to the refit in 1954. However, the averaged frequency of her firings, some 20–30 efc over a period of eight years of active life, was only around a third of the 70–80 efc typically fired by British battleships in peacetime over similar periods in the inter-war years.

GL 77 covers the 5.25in guns that were the secondary armament for *Vanguard* and the *King George Vs*. It shows *Vanguard*'s 5.25in guns fired between 5 and up to 102 efc between completion of her trials and their final inspections, which were all in 1949. The propensity to use only the forward 5.25in turrets for practice is very marked. Between 24 January and 4 September 1949 gun number 362 in S1 turret fired 70 efc, gun number 384 in S2 turret 73, and the guns in S3 and S4 only 5 efc at most.

The gun logs also show that the UK maintained an international infrastructure of ordnance stores to support battleship operations through to the late 1950s. The 15in production gun number 43, kept for proof firings at the ordnance depot at Shoeburyness, was still firing on 17 March 1949, by which stage it had reached a staggering 810 efc. The two trial guns, E596 and E597, also kept at Shoeburyness had also well exceeded the design life expectation, having fired an 417 efc over a life of thirty-eight years up to 1951, and were still reckoned to have a PRL of 100 efc. Two guns remained at Shoeburyness in Army service until the mid-1960s, and were eventually rescued to be preserved at the Imperial War Museum in Lambeth. There were spare 15in guns kept at Singapore, Sydney and Durban until 1951, and Malta, where *Vanguard* was deployed in 1949, until at least 1954. Guns numbers 148 and 165 had been captured intact by the Japanese at Singapore in February 1942. After their recapture in 1945, they were initially written off as unserviceable in 1947, but were eventually repaired in 1948 as 'decided gun now worthwhile repairing since reserve 15in will be wanted at Singapore, and it will be cheaper to repair this one than move it'.[1] There was still a full 14in outfit of ten spare guns for the *King George Vs* at Sydney until mid-1957, eighteen months after the ships went into extended reserve and after the decision to scrap them had been taken, and one gun lingered on there until February 1958.

GL4 covering the 14in guns is generally less thorough than the records made before the war. Absence of evidence is not conclusive, but when cross-referenced to the ships' logs it might give a fair indication of how often the main armaments were fired. The parallel evidence for *Vanguard*, and from GL 77 for the 5.25in secondary armament guns mounted on all these ships, and on *Dido*-class cruisers, show regular records for individual guns being maintained at Priddy's Hard until the 1950s, so it is likely that the 14in records are as thorough. There is no record of inspection for *Howe*'s guns after 23 August 1945 or *Anson*'s after 11 August 1945, at which points they had fired around 75 efc during the Second World War. This chimes with the other evidence that, as training battleships after 1946, they were de-ammunitioned and, apart from *Anson*'s brief A turret firing at Hong Kong in November 1945 (Chapter Two) probably did not fire their 14in battery at all after the war. GL77 for 5.25in guns suggests that they might have fired a few 5.25in rounds after September 1945, but this evidence is not conclusive.

King George V fired only 5 efc per 14in gun from 11 October 1945 until inspection at Devonport on 3 November 1947, probably during her passage home in the South Atlantic in February 1946, and she was not inspected thereafter. A few of her 5.25in guns, however, recorded between 33 and 90 efc firings after the war. *Duke of York*, serving with the Home Fleet for much of this period, was more active, firing three 14in efc per gun from Y turret, and between 2 and 8 per gun from A turret, from late 1945 to 3 November 1949. B turret was used much more frequently (maybe because as a twin mounting it required a smaller crew than the quadruple A and Y turrets), and, for example, the ship's log mentions firings from it in the English Channel on 6 and 15 October 1947. B turret's two guns, numbers 108 and 116, recorded 27 and 19 efc respectively between late 1945 and inspection on 10 March 1948. Although the ship's logs for later in 1948 and 1949 seem to be missing, GL4 indicates that a further 11 efc were fired from both of the B turret guns between March 1948 and the final inspection on 28 September 1949 while she was flagship of the Home Fleet. Most of the 5.25in guns aboard *Duke of York* fired between 50 and 90 efcs after the war. On 17 April 1947 the barrel on gun number 340 had to be replaced after a projectile seized in the bore, and gun number 347 was condemned after a premature explosion on 27 November 1946.

Taken together, the evidence of the ships' logs and the gun logs confirms that while six British battleships remained active for prolonged spells in the late 1940s, and one well into the 1950s, firings of their principal armaments were much rarer than for battleships before the war, and almost all firing was by *Duke of York* and *Vanguard*, the two most active ships. Even in them, manning and maintenance difficulties were reflected in a propensity to concentrate firings from a small proportion of the armament. But, reflecting their anticipated war role, significant efforts were made to keep these battleships effective, and the infrastructure to support battleship ordnance endured at least as long as the ships themselves.

Bibliography

Abbey, Lester, *The Iowa Class*, Seaforth, 2012.

Bosi, Rumen, *The End of the War*, Marshall Cavendish, 2005.

Brescia, Maurizio, *Mussolini's Navy*, Naval Institute Press Annapolis, 2012.

Breyer, Siegfried, *Battleships and Battlecruisers 1905–1970*, MacDonald and Jane's, 1973.

Brown, David K, *Nelson to Vanguard*, Chatham Publishing, 2000.

Brown, David K and Moore, George, *Rebuilding the Royal Navy*, Seaforth, 2012.

Burr, Lawrence, *US Fast Battleships 1938–1991: The Iowa Class*, Osprey, 2010.

Burt, R A, *French Battleships 1876–1946*, Arms and Armour Press, 1990.

Burt, R A, *British Battleships of World War Two*, Seaforth, 1993.

Burt, R A, *The Last British Battleship: HMS Vanguard 1945–1960*, Seaforth, 2019.

Buxton, Ian, *Shipbreaking at Faslane*, World Ship Society, 2020.

Caresse, Philippe, *The Battleships of the Iowa Class*, Naval Institute Press Annapolis, 2019.

Delgado, James P, *The Archaeology of the Atomic Bomb*, Santa Fe, New Mexico, 1991.

Dumas, Robert, *Le Cuirasse Richelieu*, Nantes Marine Edition, 2001.

Field, James A, *History of US Naval Operations in Korea*, Washington, Department of the Navy, 1962.

Gardiner, Robert (Ed), *The Eclipse of the Big Gun*, Conway Maritime Press, 1992.

Garzke, William H and Dulin, Robert O, *Axis and Neutral Battleships of World War Two*, Jane's, 1985.

Garzke, William H and Dulin, Robert O, *United States Battleships of World War Two*, MacDonald and Jane's, 1976.

Garzke, William H and Dulin, Robert O, *British, French, Soviet and Dutch Battleships of World War Two*, Jane's, 1980.

Groner, Erich, *German Warships 1815–1945 Vol. 1 Major Surface Vessels*, Naval Institute Press Annapolis, 1990.

Grove, Eric, *Vanguard to Trident*, Bodley Head, 1987.

Hamer, David, *Bomber Versus Battleship*, Conway Maritime Press, 1998.

Hough, Richard, *Dreadnought*, Patrick Stephen Ltd, 1975.

Jane's Fighting Ships, 1953/4, 1954/5, 1955/6, 1956/7, 1957/8, 1958/9 and 1971/72 editions.

Johnston, I and Buxton, I, *The Battleship Builders*, Seaforth, 2013.

Jordan, J and Dumas, R, *French Battleships 1922–1956*, Seaforth, 2020.

Marr, David G, *Vietnam: State, War and Revolution 1945–1946*, University of California Press, 2013.

McLaughlin, Stephen, *Russian and Soviet Battleships*, Naval Institute Press Annapolis, 2003.

Melson, P J (Ed), *White Ensign Red Dragon*, Edinburgh Financial Publishing (Asia) Ltd, 1997.

Middlebrook and Mahoney, *Battleship*, Penguin, 1977.

Muir, Malcolm, *The Iowa Class Battleships*, Blandford Press, 1987.

Padfield, Peter, *The Battleship Era*, Pan Books, 1972.

Parkes, Oscar, *British Battleships*, Seeley Service, 1957.

Prager, Hans Georg, *Panzerschiff Deutschland, Schwerer Kreuzer Lützow*, Koehler, Hamburg, 2002.

Raven, A and Roberts, J, *British Battleships of World War Two*, Arms and Armour Press, 1976.

Rowher, Jurgen and Monakov, Mikhail S, *Stalin's Ocean Going Fleet*, Frank Cass, 2001.

Shurcliff, W A, *Bombs at Bikini*, William H Wise & Co., New York, 1947.

Silverstone, Paul, *US Warships of World War II*, Ian Allan, London, 1965.

Simpson, Michael, *A Life of Admiral of the Fleet Sir Andrew Cunningham*, Frank Cass, 2004.

Smith, Peter C, *The Great Ships Pass*, William Kimber, 1977.

Smith, Peter C, *Battleship Royal Sovereign and Her Sister Ships*, William Kimber, 1988.

Strauss, Lewis, *Men and Decisions*, Doubleday, Garden City, New York, 1962.

Sumrall, Robert F, *Iowa Class Battleships*, Conway Maritime Press, 1988.

Tarrant, Victor, *Battleship Warspite*, Arms and Armour Press, 1990.

Taylor, Bruce, *The World of the Battleship*, Seaforth, 2018.

Tucker, Spencer, *The Encyclopaedia of the Vietnam War*, Santa Barbara, California, 2011.

Whitley, M J, *Battleships of World War Two*, Cassell, 1998

Sources and Notes

Chapter One: 2 September 1945

1 Named after HMS *Dreadnought*, completed in 1906, the first battleship to establish the pattern of all-big gun armament instead of a mixture of calibres.

2 See Malcolm Muir Junior, the *Iowa Class Battleships*, Blandford Press, 1987.

3 Details of timings and a list of officers present from *Missouri*'s deck log for 2 September 1945, RG24, US National Archives, accessed online.

4 The details in this section are drawn from a wide variety of published sources that are referenced later on in more specific contexts. The US Navy details come from the Dictionary of American Naval Fighting Ships available online from the US Navy History and Heritage Command at history.navy.mil. The Royal Navy details are supplemented by reference to the ship's logs held at the National Archives, Kew.

5 Admiral Sir Bruce Fraser was aboard observing these operations and escaped with his life but the *New Mexico*'s Captain Robert Fleming, and Lieutenant General Sir Herbert Lumsden, Senior British Liaison Officer with General MacArthur's command, died, along with twenty-eight others. Lumsden was the most senior British military fatality of the war.

6 Tarrant, Victor, *Battleship Warspite*, Arms and Armour Press, 1990.

7 R A Burt, *British Battleships of World War Two*, Seaforth Publishing, 1993.

8 'Modern' I define as meaning laid down after the London Naval Treaty of 1930.

9 Johnston and Buxton, *The Battleship Builders*, Seaforth Maritime Press, 2013.

10 Siegfried Breyer, *Battleships and Battlecruisers 1905–1970*, MacDonald and Jane's, 1973.

11 John Jordan and Robert Dumas, *French Battleships 1922–1956*, Seaforth Publishing, 2020.

12 One of the unexploded bombs was discovered in the canal in 2020 and detonated by Polish ordnance disposal teams.

13 Breyer, op cit, says until at least 1965, and Erich Groner, *German Warships 1815–1945 Vol. 1 Major Surface Vessels*, Annapolis: Naval Institute Press published in 1990, says she was still visible then.

Chapter Two: Still Work to do

1 Fraser's despatch is in the National Archives at ADM 199/1478. All ADM references are from the UK National Archives at Kew.

2 See *Idaho*'s deck logs, September, October 1945, RG24 US National Archives.

3 Details from *Missouri*'s September 1945 deck log, RG24, US National Archives.

4 Muir, op cit.

5 *Pennsylvania* deck logs for September, October 1945, in RG 24, US National Archives.

6 See Rumen Bosi, *The End of the War – Singapore's Liberation and the Aftermath of the Second World War*, Marshall Cavendish, 2005.

7 Details from *Nelson*'s ship's logs, ADM 53/121889–121193.

8 Details from ADM 53/121508–121512.

9 The Priddy's Hard Gun Logs (see Appendix) record that the wear on the guns was measured at Sydney on 11 October 1945, and that she fired between 5 and 9 effective full charges between that date and the next measurement on 3 November 1947.

10 ADM136/31 and ADM 53/121606–121610.

11 *King George V* ship's log, ADM 53/123067.

12 Naval History Net.com, normally a good source for Royal Navy casualties, is therefore probably wrong when it says that this happened during a storm and that May was in charge of a working party securing the anchor chains on the fo'c'sle during heavy weather when the group was swept overboard by a heavy sea. 'All the other men were recovered, but Lt Cdr May could not be found.' Naval History Net.com, accessed 9/1/19.

13 Details from ship's book, ADM 136/33 at National Archives.

14 For more detail of the liberation see *White Ensign Red Dragon*, edited by Commodore P J Melson, CBE RN, Edinburgh Financial Publishing (Asia) Ltd, 1997.

15 Details of *Anson*'s time in the Far East from her ship's log, ADM 53/120839–120843 and ADM 53/122588–122599 and her ship's book, ADM 136/32.

16 John Jordan and Robert Dumas, op cit.

17 L'histoire du Richelieu, netmarine.net accessed 28/11/18.

18 Sources disagree about the details of her involvement. Garzke and Dulin (*British, French, Soviet and Dutch Battleships of World War Two*, Jane's, 1980) say that the landing and bombardment were on 17 November 1945, and that only the 100mm and 152mm battery was used. Netmarine.net says she fired again on 2 December, expending a further 400 152mm and 1,200 100mm rounds. Jordan and Dumas, op cit, say that a total of 391 rounds of 152mm and 1,622 of 100mm were fired at Na Trang between 20 and 26 November.

19 For more general background and Richelieu's involvement see also *Vietnam: State War and Revolution 1945–1946*, by David G Marr, University of California Press, 2013, and *The Encyclopaedia of the Vietnam War* by Spencer Tucker, Santa Barbara, California, 2011.

Chapter Three: Post-War Planning and the Battleship

1 This section draws on an unpublished paper 'Post-war Naval Force Reductions 1945–1950: Impact on the Next War' by Commander George T Hodermarsky USN, Advanced Research Programme, US Naval War College, Newport, R I, June 1990, accessed on internet via dtic.mil. on 1 October 2018.
2 See Congressional record et seq, 18 August 1945, p 1207.
3 See wwiiafterwwii.worldpress.com, accessed 26/11/18.
4 USS *Tennessee* deck logs September 1946–December 1946, RG24, US National Archives.
5 ADM167/121, a memorandum noted by the Admiralty Board on the Empire's post-war fleet dated 15 May 1944.
6 WP 44/764 dated 29 December 1944, in ADM 205/53 21/45.
7 D K Brown, *Nelson to Vanguard*, Chatham Publishing, 2000, p 37, extracts from Sir Stanley Goodall's diaries where the Director of Naval Construction bemoans what he saw as the conservative thinking at the top of the Admiralty.
8 CP(45)57 in CAB 66/67 at the National Archives.
9 See ADM 205/53.
10 See ADM 205/53 1st Sea Lord docket 21/45 Planning for The Post War Fleet.
11 DFSL 10027/51 on ADM 205/53 ISL docket 21/45.
12 The papers are in ADM 1/16670.
13 ADM 116/5864, Future policy for Obsolete Warships, Memorandum DO(45)22, taken at DO(45)11th meeting 29/10/45.
14 See ADM 1/18659.
15 See ADM 1/17251.
16 M324/5 dated 9 April 1945 in PREM 32/7, National Archives.
17 See CP(45)54 'The New Construction programme 1945' in CAB 66/67 at the National Archives.
18 See ADM 116/5864 and ADM 167/124.
19 CAB 129/4/41 at National Archives.
20 The notes of the Sea Lords meeting are on ADM 205/64.
21 PD 061/46 dated 16 December 1946 on ADM 1/20906.
22 PD/OL 0204/45 (revised 12/9/46), which reiterated that PD 0140/45 (see above) remained the basis for planning the post-war fleet.
23 David K Brown and George Moore, *Rebuilding the Royal Navy: Warship Design Since 1945*, Seaforth Publishing, 2012.
24 ADM1/20970, and also 'Penultimate Battleships: The Lion class 1937–1946' in *Warships*, Vol. V, Ed John Roberts, Conway Maritime Press 1981.
25 DO(46)20 dated 13 February 1946 in CAB 131/2 and DO(46) 5th meeting 15 February 1946 minutes in CAB 131/1, National Archives.
26 DO(46)135 dated 8 November 1946, paragraph 17, in CAB 131/3, National Archives.
27 See papers on ADM 205/66 and 205/69.
28 ADM1/25853, which includes the Ordnance Board summary report of the trials, APP Special Serial 30 dated 13 March 1948.
29 Étude sur la reconstitution organique et technique des forces aero-navale françaises, May 1945, held at Service Historique de la Defense, Chatellerault, ref 3BB8/CSM, referenced by Philippe Querel in L'Echec du PA-28, Premier Porte-Avions Français de L'après Guerre, at www.stratisc.org, 2005, accessed 18/1/21.
30 Étude d'un plan d'armament pour les premier années d'après guerre, 1 January 1946, referenced by Querel, op cit.
31 'Memoire au sujet de programme navale, 2 juin 1949', Archives Ramadier carton 52J83, referenced by Querel, op cit.

Chapter Four: Bikini Atoll

1 Lewis Strauss, *Men and Decisions*, Doubleday, Garden City New York, 1962.
2 Quoted in the report of the UK Joint Services Team despatched to observe the tests, ADM 234/584 dated 10 October 1946.
3 ADM 234/584.
4 See papers on ADM 1/17259.
5 This and other details from the official public United States report 'Bombs at Bikini' by W A Shurcliff, William H Wise and Co., New York, 1947.
6 James P Delgado, *The Archaeology of the Atomic Bomb*, Santa Fe New Mexico, 1991, and CAB122/375 at National Archives.
7 Deck log of USS *Pennsylvania* BB-38, January to May 1946 in RG 24, US National Archives.
8 Deck Log of USS *Pennsylvania*, June 1946.
9 Sources differ slightly as to distances. These are the ones recorded by the UK eyewitnesses in ADM 234/584, which ought to be authoritative.
9 ADM 234/584, op cit.
10 *Bulletin of Atomic Scientists*, Vol. 1 No. 5, 15 February 1946.
11 Deck Log USS *Pennsylvania*, July 1946.
12 See James P Delgado, op cit, for details and pictures of all the wrecks.
13 USS *Pennsylvania* deck Log, August 1946.
14 Ibid.
15 Papers on CAB 122/375 in the National Archives.
16 Exercise Trident papers are ADM 239/489.

Chapter Five: Thinning the Ranks

1 See the paper prepared for Lord Hall dated 31/12/1947 on ADM 205/69.
2 Bob Hackett and Sander Kingsepp, combinedfleet.com, accessed 21/2/20.
3 See website bcofremembered.com, accessed 2/12/2020.
4 Whitley M J, *Battleships of World War II*, Annapolis, Naval Institute Press, 1998.
5 Hans Georg Prager, *Panzerschiff Deutschland, Schwerer Kreuzer Lützow*, Koehler, Hamburg, 2002.
6 See website wrecksite.eu, accessed 21/2/20.
7 Groner, and Garzke & Dulin, *Axis and Neutral Battleships of World War Two*, Jane's, 1985.
8 Maurizio Brescia, *Mussolini's Navy*, Naval Institute Press, Annapolis, Maryland, 2012.
9 Whitley, op cit.

10 For more details see Aidan Dodson, 'Derfflinger: An Inverted Life' in Warship Notes, *Warship 2016*, Bloomsbury Publishing, pp 175–8, and Ian Buxton, *Shipbreaking at Faslane*, World Ship Society, 2020.

11 Memorandum DO(45)22 taken at DO(45)11th meeting, 29 October 1945, on ADM 116/5864.

12 Hansard, House of Lords Debates 29 January 1947, Vol. 145, Column 281.

13 Hansard, House of Lords Debates 8 March 1948, Vol. 154, Column 510–511.

14 See ADM 1/18014.

15 Hansard, House of Commons Debates Vol. 432, column 189W.

16 Tarrant, op cit.

17 Burt, op cit; Buxton, *Shipbreaking at Faslane*, op cit.

18 See the catalogue description of the records of the HMS *Warspite* Project, National Archives Reference 1000/1/3/4, held at Walsall Archives.

19 Details of the drafts and dates of ships demolished at Troon from clydemaritime.co.uk/troonlistings, accessed 23/2/20.

20 HMS *Ramillies* Association Website, accessed 17/4/2019.

21 Website lepetitbedouin.blogspot.com, accessed 24/2/20.

22 According to Jean Meirat, *FPDS Newsletter*, Akron, Ohio, Vol. VI, pp 5–6. But R A Burt (*French Battleships 1876–1946*, Arms and Armour Press, 1990) says that she was not scrapped until 1959 'long after 90 percent of all dreadnoughts had vanished from the oceans'. French online sources refer to sale for scrapping in December 1945.

23 Don Gammill, NewsOK.com, Archive ID 487006, accessed 13/3/18.

24 USS *Idaho* deck logs, June, July 1946, in RG24 at US National Archives.

25 *Dictionary of American Naval Fighting Ships*, USS *New Mexico*; and ww2db.com, accessed 24/6/21.

Chapter Six: Peacetime in the Royal Navy

1 *Queen Elizabeth* details from ADM 136/10 and ADM53/122075 and ADM53/123350–123359.

2 See Syfret's opinions on ADM 1/19368.

3 See ADM 1/19658 for details of these exercises.

4 The report on this visit is at ADM 1/19525.

5 *King George V*'s log, ADM 53/124007.

6 Necessary to ensure that the ship's magnetic signature was cancelled out by the electric current run through her degaussing cable, as a defence against the magnetic mine.

7 Ship's log, ADM 53/124843 to 124851 (although *King George V*'s logs for October to December 1948 are missing from the series at the National Archive).

8 See ADM 1/19225 for the establishment of the Rear Admiral Training Battleships.

9 *Nelson*'s log, ADM 53/123188–199.

10 *Howe*'s log for this day is in ADM 53/123925. *Duke of York*'s is ADM 53/123834, and the Home Fleet Orders are on ADM 1/20606.

11 Authorised complements for *Howe* are in the ship's book, ADM 136/31.

12 *Howe*'s logs for 1946, ADM 53/122988–122999.

13 Correspondence on ADM 1/21473.

14 *Anson*, ship's log, ADM 53/123710.

15 *Vanguard* ship's book, ADM 136/47 The ship's books, for example ADM 136/131 show that similar restrictions had to be placed on the *King George V* class in November 1947. They too had accumulated weight steadily through the war, and were restricted to a mean draught of 34ft 8in.

16 *Vanguard* ship's log for April 1946, ADM 53/123577.

17 See ADM 53/123578 and Commemorative Brochure produced for 1947 Royal Tour, reproduced on maritimequest.com, accessed 2/1/2019.

18 R A Burt, *The Last British Battleship, HMS Vanguard 1946–1960*, Seaforth Publishing, 2019, p 46.

19 Priddy's Hard Gun Log 4 held at the Hampshire County Archives, Winchester. For more detail on the Royal Naval Armaments Depot Priddy's Hard gun logs and the light they shed on battleship history see Appendix One.

20 *Vanguard*'s log, ADM 53/123578 and 53/123579, plus ship's book, ADM 136/47 and Alan Raven and John Roberts, *British Battleships of World War Two*, Arms and Armour Press, 1976.

21 See maritimequest.com, accessed 2/1/2019.

22 ADM 136/47.

23 ADM 1/20593.

24 *Vanguard* logs January to May 1947, ADM 53/124379–124384.

25 ADM 205/67.

26 The report is on ADM 205/67.

27 The Commander-in-Chief's report of proceedings is on ADM 1/20747, 1947 summer cruise to Scandinavia.

28 *Duke of York*'s logs for this period are at ADM 53/123834–123838.

29 See ADM 116/5601 for the papers on the Clyde Review plans.

30 See papers on ADM 205/69.

31 See the ship's book, ADM 136/33.

32 ADM 136/33.

33 ADM 205/69.

34 The *report* on Exercise Sunrise and analysis by C-in-C Home Fleet is on ADM 116/5779 and ADM 116/5780.

35 ADM 136/34.

36 ADM 136/32.

37 These details from Raymond Forward, Hearts of Oak, on freepages.rootsweb.com accessed 2/1/20.

38 Details from the Exercise Verity Joint report by AOCinC Coastal Command, CinC Home Fleet and CinC Portsmouth dated 27 July 1949 in AIR 20/6788 in the National Archives.

39 ADM136/47.

40 *Vanguard*'s log, ADM 53/125255.

41 Ship's log, ADM 53/127179.

42 These details from *Vanguard*'s ship's book, ADM 136/47 and ship's log for 1949 ADM 53/127179–127189.

Chapter Seven: Peacetime for the United States and France

1 Details for *Mississippi* from the *Directory of American Naval Fighting Ships*.
2 Malcolm Muir, op cit.
3 Malcolm Muir, ibid.
4 Detail from Muir, ibid.
5 Details of movements from USS *Missouri* ship's log, RG24, US National Archives.
6 Muir, op cit.
7 Muir, ibid.
8 For details see the report on the incident, Nav Ships 250-694-3 dated 1 June 1950, quoted in Whitley, op cit; and Muir, op cit.
9 Garzke and Dulin, *British, Soviet, French and Dutch Battleships of World War Two*, Jane's, 1980. More recent sources, Querel and Jordan/Dumas, do not mention such a possibility.
10 Jordan and Dumas, op cit.
11 Jordan and Dumas, op cit.
12 Étude sur le programme d'aviation navale, État Major general de la Defence nationale, 20/6/45, referenced by Querel, op cit.
13 SHM 3BB/CSM Note 45 386 CAN/O dated 2/10/45 referenced by Querel, op cit.
14 Querel, op cit.
15 Garzke and Dulin, *British, French, Soviet and Dutch Battleships*, op cit.
16 The main sources for the story of *Jean Bart* are the monograph produced by Service Historique de la Defense, Centre des Archives de l'armament et du personnel, Serie 51, Chatellerault 2017, and Jordan and Dumas, op cit. There is some confusion about dates in 1949 and 1950, but it seems clear that she experienced quite a long quiescence in 1949–50.
17 Querel, op cit.

Chapter Eight: Cuts to the Royal Navy

1 Admiralty Board memoranda dated 26/7/47 and 28/7/47 on ADM 167/129.
2 Admiralty Board minutes 31st July 1947, item 4171, on ADM 167/128.
3 In ADM 1/16670.
4 The 1948 scrapping announcement source is mainly PREM 8/896, National Archive.
5 In the end they actually got £169 million for 1948–49, but it was a real terms reduction of nearly 20 per cent from the previous year, and the nadir of post-war Royal Navy expenditure. See Eric Grove, *Vanguard to Trident*, Bodley Head, 1987, Appendix 5.
6 ADM205/66.
7 DO(47)27th meeting, 19 December 1947 in CAB 131/5 at National Archives.
8 HC Debates 21 January 1948 Vol. 446 Col. 211–215.
9 See ADM 1/14983, PM memo dated 2 October 1943.
10 ADM116/5211.
11 CP(45)74 in CAB 66/67, National Archives.
12 Letter in ADM 205/66.

13 Arrigo Velicogna in *The World of the Battleship*, ed Bruce Taylor, Seaforth, 2018.
14 171555/Sept dated 17 September 1947 on ADM 205/68, plus unreferenced briefing note.
15 These papers are in PREM 8/593 at National Archives.
16 EPC(47)3rd meeting.
17 Velicogna, op cit
18 US Department of State, Office of the Historian, Foreign Relations of the US 1948, Western Europe Vol. III, documents 611–629, accessed online at history.state.gov 3/11/21.
19 Peter C Smith, *The Great Ships Pass*, William Kimber, London 1977.
20 Troon listings op cit.
21 *Valiant*'s logs, ADM 53/123573-6.
22 See ADM 1/18014, ADM 1/18650 and ADM 280/843.
23 Although the record in the National Archive (ADM 280/412, Report by Naval Construction Research Establishment Rosyth dated 1st October 1951) rather more mundanely names it Ship Target Trial 2H.
24 Burt R A, *British Battleships 1919–1939*, op cit.
25 Burt, ibid.
26 shipsnostalgia.com, accessed 23/7/2018.
27 History.state.gov, op cit.
28 HL Deb Vol. 161 Col. 211–17.
29 Peter C Smith, *Battleship Royal Sovereign and her Sister Ships*, William Kimber, 1988, p 187.
30 Maritime Intelligence Report No. 32 quoted in 'The Royal Navy and Soviet Seapower 1930–1950', Joseph Francis Ryan D Phil thesis, January 1996, accessed via core.ac.uk on 29/4/21.
31 'Husband on the Jodrell Bank Telescope', paper No. 6270 The Jodrell bank Radio Telescope by Henry Charles Husband B Eng, MICE, MI Eng, 1958, available online at civil.dept.shef.ac.uk accessed 14/11//2020.
32 DO(49)48, Summary of the Harwood Report in DEFE 7/592 at the National Archive.
33 See Harwood papers on ADM 205/83.
34 The Exercise Trident scenarios are on ADM 239/489.
35 Transcript on ADM 205/72.
36 PDR 51/107 on ADM 205/83.
37 See DO(49)51 on DEFE 7/592.
38 Minutes of DO(49) 19th, 20th, 21st and 22nd meetings on CAB131/8, National Archives.
39 See D.O.(49)43 in PREM 8/1245 at National Archive.
40 See scheme of complement dated 21/4/49 in ADM 136/31.
41 Papers in ADM 1/21477.
42 See ADM 205/74.
43 The First Lord's 7 February note is on ADM 205/74.

Chapter Nine: Stalin's Oceanic Navy: Soviet Battleship Ambitions

1 Stephen McLaughlin, *Russian and Soviet Battleships*, Naval Institute Press, Annapolis, 2003.

2 For the evolution of Soviet plans see Jurgen Rowher and Mikhail S Monakov, *Stalin's Ocean Going Fleet*, Frank Cass, 2001, and McLaughlin, op cit.
3 Garzke and Dulin, *British, French, Soviet and Dutch Battleships of World War Two*, op cit.
4 Rowher and Monakov, op cit.
5 See list in Chapter Two, although Robert F Sumrall estimates two ships as up to 75 per cent complete by the time work stopped. *The Eclipse of the Big Gun*, Conway Maritime Press History of the Ship series, 1992.
6 Sumrall, op cit, suggests they may have been as much as 50 per cent complete.
7 McLaughlin, op cit.
8 McLaughlin, ibid.
9 McLaughlin, ibid.
10 Garzke and Dulin, op cit, quote the naval attaché evidence.
11 Breyer, op cit.
12 Breyer ibid, who was researching before 1973 and calls this the *Tretij Internationale* class and attributes other possible names to the ships. He does not mention the Molotovsk facility or the second two *Sovietskii Soyuz* ships.
13 McLaughlin, op cit.
14 Calibre is the measure of the length of a gun in relation to its bore – so a 61-calibre 12in gun would be 61ft long.
15 Stephen McLaughlin, 'Project 82: The Stalingrad Class', in *Warship 2006* (Ed John Jordan), Conway Press.
16 JI(946)1(O) Final in CAB 81/132, quoted by Ryan, op cit.
17 March 1946 Monthly Intelligence Report, cited by Ryan, op cit.
18 JIC(46)96(O) dated 29 October 1946 in CAB 81/134, quoted by Ryan, op cit.
19 In WO 208/4111 cited by Ryan, op cit.
20 See for example FO371/106561 at National Archives.
21 J P L Thomas memo to Cabinet dated 2/7/53 on ADM 1/27600.
22 Breyer, op cit.
23 History.state.gov, op cit.
24 See McLaughlin, op cit, for details about *Cesare* and Project 27. Kuznetzov's role in its cancellation in 1946 may be questionable as he had already been purged from the Commissariat by this date.
25 See *Warship International*, Vol. XXXIV(1), pp 22–34.

Chapter Ten: Conflict in Korea

1 Lawrence Burr, *US Fast Battleships 1938–1991: The Iowa Class*, Osprey Publishing, 2010.
2 Muir, op cit.
3 Muir, ibid.
4 Muir, ibid.
5 Muir, ibid.
6 James A Field, *History of US Naval Operations in Korea*, Washington, 1962.
7 According to Burr and Muir, op cit.
8 Muir, op cit.
9 Muir, ibid.
10 Muir, ibid.
11 Burr, op cit, says this happened on 18 March.
12 Muir, ibid.
13 Muir, ibid.
14 Muir, ibid.
15 Muir, ibid.
16 Details and analysis from 'Naval Gunfire Support of Amphibious Operations – Past, Present and Future' by Major General (Rtd) Donald M Weller USMC – 1977, Dahlgren, Virginia published online by DTIC.MIL, accessed 12/12/2019.
17 DO(50)50 dated 5 July 1950 on CAB 131/9 at the National Archives.
18 See Admiralty Director of Plans paper dated 11 November 1950 on ADM 205/74.

Chapter Eleven: Cold War – Rearming and Deterring in the Early 1950s

1 Logbook of Master Signaller R V Wilks RAF, by kind permission of his son, Professor T V Wilks.
2 See files FO 371/108852 and FO 128/476 at the National Archives.
3 Board of Trade Wreck Report for *Sao Paulo*, 14 October 1954.
4 Metal Industries Ltd Minute Book, at MTSC, Newcastle University.
5 Carlos Tromben Corbalen & Fernando Wilson Lazo, 'Latorre' in *The World of the Battleship*, Ed Bruce Taylor, op cit.
6 In ADM 205/68.
7 See FO 371/90662 at National Archives.
8 Corbalen and Lazo, op cit.
9 See ADM 1/25807.
10 See FO371/81337 and FO371/97464 at the National Archives.
11 Corbalen and Lazo op cit, and Battleship Mikasa Restoration, Colin Randall at navyhistory.org.au Sept 2019, accessed 29/1/21.
12 *Vanguard*'s July–December 1950 logs are ADM 53/129230–129235.
13 See ADM 53/131424–131435, *Vanguard* logs for January to December 1951.
14 ADM 136/47.
15 ADM 116/6347 and ADM 116/6348, UK Exercise Mainbrace reports and analysis.
16 See ADM 1/24889, Report of Proceedings of the Home Fleet Spring Cruise, January to March 1953 by Sir George Creasy.
17 The British Naval Attaché in Moscow thought the whole thing deplorable, as the disproportionate interest in *Sverdlov* completely overshadowed the participation of other foreign and Allied ships, and handed Russia a huge propaganda triumph – see his Quarter 2 1953 report on FO 371/116736 at National Archives.
18 Figures in First Lord of the Admiralty's Coronation Naval Review Papers ADM 1/25087.
19 For *Vanguard* and the Bermuda Conference see papers on ADM 205/87.
20 *Vanguard* ship's log, ADM 53/136965, ADM 53/136936 and UK's Mariner post-exercise reports and analysis on ADM 116/6327.

21 *Vanguard* ship's logs for 1953 ADM 53/136962–136968, and for 1954 ADM53/139823–128834.
22 See DO(50)81 on PREM 8/1381, National Archives.
23 ADM 116/5779 and ADM 219/335, Exercise Sunrise, and ADM 1/21416 Proceedings of the Home Fleet cruise to South Africa and the West Indies, 1948.
24 Annex D to PD 033/48, Template for 1955 Fleet, on ADM 116/5727.
25 ADM 1/21305.
26 See paper on ADM 205/74.
27 See paper on ADM 205/75.
28 DO(52)41, Defence programme dated 29 September 1952 in CAB 131/12, National Archives.
29 Papers on ADM 205/89.
30 1SL No. 1808 dated 28/7/53 on ADM 205/87.
31 On ADM 205/90.
32 See ADM 1/25103.
33 Memo RDP/P(53)28 in ADM 1/24695.
34 Churchill to First Lord of the Admiralty, Personal Minute M301/53 dated 18 September 1953 on PREM 11/1507 at the National Archives.
35 ADM1/25103.
36 Churchill quoted in Grove, op cit.
37 See ADM 205/87.
38 Director of Plans note dated 4/12/53 under 'Size and Shape of the Fleet', ADM 205/87.
39 ADM 116/6327 at National Archives. Creasy's report is HF 1459/2014/22 dated 30 November 1953.
40 See ADM 205/102.
41 Burt, *HMS Vanguard, Britain's Last Battleship*, Seaforth Maritime, 2018.
42 Correspondence on PREM 11/1507 at National Archives.
43 Grove, op cit.
44 Quoted by First Lord of the Admiralty in a minute dated 24 August 1955, on PREM 11/1507, at the National Archives.
45 See ADM 1/22320, GD 02164/45.
46 DO(47)5 dated 7 January 1947 on CAB 131/4 and DO(49)8 on CAB 131/7.
47 See papers on ADM 205/69.
48 See ADM 281/62 for the modelling analysis of Sea Slug vs Sverdlov.
49 See DCNS/294/53 on ADM 205/87
50 Brown and Moore, op cit.
51 ADM1/25425 Sea Slug Ship.
52 I have drawn for some of this section on Eric Grove, 'The Royal Navy and Guided Weapons', in Ed Harding, and Brown and Moore, *The Royal Navy 1930–2000: Innovation and Defence*, op cit.
53 See the papers on ADM 1/26924.
54 See ADM 1/26026 Development of Naval Ballistic Missile.

Chapter Twelve: End of the Line? The Late 1950s and '60s

1 *Mississippi* details from the *Dictionary of American Naval Fighting Ships*.
2 Details of the 1950s *Iowa*-class deployments from Muir, and Burr, op cit, Robert F Sumrall, *Iowa Class Battleships*, Conway Maritime Press, 1988; Lester Abbey, *The Iowa Class*, Seaforth, 2012, and

Philippe Caresse, *The Battleships of the Iowa Class*, Naval Institute Press, 2019.
3 Burr, op cit.
4 More details of Mark 23 programme from navweaps.com, op cit.
5 Whitley, op cit.
6 Sumrall, op cit.
7 Garzke & Dulin, *US Battleships of World War Two*, McDonald and Jane's, 1976 and Whitley, op cit.
8 Garzke & Dulin, op cit.
9 Sumrall, Muir, op cit.
10 Admiralty Gunnery Establishment report R1.A55 on ADM 263/19.
11 Correspondence on ADM 205/74.
12 Whitley, op cit.
13 rusnavy.com, accessed 9/3/2020.
14 McLaughlin, op cit, Sergei Karamaev, rusnavy website, op cit.
15 ADM53/130269–271 and ADM 53/132620–625.
16 See ADM 1/24477 on the material state of the reserve fleet.
17 *King George V* ship's book, ADM 136/31.
18 Hansard, 7 March 1956, Vol. 549 Col. 2084.
19 Correspondence on PREM 11/1507 at National Archives.
20 T225/589 at National Archives.
21 Clydemaritime.co.uk/troon listings, accessed 20/3/20.
22 Hansard, Vol. 618 Col. 1193.
23 *Anson*, ship's book, ADM 136/32.
24 Metal Industries Outturn summary for job 75, Newcastle University Marine Technology Special Collection.
25 ADM 136/33.
26 See Last Days of HMS *Duke of York*, Hearts of Oak on Rootsweb, accessed 19/3/2020.
27 Burt, op cit, says February 1950.
28 ADM 136/34.
29 SBMA4336 on ADM 136/47.
30 First Lord of the Admiralty to Prime Minister, 24/8/55, on PREM 11/1507 at National Archive.
31 Ibid.
32 Hansard, 7 March 1956, Vol. 549 Col. 2084.
33 See paragraph 15c of C.(57) 69 dated 15 March 1957, and paragraph 45 of C.(57)79 in CAB 129/86, National Archives.
34 White Paper drafts and Admiralty deliberations on ADM 205/114.
35 Admiralty Board Minutes paragraph 5202 13 February 1958 on ADM 205/176.
36 Hansard extracts and newspaper clippings on T225/587 at National Archive.
37 Hansard, Vol. 601 Col. 1163.
38 Michael Simpson, *A Life of Admiral of the Fleet Sir Andrew Cunningham*, Frank Cass, 2004.
39 Hansard, 24 February 1960, Vol. 618 Col. 361.
40 Metal Industries Vanguard folders, courtesy of Ian Buxton at Newcastle University Marine Technology Special Collection.
41 Lest it be thought that *Bustler* was jinxed, it should be recorded that she had an outstanding record of service in the war and after, including laying the

PLUTO pipeline to the Normandy beachhead in 1944.

42 *Vanguard* folders, MTSC Newcastle University, op cit.

43 Buxton, Ship Breaking at Faslane, op cit.

44 netmarine.net accessed 21/3/2020 and Jordan and Dumas, op cit.

45 www.navweaps.com accessed 17/3/2020 and Robert Dumas, *Le Cuirasse Richelieu*, Nantes, Marine Edition, 2001.

46 Service Historique de la Defense, Serie 51, op cit.

47 Robert Dumas, Cuirasse Jean Bart, 1970, and Jordan and Dumas, op cit.

48 Garzke and Dulin, British, French, Soviet and Dutch Battleships, op cit, mention this possibility.

49 Jordan and Dumas, op cit.

50 See *Warship International* Vol. 6 No. 4, Fall 1969, pp 259–261, accessed via www.jstor.org/stable/44887375 on 2/2/21.

51 Ed Taylor, *The World of the Battleship*, op cit.

Chapter Thirteen: Vietnam, 1967–69

1 See Abbey and Muir, op cit.

2 Sumrall, op cit.

3 Muir, op cit.

4 Whitley, op cit.

5 Muir, op cit.

6 Muir, ibid.

7 *Jane's Fighting Ships, 1971–72*, Marston Low; and Burr, op cit.

8 navweaps.com accessed 23/12/2018.

9 Details for *New Jersey* commissioning and work-up from her deck logs at RG24, US National Archives.

10 Caresse, op cit, and www.battleshipnewjersey.org, accessed 1/9/21.

11 Narrative 1968 history of the USS *New Jersey* B62, Ships Histories Branch, Naval Heritage Command.

12 Muir, op cit.

13 Muir, ibid

14 Muir, ibid.

15 Details of operations from USS *New Jersey* Deck Log, RG 24, US National Archives.

16 Quoted in Burr, op cit.

17 Abbey, op cit.

18 Quoted by both Sumrall and Abbey, op cit.

19 Howard W Serig Jnr, Naval Institute Proceedings 1982, p 138.

Chapter Fourteen: Revival – The 600-Ship Navy

1 Writing in *Jane's Fighting Ships 1971–72*, p 493, Norman Polmar.

2 Serig, op cit.

3 Serig, op cit, says 458 active in 1979.

4 *Flight International*, 8 March 1980, p 726.

5 *Aviation Weekly and Space Technology*, 26 May 1980.

6 US News and World Report, quoted in Sumrall, op cit.

7 Muir, op cit.

8 Arthur R Romano, Director, Gun Division, Naval Sea Systems Command: Reactivation of 16in three gun turrets in the battleship, March 1987, accessed

via apps.dtic.mil accessed 29/2/2020.

9 Muir, op cit.

10 Romano, op cit. There are more details on navweaps.com, accessed on 1/3/2020.

11 battleshipnewjersey.org accessed 2/3/2020.

12 Burr, op cit.

13 Sumrall, op cit.

14 Details of the investigations mainly from US Navy History and Heritage Command publication 'H-Gram 029-4 USS *Iowa* turret explosion' by Samuel J Cox, Director, dated 3 May 2019. This is a balanced factual account, and it also draws attention to other published analyses that are far more critical of the US Navy approach.

15 USS *Wisconsin* Association website on web.archive.org accessed 3/3/2020.

16 Burr, op cit.

17 Sumrall, op cit.

18 See 2006 Act – section 1014 authorises Sec Nav to strike the vessels and transfer *Iowa* to a transferee in California and Wisconsin one in Virginia. 1996 act 104–106 section 1011 repealed, and 1999 act 105–261 section 1011.

Chapter Fifteen: Preservation, Historic Ships and Relics

1 Burt, *The Last British Battleship – HMS Vanguard 1946–1960*, op cit.

2 For the full story see DEFE24/462 at the National Archive.

3 Texas Parks and Wildlife Department Website, accessed 24 /12/2018, and subsequently source for details of preservation efforts.

4 tpwd.texas.gov and battleshiptexas.org accessed 3/3/2020, 4/2/21 and 5/11/21.

5 Commemorative Landscapes of North Carolina at docsouth.unc.edu accessed 31/12/2018.

6 Website battleshipnc.com accessed 31/12/2018.

7 Memorial Park website ussalabama.com accessed 2/1/2019.

8 www.battleshipcove.org accessed via web.archive.org 15/1/2019.

9 www.battleshipnewjersey.org, accessed 30/1/2019.

10 pacificbattleship.com accessed 2/1/2019.

11 Nauticus.org accessed 4/2/21.

Appendix: The Royal Naval Armaments Depot Priddy's Hard Gun Logs

1 D13519 dated 11 August 1948 quoted in Priddy's Hard GL3.

Index

411